LITERARY

CRITICISMS

AND

OTHER PAPERS.

BY THE LATE

HORACE BINNEY WALLACE, ESQUIRE,

OF PHILADELPHIA.

PHILADELPHIA:

PARRY & McMILLAN,

SUCCESSORS TO A. HART, LATE CAREY & HART.

1856.

STEREOTYPED BY GEORGE CHARLES. PRINTED BY T. K. & P. G. COLLINS.

TO

GEORGE P. MORRIS,

THE TONES OF WHOSE LYRE HAVE WAKED, IN FOREIGN LANDS, A RESPONSE FROM

"Those chords of pervading Nature,
Which fraternize multitudes of differing nations;"

AND OF WHOM THE AUTHOR OF THESE WRITINGS SAYS:

"Search the wide world over, and you shall not find among the literary men of any nation, one on whom the dignity of a free and manly spirit sits with a grace more native and familiar: whose acts, whether common and daily, or deliberate and much considered, are wont, at all times, to be more beautifully impressed with those marks of sincerity, of modesty, and of justice, which form the very seal of worth in conduct;"

THESE PAGES ARE AFFECTIONATELY INSCRIBED

BY THE EDITOR.

"Tell Mr. H. B. Wallace I am proud of his praise. He is one of the few in this our day and generation, who can appreciate the solution of a black letter question."—*Letter of Chief Justice Gibson, of Pennsylvania, July* 7, 1851.

Je dois maintenant achever cette préface en déplorant la catastrophe exceptionnelle qui me priva récemment d'un éminent disciple, destiné, sans doute, à devenir l'un des meilleurs appuis du positivisme. En signalant, dans la préface du volume précédent, la digne adhésion d'un noble citoyen de Philadelphie, j'étais loin de prévoir qu'une fatale maladie allait m'enlever Wallace, à l'âge de trente-cinq ans.

Quoique nos relations se soient bornées à trois entretiens décisifs, séparés par une correspondance aussi courte que précieuse, elles m'ont permis de juger la perte que fait en lui l'Humanité. D'après un rare concours entre le cœur, l'esprit, et le caractère, il devait puissamment seconder la difficile transition réservée au dix-neuvième siècle. Exempte de toute affectation, sa culture spéculative, tant esthétique que scientifique, correspondait pleinement à sa belle organisation. Mais ses confidences spontanées m'autorisent à penser, malgré les essais littéraires de sa jeunesse, qu'il se serait surtout illustré par la vie active, dans un pays où les grands citoyens prévalent sur les magistrats. J'ose résumer sa véritable appréciation en le comparant au plus éminent des hommes d'Etat américains. * * * *

Chaque fois que je vois ainsi disparaître, avant le temps, un être vraiment supérieur, je déplore la fatale impuissance de l'Humanité contre les lois extérieures qui lui ravissent ses meilleurs organes. Quoique l'influence subjective perpétue les services objectifs, elle n'empêchera jamais de sentir que nous fûmes privés de Bichat, de Vauvenargues, de Bellini, etc., sans avoir pu subir leur principal ascendant.—*Auguste Comte. Pref., vol. 3eme, du Systeme de Politique Positive, p. xvii.*

"Horace Binney Wallace, of Philadelphia, is a son of the late John B. Wallace, and nephew of Mr. Binney. He is a young man of as much ability and power as any I know. His father was one of my best, warmest, truest friends. He died eight or nine years ago. I have cultivated the acquaintance of this son, and if I had the power I would most cheerfully bring him into public service."—*Letter of Daniel Webster to Hiram Ketcham, of New York, February* 22, 1849.

ADVERTISEMENT.

THE papers which are contained in this volume are the productions of a young man, whose career was terminated in a foreign country, at the age of thirty-five. Much of the last year of his life had been occupied in the pursuit of health. He had previously passed a considerable time in foreign travel, and when at home and while discharging, with remarkable interest and fidelity, all the duties of his social and civil station, had been a constant laborer in his profession, the law, to which science he had contributed some of the best known and most authoritative publications which American Jurisprudence now owns. A volume, entitled "Art, Scenery and Philosophy in Europe," was published in 1855, from manuscripts found in his port-folio at Paris, after his death; but, as a literary writer, he was not during his life-time ever publicly known, nor at all willing to be known. No one of the papers, printed since his death, was ever acknowledged by him in any way; and outside of his profession every thing that he either wrote or printed was given off by him in the most perishable form, and without the least idea of ever claiming or acknowledging it himself, or of its being at any time presented by others as his. These facts are proper to be stated in order that the reader may understand the true relation of Mr. Wallace, to what is here presented as the production of his pen. It is probable that occasional passages in the present volume ought not to be regarded as the completed or final expression of his judgment: and it is certain, from what has been already said, that he did not regard any of the pieces as a satisfactory expression of literary effort. Many of them, as will be seen by the indication placed at the head of each page were written at the age of twenty-one or below it, and were merely tentative; "the flights of a noble bird for the first time essaying his own wings." Indeed his life, up to its close, seemed to have been one chiefly of study and preparation: and it was one of the sad circumstances connected with his death, that his fine powers seem to be arranging themselves, with confidence in their own strength, for great, sustained, and systematic labor in the departments of literature, philosophy and politics, when they were paralyzed at their source.

The pieces, it will be perceived, are different in extent and character. Several of them are fragmentary. A few have been printed in an ephemeral and limited form. Of these several were designed as expressions of friendly feeling to literary men of our country who are the subjects of them, and who till now, it is probable, have never known, except as they may have inferred it from internal evidence, the pen from which they came. Some were contributions, spontaneous or solicited, to the enterprises of unfriended merit seeking subsistence in the scanty fields of our native literature: A few have appeared in newspapers or other journals, the editors of which, while generally ignorant of their source, were usually impressed by the genius whose stamp they bore: And the residue appear to have been written chiefly in obedience to that law which declares that "genius *will* labor." "He wrote and thought," said one of the guides and exponents of the best public opinion in Philadelphia,* in speaking of Mr. Wallace after his death, "with the most unselfish indifference to the immediate results to his own fame or fortune. To a limited circle of his personal and professional friends and of people who detected his unusual intelligence even in its retirement, was he known: and it was only after his death, when the admiration of these was expressed along with their grief, that the public at large discovered that a man of extraordinary talents had been born and bred among them."

The "Art, Scenery and Philosophy" already referred to, and the volume now printed, form but a small part of Mr. Wallace's literary productions. Other portions of them, along with parts of his correspondence, may hereafter, it is possible, be communicated to the public.

Philadelphia, February 26th, 1856.

* "The Evening Bulletin," November 25, 1854.

LITERARY CRITICISMS.

THE PROSE WRITERS OF AMERICA: WITH AN INTRODUCTORY SURVEY OF THE INTELLECTUAL HISTORY, CONDITION, AND PROSPECTS OF THE COUNTRY: with Portraits from Original Pictures. By RUFUS WILMOT GRISWOLD.* Second edition.

No man is more deserving of the public gratitude than he who teaches a nation to respect itself. A proper confidence in one's own standards, in one's own judgment, and in one's own abilities, is so important for the full development of intellectual capacity, and social dignity and happiness, and moral power, that it ought to be considered a duty of every one who holds the place of a guide or teacher to implant and cultivate it in the subjects of his care, whether communities or individuals. Personal or national vanity, indeed, may become even bloated upon the contempt and ridicule of the rest of the world; but an honorable self-dependence, a manly self-reliance, can be inspired only by contemplating, as external, the monuments of one's own character and ability, or by seeing that others regard them with esteem and deference and admiration. For either purpose, of enabling the literary genius of the country to know itself, objectively, or of causing other countries to receive the complete impression of its power, we hold such efforts as have been made by Mr. Griswold to be of great value. He has done a useful work, and he has done it well. The book now before us is more than respectable; it is

* This volume, greatly enlarged and improved by the numerous editions through which it has passed since the present notice of it was written, now forms part of a series of works, comprising, with it, "The Poets and Poetry," and "The Female Poets of America," and likely to do honor to our country, under the title of "A Survey of American Literature."—ED.

executed ably, and in many parts brilliantly. In some respects it is an extraordinary work; such as few men in America, perhaps, besides its author, could have produced, and he only after years of sedulous investigation, and under many advantages of circumstance or accident. He has long shown himself to be of Cicero's mind: "*Mihi quidem nulli satis erudito videntur, quibus nostra ignota sunt.*" The distribution of the various writers into their classes, and the selection of representatives of each class or type, exhibit much skill. Many passages present fine specimens of acute, original and just criticism, eloquently delivered. We differ from Mr. Griswold sometimes, but never without a respect for his judgment, and never without feeling that we owe it to the public in all cases to give a reason why we do not assent to the conclusions of so candid and discriminating a judge. We acknowledge Mr. Griswold to be a good critic; and if his personal friends or others claim for him the title of a writer of first-rate merit, we make no other hesitation than that we have not yet seen quite enough of original matter from his pen. "The strength of the eagle," says Mr. Hallam, "is to be measured, not only by the height of his place, but by the time that he continues on the wing." If the editor of "The Prose Writers" will produce an entire volume on some continuous subject, in the same style of fearless and acute discussion, and of graceful and elegant composition, which is displayed in some of the paragraphs here—which we do not question his ability to do—we shall readily admit his right to take a place among the foremost authors of the country. The present volume we have read with constant interest and frequent admiration. We have derived more instruction from it than it would be becoming in a reviewer to admit. The reader is here brought for a time into society with the greatest and most accomplished of the minds of this country:

> "Et varias audit voces fruiturque deorum
> Colloquio."

It is much to admit that we pass to the comments of the author without any very sensible diminution of interest or respect.

The benefits to be expected from a compilation like this are several. In the first place, by exhibiting in concentrated brightness, "the ancestors' fair glory gone before," it will stimulate the youthful energy of the day to more earnest action in this great field of exertion and renown. In the next place, it will tend to ascertain and illustrate, by a kind of induction, more reliable than any speculation or random experiment, the natural and proper tone and character of American literature. We wish, as perhaps all wish, and we believe, as certainly many do not believe, that there is, or is to be, a literature peculiarly and distinctively *American.* This country in its origin was little else than a concourse of individual persons, aggregated but not associated, and of companies clustered but not combined; gradually this "dust and powder of individuality" has tended to an organization: a definite principle of social life has been evolved, or is evolving; characteristics of a national existence have been perceived, and have deepened and multiplied as time has gone on. In every thing the dead-reckoning, which carried forward the old wisdom into the new region, has failed or begun to fail, and new observations have required to be taken. A thousand tokens in every thing from which we can prognosticate, make it manifest that a spirit, indigenous and self-vital, inhabits our country; a spirit of power, *ipsa suis pollens opibus.* If all this be so, there is an end of the question about a national literature; for this creative vigor, breathing and burning in the bosom of the nation, must find an issue in art as well as in action. The flower of literature will blow, and the fruit of science bloom, upon the tree of national life, as surely as the branches and leaves of business, politics or war expand and strengthen. It is then of the first consequence that every one interested in associating his name with his land's language, should apprehend correctly the tendencies of the literary spirit of the country, in order that he may divine the nature of that literature in its perfect development; for it is only as his productions embody and represent that native spirit of art, that they will have a permanent life. He must look backward, and catch a prophecy of the future from the performances of the past. He must listen to the various notes that have been struck; observe which sound falsely, which have died away and become inaudible, and which rise and flow and swell upon the ear, the true key-notes of the symphony. Of one thing, however, even a hasty glance gives us a gratifying assurance; that of whatever nature or quality the new literature may be, it will bear no resemblance to the productions of "Young America;" a fraternity young only in wisdom, and incapable of representing any thing of America but its vulgarity. Following the order of Mr. Griswold, we shall, in the discursive observations which we propose, attempt a hasty review of the several departments in which monuments of the mental vigor of America remain for the instruction and delight of mankind: beginning with her statesmen and orators.

The Congress which, having vindicated by arms those principles of liberty that are constitutional in Anglo-Saxon society, afterward assembled to define and institute them in abiding forms of legislation, brought together, to use the language in which Warburton spoke of the Long Parliament, "the greatest set of geniuses for government that ever embarked in a common cause." And to this day, that high lineage has never failed. Political and legal ability, in fact, seem to be an instinct of the American people; and those faculties, implying an action, present, personal and persuasive, admit of scarcely any effective literary *sortie* but in oratory. Accordingly, the eloquence of the bar, the legislative hall and the popular assembly constitutes the most characteristic display of American intelligence, and of itself sustains our pretension to take a rank among the great intellectual nations of the world. In the night of tyranny the eloquence of the country first blazed up, like the lighted signal-fires of a distracted border, to startle and enlighten the community. Every where, as the news of this or that fresh invasion of liberty and right was passed on through the land, men ran together and called upon some speaker to address them. It is a striking evidence of the dignity and elevation of this noble gift, that at seasons demanding deep wisdom, and varied resources of suggestion and experience, and consummate judgment, oratory was the most commanding influence in the state, and that it was then more splendid, more finished, more truly classical, than it has been in any times of less excited interest. Eloquence is the enthusiasm of reason, the passion of the mind; it is judgment raised into transport, and breathing the irresistible ardors of sympathy. It contributed in a great degree to the adoption of the Federal constitution; and never let it be forgotten, that when the same perverse and fatal spirit, against which the constitution in its infancy had prevailed, again appeared in the councils of the nation, inflamed by interest and ambition, and at once insidious and dómineering, to betray the system which it could not overthrow, it was the same divine energy that, with the indignation of truth, the power of argument, and a torrent-rush of resistless feeling, swept forth to scatter and punish the foe. The eloquence of Hamilton, spoken and written, did much to establish our national system; the eloquence of Webster did more to defend and save it.

"Duo fulmina belli,
Scipiadas, cladem Libyæ!"

Looking then at the monuments of American eloquence, even with the severe eye of scholars and critics, there is cause for satisfaction and a just pride. There is Henry, not fulminating from the clouds, like Demosthenes, to terrify men into sense and virtue; not sending up a flash, like Cicero, to be a signal to distant ages, rather than a fire of present energy; but first drawing his hearers' sympathies to him by a delightful conciliation, and then charging them with the fervor of his own bosom; familiar, simple and near, yet intense, vehement and thrilling; converting his hearers first into friends, and then animating them into partisans, and finally hurrying all along with him in one united fellowship of feeling; not surpassing in intellect, rarely analytical, never ascending to the illuminated heights of abstract wisdom; but setting before his mind usually some one definite object, and piercing it through and through by the shaft of a sound understanding, pointed by an honest purpose, and driven by all the force of devoted passion. There is Ames, whose speech was enchantment, and his pen a subtler magic; possessed by nature of "the delicacy which distinguishes in words the shades of sentiment, the grace which brings them to the soul of the reader with the charm of novelty united to clearness;" whose dignified and pure spirit, apprehending a corrupt triumph as the most fatal of failures, and unprincipled success as only a keener disgrace, desponded, not because it did not see justly and foresee clearly, but because its hopes had been so high and its feeling so refined; as the common air would cloud and sully an atmosphere of more essential ether; who, had he lived to see what we see, with his quick sensibilities of honor and his far-reflective sagacity, instead of recalling one of his gloomy anticipations, would perhaps have pointed to the most despairing omens of his eloquence, and have said in anguish: "This day is this scripture fulfilled in your ears!" There is Otis the elder, impetuous, uncompromising, kindling; Marshall, who could vindicate the power of reason in discussion as impressively as he could illustrate its dignity in judgment; whose only surviving oration stands like the cyclopean structure of a superior race; Rutledge, Adams. Coming down to later times, Quincy, Stockton, Wirt, and afterward Clay, Calhoun, Everett, are truly orators of the early heroic age of our statesmen, the ἡμιθεοι of our history. Mr. Griswold has properly chosen Hamilton as the principal and representative. He closes an animated survey of his life with these discriminating remarks:

> "In every page of the works of Hamilton we discover an original, vigorous and practical understanding, informed with various and profound knowledge. But few of his speeches were reported, and even these very imperfectly; but we have traditions of his eloquence, which represent it as wonderfully winning and persuasive. Indeed, it is evident from its known effects that he was a debater of the very first class. He thought clearly and rapidly, had a ready command of language, and addressed himself solely to the reason. He never lost his self-command, and never seemed impatient; but from the bravery of his nature, and his contempt of meanness and servility, he was perhaps sometimes indiscreet. His works were written hastily, but we can discover in them no signs of immaturity or carelessness; on the contrary, they are hardly excelled in compactness, clearness, elegance, and purity of language."

Mr. Webster is properly selected as the representative of the best sense and highest wisdom and most consummate dignity of the politics and oratory of the present times. With elements of reason, definite, absolute and emphatic; with principles settled, strenuous, deep and unchangeable as his being; Webster's wisdom is yet exquisitely practical: with subtlest sagacity it apprehends every change in the circumstances in which it is to act, and can accommodate its action without loss of vigor, or alteration of its general purpose. Its theories always "lean and hearken" to the actual. By a sympathy of the mind, almost transcendental in its delicacy, its speculations are attracted into a parallelism with the logic of life and nature. In most men that intellectual susceptibility by which they are capable of being reäcted upon by the outer world, and having their principles and views expanded, modified or quickened, does not outlast the first period of life; from that time they remain fixed, rigid in their policy, temper, characteristics; if a new phase of society is developed, it must find its exponent in other men. But in Webster this fresh suggestive sensibility of the judgment has been carried on into the matured and determined wisdom of manhood. His perceptions, feelings, reasonings, tone, are always up to the level of the hour, or in advance of it; sometimes far, very far in advance, as in the views thrown out in his speech at Baltimore, on an international commercial system, in which he showed that he then foresaw both the fate of the tariff and the true nature of free-trade. No man has ever been able to say, or now can say, that he is before Webster. The youngest men in the nation look to him, not as representing the past, but as leading in the future. This practicalness and readiness of adaptation are instinctive, not voluntary and designed. They are united with the most decided preference for certain opinions and the most earnest averseness to others. Nothing could be less like Talleyrand's system of waiting for events. He has never, in view of a change which he saw to be inevitable, held himself in reserve and uncommitted.

What Webster is at any time, that he is strenuously, entirely, openly. He has first opposed, with every energy of his mind and temper, that which, when it has actually come, he is ready to accept and make the best of. He never surrenders in advance a position which he knows will be carried; he takes his place, and delivers battle; he fights as one who is fighting the last battle of his country's hopes: he fires the last shot. When the smoke and tumult are cleared off, where is Webster? Look around for the nearest rallying point which the view presents; there he stands, with his hand upon his heart, in grim composure; calm, dignified, resolute; neither disheartened nor surprised by defeat. "Leaving the things that are behind," is now the trumpet-sound by which he rallies his friends to a new confidence, and stimulates them to fresh efforts. It is obvious that Webster, when contending with all his force for or against some particular measure, has not been contemplating the probability of being compelled to oppose or defend a different policy, and so choosing his words warily, in reference to future possibilities of a personal kind; yet when the time has come that he has been obliged to fight with his face in another direction, it has always been found that no one principle had been asserted, no one sentiment displayed, incompatible with his new position. This union of consistency with practicability has arisen naturally from the extent and comprehensiveness of his views, from the breadth and generality with which the analytical power of his understanding has always led him to state his principles and define his positions. From the particular scheme or special maxim which his party was insisting upon, his mind rose to a higher and more general formula of truth.

Owing to the same superior penetration and reach of thought, the gloom of successive repulses has never been able to paralyze the power which it has saddened. The constitution has been so often invaded and trampled upon, that to a common eye it might well seem to have lost all the resentments of vitality. But Webster has distinguished between the constitution and its administration. He has seen that the constitution, though in bondage, is not killed; that the channels of its life-giving wisdom are stuffed up with rubbish, but not obliterated. He has been determined that if the rulers of the country will deny the truth, they shall not debauch it; if they depart from the constitution, they shall not deprave it. He has been resolved, that when this tyranny of corruption shall be overpast, and the constitution draws again its own free breath of virtue, truth and wisdom, it shall be found perfect of limb and feature, prepared to rise like a giant refreshed by sleep.

What task would seem more barren of present encouragement than that of confuting Mr. Polk's notion of the unconstitutionality of "The Harbor and River Bill?" But Mr. Webster, vividly alive to every wound or even sting against that sacred form in whose life lives all the promise of the future, takes the subject up with all the warmth of the dearest interest of his thoughts, and exhausts the power of his logic in enlightening the honest shopkeepers of Philadelphia on a subject which they probably cared for as little as they understood; delivering with judicial emphasis, on a subject of great importance, that which posterity will receive as an oracle of truth. What an impressive display of public duty is here given! what inherent dignity of nature is thus attested! what a lesson to the younger men of the country to persist, and to "steer up-hill-ward," and never to compound! But the capacity thus to be loyal to dethroned Truth; to feel this enthusiasm of reverence for Right in captivity, belongs to those spirits only which nature has touched with her most ennobling influences. The mental ability to be thus freshly and earnestly interested in each new scene of a most discouraging strife; to rise from defeat with the flushed energy of triumph; shows a large measure of the divine power of genius, and a spirit, the fountains of whose being are copiously refreshed from the eternal sources of strength and hope.

Mr. Griswold, we suppose, is quite right in suggesting that the only name in modern times to which reference can with any fitness be made for purposes of analogy or comparison with Webster is that of Burke. In many respects there is a correspondence between their characters; in some others they differ widely. As a prophet of the truth of political morals, as a revealer of those essential elements in the constitution of life upon which or of which society is constructed and government evolved, Burke had no peer. In that department he rises into the distance and grandeur of inspiration; *nec mortale sonans.* Nor do we doubt that the Providence of God had raised him up for purposes of public safety and guidance, any more than we doubt the mission of Jeremiah or Elisha, or any other of the school of the Lord's prophets. But leaving Burke unapproached in this region of the nature and philosophy of government, and looking at him, in his general career, as a man of intellect and action, we might indicate an analogy of this kind, that the character, temper and reason of Burke seem to be almost an image of the English constitution, and Webster's of the American. To get the key to Burke's somewhat irregular and startling career, it is necessary to study the idea of the old whig constitution of the English monarchy: viewing his course from that point of view, we comprehend his almost countenancing and encouraging rebellion in the case of the American colonies; his intense hostility to Warren Hastings' imperial system; his unchastized earnestness in opposition to French maxims in the decline of his life. The constitution of the United States, that most wonderful of the structures of human wisdom, seems to be not only the home of Webster's affections and seat of his proudest hopes, but the very type of his understanding and fountain of his intellectual strength:

—— "hic illius arma;
Hic currus."

The genius of Burke, like the one, was inexhaustible in resources, so composite and so averse from theory as to appear incongruous, but justified in the results; not formal, not always entirely perspicuous. Webster's mind, like the other, is eminently logical, reduced into principles, orderly, distinct, re-connecting abstraction with convenience, various in manifestation, yet pervaded by an unity of character.

Mr. Webster has not merely illustrated a great range of mental powers and accomplishments, but has filled, in the eye of the nation, on a great scale, and to the farthest reach of their exigency, a diversity of intellectual characters; while the manner in which Burke's wisdom displayed itself was usually the same. We cannot suppose that Burke could have been a great lawyer. Webster possesses a consummate legal judgment and prodigious powers of legal logic, and is felt to be the highest authority on a great question of law in this country. The demonstrative faculty; the capacity to analyze and open any proposition so as to identify its separate elements with the very consciousness of the reader's or hearer's mind; this, which is the lawyer's peculiar power, had not been particularly developed in Burke, but exists in Webster in greater expansion and force than in any one since Doctor Johnson, who, it always appeared to us, had he been educated for the bar, would have made the greatest lawyer that ever led the decisions of Westminster Hall. We should hardly be justified in saying that Burke would have been a great First Lord of the Treasury. Mr. Webster, as Secretary of State, proved himself to be a practical statesman of the highest, finest, promptest sagacity and foresight that this or any nation ever witnessed. Who now doubts the surpassing wisdom, who now but reverences the exalted patriotism, of the advice and the example which he gave, but gave in vain, to the whig party at the beginning of Mr. Tyler's administration? His official correspondence would be lowered by a comparison with any state papers since the secretaryship of John Marshall. Does the public generally know what has become of that portentous difficulty about the Right of Search, upon which England and America, five years ago, were on the point of being "*lento collisa duello?*" Mr. Webster settled it by mere force of mind: he dissipated the question *by seeing through it*, and by compelling others to see a fallacy in its terms which before had imposed upon the understandings of two nations. In the essential and universal philosophy of politics, Webster is second only to Burke. After Burke, there is no statesman whose writings might be read with greater advantage by foreign nations, or would have been studied with so much respect by antiquity, as Webster's.

In a merely literary point of view, this perhaps may be said of Mr. Webster, that he is the only powerful and fervid orator, since the glorious days of Greece, whose style is so disciplined that any of his great public harangues might be used as models of composition. His language is beautifully pure, and his combinations of it exhibit more knowledge of the genius, spirit, and classic vigor of the English tongue, than it has entered the mind of any professor of rhetoric to apprehend. As the most impetu-

2

ous sweeps of passion in him are pervaded and informed and guided by intellect, so the most earnest struggles of intellect seem to be calmed and made gentle in their vehemence, by a more essential rationality of taste. That imperious mind, which seems fit to defy the universe, is ever subordinate, by a kind of fascination, to the perfect law of grace. In the highest of his intellectual flights—and who can follow the winged rush of that eagle mind?—in the widest of his mental ranges—and who shall measure their extent?—he is ever moving with the severest tone of beauty. No one would think of saying that Mr Webster's speeches are thrown off with ease and cost him but little effort; they are clearly the result of the intensest stress of mental energy; yet the manner is never discomposed; the decency and propriety of the display never interfered with; he is always greater than his genius; you see "the depth but not the tumult" of the mind. Whether, with extended arm, he strangles the "*reluctantes dracones*" of his adversary, or with every faculty called home, concentrates the light and heat of his being in developing into principles those great sentiments and great instincts which are his inspiration; in all, the orator stands forth with the majesty and chastened grace of Pericles himself. In the fiercest of encounters with the deadliest of foes, the mind which is enraged is never perturbed; the style which leaps like the fire of heaven is never disordered. As in Guido's picture of St. Michael piercing the dragon, while the gnarled muscles of the arms and hands attest the utmost strain of the strength, the countenance remains placid, serene, and undisturbed. In this great quality of mental dignity, Mr. Webster's speeches have become more and more eminent. The glow and lustre which set his earlier speeches a-blaze with splendor, is in his later discourses rarely set forth; but they have gained more in the increase of dignity than they have parted with in the diminution of brilliancy. We regard his late speech before the shop-keepers, calling themselves merchants, of Philadelphia, as one of the most weighty and admirable of the intellectual efforts of his life. The range of profound and piercing wisdom; the exquisite and faultless taste; but, above all, the august and indefectable dignity, that are illustrated from the beginning to the end of that great display of matured and finished strength, leave us in mingled wonder and reverence. There is one sentence there which seems to us almost to reach the *intellectual* sublime; and while it stirs within us the depths of sympathy and admiration, we could heartily wish that the young men of America would inhale the almost supra-mortal spirit which it breathes: "I would not with any idolatrous admiration regard the Constitution of the United States, nor any other work of man; but this side of idolatry, I hold it in profound respect. I believe that no human working on such a subject, no human ability exerted for such an end, has ever produced so much happiness, or holds out now to so many millions of people the prospect, through such a succession of ages and ages, of so much happiness, as the Constitution of the United States. We who are here for one generation, for a single life, and yet in our several stations and relations in society intrusted in some degree with its protection and support, what duty does it devolve, what duty does it *not* devolve, upon us!" In the name of distant ages, and a remote posterity, we hail the author of this and similar orations, as Webster the *Olympian.*

But we leave a subject which we have incidentally touched, sincerely disclaiming any attempt to estimate the character or define the greatness of Webster. In reference to him we feel, as Cicero said to Cæsar, "*Nil vulgare te dignum videri possit.*"

First among the great theologians of the country must be ranked Jonathan Edwards, whose sincerity, courage and extraordinary skill in dialectics have commanded the admiration of all parties for nearly a century. Robert Hall, in one of his bursts of enthusiasm, declares him the "greatest of mankind;" and Mackintosh, the range and profoundness of whose studies qualified him to judge of his relation to the other masters of reason, does not scruple to say that "in power of subtle argument he was unsurpassed among men." Dugald Stewart, Hamilton, Chalmers, and indeed nearly all the leading ethical and theological writers of the old world, have endorsed these opinions. The "Treatise on the Will" is regarded as his greatest production, and its amazing power has contributed scarcely more than its perfect sincerity and conscientiousness to its celebrity. There is no trick of words, no subterfuge, no verbal sophism, no petulance or dogmatism, in his argument. He reasons of "fixed fate, free-will, foreknowledge absolute," not as one wishing to secure to himself a triumph, but as if anxious to remove all stumbling-blocks from the way of truth. His treatise on original sin was published ninety years ago, in reply to Dr. Taylor, of Norwich, the leader of the Arminians of that day, who had boasted that his own book on this subject was unanswerable, but was compelled to admit that no rejoinder could be made to the American Calvinist. "The grasp of his antagonist was death," literally; for he died of mortification at his defeat. Mr. Griswold says of Edwards:

> "Born in a country which was still almost a wilderness; educated in a college which had scarcely a local habitation; settled, a large part of his life, over a church upon the confines of civilization, and the rest of it in the very midst of barbarism, in the humble but honorable occupation of a missionary, he owed nothing to adventitious circumstances. With a fragile body, a fine imagination, and a spirit the most gentle that ever thrilled in the presence of the beautiful, he seemed of all men the least fitted for the great conflict in which he engaged. But He who, giving to Milton the Dorian reed, sent out his seraphim to enrich him with utterance and knowledge, with fire from the same altar purified the lips of Edwards, to teach that 'true religion consists in holy affections,' the spring of all which is 'a love of divine things *for their own beauty and sweetness.*'"

A history of theological opinions in America would have no completeness unless it included the names of the younger Edwards, Chauncey, Mayhew, Hopkins, Bellamy, Seabury, Dwight, and that independent and shrewd dogmatist, Emmons, "the last of the cocked hats," who died recently, after a conflict of nearly three-quarters of a century with all the forms of opposition to the most ultra doctrines of Geneva. These giants of the last age have been succeeded, in many places, by a race of preachers who present to us, under the name of sermons, discourses on moral subjects which have been handed down by Cicero, Seneca, and "The Spectator;" with "little more of the Gospel in them than is to be found in the heathen philosophers." Except Edwards, Dwight is the only New England divine of the Puritan stock to whom Mr. Griswold has devoted an essay. He came upon the stage while the smoke of the great battles of the last century was clearing away; and though a Calvinist, the "five points" of his doctrine were so rounded off that he suited perfectly his place and time. His writings have been extremely popular, and he was an orator of no mean reputation; but his style nevertheless was decidedly bad. He never learned the saying, "*Apud oratorem vero nisi aliquid efficitur, redundat;*" and his diffuseness and bad taste will prevent the continuance of his name in the select list in which it has been written. Very different from the celebrated president of Yale was his contemporary Buckminster, who, with fit opportunity and long life, would have carved his name in enduring letters upon his age. Of the character and eloquence of this youthful divine Mr. Griswold says:

"With a face remarkable for its pure intellectual expression, and a silvery voice, the tones of which won the devout attention and haunted the memories of all who listened, it is not surprising that in a community where mental power is so highly appreciated as in Boston, the weekly addresses of the youthful divine attracted large and enthusiastic audiences. His manner was artless and impressive, and there was something about the whole man that irresistibly fascinated the taste at the same time that it inspired respect and love. In social life he was remarkable for his urbane spirit, quick intelligence, and refined wit. He was the centre of a rare circle of the good and cultivated, and his death fell upon the hearts of his numerous friends with the solemn pathos of a deep calamity. To the readers of his discourses in whose minds they lack the charm of personal associations, there is perhaps a coldness in their very beauty. Yet few sermons equal them for a happy blending of good sense and graceful imagery. Truth is enforced with a simple earnestness, and pious thoughts are clothed in language strikingly correct and impressive. One of the most characteristic of these essays is the one on "*The Advantages of Sickness.*" It was composed after a dangerous illness of several weeks. On the Sabbath morning when Buckminster was to reäppear before the anxious congregation, at an early hour, before rising, he called for the necessary materials, and wrote the entire sermon in bed, after having meditated the subject during the night. The bell had ceased tolling when his diminutive figure was seen gliding up the aisle of the church, thronged with expectant faces. He ascended the pulpit stairs with feeble steps, and went through the preparatory exercises in a suppressed voice. Still weak from long confinement, as he leaned upon the desk and gave out his theme, every ear hung upon the cherished accents. The effect of his address is said to have been affecting in the highest degree. As it proceeded, he kindled into that calm and earnest ardor for which he was remarkable, and vindicated the benignity and the wisdom of the heavenly Father who had so recently afflicted him, in a strain so exalted and sincere that to this day all who heard him dwell with enthusiasm upon the scene."

Of the living lights of Andover, New Haven, Hartford, and Cambridge; of the learned and accurate Stuart; of Bacon and Bushnell, with their light but shining armor, Jarvis with his vast erudition, and Norton, whose exact and comprehensive scholarship, clear, compact and beautiful style, and masterly discussions of the evidences and genius of Christianity are fitly applauded by Mr. Griswold, our limits forbid a particular characterization. Coming from New England into New York, we find in the last generation the wise and pious Hobart, and his Presbyterian contemporary, Dr. Mason, who deserves to be classed among the most eloquent preachers since Bourdaloue and Massillon entranced the gay world of Paris, or Barrow and Taylor warmed and invigorated the colder hearts and minds of London. It is related that the celebrated Robert Hall, after listening to a sermon by Mason, while the American orator was in England, declared that his "occupation was gone;" he could never hope to approach so great a master; and was so impressed by his superiority that he could not be prevailed upon for nearly two months to erënter a pulpit. Mason has left us no compositions to sustain his great reputation; but we know that his mind was thoroughly furnished with the best learning; that the fulness of his mind gave him his powerful and fit command of language; justifying the words of Horace:

—— "cui lecta potenter erit res,
Nec facundia deseret hunc, nec lucidus ordo."

Passing from the theologians, eminent as such, to those who have been more especially distinguished as religious moralists, we meet first the venerated name of Dr. Channing, whom we have always regarded as one of the most interesting and remarkable characters that this nation has produced. He was not distinguished for those qualities that usually confer celebrity in this country; for his nature was in fact a complete antagonism to all the characteristics of our people and our day. In all wherein the ordinary great of these times are strongest, he was nothing; and that which constituted the mystery of his undying influence, was what the popular mind was little able to analyze, however quick it might be to feel. He was not eminent for keenness of intellectual penetration, for closeness of logic, dexterity of argument, or copious strength of passionate eloquence: the magic of his power consisted in the exquisite sensibility of his moral apprehension, in his subtlety of spiritual perception, in the fineness and freedom and fervor of his sympathies with nature and man and truth. His greatness was in an unusual way. In meeting him in society, the first impression undoubtedly was disappointing. Certainly, he was not great after the same fashion that Webster is. Of the logical analysis,—the demonstrative power,—the piercing and all-pervasive ratiocination that, like the formulas of the higher mathematics, is at once comprehensive and exact,—which Webster has in such prodigious perfection,—Dr. Channing, as we have intimated, possessed little or nothing. When for the first time you "coped" him, to use the Duke's expression,—prepared, of course, more or less, for that re-active, wrestling vigor that you look for commonly, from a strong mind, there was absolutely no re-action at all; and the sort of shock was felt, which one experiences when he has braced his muscles for a strenuous effort and finds that the object he opposes, offers no resistance whatever. You got a fall It was not, that the display of mental force was toned down by a peculiar delicacy of taste or an unwonted suavity of temper; the mental force, nay, even the ability to understand and reply, seemed quite to be wanting. Of course, the visitor had no mind to appreciate what proceeded from one who appeared to have no sympathy with his perceptions. If he were a quick and confident man, he went hastily away in contempt; and remained, forever after, intolerant of the praises of so unimpressive a companion. But if he chanced to be of a more patient and inquiring temper, and remained to observe and consider, his curiosity was soon engaged by something altogether unexpected; and out of his first disappointment grew the capacity to comprehend those qualities which, when once comprehended, were sure to be admired. He made acquaintance with a character wholly new and singular, in whose developments he soon felt himself intimately interested; a character which first puzzled, and then charmed. He beheld mental capacities, not so much rare in order, as novel in kind; sentiment doing the work of understanding, and doing it with infallible accuracy; feeling made rational, and reason warmed and animated by sensibility. It seemed as if, a Des Cartes in morals, Dr. Channing had by some fundamental conception, reconciled two faculties and two domains, before separated and antagonist, and had reduced affection and intellect to one; originating, in effect, a new analysis. So simple, quiet, and even loose, did this new method seem,—so little of the old geometrical formality had it, that you might doubt its power and efficacy; but when you saw it decomposing with ease the insoluble problems of philosophy, developing social theorems of immense application, and without any failing cases at all; and, if not explicating all political difficulties, at least turning their flank and taking them in the rear, and thus provisionally determining them,—then your doubt turned into wonder, and your wonder grew to confidence and the enthusiasm of admiration. He formed, in truth, a new centre of opinion and action in this country; he might almost be said to have introduced a new element into our civilization, and to furnish a new variety of character in our history. The effects of his career upon American society will never cease; and whatever fresh commotions may disturb the waters of life among us, the gentle wave that emanated in expanding circles from the sphere of his operations will be reproduced in larger and broader sweeps throughout all times, and that agitation will be for the healing of the nations.

In the same dignified company, a high place is justly given to Dr. Wayland, whose vigor and originality are appreciated. In regard to the literary characteristics of this distinguished writer, Mr. Griswold has been guilty of an infelicity, which he will probably correct in a new edition; he has given a description that is applicable only to Dr. Wayland's later productions, and added specimens from his early works which are marked by qualities of a very different kind.

Of American novelists, the earliest that attained general distinction and enjoys a still-living reputation, was Charles Brockden Brown. In some of his characteristics he resembled the school of Godwin; in some qualities, he bore the stamp of decided originality and power. His narratives exhibit great ingenuity of mental contrivance; his characters are analyzed with a morbid acuteness; both are so vivid in their impression, and so connected in the sequence of the parts, that if the reader's interest is once engaged, it is held by a kind of fascination to the end. His writings, however, want relation to nature and ordinary life; they lack the invigoration of human sympathy, and the grace of familiar and domestic sentiment. They look like wonderful pieces of mechanism; they excite our respect and wonder, but do not attract affection. The decorations of his style resemble cast-iron ornaments, more than the genuine flowers of imaginative feeling.

But the writer who in this department has risen to the highest order of greatness, and in a style of narrative entirely his own exhibited the fullest luxuriance of creative vigor in art, is Mr. Cooper. With all that is impressive and splendid and peculiar in the condition and character of this continent; with the prairie, the solemn forest, the lake, the wild and boundless ocean; his genius is associated in enduring connection. The influences which in the silent mighty regions of the west act upon the character of man till they inspire it insensibly with a force and sublimity kindred to their own; the enthusiasm that "thrills the wanderer of the trackless way" of waters; are subjects of the first magnitude and difficulty in romance; and the pen of Mr. Cooper has been equal to them. If you consider the variety of subjects over which his fancy has cast an illustrative ray, and the novelty of the effects which he has accomplished in fiction; if you follow him through the long range of characters and scenes; the Indian, the revolutionary soldier, the western adventurer, the sailor, the pirate, and many others; in all of which he is superior, and in some of which he is supreme; it will be acknowledged that he possesses a copiousness and energy of imagination which few in any day have exceeded. Few have been gifted with a larger share of the idealizing faculty, and none have exercised the faculty with more exquisite taste and judgment. The elevation and lustre of romance are given to every subject which his narrative takes up, yet the impression of reality is always preserved undiminished. The truth of the scene is always closely kept; the character, effect and tone of nature are never sacrificed. He never indulges in false creations; he never resorts to distortion from a want of strength to render the simple and genuine impressions. Persons and incidents and circumstances are described with minuteness enough to individualize and bring them vividly before us, but without that painful subtlety of characterization and description which forget that they are addressed, not to the intellect, but to the imagination and the taste. It must be remembered, too, in estimating the creative power of his genius, that in the cases in which his success has been most brilliant he was not dealing with scenes around which traditionary narrative had thrown a romantic charm, or incidents and characters that national feeling had invested with a sentiment which the novelist is called upon merely to render and not to impart; that he was not occupied with the "old poetic mountain," which "inspiration breathes around," nor with the valley or the stream on which the shadows of the past linger and sport, but with regions bare of association; with plains and hills and rivers not glittering in the ray of any noble recollection; with characters known to us only in connection with vulgar or repulsive or disgusting accompaniments. He was called upon first to drive away the atmosphere of familiarity that surrounded and degraded the landscape, and then to breathe through all the region, from his own resources of fancy and feeling, the roseate air of romance.

Next to Mr. Cooper, in the walks of fiction, and in the power to invest familiar narrative with ideal grace and sentiment, we are disposed to place the authoress of "Hope Leslie." There is a charm of imaginative purity and a beauty of refined thoughtfulness in all her writings, which have caused us to read them again and again without diminution of interest or admiration. When woman becomes an original and vigorous author, without ceasing to be a delicate and gentle woman, authorship is seen in its most delightful lineaments. We are glad to find Mr. Griswold thus appreciating the higher part of a character in which all is excellent and all is lovely:

"Miss Sedgewick has marked individuality. She commands as much respect by her virtues as she does admiration by her talents. Indeed, the rare endowments of her mind depend in an unusual degree upon the moral qualities with which they are united for their value. She writes with a higher object than merely to amuse. Animated by a cheerful philosophy, and anxious to pour its sunshine into every place where there is lurking care or suffering, she selects for illustration the scenes of every-day experience, paints them with exact fidelity, and seeks to diffuse over the mind a delicious serenity, and in the heart kind feelings and sympathies, and wise ambition and steady hope. A truly American spirit pervades her works. She speaks of our country as one "where the government and institutions are based on the *gospel principle* of equal rights and equal privileges to all," and denies that honor and shame depend upon condition. She is the champion of the virtuous poor, and, selecting her heroes and heroines from humble life, does not deem it necessary that by tricks upon them in the cradle they have been only temporarily banished from a patrician caste and estate to which they were born.

"Her style is colloquial, picturesque, and marked by a facile grace which is evidently a gift of nature. Her characters are nicely drawn and delicately contrasted. Her Deborah Lenox has remarkable merit as a creation and as an impersonation, and it is perfectly indigenous. The same can be said of several others. Miss Sedgewick's delineations of New England manners are decidedly the best that have appeared, and show both a careful study and a just appreciation."

We are happy also to agree with the present editor in our estimate of the historical novels of Dr. Bird, especially the novel of "Calavar;" but Mr. Griswold has not observed his entire and hopeless inferiority in other classes of fiction, when he who was dignified, brilliant and classical, becomes commonplace, tedious and inelegant. The reason of the difference appears to be that the talent of the author lies not in the delineation of character, not in humor, nor in narrative, but in costume, picturesque impression and dramatic effect. "Calavar and The Infidel," says Mr. Griswold, in his introduction, "were the first novels of Dr. Bird, and there are few American readers who need to be informed of their character or desert; though, as their accomplished author has been so long in retirement, the inference is reasonable that their reception was equal neither to their merits nor his expectations. Dr. Bird has great dramatic power, and has shown in several instances considerable ability in the portraiture of character. His historical romances are deserving of that title. His scenes and events from actual life are presented with graphic force and an unusual fidelity. He had the rare merit of understanding his subjects as perfectly as it was possible to do so by the most persevering and intelligent study of all accessible authorities; and in the works I have mentioned has written in an elevated and effective style."

Of Mr. Kennedy, the author of "Horse-Shoe Robinson," etc., Mr. Griswold has spoken more highly, we think, than an unbiassed examination of his writings would justify. Of Mr. Paulding he says with considerable felicity:

"Mr. Paulding's writings are distinguished for a decided nationality. He has had no respect for authority unsupported by reason, but on all subjects has thought and judged for himself. He has defended our government and institutions, and has imbodied what is peculiar in our manners and opinions. There is hardly a character in his works who would not in any country be instantly recognized as an American. He is unequalled in a sort of quaint and whimsical humor, but occasionally falls into the common error of thinking there is humor in epithets, and these are sometimes coarse or vulgar. Humor is a quality of feeling and action, and like any sentiment or habit, should be treated in a style which indicates a sympathy with it. He who pauses to invent its dress will usually find his invention exhausted before he attempts its body. He seems generally to have no regular schemes and premeditated catastrophies. He follows the lead of a free fancy, and writes down whatever comes into his mind. He creates his characters, and permits circumstances to guide their conduct. Perhaps the effects of this random and discursive spirit are more natural than those of a strict regard to unities. It is a higher achievement to maintain an interest in a character than to fasten the attention to a plot."

Mr. Dana may be considered as standing at the head of the literary men of New England; and as being, past all question, one of the brightest, purest and highest intelligences that this land has yet produced. The delicacy of his mental perceptions, the strength of his reflective powers and the richness of his genius in composition, render him almost unrivalled in the high field of the philosophy of criticism, and in the department of art have made him especially able to trace with a learned eye, the law of that mysterious process by which, as in the case of Allston and of all who have reached the heights of genius, spiritual sensibility passed into an exalted æsthetic power under the animating guidance of thoughtful self-control. In regard to his mental characteristics, Mr. Dana may be called the American Coleridge. There is the same union of the keenest intellectual subtlety—the most piercing philosophical analysis—with the wealth and glory of practical imagination. Looking at life and nature with the same blending of the moralist's with the artist's view, both of these remarkable men habitually regarded truth as the beauty of reason, and beauty as the truth of taste. As in the case of Coleridge, Mr. Dana's views and discoveries have been chiefly communicated in conversation—by living action upon the understandings of those who afterwards, in their most shining displays, have only reflected the rays of his intelligence. Hence his public reputation, great as it is and always was, has been of a reflective and secondary sort; that is to say, it rested not so much upon any actual impression which the public had received from Mr. Dana's productions, as upon the testimony of an intermediate class of writers and students, who have appreciated his merit and propagated his fame. He has been more the author of authors, than the author of the public. The greatness of such men becomes known, as the ores of Mount Truolus were discovered, from the golden particles that were borne along with the current that passed by.

In Mr. Griswold's estimate of the characteristics of the author of "The Idle Man," there is just perception and discrimination.

"The strength of Mr. Dana lies very much in the union of sentiment with imagination, or perhaps in an ascendency of sentiment over his other faculties. It is this which makes every character of his so actual, as if he entered into each with his own conscience, and in himself suffered the victories over the will, and the remorse which follows them. There are beautiful touches of fancy in his tales; but, as in his poems, the fancy is inferior and subject to the imagination. He has a solemn sense of the grandeur and beauty of nature, and his descriptions, sometimes by a single sentence, have remarkable vividness and truth. His observations on society are particular and profound, and he brings his characters before us with singular facility and distinctness, and invests them, to our view, with the dignity and destiny of immortal beings. His mind is earnest, serious and benevolent, delicately susceptible of impressions of beauty, and apt to dwell upon the ideal and spiritual. Its characteristics pervade his style, which is pure English, and has a certain antique energy about it, and an occasional simple but deep pathos, which is sure to awaken a kindred feeling in the mind of the reader."

Mr. Griswold has scarcely spoken with sufficient distinctness and emphasis of the extraordinary merit of Allston's "Monaldi," as a work of fiction. The wonderful mind which was oftener and so perfectly exhibited by the pencil, was here revealed, not indeed upon a great scale, but with entireness of moral and intellectual effect. Indeed, we may say that it is as perfect a picture as Mr. Allston ever painted; for the genius which it displays, though employing "the instrument of words," is essentially pictorial in its character and impression. We may apply to it the criticism made in the work itself of a picture of the crucifixion by an old artist: "Though eccentric and somewhat capricious, it was yet full of powerful expression, and marked by a vigor of execution that made every thing around it look like washed drawings." The various persons of the tale are not revealed to us by an illumination seemingly proceeding from the author's mind, but flash their characteristics upon us with a vividness which almost renders us uncomfortable by its nearness and force. To display the operation of the passions with that intensity and clearness which his plan contemplated, it was necessary to represent the subjects of the narrative as endowed with sensibilities very greatly more susceptible and active than ordinary people; yet with consummate skill these characters are held firmly to nature and probability. Nothing is morbid or overwrought; but all healthful, genuine and actual. To exhibit a series of telescopic views which, though greatly magnified, are never indistinct, and which first studied inseparate particularly, are afterward reduced to a common centre and point of view, is a surprising exhibition of genius and skill. Indeed, we venture to suggest, that scarcely any work in modern times, if properly examined, would exhibit the resources of literary art more wonderfully than the tale of "Monaldi."

In speaking of Mr. Allston's moral nature, we ought not in fact to separate his literary productions from the revelations of his pencil. Mr. Griswold appears to be fully conscious of this. The opportunity which the period that has elapsed since Allston's death, has afforded of weighing, coolly and comparatively, the opinions formed of his abilities during his life, has confirmed the impression that his genius was superior, not only to all that has appeared in this country, but to anything that can be found in Europe, until you get back to the great immortal names of Italian glory, the heroes of art, the half-divine. No man ever had juster, deeper, clearer views of the character of art, and the splendor of his success as a painter, is principally due to the fidelity with which he worked out that conception, within himself and in his works. He understood the nature of art as it exists, distinguished from a transcription of the real, on the one hand, and from a metaphysical idea on the other. He had apprehended, with a profound insight, the relation which a spirit and temper of art bear to moral virtue; the fine, but vital links, by which it is allied to all that is good and all that is lovely in human sentiment and human conduct; he felt the purity of its profession and the dignity of its practice. Mr. Griswold informs us that a memoir of the life of Allston is now in the course of preparation by his brother-in-law Mr. Dana. We hope that this statement is not mistaken nor premature. The dissemination of views like Allston's upon art, under the living illustration of a career so beautifully true to that worship of excellence in art, to which early love had deepened, in the bosom of this elevated man, would be of inappreciable value at this time in its influence on literary and pictorial art in the United States, and upon the characters of those who profess it. It would raise and illumine their aspirations. It would teach them what to desire, and how to strive for it. There is abundance of intellectual action and of willing energy of mind in this country; but it is essentially uninstructed as to the objects of its interest, and the nature of the service which it professes. It has not been told of the character of that Unknown God whom it ignorantly worships. In Allston was seen the true artist; one to whom the ineffable beauty had been revealed, and whose soul that sight had forever rapt and consecrated; thenceforth his vowed and single purpose was to reproduce that celestial vision in forms of existence, of thought, and of feeling—to develop the infinite from beneath the disguises of the actual, and shed around the things of time those rays which are a lustre of eternity.

We have here alluded to the close connection between the forms of mental and moral power or grace, as exhibited by the great artist and the great writer. The subject is profoundly interesting. It has so presented itself to Mr. Griswold, who, in closing his preliminary view of The Intellectual Condition of the Country, observes that the relation of the plastic arts to the higher forms of literature is so immediate that "the shortest survey of our intellectual history would be incomplete, without some reference to the noble works of our painters and sculptors." He accordingly touches in outline, though effective, strokes, the history of the higher forms of American Art, as shown in the productions of the pencil and chisel. The topic may be commended to his thoughts for future essay and enlargement in some independent form. It is one which would grow greatly under the consideration: and form a fine subject for a delicate and discriminating pen. It is a superficial opinion which represents art as subservient only to the delights of the senses, or the diversion and amusement of the vacant mind. Its truest ministration, as we have remarked in speaking of Mr. Allston, is essentially moral; and of the subtlest and most intimate operation. The highest forms of art, whether in music, painting, or architecture, touch sensibilities of our nature that are reached by no other mortal agency. They react on our inmost sympathies, in which they become melted in a transport of spiritual fruition. The benefits of such experiences, in developing and educating the nature, and bringing one part of our being acquainted with another, are highly to be valued. There are those whose various mental qualities seem not to be in a state of communication, and in whom intellect, sentiment, conscience, passion, seem to dwell in unconnected chambers, and move in separate channels! This is an imperfect state of life—an immature condition of existence. That emotion which proceeds from an intense sympathetic enjoyment, is the natural provision for breaking down these detaching barriers, opening clear passages from one department of the soul to another, and mingling them all in the unity of a combined and entire character. The affections ordinarily are the appropriate solvent for the crude and isolated elements of the individual constitution. They liquefy the rude masses of consciousness, precipitating in dross the impure combinations, and causing the essential parts to flow forth together in one clear, blended stream of sensibility. But it is not every one who has the happiness to be subjected to the forges of affection; and the range of its reactive energy is somewhat low and limited. Those more interior and abstract sympathies which fuse only at a very high point, yield to nothing perfectly but the appeals of that power which dwells in consummate art. The appreciation and enjoyment of art is, in fact, but an action of affection in its finest and most transcendental phase; and that action is vivid in proportion as it is exquisite. It flashes, like a harmless lightning, from point to point of our complex nature—illuminates depths of being that before were unknown to ourselves—traces with rapid certainty the tangled chain of mental correspondences—interprets between opposite and remote regions of our spirit in signals of light—and kindles in momentary splendor the visionary conflagration of inspired intelligence.

Mr. Griswold does well, therefore, in speaking as he does of "Greenough, whose majestic Washington sits in repose before the capitol;" and of "Powers, in whom Thorswalden saw the restorer of a glory to the marble it had scarcely known since the days of Praxiteles." Such men, he declares, "promise to make our country a resting-place for the eyes of future generations as they travel backward toward Rome and Athens." The prospects of American Art in its ethnological characteristics deserve, as Mr. Griswold truly remarks, a large consideration in immediate connection with its letters. Let us, therefore, profiting by the hint thus given us, say a few words on this subject.

A judicious critic, in distinguishing the characteristics of ancient and modern Art, has referred to Sculpture as the type of the former, and to Painting as a symbol of the latter. The illustration is, to some extent, well chosen. Classic art is, in its nature and impression, single, definite, substantial, satisfying the sense: Christian art is complex, vague, ideal, kindling the imagination. Form is the element of one; effect is the object of the other. The older style indicates nothing beyond what it exhibits; the latter school is essentially suggestive, and it conciliates the eye, only that it may command the mind. Natural emotion is therefore the region of the former. Moral conception is the peculiar province of the other. Modern art, throughout all its range, addresses the reflective powers; it speaks to our spiritual being; by an indirect, but sure appeal, it wakes to an intense sensibility, remote, undefined and slumbering sympathies. It might of course be looked for, that the ancients and the moderns should excel, severally, in that kind of production which is referred to as the representative of their respective genius; and so indeed we find it. The statuary of Greece stands as lonely, as lofty, as eternal in its perfection, as the stars of heaven: in literature, architecture and music, the emanations of modern intelligence have been recognized as genuine, distinctive and admirable; but in sculpture, Europe has never risen above a cold and stiff imitation of the antique. On the other hand, painting among the Athenians seems never to have gone beyond a vivid and illusory transcription of sensible objects, if we may credit the anecdote of the curtain and the fruit in the rivalry of Xeuxis and Parrhasius; it probably made no approach whatever to the comprehensive, sublime, resistless creations of Angelo, Raphael and Guido.

The question whether Art is likely ever to be enriched by a style of sculpture essentially modern, resolves itself, then, into an inquiry whether the marble is capable, in groups or in single figures, of developing an interest predominantly moral. In order that the pure influence of thought or feeling should be impressed upon the mind, through the medium of a work of art, it is necessary that the obtrusive definiteness of form should be kept back from view: the Italian painter and the Gothic architect, accordingly, conceals, confuses, and shades away the shapes he is dealing with, until the realizing keenness of the senses is bewildered and fascinated, and the mental conception which lay insphered within the work is poured in upon the spirit in unopposed intensity. The sculptor's difficulty is, that he has no element to operate with but distinct and simple form; and that form the human figure. The sense is therefore always addressed; the idea of imitation is always present. If the mind wanders away for a moment in dreamy apprehension of the sentiment which the stone appears to typify, material consciousness quickly calls it back to trace the natural beauties of the limbs, the face, the attitude. In order, also, that the scrutinizing taste of the eye may never be offended, these last must be perfect in their inherent and visible grace: to accomplish this, and at the same time to charge the figure with a glow of spiritual significance, which shall eclipse the brightness of physical perfection, is the profoundly delicate task which modern sculpture is called upon to execute. The Greek never attempted it: satisfied with the merely natural elegance of his Apollo and Venus, he excluded from their faultlessness every conception not material and mortal. It appears to us that in recent times, this fine problem of creative skill has found an abler solution, in the galleries of *American* genius, than in those of any country; and this chiefly in two works, which Mr. Griswold selects as representatives of the national power in this department—Powers' Greek Slave, and Greenough's Washington. Both are representations of real objects; yet in both, the paramount impression is ideal and moral. Both exhibit forms of surpassing merit—one, of commanding grandeur—the other, of melting grace: but in both, all sense of physical proportions is merged and lost in mental sympathy with the thought that radiates from the image with a power to awe, to elevate and to refine the mind. Greenough's statue, of course, is not intended to be a portrait statue, as Houdon's is; in which, so far as imitative art can aid the imagination, we behold the Father of his Country "as he lived;" but is a representation of the *historic idea* of Washington, a personal type of the moral grandeur that is associated with that conception. It is designed to embody in a form of appropriate majesty the impression due to his towering and awful superiority above ordinary men. Borrowing the antique conception of the divine, the figure is colossal; the attitude and expression those of a god. In its sublime entirety, it sets before the eye such an image as posterity will call up to its mind when it thinks of the mighty and unapproached career of Washington. In approaching the delicate creation of chaste imagination which Mr. Powers gives us in his Greek Slave, after the first shock of delight from the gentle rush of her beauty, wave-like, upon the spirit, is past, we are arrested and enchained by the profound and lofty interest of her countenance. The conception is as exalted, as the execution of it is exquisite. It is an expression of offended dignity —of expostulating rebuke—of placid and pitying contempt. Confident in an unassailable moral safety—feeling that no material subjugation or injury can ever harm the soul—she stands in the pride of her unapproachable purity; insulted, but not abased—outraged, but not degraded. There is no touch of shame in her features; she feels that she is not responsible for the condition in which she is placed: an instinctive gesture of self-protection—an involuntary averting of the head from the spectacle of the wrong that is done her by such exposure—are tributes to the natural delicacy of her character. There is no shade of fear in her attitude; her whole being, absorbed into intense consciousness of an impregnable spiritual existence, dwells in serene composure upon the calm heights of a more intimate and essential life. Never was the native majesty of the chaste, refined, and high-toned soul of a woman, embodied in nobler force and more enchanting grace. Never was it more admirably shown, with what energetic sincerity virtue can look down upon her oppressors, and chastise their unworthiness: never was the contrast between humiliating circumstances and a mental elevation more gloriously flashed forth. Over those who are disgracing themselves by this treatment of a woman, she seems to feel such infinite superiority, that reflection interposes to temper its excess by some infusion of compassion. Her look reproaches them for exhibiting conduct so ineffably dishonoring to them. She appears to blush for the degradation of her race, by the display of a behavior so discreditable to men. What, in a critical point of view, we chiefly admire, is the moderation which the sculptor has imposed upon himself in the material working out of this conception—the exquisite temperance which he has observed in the degree in which a temporary feeling is allowed to prevail over the native and habitual repose of the features. Fixing the expression unmistakably upon the countenance, he has with consummate taste abstained from interrupting the serene beauty of loveliness and grace, further than to waken in the observer a train of emotion which no heart can fail to carry out to its full result. Such is the impression which this divine emanation of the artist's power gives to us. It is well called the *Greek* Slave, for it is the bondage of that ethereal essence whose incarnation is identified with Attica; it is an everlasting vindication of that supremacy of mind over condition which Greece first taught, and Grecian fame forever attests.

But we return from this digression upon American Art, which the name of Allston—great both in letters and in Art—and the close connection pointed out by Mr Griswold, between letters and the expressions of high art, have naturally inspired.

Of Hawthorne, an old and favorite correspondent of the Knickerbocker Magazine, appropriate specimens are given, and his manner is happily illustrated.

Fay, Miss Leslie, Simms, Neal, Hall, and others, pass in review before the author, and receive each a measure of commendation.

In passing from the writers of fiction to the historians and essayists, we are detained by the name of Mr. Irving, which, shedding an equal lustre over all these departments, receives from all of them an equal reflection of honor; "focus at once of all the rays of Fame." This eminent person ought ever to be followed by the respect and gratitude of his countrymen; for he was the first who led American literature to the sympathies of the English people, and conciliated or commanded the deference and applause of literary factions in that country, who, rivals in every thing, seemed especially to vie with each other in contempt for America. No man ever succeeded so perfectly in rendering literature *delicious*. Elevated, pure, of pervading refinement and chastity, his writings give us a pleasure which is almost sensuous, in its fulness and directness. Without apparent arts, without affectation or tricks, they fascinate, enchant, bewitch us.

Subduing our affections, and reigning over them with an absolute power, they always command the respect of our taste, and receive the approbation of our judgment. The charm is obviously not the result of an assumed manner, an acquired style, or a contrived dress; but springs from a source in nature, and emanates from instinctive and essential gracefulness of temper and spirit and feeling:

> "Illum quidquid agit quoquo vestigia movit,
> Componet furtim subsequiturque Decor."

The richness and delicacy of his fancy, the ethereal flow of his humor, which like the dew of summer refreshes and brightens every flower and leaf and branch; the constant and quiet good sense; the playfulness of temper which never betrays from decorum, and never beguiles from seriousness of purpose; the familiarity mingled with native reserve; the inborn elegance of mind which renders gayety dignified, and gives attraction to grief and sadness, and throws an atmosphere of interest around occasions the most barren; all these combine to form a talent for agreeable writing, which in extent and quality perhaps has never been exceeded. Through how wide a range, also, have these admirable resources of imagination and taste been exhibited in unfailing brilliance! With surprising versatility of character, this exquisite genius first yields to the spirit of the subject or scene, and then glorifies it with the illumination of its own glowing life. It becomes grotesque, and revels quaintly amid the burgomasters of New Amsterdam; in the scenes of Moresco chivalry, it assumes the forms and colors of imaginative passion: at once gorgeous and delicate, and so perfectly as to become almost the express image of Saracenic character and art; in the lanes and parks of the merry England, it becomes simple, decent, homely; in all its tone and temper and intelligence, more English than England itself; a Chaucer in prose; in the daring, dashing life of the west, who throws himself into the *abandon* of adventure with more genial earnestness than the Tourist of the Prairies?

In another sphere, this frolic spirit can assume, with native majesty, the buskined tread of the historian. Not only can he do justice to every subject, however peculiar or difficult, which is given to him, but he can write delightfully when he has no subject at all. "Astoria" has always seemed to us to be the triumph of his skill; for the subject there, if not nothing, was certainly worse than nothing. For purposes of romantic art and elegant literature, what theme could be more jejune and impracticable than the journal of a trading voyage to the Pacific, and a trading journey across the Rocky Mountains, by persons whose characters and objects and adventures had scarcely a ray of dignity or interest? Yet, by mere power of style, and mere grace of manner and embellishment, he has made the narrative as delightful as a tale of genii, and transformed the desert into a garden of fairy loveliness. Mr. Irving in fact possesses that natural fertility of sentiment, that delicate observation and selection, that truth of judgment and gentle animation, which supplied in Goldsmith the want of almost every qualification, and constitute a faculty of which it is correctly said that, "*Nullum quod tetigit non ornavit.*"

Among American historians, we are glad to find that Mr. Griswold appreciates the supremacy of Prescott:

"Mr. Prescott is undoubtedly entitled to a prominent place in the first rank of historians. With extraordinary industry he explores every source of information relating to his subjects, and with sagacity as remarkable decides between conflicting authorities and rejects improbable relations. His judgment of character is calm, comprehensive, and profoundly just. He enters into the midst of an age, and with all its influences about him, estimates its actors and its deeds. His arrangement of facts is always effective, and his style flowing, familiar, singularly transparent, and marked throughout with the most felicitous expressions.

"Whatever may be the comparative merits of the two great histories he has already published, as intellectual efforts, there is little room to doubt that 'The Conquest of Mexico' will continue to be the most popular. It is justly remarked in the Edinburgh Review, that, considered merely as a work of amusement, it will bear a favorable comparison with the best romances in the language. The careful, judicious, and comprehensive essay on the Aztec civilization, with which it opens, is not inferior in interest to the wonderful drama to which it is an epilogue. The scenery, which is sketched with remarkable vividness and accuracy, is wonderful, beautiful, and peculiar. The characters are various, strongly marked, and not more numerous than is necessary for the purposes of art. Cortez himself is a knight errant, 'filled with the spirit of romantic enterprise,' yet a skilful general, fruitful of resources, and of almost superhuman energies; of extraordinary cunning, but without any rectitude of judgment; a bigoted churchman, yet having no sympathy with virtue; of kind manners, but remorseless in his cruelties. His associates, Valasquez, Ordaz, Sandoval, Alvarado, the priest Olmedo, the heroine Dona Marina, and others of whom we have glimpses more or less distinct, seem to have been formed as well to fill their places in the written history, as to act their parts in the crusade. And the philosophical king of Tezcuco, and Montezuma, whose character and misfortunes are reflected in his mild and melancholy face, and Guatemozin, the last of the emperors, and other Aztecs, in many of the higher qualities of civilization superior to their invaders, and inferior in scarcely any thing but a knowledge of the art of war, are grouped and contrasted most effectively with such characters as are more familiar in the scenes of history. . . Mr. Prescott perhaps excels most in description and narration, but his histories combine in a high degree almost every merit that can belong to such works. They are pervaded by a truly and profoundly philosophical spirit, the more deserving of recognition because it is natural and unobtrusive, and are distinguished above all others for their uniform candor, a quality which might reasonably be demanded of an American writing of early European policy and adventure."

We do not, however, agree with Mr. Griswold in considering Mr. Bancroft's history as "one of the great works of the age." Transcendentalism, so long as it keeps itself in the cloudy regions of metaphysics and moral sentiments, may escape confutation or exposure; you cannot *prove* its worthlessness, because you cannot bring it to any absolute and settled test. But when it comes down into the *terra firma* of actual life and historical reality, and gives its views of national interests, and traces the connections of human events, and enables us to see it against a background of experience, we then discover the shadowy vanity of the imposture; for these are matters with which sense and reason and logic, only can properly deal. "*Qui Bavium non odit,*" etc.; he who can understand Mr. Emerson, may value Mr. Bancroft. But a man of merely common sense may read the three volumes of "The History of the United States," and he will find at the end of his lessons that he has not acquired one clear, definite notion; one distinct apprehension of fact or thought. A series of dreamy forms has passed before his mind; a procession of vaporous images has beguiled his attention; but they came like shadows, and so they have departed; leaving no impression, and no benefit behind them. The understanding of the reader is neither enriched, nor informed, nor quickened.

In that class of essayists, and authors of fugitive pieces, who are conveniently designated as miscellaneous writers, Mr. Poe deserves a place. Narratives which rivet the interest, and sway the passions as powerfully as his do, indicate a vigor of imagination that might send its productions forward far along the line of future life. Many of his tales, we have no doubt, will long survive, as among the ablest and most remarkable of American productions. In the perfect contrivance of the plans, which, though complex, are never embarrassing or perplexing, and in the orderly evolvement of all the incidents, they bear a resemblance to the dramatic plots of Ben Jonson, which, of themselves, without reference to the treasures which they wrap up in them, have been considered as giving him a very eminent rank. Of talents such as Mr. Poe is blessed with, the true employment is in original composition; in a genial exercise of the creative faculties of imagination and feeling, in extending through a space which is else void and silent, the limits of the region of living and lovely forms, and augmenting the trophies of the genius of his nation and his race. To one who possesses the powers of close, logical reasoning, and of pointed and piercing sarcasm, the "*torva voluptas*" of literary and social controversy is often a fatal fascination. But a man who is conscious within himself of faculties which indicate to him that he was born, not to wrangle with the men of his own times, but to speak truth and peace to distant ages and a remote posterity, ought to make a covenant with himself, that he will be drawn aside by no temptation, however vehement, from that calm dedication of his thoughts to literary art, which is the service he owes to that Spirit which has given him power to become one of its ministers.

As an analytical critic, Mr. Poe possesses abilities quite unrivalled in this country, and perhaps on either side of the water. We have scarcely ever taken up one of his more careful critical papers, on some author or work worthy of his strength, without a sense of surprise at the novel and profound views from which his inquiries began, nor followed their development without the closest interest, nor laid the essay down without admiration and respect for the masculine and acute understanding with which we had coped during the perusal. But in the case of inventive genius so brilliant and vigorous as is shown in his poems, and in the papers to which we have alluded, and of which Mr. Griswold also speaks, we feel that even criticism of the highest kind is an employment below the true measure of its dignity, and, we may say, its duty; for to be a tender of the light in another man's tomb, is no fit occupation for one who is able to kindle a lamp of his own, whose ray may abide against all the force of night, and storms, and time. The poet's is a consecrating gift. A man who can produce such a work as "The Raven," ought to feel that it was his office to afford subjects, and not models, to criticism.

In the same class of writers, Willis has a prominent rank given to him by Mr. Griswold. To such he is fully entitled. The world has lately, with some diligence, been set wrong in his matter, but it is already, by a certain instinct, bringing itself right in the main.* Indeed it is a mistake to accuse the world of injustice or malignity. It is an honest world, at heart; its faults proceed in reality from want of knowledge, or from defects in judgment. Like the rest of us, it is liable at times to bald misapprehension; it is subject to the imposture of appearances; it is prone to decide precipitately; on many subjects, it is not well informed, and so is exposed to the arts of charlatanism and the arrogance of pretenders; nay, what was hardly to be looked for in so old a subject, it suffers from an extreme of diffidence, and, from a want of confidence in its own clearest impressions, will believe one thing when it knows another, and will be dictated to by men who well might go to school to it. As respects

* These remarks were written at a time when several of the English Reviews had conspired to make a virulent and unjust attack upon Mr. Willis's literary pretensions; the result, no doubt, in a large degree, of English insularity and national dislike. On this account especially, the author gives to Mr. Willis's merits, as identified with America, a special and elaborate consideration.—ED.

sagacity, it cannot be characterized as weak, but it is slow. A subject must be removed some distance into the past, before its myriad eyes can get the focus. When it does see, we must all give up to it. The rectification of popular opinions is, therefore, a process of anticipation rather than of change; and, in venturing upon the task of correction, we profess not to have thought better, but a little faster.

With Mr. Willis we have never had the pleasure of any personal acquaintance or relations. But speaking of him as a literary man, by what, in common with the whole country, we have seen and known, we may affirm with certainty that no man is of a more open and prompt disposition in respect to the appreciation and encouragement of other literary men, who are always, of course, in some degree literary rivals. His hand is as ready to aid them when struggling toward distinction in letters, as his pen is to recognize them when they have emerged into it, to explain their merits and expand their reputation. Those who have needed him have seen his benevolence; those who have trusted him have found him faithful; those who have favored him know that he is grateful. Conduct such as he has exhibited, and such a character as he enjoys among those who know him, a superficial or spurious virtue could neither inspire nor sustain. The world has a distrust of too much refinement—which it refers to a tainted heart or a feeble head—and the distrust is not unnatural; but in the present case, if the testimony of friends is of any credibility—it is grafted on a wild stock of sense and feeling. Willis is a man who, if he possessed more cant, would be thought to have more virtue; whose morality has not pretension enough to be popular, and who, if he had more hypocrisy of speech, would undoubtedly be credited for a better heart.

The causes of the misapprehensions which have been prevalent on his subject might easily be discovered. One of them arose out of circumstances more honorable to his spirit and independence than altogether prudent. In the beginning of his career, he quarrelled with the reviewers; and it is generally agreed that a man had better have a bad epitaph after his death than their ill report while he lives. His taste, his good feeling, his disgust at imposition, and his hatred of oppression, drove him into that quarrel, and his ability and the justice of his cause carried him triumphantly through it. He spoke of Captain Marryat, in the high day of his popularity, as the whole world now acknowledges that Captain Marryat deserved to be spoken of; and he retorted with memorable vigor upon Mr. Lockhart, who, having violated the law of decorum himself with the shamelessness of a prostitute, now stickled for its strictness in others with the fastidiousness of a prude.

Those who do not taste the peculiarities of Mr. Willis's merit, or are willing to be thought difficult, have imputed to his style the faults of affectation and conceit. *Fineness* of sense and feeling is undoubtedly the Delilah of his taste, under whose fascination he is sometimes shorn of his strength. Hence often he is not natural. He is too frequently "upon the rack of exertion." This must be conceded: and if the suggestions of an unknown counsellor are worthy of being followed, we would urge, above all things, upon this fine writer to achieve, as an all-essential element of true literary style, the merit of *simplicity*. But we shall not here enlarge upon what we may be permitted to regret. We can pardon something to the exuberance of youthful faculties, more to circumstances, and a great deal to the natural excesses of human temper, by which a man in pursuit of refinement may verge upon effeminacy. Where there is uncommon merit, a liberal mind will overlook and forget defects and weaknesses in the glow of enjoyment and admiration. Has anybody yet found out how to defend Shakspeare's quibbles and clenches, or Dryden's freedoms, or Pope's unvarying monotony? We believe not; yet nobody is on that account less moved when Othello rages over the scene, or less open to the influence of brilliant sense and lively passion in the writings of the other two. We have not labored to acquire that waterish judgment which, under the name of critical, bears up and floats upon its surface all the light straws and empty rubbish with which valuable things are often surrounded, and lets every thing that is weighty sink out of sight. Mr. Willis's literary failings proceed out of a worthy, or, at least, a pardonable cause: a hatred of parade, and a contempt for the arts of pedantry and professional mystery. In truth, the old dignified and solemn style was so thoroughly done to death, that, for our own parts, we like even the extravagances of this natural and simple school. Let us, then, with a certain candor which becomes men who would judge, estimate the nature and extent of his capacities.

No man has appeared in our literature, endowed with a greater variety of fine qualities. He possesses an understanding, quick, acute, distinguishing even in excess; enriched by culture, and liberalized and illuminated by much observation. He commands all the resources of passion; at the same time that he is master of the effects of manner. The suggestions of an animated sense are harmonized by feeling, and are adorned by a finished wit. His taste is nice, but it is not narrow or bigoted, and his sympathies with his reader are intimate and true. His works exhibit a profusion of pointed and just comment on society and life; they sparkle with delicate and easy humor; they display a prodigality of fancy, and are fragrant with all the floral charm of sentiment. He possesses surprising saliency of mind, which in his hasty effusions often fatigues, but in his matured compositions is controlled to the just repose of art. But distinct from each of these, and sovereign over them all, is the vivifying and directing energy of a fine poetical talent; that prophetic faculty in man whose effects are as vast as its processes are mysterious; whose action is a moral enchantment that all feel, but none can fathom. This influence it is which, entering into and impregnating all his other faculties, gives force to some, elevation to others, and grace and interest to them all.

A peculiarity of Mr. Willis consists in his having united in himself, and reconciled in art, two powers which are so distinct and even inconsistent that not only do they scarcely ever enter into the same genius, but rarely can be appreciated and enjoyed by the same taste. If the ideal faculty has, in any author, coexisted with the opposite talents of wit and observation, the two have yet been distinct, and have been exercised upon separate works; but in Willis they seem to be identified to a great degree, and in his productions their influence is interfused and blended together. In his tales, for example, he leads us into a drawing-room; the persons of the story are mere human gentlemen in coats and stocks, and ladies, not "in beauty dight" *alone*, but appareled with the aid of strings and hooks and so forth. The beginning of the tale is simple, its progress easy, and its end satisfactory. Here the function of an ordinary story-teller would cease; but it is precisely here that Willis's art begins. What he has of remarkable lies beyond this; it lies in the faculty which can add the loftier without taking away the less; which can create the wonderful without destroying the familiar; which can make the scheme ideal without its ceasing to be real; can shed the rich lights of glowing fancy over the unaltered forms of common life; can carry us through a romance without tasking our invention, and delight us with all the interests of poetry without starting our most common sympathies.

Mr. Willis's genius does not affront the sterner shapes of imagination that wait to be bodied by the poet: it woos the lighter and lovelier forms of fancy which are not less abiding in their beauty. The author seems to let his fancy wander at its own quaint will, and to contemplate no loftier end than his own amusement. But when we return to consider the impression which has been produced and remains; when we observe the essential truth that is wrapped up in the careless comment, and what deep experience breathes in that which seemed but the wantonness of a capricious pen, then we recognize that this seeming negligence is real toil; that there is an earnest purpose in this apparent trifling, and that much art has been concealed with more artifice.

After all, the basis of the literary character of Mr. Willis, and the most valuable of all his qualities, is *common sense;* out of which we shall always believe, that the best literature must proceed. He gets very thoroughly at the truth of life; his perceptions are not blinded by the pre-judgments of a visionary philosophy, and his conclusions are neither warped by his own passions nor racked to fit the prejudices of a faction. He is not forever dealing with sublimated theories, and bewildering reality with transcendental fallacies. His conceptions possess that spontaneous force and interest, that native vigor and richness which recalls the strong days of England, when her literature spoke the language of nature, and not the cant of systems; breathed the fresh air of life, and not the sickly atmosphere of schools.

There is an intimate connection between genius and language, or, in more general terms, between the powers of conception and those of expression. Phrenology has recognized the latter as distinct, intellectual faculties; and the law of the relation between the two and their mutual reaction is one of the contributions which knowledge expects from that science. As to no man are given the trembling sensibilities, the thrilling sentiments, the delicate apprehensions of the poet, but with them is given the power to impart every nicety of his impressions in the appropriate dialect of his art, so upon none is bestowed this marvelous gift of tongues but those to whom is given a higher inspiration which it is their privilege to set forth. Indeed, it is only when the divinity of genius rides upon the language, that the vehicle thus becomes, like the car of Kehama, itself animated with life. What magic sits upon the syllables of Shakspeare! how the phrases of Bacon glitter and ring, like the arrows of Apollo! What rich and dazzling influence in the purple words of Thomson, and the jeweled speech of Gray! Expression, then, is one certain test of genius; and Mr. Willis satisfies that test more entirely, perhaps, than any of his contemporaries. He is a master of the hidden sorceries of speech. He can unbind the rainbow hues that are wrapt up and hidden in the colorless light of our common language, and shed their lustre over thought and passion. Like the great authors of an earlier day, he aims to attain those fine and rich impressions which dwell only in language, and have no being but in words. An error is made by those who do not discriminate between science and art. In matters of reason, the thought is everything, the setting forth of it nothing. But with the fine arts, the expression is a great part of the creation. The fine arts exist at that point where mind and matter coalesce; they are the issue of spirit embracing with sense; hence their most genuine effects flash into existence only when the inward thought passes forth into the outer medium, be it sound, color, form, or language, and the two have become incorporate forever.

Mr. Willis's early poems on Scripture subjects are marked by an exquisiteness of moral perception—a delicacy of penciling, like the touches of the morning light along the heavens, and a noble sympathy with truth and virtue. The snowy gleams of morning hope are joined to a glow of passion as golden as sunset; and the mingled ray flushes everything into beauty. To equal the best that America has yet done, Willis needs only that profound study of poetry as a great art, and that patient and energetic development of his faculties, without which the old sublimities of verse were never reached.

For ourselves, bred in a school of letters too severe, perhaps, in the extent and nicety of its exactions, we are not apt to throw our admiration about promiscuously. To that which is modern and popular, we yield it not unreluctantly. At the same time we ask, who is the writer now in England that combines upon his pages so many of the qualities that contribute to form that copious, rich and mellow composition which characterizes the old models of strength and beauty? The literature of England has, in modern times, degenerated: it has become factitious, feeble, and false; technical, narrow, and dogmatic. The strong, bold music which once rose from it, and shook the heavens with its kingly tones, is changed to a lean and scrannel pipe, whose thin sounds tinkle in the chambers of the ear, but neither reach the understanding nor rouse the heart. Mr. Willis very wisely turned away from the irretrievable barrenness of this metaphysical school, to refresh his faculties at the fountains of a more genuine inspiration. The type of his manner might be found in the writings of the best class of those choice spirits who flowered into literature a little before and after the period of the Restoration; men of thought and of action; at once geniuses, scholars and courtiers. He possesses that delicate propriety of sentiment, instinctive grace, and truth combined with refinement of perception, together with a rare felicity of words, which drew down on Waller the weighty praise of Dryden, who often called him the father of our English elegance, and taught Pope, in the next age, to appreciate and enlarge his merit. There is the same usage of actual life in its best phases; the same knowledge of the heart, if not in its deeper aud darker workings, yet in all the wide range of healthful, fine and pleasurable emotion; the same spontaneous good sense, suavity of manner, and perpetual soft play of wit. We must confess that this school of letters has in it something very charming: it addresses our sympathies, if not with the force of some which went before it, yet with an intelligence, breadth, and distinctness which none that have succeeded it have reached. It is the literature of gentlemen. Those who are familiar only with the violent tribunitian style of this time will not at once recognize its strength; and those who have had their virtue stretched upon the theological racks of the age, will hardly give it credit for the solid and genuine integrity which it conceals under an entire simplicity of manner.

Though never disposed to dogmatize where it is at all reasonable to doubt, we have no idea of suffering any of the modern school of England to dictate judgments to us upon literary subjects. We see nothing in their performances which should make us afraid of their opinions. This is a world in which nations, like individuals, must take care of themselves. Whenever America chooses to claim her own, she may hold forth the name of this gifted person, as that of a writer, who has felt and been faithful to the great mission of art; which is, not to lend itself to the perversions of schemes and theories, but to develop, to animate, and to beautify the native, spontaneous, deathless sympathies and aspirations of humanity. Above all, this is his peculiar characteristic as an author, that, while others touch but one string, or entertain us with the echoes of a single note, there proceeds from his productions a rich and varied chime of reason, passion, sentiment, and fancy, whose tones enrich the air with charming melody, and long will float upon the breezes of the future.

In a special department of this same class of miscellaneous writers, in which Mr. Willis is presented, the editor of "The Prose Writers" includes Mrs. Kirkland, the well-known authoress of "Western Clearings," "A New Home," "Forest Life," and other tales descriptive of American frontier character and homes. This particular department of writers is likely to receive new honor, we are told, in a production called "Leavenworth," a story of the Mississippi and the Prairies, by Mr. J. D. Nourse, of Kentucky.

This is a field of literature all our own, and which we specially note, because we desire to see it specially cultivated. As we have stated in the opening and in other parts of this paper, we entertain a confident opinion that the progress of life and action in our country will develop, in every department of taste, a style essentially native and original. We constantly have prophesied of a national literature that should be equally genuine, in its relations to truth and beauty, with those elder schools which criticism has sealed with its approbation, and yet be stamped with the marks of a new and individual creation; a style of composition that should symbolize, in the richness of its resources, the variety of its effects, and the energy of its tone, those characteristics of force and freedom and expansion that mark the physical scenes amid which we are placed, and the spirits and minds of the men who inhabit them. To be American without falling into Americanisms—to catch that which is peculiar among us through exuberance of youthful power and not through distortion of ancient forms—to derive from the promises of the Future an ideality more trancing than the memories of the Past, and to find in Hope an inspiration more kindling than was ever drawn from Fancy—is the noble task that is set before him that would be in letters the type and idol of a nation which is just rustling its wings in preparation for the limitless flight that awaits its energies. Some of our ablest authors, fascinated, very excusably, with the faultless models of another time, have declined these new conditions of distinction entirely; they have given us merely Spectators and Tattlers with false dates, and developed a style of composition whose very merits imply an *anachronism,* even in the proportion of excellence. Others have understood the result to be attained better than the means of arriving at it. They have failed to take the difference between those peculiarities in our society, manners, tempers and tastes, which are genuine and characteristic, and those which are merely defects and errors upon the English system; they have acquired the force and gayety of liberty, but not the dignity of independence, and are only provincial when they hoped to be national. Mr. Cooper, hitherto, appears to us to have been more happy than any other writer in reconciling those repugnant qualities which are indicated in our opening remark; and displaying the features, character and tone of a new and great national style in letters, which, original and unimitative, is yet in harmony with the truth of nature and ancient models. And it is on that account that we have always considered Mr. Cooper's greatness as resting on quite another platform from that of several of our eminent men of letters. "There is but one way," says Mr. Griswold, "in which we can be rightly and advantageously free from the tyranny of British examples. Truth of understanding and truth of feeling must be the only directors to real excellence in untried courses. In literary art, as in the higher one of virtue, it is only when 'the *truth* shall make us free,' that we can become 'free indeed.'"

The past of America—both that which brings us in contact with the early Indian races, and that which is illustrated by the heroism of our revolutionary struggle—has already yielded a copious harvest to the sickle of the Romancer. But the America of the present hour—the America whose history is to be found only in the columns of the morning newspaper, or in the Extra which brings our annals up to the present moment, is abounding in occurrences of startling and profound interest, and in characters full of the power and passions that tell with enduring effect upon the condition of the world. The tree of our national life, however dry and wooden it may seem in the *hortus siccus* of the north and east, shoots out in the opposite directions into a wild luxuriance, characteristic of a climate whose forest growths are brightened with tints with which nothing among us but the splendors of the heavens can compete. That Gothic fervor of invasion which had so long been abeyant in the civilization of England, there swells once more within our blood: as in the days of Alaric, the stream of an irrepressible population sweeps down in tumultuous current upon the plains of the south, and encountering the adverse current of another race, the shock sends the waters of strife foaming into forms that glitter with the dazzle of romance and wonder.

The difficulty in dealing with the incidents of our western progress in recent times, is that their inherent and substantial interest is so powerful, that the task of idealizing them becomes almost impracticable. Herein consist the merits of both the authors we have named in this particular connection. Of Mrs. Kirkland's Western Clearings, Mr. Griswold thus speaks:

> "It has the strength, freshness, effect and brilliancy, which we associate with the best conception of our native character, and is uniformly saved from those kindred faults which lie so fatally near to this bold class of virtues, by the inborn refinement, practised taste, ready tact, and varied resources which are the special and rare accomplishment of this delightful writer. In the roughest scenes, she is never coarse; amidst the least cultivated society, she never is vulgar. She interests us in the wild men and in the wild occurrences of border life, by identifying them with the fortunes and feelings of that humanity of which we are a part. Her sympathies are sensitive, and various in their range, but always sound and healthful, and neither extravagant in their objects, nor excessive in their degree. The constant presence of strong, active sense, on the part of the author, carries us through the monotonous incidents of western settlement with animation, amusement, and instruction. These narratives have, throughout, that simplicity, vigor, and inherent beauty, which a superior mind, if it be faithful to the great law of genuineness and honesty, never fails of attaining in its representations of the actual."

Mr. Nourse, instead of gazing at the views before him through the medium of a dreamy sentiment merely, has looked upon them through the atmosphere of those mighty feelings and kindling thoughts and fervid expectations which, to the appreciant eye, hang ever around them—the only medium capable of refracting such stern realities into a picturesque harmony. The visionary faculty of anticipation and reflection has been the influence by which he has transmuted the actual into the poetic. A conspiracy of land speculators, viewed as the origin of a nation, acquires grandeur under the pen of the philosophic narrator: the character of the huntsman of the backwoods looms up into something of classic majesty, when we consider that the rovings of his impatient steps are the march of an empire: the rough experiences of this border life are clothed with elevation and refinement by a conception of the immense social results that are mingled with the fortunes of these daring wanderers. The coarseness of the materials wrought with, is rescued from offensiveness, sometimes by a gleam of profound thought, sometimes by an exhibition of exquisite feeling, and, occasionally, by a highly-wrought description of scenery. The singular contrasts produced by the rapid cross-motions of the elements of life upon a scene where, so far as the structure of society is concerned, the work of creation may be said to be yet going on; the strange lustre which a mature political system assumes, when seen in relief against a state of savage turbulence, which it is extending over and redeeming; the thrilling spectacle of the magnificence of the phenomena of nature, in that vast region, being overborne, and even dwarfed, by the greater sublimity of human audacity and achievement: all these are characteristic circumstances of a society which belongs to no country but our own;—a society at once American and the most wonderful now existing upon earth.

Mr. Griswold's characterization of Chief Justice Marshall is one of the most extensive in the book. We copy it entire:

"Mr. Marshall's career as Chief Justice extended through a period of more than thirty-four years, which is the longest judicial tenure recorded in history. To one who cannot follow his great judgments, in which, at the same time, the depths of legal wisdom are disclosed and the limits of human reason measured, the language of just eulogy must wear an appearance of extravagance. In his own profession he stands for the reverence of the wise rather than for the enthusiasm of the many. The proportion of the figure was so perfect, that the sense of its vastness was lost. Above the difficulties of common minds, he was in some degree above their sympathy. Saved from popularity by the very rarity of his qualities, he astonished the most where he was best understood. The questions upon which his judgment was detained, and the considerations by which his decision was at last determined, were such as ordinary understandings, not merely could not resolve, but were often inadequate even to appreciate or apprehend. It was his manner to deal directly with the results of thought and learning, and the length and labor of the processes by which these results were suggested and verified might elude the consciousness of those who had not themselves attempted to perform them. From the position in which he stood of evident superiority to his subject, it was obviously so easy for him to describe its character and define its relations, that we sometimes forgot to wonder by what faculties or what efforts he had attained to that eminence. We were so much accustomed to see his mind move only in the light, that there was a danger of our not observing that the illumination by which it was surrounded was the beam of its own presence, and not the natural atmosphere of the scene.

"The true character and measure of Marshall's greatness are missed by those who conceive of him as limited within the sphere of the justices of England, and who describe him merely as the first of lawyers. To have been 'the most consummate judge that ever sat in judgment,' was the highest possibility of Eldon's merit, but was only a segment of Marshall's fame. It was in a distinct department, of more dignified functions, almost of an opposite kind, that he displayed those abilities that advance his name to the highest renown, and shed around it the glories of a statesman and legislator. The powers of the Supreme Court of the United States are such as were never before confided to a judicial tribunal by any people. As determining, without appeal, its own jurisdiction, and that of the legislature and executive, that court is not merely the highest estate in the country, but it settles and continually moulds the constitution of the government. Of the great work of constructing a nation, but a small part, practically, had been performed when the written document had been signed by the convention: a vicious theory of interpretation might defeat the grandeur and unity of the organization, and a want of comprehension and foresight might fatally perplex the harmony of the combination. The administration of a system of polity is the larger part of its establishment. What the constitution was to be, depended on the principles on which the federal instrument was to be construed, and they were not to be found in the maxims and modes of reasoning by which the law determines upon social contrasts between man and man, but were to be sought anew in the elements of political philosophy and the general suggestions of legislative wisdom. To these august duties Judge Marshall brought a greatness of conception that was commensurate with their difficulty; he came to them in the spirit and with the strength of one who would minister to the development of a nation; and it was the essential sagacity of his guiding mind that saved us from illustrating the sarcasms of Mr. Burke about paper constitutions. He saw the futility of attempting to control society by a metaphysical theory; he apprehended the just relation between opinion and life, between the forms of speculation and the force of things. Knowing that we are wise in respect to nature, only as we give back to it faithfully what we have learned from it obediently, he sought to fix the wisdom of the real and to resolve it into principles. He made the nation explain its constitution, and compelled the actual to define the possible. Experience was the dialectic by which he deduced from substantial premises a practical conclusion. The might of reason by which convenience and right were thus moulded into union, was amazing. But while he knew the folly of endeavoring to be wiser than time, his matchless resources of good sense contributed to the orderly development of the inherent elements of the constitution, by a vigor and dexterity as eminent in their kind as they were rare in their combination. The vessel of state was launched by the patriotism of many: the chart of her course was designed chiefly by Hamilton: but when the voyage was begun, the eye that observed, and the head that reckoned, and the hand that compelled the ship to keep her course amid tempests without and threats of mutiny within, were those of the chief justice. Posterity will give him reverence as one of the founders of the nation; and of that group of statesmen who may one day, perhaps, be regarded as above the nature, as they certainly were beyond the dimensions of men, no figure, save ONE alone, will rise upon the eye in grandeur more towering than that of John Marshall.

"The authority of the Supreme Court, however, is not confined to cases of constitutional law: it embraces the whole range of judicial action, as it is distributed in England into legal, equitable, ecclesiastical and maritime jurisdictions. The equity system of this court was too little developed to enable us to say what Marshall would have been as a chancellor. It is difficult to admit that he would have been inferior to Lord Eldon: it is impossible to conceive that he could at all have resembled Lord Eldon. But undoubtedly the native region and proper interest of a mind so analytical and so sound, so piercing and so practical, was the Common Law, that vigorous system of manly reason and essential right, that splendid scheme of morality expanded by logic and informed by prudence. Perhaps the highest range of English intelligence is illustrated in the law: yet where in the whole line of that august succession will be found a character which fills the measure of judicial greatness so completely as Chief Justice Marshall? Where in English history is the judge, whose mind was at once so enlarged and so systematic, who so thoroughly had reduced professional science to general reason, in whose disciplined intellect technical learning had so completely passed into native sense? Vast as the reach of the law is, it is not an exaggeration to say that Marshall's understanding was greater, and embraced the forms of legal sagacity within it, as a part of its own spontaneous wisdom. He discriminated with instinctive accuracy between those technicalities which have sprung from the narrowness of inferior minds, and those which are set by the law for the defence of some vital element of justice or reason. The former he brushed away like cobwebs, while he yielded to the latter with a respect which sometimes seemed to those 'whose eyes were' not 'opened' a species of superstition. In his judicial office the method of Marshall appeared to be, first to bow his understanding reverently to the law, and calmly and patiently to receive its instructions as those of an oracle of which he was the minister; then, to prove these dictates by the most searching processes of reason, and to deliver them to others, not as decrees to be obeyed, but as logical manifestations of moral truth. Undoubtedly he made much use of adjudged cases; but he used them to give light and certainty to his own judgment, and not for the vindication or support of the law. He would have deemed it a reproach alike to his abilities and his station, if he should have determined upon precedent what could have been demonstrated by reason, or had referred to authority what belonged to principle. With singular capacity, he united systematic reason with a perception of particular equity: too scrupulous a regard for the latter led Lord Eldon in most instances to adjudicate nothing but the case before him; but Marshall remembered that while he owed to the suitor the decision of the case, he owed to society the establishment of the principle. His mind naturally tended, not to suggestion and speculation, but to the determination of opinion and the closing of doubts. On the bench he always recollected that he was not merely a lawyer, and much less a legal essayist; he was conscious of an official duty and an official authority; and considered that questions might be discussed elsewhere, but came to be settled by him. The dignity with which these duties were discharged was not the least admirable part of the display. It was Wisdom on the seat of Power, pronouncing the decrees of Justice.

"Political and legal sense are so distinct from one another as almost to be irreconcilable in the same mind. The latter is a mere course of deduction from premises; the other calls into exercise the highest order of perceptive faculties, and that quick felicity of intuition which flashes to its conclusions by a species of mental sympathy rather than by any conscious process of argumentation. The one requires that the susceptibility of the judgment should be kept exquisitely alive to every suggestion of the practical, so as to catch and follow the insensible reasonings of life, rather than to reason itself: the other demands the exclusion of every thing not rigorously exact, and the concentration of the whole consciousness of the mind in kindling implicit truth into formal principles. The wonder, in Judge Marshall's case, was to see these two almost inconsistent faculties, in quality so matchless and in development so magnificent, harmonized and united in his marvellous intelligence. We beheld him pass from one to the other department without confusing their nature, and without perplexing his own understanding. When he approached a question of constitutional jurisprudence, we saw the lawyer expand into the legislator; and in returning to a narrower sphere, pause from the creative glow of statesmanship, and descend from intercourse with the great conceptions and great feelings by which nations are guided and society is advanced, to submit his faculties with docility to the yoke of legal forms, and with impassible calmness to thread the tangled intricacies of forensic technicalities.

"There was in this extraordinary man an unusual combination of the capacity of apprehending truth, with the ability to demonstrate and make it palpable to others. They often exist together in unequal degrees. Lord Mansfield's power of luminous explication was so surpassing that one might always say that he made others perceive what he did not understand himself; but the numerous instances in which his decisions have been directly overthrown by his successors, and the still greater number of cases in which his opinions have been silently departed from, compel a belief that his judgment was not of the truest kind. Lord Eldon's judicial sagacity was a species of inspiration; but he seemed to be unable not only to convince others, but even to certify himself of the correctness of his own greatest and wisest determinations.

But Judge Marshall's sense appeared to be at once both instinctive and analytical: his logic extended as far as his perception: he had no propositions in his thoughts which he could not resolve into their axioms. Truth came to him as a revelation, and from him as a demonstration. His mind was more than the faculty of vision; it was a body of light, which irradiated the subject to which it was directed, and rendered it as distinct to every other eye as it was to its own.

"The mental integrity of this illustrious man was not the least important element of his greatness. Those qualities of vanity, fondness for display, the love of effect, the solicitation of applause, sensibility to opinions, which are the immoralities of intellect, never attached to that stainless essence of pure reason. He seemed to men to be a passionless intelligence; susceptible to no feeling but the constant love of right; subject to no affection but a polarity toward truth."

Of Mr. Legaré Mr. Griswold says:

"The impression left by his collected writings is, that his mind was of the first order, but that it did not hold in that order a very prominent place. He had that rectitude of judgment, that pervading good sense, that constant natural sympathy with truth, which is a characteristic of the best class of intellects, but he was wanting in richness, fervor, and creative vigor. He possessed the forms of fine understanding, but the force of intellectual passion, or the fire of genius, are not found. His perception of truth was superior to his power of illustrating it. We follow the difficult and somewhat languid processes of his thoughts, and, surprised at last at finding him in possession of such admirable opinions on all subjects, we imagine that he must have discovered his conclusions by different faculties from those which he uses to demonstrate them. That splendid fusion of reason, imagination, and feeling, which constitutes the inspiration of the great, is not visible; the display is meagre, laborious, and painful. He fills the measure of his subject, but it is by the utmost stretch of his abilities; we do not observe the abounding power, the exuberant resources, the superfluous energy, which mark the foremost of the first.

"In his own profession Mr. Legaré had, with many, discredited his reputation by the devotion which he avowed to the civil law. It is understood that no one who has been able thoroughly to master and comprehend the common law, is disposed to give much time to the civilians. I am inclined to believe that no man ever yet took up the Code, because having sounded the common law through its depths, he had found it wanting: many have cheaply sought the praise of having gone through the common law, by appearing to have attained to something beyond it, upon the principle that if you 'quote Lycophron, they will take it for granted that you have read Homer.' In Mr. Legaré's case, such suspicions are probably without justice. He was attracted to the 'first collection of written reason' chiefly by the interest which the scholar feels in that majestic philosophy of morals which is the 'imperium sine fine' of Rome. His remarks in a review of Kent's Commentaries, show that he understood what advantages the common law had attained over the civil law, as a practical system, by its constant regard for certainty, convenience and policy. As a common lawyer, Mr. Legaré was respectable; and in great cases, his elaborate style of preparation made him a formidable opponent.

"As a statesman I think the finest monument of his powers is his speech in Congress on the Sub-Treasury. It is formal, elementary, and scholastic, but able, and at times brilliant. His politics, as displayed in various essays and reviews, were profound and intelligent; but it always seemed as if he had settled his views of the present times upon opinions derived from history, and not that, like Machiavelli, he had informed his judgment on occurrences in history by suggestions drawn from his own observation. Still, by any method to have formed sound principles on government and society, in the unfavorable circumstances in which he was placed, was an indication of extraordinary powers. He triumphed over disadvantages of position, connections, and party; and was among the wisest men of the South. Yet he appears, like Mr. Hamilton and Mr. Ames, to have been of a too desponding temperament; to have magnified dangers that threatened our young energies, and to have lacked faith in our system, after it had passed some of the strongest trials to which it was reasonable to suppose it would ever be subjected.

"As a classical scholar Mr. Legaré made great pretension, but there is nothing in his works to prove that he was here superior or even equal to several of his countrymen. His proficiency partook of the dryness and severity of his character. He studied rather as a grammarian than as a man of taste. He may have been accurate, but he was not elegant. He writes often about the Greeks and Latins, but he had never caught the spirit and sentiment of classical enthusiasm. We miss the fine felicity of illustration, the apt quotation, the brilliant allusion, which are so attractive in the writings of one whose heart and fancy have dwelt familiarly in the clime of antiquity. He is not betrayed as a visitor to the halls of the past by the smell of aloes and cassia hanging about his garments, caught from the ivory palaces whereby they have made him glad. We know the fact by his constantly informing us of it, and because he describes the localities with the precision of one who must have observed, chiefly for the purpose of making a report. The most striking passage in his writings on a classical subject is that relating to Catullus, in his criticism of Dunlap's History of Ancient Literature. The remarks on that poet are original, beautiful, and undoubtedly just."

But our limits forbid us to pursue more extensively this survey of American writers. Of Longfellow, Sanderson, Hooker, Hoffman, and others, Mr. Griswold has given interesting and generally accurate estimates; and as he always presents a specimen of the author whom he judges, so as to submit himself to the test of direct verification by the reader, he deserves to be called, since Luke Milbourne, "the fairest of critics."

The data which he gives are sufficient to bring before the reader the history of American letters through the departments of Statesmanship, Philosophy and Religion, as well as the history, condition and prospects of our Legal, Historical, Romantic, Æsthetical and Miscellaneous literature; and to show the justness of his assumption, that thus far, despite of all that has been said to the contrary and in the face of all the confessed obstacles to our intellectual progress, we have done more than any other nation, for the same term of time, in the various fields of investigation, reflection, imagination and taste.

We take leave with the renewal of our thanks to the editor for the spirit which prompted, and our respect for the talents and tempers which have guided, his labors. He has triumphed over many difficulties; and we have pleasure in commending his work to the perusal of all who are interested in literature and criticism.

FOREST LEAVES, AND OTHER POEMS. By MRS. LYDIA PEARSON.

A VOICE from the forest! or, rather, a pleasant sound of many voices, swelling in plaintive chaunt through the solitary woods at evening, and throbbing in delicate echoes against the hills—kept in tune by the harmony of an uniform sentiment, whose key-note still is melancholy! Nor to us does it seem wonderful, that the harp-strings of a "spirit *finely* touched," should answer to the varying airs of fortune with notes forever sad. The world, said one of its true worldlings, is a comedy for them that think, and a tragedy to those that feel: we might add, that, to the feeling heart, thought serves for little else than to open new passages to sympathy, and discover remoter sources of pain. Life—"which, to every one that breathes, is full of care"—must bring to one inheriting, as this lady does, the darkly-glorious dower of genius, such shows, such glimpses, such suggestions of fear and sadness, as the rough and bustling never dream of. So refined an atmosphere of sensibility as attends a nature like hers, must be often dimmed by clouds, whose duskiness is owing, not to their own thickness, but to the exquisite purity of the medium in which they are formed. "If you listen to David's harp, touched by the Holy Ghost," says Bacon, "you shall hear as many hearse-like airs as carolings;" and to those prophet-souls who partake a portion of the depth and foresight of the Divine existence, for whom a veil is riven, it may well seem as if a dirge was the only tribute proper for the past, and a lamentation the fit herald of the future.

We have heard it objected, as a kind of moral fault against this gentle and tender poet, that the tone of her verse is sombre; and we would defend her from so strange a reproach, by observing that the pensiveness which is complained of, is twin-born with the power which ought to be admired, and is inseparable from it. But there are readers enough to whom this plaintive tone will be welcome. Clouds are things common enough in the heaven of every man's prosperity; the ray which can turn those clouds into spots of glory, and spectacles of magnificence, is not common.

MEMOIR OF THE LIFE AND CHARACTER OF PHILIP SYNG PHYSIC, M. D. By J. RANDOLPH, M. D.

WE have been much gratified by this notice of one to whose professional sagacity, in former years, we were weightily beholden, and of whose disinterested kindness we shall always retain a grateful remembrance. It is a memorial of the greatest physician of the last generation, written by an accomplished one of this. It is able, discriminating and valuable. Our own recollections enable us to verify many features in the portrait. The career of the remarkable person who is the subject of this interesting sketch furnishes an illustration of the unquestionable truth, that to the constitution of a great practical understanding, moral qualities must contribute even more largely than intellectual ones. Indeed, in contemplating the ability of a man of the first order of professional power, we are at a loss, many times, to determine whether the peculiarities which make his superiority, ought to be referred to one class or to the other. In those lofty regions of sincere greatness, the two blend together into one. Those who looked at Dr. Physic, unreflectingly, might have thought that his capacity consisted in his habits: that it was in the obstinate scrutiny into the facts of his cases—in his prolonged and unresting consideration of those facts—and the earnest, almost devoted attention with which every case was followed up—that the true secret of the marvellous skill of this extraordinary man might be found. But that would have been to confound the power itself, with the conditions under which the development of that power necessarily took place: it would have been to mistake the elements which a plant appropriates from the air and earth in aid of its growth, for the living principle of the plant itself. The truth is, that the mental vigor of Dr. Physic was of the rarest and truest kind: his intellect was wonderfully quick and far-ranging in its suggestions, thorough in its processes, and fearless in its conclusions; but those mental habits of caution, patience and inquiry, were the only medium in which these qualities could work out their best and perfect display. Uncontrolled by that discipline, they would have resulted in an ability splendid and impracticable; but they would not have filled the sphere of the most illustrious professional excellence, in medicine, that this country has ever witnessed. It must be remembered that the power to examine minutely and reflect slowly, is, itself, a species of genius; and, perhaps, the highest. There is a class of natures, whose intellectual action is of an electrical kind—instant, intense and momentary: there is another sort, in whom the accumulation of mental energy is given forth with the gradual, steady and continuous flow of a galvanic current. One is more startling and impressive; the useful power of the other is greater; both are equally divine. The well-known observation of Sir Isaac Newton, in relation to himself, would indicate that he is to be classed, with Dr. Physic, in the latter rank.

Elegant and satisfactory as Dr. Randolph's Memoir is, in reference to the design and purpose which he contemplated, we confess that we are hardly willing that the name of this extraordinary and admirable man should go down to future times without a memorial of a different and more minute and detailed kind—such an exposition of the particulars of his life and conduct, we mean, as can be given only by a copious biography, bringing together everything that journals, correspondence, or the recollections of others, can furnish for the completion and illustration of the portraiture. We are aware that Dr. Physic was unwilling that his private letters and papers should be laid before the public; and this reluctance was characteristic of a man who was as modest as he was able—whose sensitiveness in all that concerned himself was as keen, as his energy in suppressing it, where it might be prejudicial to others, was manly and noble. But it has been doubted by many how far, in any case, the commands of the dead should operate as clogs upon the living, when the interests of society are in question: for ourselves, we think that when a prohibition of this kind has been prompted only by the extreme sensibilities of the person's own diffidence, it ought at least to be construed with the utmost strictness. We often violate the orders of the living when they tend to the unjust suppression of their proper praise and reward, and suppose it to be an act of duty on our part to do so. We would recommend the limits of Dr. Physic's order on this subject, to be very critically examined, and the best advice to be taken as to the necessity, in point of propriety and good faith, of being governed by it: for not without something like a moral necessity, would we forego the benefit of giving to the world, by the publication of letters and other documents, an exhibition of the manner in which this great man lived among his contemporaries, diffusing benefits and receiving gratitude—of the extent of his professional generosity—the incorruptible integrity of his motives—and, above all, the unremitting intenseness with which the obligations of *professional responsibility* rested upon his conscience, as a necessity of his nature, and almost as a condition of his existence. This lesson, so invaluable in this country, and at this time, is the most rarely given. For it happens, unfortunately, though perhaps as a natural result of things, that it is this class, of which the personal character and private history would be studied by the world at large, with the very highest interest and advantage, whose biographies are the most seldom written, at least with any considerable degree of minuteness and precision. The history of a soldier, or a man of letters, may be said, to some extent, to write itself: the former, in those actions which remain as monuments among mankind, and the latter, in those productions which bear upon their surface the evidence and the measure of all that was extraordinary in him from whom they proceeded. But the qualities that work themselves out in a great *professional* career, such as that of an eminent lawyer or physician, are of a less distinct and manifest sort. Silent, complex, gradual in their influence, their combined effect is seen in the commanding character which attracts the confidence, and sways with unacknowledged but boundless control, the minds and feelings of the community; but the definite, individual form and nature of these properties in their true analysis, can be known entirely by those only who have witnessed their operation long and inspected their relations closely. But, either the skill to note, or the disposition to follow, or the leisure to record observations of this kind, is commonly wanting among the friends of these eminent persons: and the interesting knowledge of that discipline by which the character has slowly been constructed, of the uses by which its perfection has been kept up, and the *traits* by which its peculiarities were wont to illustrate themselves—which the philosopher might profitably have inspected, and which the student of morals would have loved to linger upon—is lost forever; society retaining nothing of the richest treasure that it possessed, save the empty name by which it was surrounded. In the few instances in which a complete picture of the private life and daily conduct of an eminent professional man has been given to the public—as in the recent case of Lord Eldon's life—the theme has awakened an interest not inferior to that which attends the narrative of the most stirring deeds. In the case of Dr. Physic, if it can be considered as a task proper to be undertaken, no man would be more proper to do it than Dr. Randolph himself. His mind has been schooled in the professional learning of two continents: he has added the best suggestions of the science of the old world to the varied experience of the new; and is fitted by intelligence, acquisitions and situation, to do justice to all the excellence of the subject. The undertaking would be equally safe in the hands of Dr. J. K. Mitchell, so well and honorably known to our whole country as one of the most eminent of its physicians, and specially known to the younger portion of our medical practitioners, of whom so many have received instruction at his hands, as the accomplished Professor of the Theory and Practice of Medicine in the Jefferson Medical College of Philadelphia. He holds the pen of a scholar and a man of genius. Saved by his own merited distinction from any liability to professional or personal jealousies, he would approach the subject with "that candor which," according to a great authority, "always accompanies great abilities:" and the want of that minute information in respect to many things, which only a contemporary experience could bestow, would be supplied in him, to a great extent, by the superior "ardor of sympathetic genius." We commend the suggestion, heartily, to the consideration of these gentlemen.

THE POEMS OF FITZ-GREENE HALLECK. New York, Harpers.

THE dominion of poetry is as boundless as the race. Of her sceptre less cannot be said, than that its heritage is the sovereignty of the world, its possession the loyalty of every human heart. Various, therefore, of necessity, and diversified as the nature of man, are the shapes, and aspects, and characters, in which are put forth the manifestations of that influence which means to be triumphant wherever it is exerted. For ourselves, we profess a worship as catholic as the spirit of this changeful deity; for every form she takes, we own a separate taste. Poetry is, to us, like the enchanting mistress of a youthful cavalier, whose figure fascinates in every dress, whose features charm in all their moods. Whether this glorious child of heaven—majestic in exalting loveliness, unfolds her snowy robes upon the breezes of the evening, and, floating off from the earth, a re-ascended goddess, smiles down upon us from the golden sky of Spenser's imagination—or, whether, with Milton, she expands the soul into a vast and solemn cathedral, in which every mortal thought, and sentiment, and sensibility, bows down in awe, while the sounding inspiration rolls along the columned roof—and swells through every aisle, and passage, and gallery of human consciousness—or, like Shakspeare, exhibits no picture to us, but the real earth, made glorious through the medium of intense imagination—or, with Dryden's nervous hand, strikes from the lyre the ringing tones of manly sense and earnest passion—or, like Pope, masking divinity in the familiar and the mortal, and hiding celestial sensibilities beneath the lawn and velvet of a court-costume, she fashions the heaven-shed essence of immortal truth into glittering shafts of wit, and uses the choicest pearls from the paradisal streams of inspiration, for missiles to assail the multitude—whether, in some one of these, or in yet another of her myriad guises, her presence enriches the breeze with fragrance, or makes golden the air of common thought and daily feeling—we claim an ability to know, and an inclination to acknowledge her, as the apparent deity and queen of human sensibility. In some aspects, undoubtedly, she is more impressive to different persons than she is in others: to us, she approaches, in all her pomp of charms, and in the fullest luxuriance of attractions, when she seizes the trumpet of the lyric muse, and sounds forth a strain that "bids the heavens be mute."

Fitz-Greene Halleck!—The Tyrtæus of America—acknowledged master of the western lyre!—a magic name to us, for it comes charged with all the remembered and still vital enthusiasms of youth, and passion, and genial admiration. The critics may rehearse the praises of modern English bards, and we shall suffer them in patience; but until we have forgotten the intense surprise and joy with which we first heard "at school," the gorgeous yet simple ode of "Bozzaris," and learned that its author was a modern, and an American; or can read the lines of "Alnwick Castle," or "Alloway Kirk," or those on the death of Drake, without a tumult of emotions, we must be permitted to reply to all their eulogies—"Beneath the Lesbian singer!"—"That poetry is the best, which moves us most, and which comes nearest to God, who is the source of all power." We say, also, that that is the best which has the most simplicity; which is the most effective with the greatest directness; and reaches the highest flights of fancy with the least sacrifice of nature and truth. That power of pleasure which springs into our bosoms from the lines of Halleck, does not arise from remote combinations of thought or novel shapes of art, but from general and genuine feelings being disengaged in absolute entireness, and shot forth with the intenseness of perfect purity, and from the plain and ordinary phrases of daily language being charged and vivified with all the energy with which human speech can swell. He does not seek to reclude those sacred fountains of the moral muse, whose hidden sources can be unsealed only by the finger of philosophy; nor does he labor to subtilize emotion into the finest exquisiteness of thought, or impart the sensuousness of art to the quaintest apprehension of the metaphysical faculty—but, musing within his own heart, like the royal psalmist, in moody earnestness of passion, at length the fire kindles, and, rugged, vehement and irresistible, the blazing words leap forth in music, as the bolt leaps from the sombre cloud, illustrating all the sublimity of light, and sound, and motion.

The style of composition to which the powers of Halleck have been devoted, is capable of the highest and severest polish, and it so happens that many of those English poets who have excelled in it—Gray, Campbell, Collins, and, with less vigor than any of them, Wordsworth—have possessed and put forth the most extraordinary powers of delicate and faultless finish. Mere substantial strength will lift a work of art far up into the empyrean of renown; but nothing can set it safe against the shocks, and pressures, and attritions of time, but the smoothing down of every roughness, the rounding off of every turn, and the rubbing away of every adhering defect. Finish is, to works of art, the enamel which defies the corrosion of ages.

Harpers' edition of Halleck's Poems is, in respect to appearance, worthy of the poet, and creditable to the gentlemen from whose press it proceeds. The gratification of the senses has so much to do with even the mental perception of the beauties of works of elegant taste, that a poet ought to consider the style of publication of his works, part of the works themselves. A poem ill-printed, is like an overture badly played. The finest performance cannot redeem a musical composition essentially worthless; but a slovenly execution may destroy the effect of the noblest harmonies that ever flowed from the genius of a composer.

MEMOIRS OF THE ADMINISTRATIONS OF WASHINGTON AND JOHN ADAMS. Edited from the Papers of OLIVER WOLCOTT, Secretary of the Treasury. By GEORGE GIBBS. In two vols. New York, printed for the Subscribers, 1846. Philadelphia, sold by JOHN PENINGTON.

THE events which secured to this country a popular constitution as a possession forever, made every American a member of the most difficult, responsible and dignified profession which the ability or virtue of man can illustrate—the profession of politics. By the fundamental law of the government we are all "hereditary statesmen;" we are all advisers and active directors of the administration. "*La vie du plus simple particulier dans une république,*" said the elder and wiser of the Mirabeaus, "*est plus compliquée que celle d'un homme en place dans une monarchie.*" Of this calling of politics may be said what Augustus Schlegel has said of authorship, that according to the spirit in which it is pursued, it is an infamy, a pastime, a day-labor, a handicraft, an art, a science, a virtue. It is of the first importance to society, and every one in it, that the character and tone of this profession should be raised, and maintained at an elevation; that its members should be capable of dealing in it with competent ability, and with that temper of confidence that rejects and despises tricks and intrigue; that they should be always feeling that it involves principles, and not merely personalities; that it is a great moral and intellectual science, in which passions and interests must play in perpetual subordination to the permanent laws of wisdom and truth; and that all its acts and all its contests stand in such intimate relations with the lofty interests of human virtue and human greatness, that the humblest efforts in its cause partake of dignity, and its least rewards are truly honorable. Nothing would open and ventilate the politics of this day more happily—raise, expand and purify them—give them higher significance and greater weight, than a study of the characters and actions of those who founded our constitution, and watched over the earliest development of its principles. To comprehend the distinction and the permanent relation between the great parties that have divided and will always divide this country, it is indispensable to resort to the conferences and the conduct of those who, in the brighter and better time of the commonwealth, explored the depths of that subject with the sagacity of philosophers, and illustrated its extent upon the largest scale of statemanship. If we would learn how to wage war, and not to huckster it—if we would see the difference betwixt that kind of diplomacy which is suggested by honor and conducted by wisdom, and that kind which for paltry ends employs the wretched arts alternately to bubble and to bully—the public history and the private writings of those who formed the *entourage* of Washington will afford us important instruction.

"I am not fonder of simpletons in politics than other people are," says M. Capefigue, "but, for the honor of mankind, I am willing to believe that men may be clever and still retain perfect probity and good faith." This difficult art, to carry into public life the morals and the sentiments that give grace to private character; to join sincerity and directness of personal demeanor with effectiveness and force of political action; to gain the outward with neither soilure nor loss of a more sacred excellence within, seemed to be the native inspiration of these extraordinary men. They formed a band of "Happy Warriors:"

"Whose high endeavors were an inward light
That made the path before them always bright.
More skillful in self-knowledge, even more pure
As tempted more:

Who in a state where men are tempted still
To evil for a guard against worse ill,
And what in quality or act is best
Doth seldom on a right foundation rest,
Still fixed good on good alone, and owe
To virtue every triumph that they know."

Mr. Wolcott was one of the most sterling of this illustrious company: and the respect and confidence which he enjoyed, in an eminent degree, on the part of his greatest contemporaries, such as Hamilton, Ames and Marshall, have enabled his descendant to present to the public a correspondence of remarkable extent and value. He had not the inventive, or rather the creative faculties which enabled Hamilton to institute that system of finance which brought the nation out of bankruptcy, and has kept it from recurring to it; but he had a perfect comprehension of the principles upon which it was to be administered, and executive talents probably not inferior to those of Mr. Hamilton himself. On the death of Mr. Eveleigh, Hamilton solicited from Washington the elevation of Wolcott from the post of auditor to that of comptroller of the Treasury, and used this language in his letter to the President:—"Mr. Wolcott's conduct in the station he now fills has been that of an excellent officer. It has not only been good, but distinguished. It has combined all the requisites that can be desired; moderation with firmness, liberality with exactness, indefatigable industry with an accurate and sound discernment, a thorough knowledge of business, and a remarkable spirit of order and arrangement. Indeed, I ought to say that I owe very much of whatever success may have attended the merely executive operations of the department to Mr. Wolcott." That such commendation should have introduced the subject of it to the highest honors which Washington could bestow, was equally honorable to Mr. Hamilton and Mr. Wolcott.

Mr. Gibbs has written, of course, with something of inherited partiality for the system of which his ancestor formed a prominent part; but his work makes no departure from candor or fairness. The documents which he gives to the world certainly bear with not trifling weight upon some men around whose names the honor of the nation still lingers; the tone of the publication is decidedly in favor of one set of persons and against their adversaries: but, upon a careful review, we cannot discover that the biographer has, by arguments or suggestions of his own, changed or disturbed the impression which the documents themselves produce. He has been faithful to disclose the evidence on which his comments are founded, and, while he enforces it, we cannot perceive that he departs from its true character. The arrangement of the materials is judicious, and the narrative portions possess considerable brilliancy. The work is highly creditable to Mr. Gibbs in a literary point of view, and may be regarded altogether as decidedly the most valuable contribution that has been made to our historical literature in several years.*

* In no part of our national literature did the youthful author of these papers take a more sincere interest than in that which would do honor to the founders and first administrator of our Republic, by the publication of their yet inedited correspondence. His own MS. collections on this subject are of an incredible extent, considering how much his short life was engaged by other subjects. Indeed, he had drafted the "Protocol of a Society for the publication of letters and other documents of the War of the Revolution," an association which he was about to organize, and a sketch of which is given in an Appendix (A.), as a suggestion for others on this subject.

The commendation above given of Mr. Gibbs's valuable work, was thrown off for some sheet of the day. In a familiar letter he expresses himself as follows: "It is gratifying to find that the truth is at last beginning to be spoken in an audible tone about the parties and the men that distinguished the early days of our republic. There are, probably, ten thousand persons in the United States who, in their private minds, think about the Federalists precisely as Mr. Gibbs has written; but utterance is never given to such sentiments, except in a kind of confidential whisper, when two or three of them are met in social privacy. Mr. Gibbs has expressed the truth on these subjects, and what everybody knows to be the truth; and, as an example of fearless declaration of the truth, his work deserves to receive commendation and support. Nothing strikes me as of worse omen in the present condition of the country, than the circumstance that all parties have agreed to suppress all reference to Federal principles and policy, as a source of instruction and a guide in action. If redemption is ever to come to the honor and integrity of the national administration—if the country is ever to be recovered from the degradation under which it labors—if a high tone is ever again to be

WASHINGTON IRVING: HIS WORKS, GENIUS, AND CHARACTER.

IN nature, in personal character, and in every department of art, there is a quality of excellence which, even in the degree of its perfection, disappoints the efforts of description, and eludes the analysis of the critic, because it consists, not in the magnitude, energy, or splendor of the separate elements, but in

given to the counsels and the conduct of the government—the elevating and restoring influence must proceed from a recurrence to the wisdom, the purity, and the loftiness of aim, and temper, and motive, in which the Constitution was founded, and the Union at first conducted. Those who still can feel the ineffable disgrace of such a rule as we were subject to until John Tyler and his party were driven from the capitol, must convince themselves of the truth of Machiavelli's remark, that, in the decline of a state, it is necessary often to revert to the first principles upon which it was founded, for we must know the beginning of our greatness, if we would ever come to the end of our errors. We must re-organize the Federal party; not from any hope of gaining thereby possession of the government, but for the purpose of bringing the weight of an united public opinion to act upon the politics of the country. The indirect control which might thus be exercised over an administration, would be of immense service. The power of truth and honor, in every community, is very great, if there be somebody in the foreground to represent them, to invoke attention to them, to give voice to their judgments upon resolutions and measures.

"Gibbs's book, you will find, contains many important documents, now given to the public for the first time. Wolcott was on terms of close official and personal relation with most of those who made that period an age of so much greatness; and the correspondence of Hamilton, Ames, and Marshall, necessarily gives us an enlarged acquaintance with the design and characters of those who then commanded the confidence and respect of the nation. The more I learn of these extraordinary men, the more nearly I am brought to see their universal intelligence, their various and ready abilities, and their high and earnest patriotism, the more I am impressed with admiration, and the more earnestly I desire to have every record and every monument of their greatness brought out to the knowledge and attention of the country. There are many collections of papers yet in private hands, which the owners are willing to make public, but have not ability to do so. There ought to be a fund connected with the Historical Societies of Philadelphia and New York, for the purpose of printing the correspondence of early statesmen; or, at least, of aiding in the publication. A moderate annual subscription to such a fund, by members and others, would enable the society to rescue many valuable collections, which are now hidden in obscurity, and which in a few years will be entirely destroyed, to the unavailing regret of all who come after us."—ED.

the exquisiteness of the proportion, the harmony of the combination, the fineness of the pervading tone, the gentle animation with which it flatters each sympathy into delighted calmness, and wakes no uncomfortable earnestness of reaction. It absorbs and holds all our sensibilities, yet seems to be below, rather than above, the measure of power, with which our minds are familiar, and to fall within the range of our own ambition, desire, or conception. More admiration would disturb the repose of our satisfaction; a more vigorous address to our intellectual apprehension would change the nature of the enjoyment. The ordinary degrees of this character we call the agreeable; the more poignant exhibitions of it we qualify as charming.

To this class or order belong especially the writings of Mr. Irving. Their effect is uniformly pleasant:—we read with perpetual interest, and with the certainty of delight. Yet are we scarcely inclined to commend anything else than the general and composite impression resultant from the whole. We are impressed with no very vivid respect for the author's mental powers or accomplishments, and carry away no decided impressions of vigorous or dexterous or felicitous effort. We are a little annoyed at being called upon for the reasons of our exclamations of pleasure. If asked our opinion of him, in the absence of his works, our impulse would perhaps be to speak somewhat depreciatingly. Yet while we read we were fascinated; and the enchantment shall assuredly renew itself so often as we come within the action of the strains that "lap us in Elysium." They are productions which communicate pleasure, rather than excite enthusiasm, and are more enjoyed than eulogized. The mystery of the performer seems to consist, not in creating an extraordinary work, but in pre-disposing us, by some magic touch, to be ravished with that which is not greatly remote from common and moderate. The perusal of Mr. Irving's writings is like walking in some familiar lawn, or ordinary scene of nature, on a fine, soft morning in the early spring. Usual sights are around us, accustomed objects greet our senses; but to our transported nature they seem to be invested with influences, spiritual in their fineness, and spiritual in their power. A baptism from on high seems to descend upon our being, and to regenerate it into the vivid delicacy of childhood's sensibilities; and sense, as it transmits to the mind the impressions of outward things, refracts them into splendor. The grass is edged with a bright, glittering green that fairly bewilders the sight; the budding trees impregnate the air with a vital richness, which is not an odor, yet is rarer and more intoxicating than all odors; the cloudless sky, like an expanse of airy waters, wafting our consciousness into paradise, spreads around us, rather than above us; the woodsman's axe, the murmur of the full stream, the lowing of cattle,—for sounds seem to be enchanted into wandering messengers of eternity—startle us with weird impressions that carry us beyond the confines of the material, the limited and the mortal. A lustrous atmosphere brings out each object truly, yet under such strong, aerial perspective, as renders everything picture-like. The softness of a dream envelopes the scene; but "the glory and the freshness" of an existence as much more fervent than reality, as reality itself is more fervent than a dream.

The acceptableness of Mr. Irving's works—the peculiar attraction which they have for every class of readers—illustrates an important truth in criticism, too much overlooked by writers, that in literature, more depends on manner than on style; and manner is an affair of the character more than of the intellect. Power, however great, if it be turbulent and unchastised, stimulates the passions while it impresses the mind; its moral influence excites more appetency than its mental action satisfies; and it leaves the reader disappointed and discontented in the very measure in which he has been moved. On the other hand, there is a tone of decency, decorum, refined reserve, and intentional restraint in composition, which induces in the reader an answering concentration and restriction in feeling, by which he is in a situation to enjoy quiet and moderate interests with a delight at once earnest and calm. Something akin to this is felt in the company of high-bred people. The temper of moderated animation, the controlled and self-guarding attention, the avoidance of strong efforts, and the care with which each one seems to play below his full power, the subdued key to which everything is pitched, tends to create in each person a certain strenuous repose of the feelings which causes commonplace things in such a sphere to inspire pleasure and respect. That state in which sensibility is excited, and then voluntarily checked and drawn back upon itself, is the one of greatest impressibility to what is beautiful and intellectual. How remarkable and how delightful is the moral charm diffused by the mere personal deportment of a refined and thorough-bred gentleman! Very much like that is the spell of retiring dignity and elegant reserve which fascinates in Mr. Irving's writings. And when this sort of manner is found in conjunction with essential genius and genuine finished art, as in his case it undoubtedly is, the delight becomes as irresistible as it is undefinable.

Mr. Irving possesses but little invention. The attractiveness of his tales does not depend upon their material, upon their construction, upon the novelty, variety, or impressiveness of their incidents, upon an anxious crisis or a brilliant denouement, but upon the illustrative talent of the narrator, upon the innumerable occasional decorations that delight us into a forgetfulness of the purpose or want of purpose of the whole, and the pleasant sketches of costume, scenery, and manners which are hung along the conduct of the piece in such profusion, that it resembles at length a brilliant gallery of pictures, built for the display of its own treasures, and not to lead to some definite end. His conception of beauty is not rich or exquisite. In sentiment he is commonplace, dilute, and superficial. Of earnest, deep feeling, he can scarcely be said to have anything at all. Intellectual force or moral sensibility contribute little to his works. But let us not, therefore, suppose that those works are commonplace productions, or the author of them an ordinary person. Let us not imagine that because we cannot detect the seat of a power, or define its nature, components, or origin,—nay, because we can touch this point, and say it is not here, or knock upon that surface, and find for a response, that it issues not thence,—that any doubt is thrown upon the greatness, genuineness, or elevation of that power. In literature, and especially in that fine region in which the genius of Mr. Irving moves, the more subtle and elusive the interest is, the more exalted and consummate is the art; the more evanescent the charm, the more potent is it, the more certain, and the more enduring. In such a department of pure art, to accomplish the greatest result with the least visible display of exertion, is the highest triumph. To impress, and conceal the source of the impression, is mastery in its utmost. When once we are assured that a work is certainly impressive, the difficulty of detecting the reason of that impressiveness enhances the glory of the production. We may talk of the slightness of Mr. Irving's composition; it is easy to make compositions as slight, but not easy to make slightness so effective.

Beauty is a thing of form and place; it may be detected, and analyzed, and reproduced. But infinitely higher and grander in its range, degree, and order, than beauty, is grace; and that is an unsubstantial and unlocal essence. Beauty resides, definitely, in the work in which it is recognized; grace is an electric light evolved by the action of successive parts of the subject upon the mind. It is experimental, and not demonstrative. Certain and absolute in its action upon refined sensibilities, when searched out by the critical eye it is a nervous, flitting, evasive thing. It is the true Galatea of taste, which strikes us in spite of our will, and when we turn to seize it, has fled from our sight, and becomes visible only as it vanishes. It is on this account that ordinary critics, whose minds are always more active than their sentiments are delicate, generally fail to apprehend and appreciate this exalted quality. It is the source of that fresh, delightful fragrance which always exhales from Irving's writings.

In noting, therefore, the absence of great and commanding intellectual force, it will not be thought that we esteem Mr. Irving lightly; on the contrary, we regard him as an extraordinary and admirable artist, standing quite alone among his countrymen; not likely ever to be neglected, or ever to be rivalled. Of the genius of his pencil we shall speak hereafter, but looking at present only at the style and manner of his works, we find a grace as inherent as that of childhood; a gentle gayety as variable yet as unfailing and as unfatiguing as the breezes of June; an indestructible presence of good taste, simplicity, and ease; qualities which, in their separate conception, seem to be slight, yet, in their conjoint effect, are the splendor of fame and the power of immortality. What renders the merit more singular in Irving is, that successful and inimitable as the charm is, it is obviously not spontaneous or unconscious. In strenuous simplicity he almost equals the poet whose stream of verse reflects forever the dewy lustre of the morning of English civility; but what in the Pilgrim of Canterbury's scenes is the natural dazzle of the hour, is, in Irving, clearly the noonday elaboration of profound and much-taught science. Such composition is, in a great degree, a process of rejection; a labor of excision and exclusion, in which, however, excess is fatal; and the full genius and true art of Irving can never be popularly understood, until we can see the weedings of the exquisite violet banks on which he gives us to repose and be intoxicated with purity of sensual bliss, or can analyze the lees of his cup of enchantment, which alone would disclose how composite is the formation of that liquor which, in its final distillation, is as clear and natural as the crystal gushings of the rock. The "*mille decenter*," which can be seen only in the general effect, are of infinitely greater value than the "*mille ornatus*," which the eye recognizes and registers.

The prominent faculties in Mr. Irving's genius are OBSERVATION and FANCY. When they act in conjunction,—when quick and lambent Fancy touches with its quaint, kindling ray the fine particular truths which Observation has noted,—we have the brightest and most characteristic exhibitions of his powers.

The minute delicacy of his observation of outward life is remarkable. The eye has been to him a potent instrument of literary fame; it has played the part of a tireless gleaner in the fields of life, bringing in snatches of beauty and grace, trivial in themselves, but invaluable in their disposed and aggregated effect. Mr. Irving has obviously been through life a quiet yet busy watcher of the shapes, the colors, the changes of the landscape, the figures of trees, the forms, motions, and habits of birds, the looks and ways of animals, the appearances and physical peculiarities of men. So exact and special, in many instances, are the lines of description, that we cannot but suppose that it has been his custom, in viewing objects, to make notes upon the spot, or immediately after, so as to preserve the precise peculiarities of things which were afterwards to be worked up in sketches. As the subjects of the exercise of this faculty in him, however, are usually familiar or domestic, and therefore not especially dignified, the traits of observation are mostly hued by humor, or heightened by sentiment, or grouped in some inventive combination; and we meet few examples of incidents or scenes in nature, rendered with simple accuracy, as by historical portraiture of a real occurrence. Yet some such may be found, which challenge comparison with anything in literature, and which place the author in the highest class of faithful copyists of nature in her noblest simplicities, and of art in its most gorgeous complexity. The picture, in "Bracebridge Hall," of the eagle expelled from his resting-place, in the early morning, by the pinnace of Heer Antony Vander Heyden, among the Highlands of the Hudson, is unrivalled in correctness and power.

"As they coasted along the basis of the mountains, the Heer Antony pointed out to Dolph a bald eagle, the sovereign of these regions, who sat perched on a dry tree that projected over the river, and, with eye turned upwards, seemed to be drinking in the splendor of the morning sun. Their approach disturbed the monarch's meditations. He first spread one wing, and then the other; balanced himself for a moment, and then, quitting his perch with dignified composure, wheeled slowly over their heads. Dolph snatched up a gun, and sent a whistling ball after him, that cut some of the feathers from his wing. The report of the gun leaped sharply from rock to rock, and awakened a thousand echoes; but the monarch of the air sailed calmly on, ascending higher and higher, and wheeling widely as he ascended, soaring up the green bosom of the woody mountain, until he disappeared over the brow of a beetling precipice."

We have beheld that striking and impressive sight amidst the mountains of the West, and this account of it is as accurate as it is effective. The description of Henry the Seventh's chapel, in "The Sketch Book," is equally remarkable in a very different

7

style. It is a true Dusseldorff picture, minute in detail, dazzling in coloring, with a delightful bewilderment thrown over its actuality by cross-lights managed with consummate skill.

Fancy, as we have said, is the principal and most active of the creative powers of Mr. Irving, and to its predominance are due alike his most surpassing excellences and his only defects. To that it is owing that as a picturesque painter of material life in all its familiar phases, he shines without an equal. To that is owing the perpetual charm of unwearying liveliness, which commends him to us as a companion in the longest solitudes, and the best entertainer of brief moments of vacuity or gloom. But to this, also, in the exclusive way in which it exists in him, is owing that his works do little else than amuse; and that, too, only the lower and less intellectual portions of our nature. We wish not to diminish the regard that is due to a writer who has delighted us too often to dispose us to criticism; but in pleasing always he has foregone the possibility of pleasing ever in the highest degree; and in making himself perpetually liked, he has consented never to be enthusiastically admired, nor perhaps deeply respected. For the excess and over-cultivation of fancy has been fatal to the exercise of the far greater faculty of imagination. Without staying to unfold the distinction between these two qualities in their entire nature, as seen in fiction, thought, feeling, and the whole action of intelligent man, we may note their difference, as far as the present purpose requires, in reference to the field where, in this instance, the diversity is chiefly illustrated, namely, in description. In an imaginative view of a scene, the mental consciousness of the person, or the moral character of the occasion, reacts upon the outward scene with such overpowering and transfusing energy, that all things around become but types and symbols,—nay, the very complements and visible parts,—of that which is within. You behold the scene, not as it is, but as it is felt or as it appears,—not in its actual condition, but as it is cast and reproduced in a speculum of thought or passion already warped or colored by the master emotion. Everything is subordinated to one prevailing sentiment. Objects are not viewed in their details, but each part is considered in reference to the whole, and colored by the notion of the whole. The spirit of totality and unity, derived from the singleness and intensity of the intellectual medium of conception, predominates. The action of fancy, however, is the opposite of all this.

The absence of imagination is obvious throughout the whole of Irving's writings. But to illustrate, in a single scene, how entirely humor in him is dependent on fancy, and not imagination, we may take the account of the Wacht-meester of Bearn Island, when the herald who had been sent by Governor Kieft arrived at the rebellious fort of Van Rensellaerstein, in the Knickerbocker annals.

"In the fulness of time, the yacht arrived before Bearn Island, and Anthony the Trumpeter, mounting the poop, sounded a parley to the fortress. In a little while, the steeple-crowned hat of Nicholas Koorn, the wacht-meester, rose above the battlements, followed by his iron visage, and ultimately his whole person, armed, as before, to the very teeth; while one by one a whole row of Helderbergers reared their round burly heads above the wall, and beside each pumpkin-head peered the end of a rusty musket."

This separation of the wacht-meester's person into a three-storied automaton, and this display of his mimic garrison, as in a mirror which leaves their vital consciousness unreflected, is extremely diverting, but it never could be the suggestion of any but an unimaginative mind.

As a double example of the perfection of a description of natural scenery in itself and wholly apart from imagination, and the failure of an attempt to represent the same scene imaginatively, may be cited the view around Tappan Zee as Ichabod Crane rode towards it in the afternoon, and from it at midnight. The former of the two pictures is as follows:

"As he journeyed along the side of a range of hills which look out upon some of the goodliest scenes of the mighty Hudson, the sun gradually wheeled his broad disk down into the west. The wide bosom of the Tappan Zee lay motionless and glassy, excepting that here and there a gentle undulation waved and prolonged the blue shadow of the distant mountain. A few amber clouds floated in the sky, without a breath of air to move them. The horizon was of a fine golden tint, changing gradually into a pure apple-green, and from that into the deep blue of the mid-heaven. A slanting ray lingered on the woody crests of the precipices that overhung some parts of the river, giving greater depth to the dark-gray and purple of their rocky sides. A sloop was loitering in the distance, dropping slowly down with the tide, her sails hanging uselessly against the mast; and as the reflection of the sky gleamed along the still water, it seemed as if the vessel was suspended in the air."

An exquisite, a faultless piece of cabinet painting! undoubtedly drawn and colored upon the spot. It is a portraiture of the scene as it is—abstractly—without reference to any state of feeling in the observer, or any prevailing sentiment in the narrative. In the *pendant* to this, the endeavor has been to exhibit the same locality in immediate relation with a peculiar condition of mind in the hero of the tale.

"It was the very witching time of night when Ichabod, heavy-hearted and crest-fallen, pursued his travel homewards, along the sides of the lofty hills which rise above Tarry Town, and which he had traversed so cheerily in the afternoon. The hour was as dismal as himself. Far below him the Tappan Zee spread its dusky and indistinct waste of waters, with here and there the tall mast of a sloop, riding quietly at anchor under the land. In the dead hush of midnight he could even hear the barking of the watch-dog from the opposite shore of the Hudson; but it was so vague and faint as only to give an idea of his distance from this faithful companion of man. Now and then, too, the long-drawn crowing of a cock, accidentally awakened, would sound far, far off, from some farm-house away among the hills—but it was like a dreaming sound in his ear. No signs of life occurred near him, but occasionally the melancholy chirp of a cricket, or perhaps the guttural twang of a bull-frog, from a neighboring marsh, as if sleeping uncomfortably, and turning suddenly in his bed."

Not thus would these objects have appeared to one who was in such a sensitive and excited condition of mind as presently to mistake an acquaintance with a cloak over his head and a pumpkin on his saddle-bow, for the Headless Horseman of the Hollow carrying his cranium before him. The design of describing the nocturnal scene by sounds rather than by sights is a good one; but each particular noise, instead of being represented in a manner to react with augmenting terror upon the fear-stricken sense of the traveller, is described in such a way as wholly to explain it away as a source of alarm, and to deprive it of the power of affrighting. The things are described not according to the law of terror within the mind of him on whom they were to operate, but according to the law of their actual state, as coldly viewed by an unexcited observer. The mast, which should have appeared as a strange, gleaming thing, weird and spectral, raising indefinite apprehensions, becomes a familiar and calming sight by being referred to a sloop, "riding quietly at anchor under the land." The distant bay of the watch-dog is well managed; but the drowsy crowing of the cock, which might with great effect have been made to have mysterious relation to the return of wandering ghosts to their sepulchral tenements, is brought back to quotidian unmeaningness by being made to proceed from a bird "accidentally awakened." The chirp which, heard at midnight, should have been an unknown signal, is elaborately portrayed as the soothing voice of the domestic and companionable cricket; and the awful bass from the marshes which, in lonely darkness, would have been an unlocal, bodiless horror, thrilling the nerves like a galvanic shock, is divested of all terror and of all dignity, by being the snort of a frog "sleeping uncomfortably, and turning suddenly in his bed." Compare all this with one of Shakspeare's nights! Mr. Irving's failure in this case is to be ascribed to defect of imagination, and consequent excess of inappropriate and discordant detail.

Moreover, this constant following of the minutiæ of a scene to turn them into picturesque effect—this constant subordination of reflective action to outward appearance—damps and enfeebles the intellectual power. The fine, strong, manly thought—the vigorous moral reflection—the commanding tone of rational sense—which form so potent and grand an element in the magic of Scott's creations, are not found in Irving. However, it is a false system to criticise a literary work according to what it has not. So viewed, it is seen erroneously as the complement of some imagined whole, and has all its signs reversed. It is wiser as well as kindlier to consider a production of art under the view of what it is and has, and not of what it lacks.

In ideal pictures of inanimate nature, and of animals, trees, and landscapes, Mr. Irving's microscopic fidelity in limning accomplishes some remarkable effects. He does not bring a scene before you by giving the general expression of it, or the leading characteristics, under the form of a mental conception, here and there rendered definite and particular by certain touches of detail. He paints every object separately and exquisitely, fixing your attention upon each in succession, and making the whole a series of special studies. He is in description what Backhuysen is in painting. So prominent is the perspective, so absolute the verisimility, that you seem to have the thing itself, rather than a representation of it. As a specimen of consummate skill in this way, we may take the picture of the inn-yard on a wet Sunday, in the story of "The Stout Gentleman."

"I know of nothing more calculated to make a man sick of this world, than a stable-yard on a rainy day. The place was littered with wet straw, that had been kicked about by travellers and stable-boys. In one corner was a stagnant pool of water, surrounding an island of muck; there were several half-drowned fowls crowded together under a cart, among which was a miserable, crest-fallen cock, drenched out of all life and spirit; his drooping tail, matted, as it were, into a single feather, along which the water trickled from his back; near the cart was a half-dozing cow, chewing the cud, and standing patiently to be rained on, with wreaths of vapor rising from her reeking hide; a wall-eyed horse, tired of the loneliness of the stable, was poking his spectral head out of a window, with the rain dripping on it from the eaves; an unhappy cur, chained to a dog-house hard by, uttered something every now and then, between a bark and a yelp; a drab of a kitchen-wench tramped backwards and forwards through the yard in pattens, looking as sulky as the weather itself; everything, in short, was comfortless and forlorn, excepting a crew of hardened ducks, assembled like boon companions round a puddle, and making a riotous noise over their liquor."

Certainly this is nature itself,—only more so, as Hudson would say. That "more so," is just the difficulty.

The description in another part of "Bracebridge Hall," of Lady Lillicraft's dogs, is hardly inferior.

"One is a fat spaniel, called Zephyr—though Heaven defend me from such a Zephyr! He is fed out of all shape and comfort; his eyes are nearly strained out of his head; he wheezes with corpulency, and cannot walk without great difficulty. The other is a little, old, gray-muzzled curmudgeon, with an unhappy eye, that kindles like a coal if you only look at him; his nose turns up; his mouth is drawn into wrinkles, so as to show his teeth; in short, he has altogether the look of a dog far gone in misanthropy, and totally sick of the world. When he walks, he has his tail curled up so tight, that it seems to lift his feet from the ground; and he seldom makes use of more than three legs at a time, keeping the other drawn up in reserve. This last wretch is called Beauty."

In the same line of excellence may be placed the picture of the landscape, in the chapter of the Angler in The Sketch Book."

"I have them at this moment before my eyes, stealing along the border of the brook, where it lay open to the day, or was merely fringed by shrubs and bushes. I see the bittern rising with hollow scream, as they break in upon his rarely invaded haunt; the kingfisher, watching them suspiciously from his dry tree, that overhangs the deep, black mill-pond, in the gorge of the hills; the tortoise, letting himself slip sideways from off the stone or log, on which he is sunning himself; and the panic-struck frog, plunging in headlong, as they approach, and spreading an alarm throughout the watery world around."

These are remarkable illustrations of the completeness and vividness with which an object or a scene can, by mere imitative description, be realized under your eye. This faculty we take to be Mr. Irving's *forte;* and its successful exercise by him has given rise to a school of writers, who, with less taste, but in some cases more power, have carried the style to an unlimited height of popularity, but quite beyond the domain of genuine art. We regard Mr. Irving's works as having furnished the original and model of Dickens's descriptive manner; and, if the former has more delicacy, softness, and grace, the other excels in force, range, and vividness. Has not the general portraiture of the species "English Stage-coachman," in "The Sketch Book," served as a preliminary study for the elder Weller in Pickwick?

"He has commonly," says Irving, "a broad, full face, curiously mottled with red, as if the blood had been forced by hard feeding into every vessel of the skin; he is swelled into jolly dimensions by frequent potations of malt liquors, and his bulk is still further increased by a multiplicity of coats, in which he is buried like a cauliflower, the upper one reaching to his heels. He wears a broad-brimmed, low-crowned hat; a huge roll of colored handkerchief about his neck, knowingly knotted, and tucked in at the bosom; and has, in summer-time, a large bouquet of flowers in his button-hole," &c., &c.

There can be no doubt of Mr. Irving's supremacy in this class or school. The only question is as to the comparative dignity and elevation of the school itself. For ourselves, we may as well say at once that we do not regard it as belonging to a high order of art. It implies an extremely nice observation, constantly and painfully engaged upon its task; but it involves no act of true creation, no exercise of veritable poetic power. The pictures have no atmosphere; the objects glare directly upon you without passing through any mental medium. Amused, astonished, and perhaps delighted with the work, you feel little respect or interest for the author. His character is not in his production. This is the style of all recent art. It is the school of Backhuysen, Achenbach, and Birkel. We make our protest against the whole cabal. We design, at a convenient opportunity, to deliver a full confession of our critical faith upon these topics. We deem an exposure of the pervading feebleness and falsity of the principle of this style, indispensable to rescue the youthful genius of our country from a fatal seduction. The vice of the art of this day, literary and pictorial, poetical and prose, and infecting authors and readers alike, consists in the excess of fancy, and the deficiency of imagination.

In respect to personal portraiture, Mr. Irving is an exquisite delineator of external manners, but has no power of representing character. He paints, not to the mind, by those intellectual touches which flash a complete subject into existence; nor to the conceptive faculty, by seizing those leading traits which draw all the accessories and dependents after them; but to the eye, by the transcription of every individual peculiarity in succession, each of which adds a modifying influence to those that went before, so that the effect is not complete until each stroke has been noted. He never gives you the interior, living, conscious man. You never get hold of the moral being of the creature. You have the mere *larva* of the person; the filmy shell of dress, carriage, and deportment, according to their pictorial impression. There is a complete absence of materiality from his people. They make no noise in walking. When they cross the mead, the grass is not pressed down under their feet. They seem, like Chinese figures in a landscape, to hang a foot or two up in the air. They are shadows; visionary toys in human shape; moving their limbs according as the author of their being draws the strings upon which they are hung; airy forms, flitting in an airy scene.

How different is the nature of Scott's creations! He seizes the moral and mental being of the subject of his pencil, and sets him before you as a real, breathing, earnest man. He brings out the exterior impression as strikingly and particularly as Irving; but he approaches it from within, and compasses it by associating outward indications with inward and characteristic qualities. Compare the picture of Touchwood with that of General Harbottle! How clear and marked are the face, figure, and bodily peculiarities of the former; yet how living he is! How you feel his breath as he passes by; how uncomfortably his eye lies upon you! The elaboration of General Harbottle's exterior is infinitely greater; and, as a piece of outward picturing, nothing can be more complete:—"A soldier of the old school, with powdered head, sidelocks, and pig-tail:—his face shaped like the stern of a Dutch man-of-war, narrow at top, and wide at bottom, with full rosy cheeks, and a double chin;"—then, the meeting between himself and Lady Lillicraft: "The graciousness of her profound courtesy, and the air of the old school with which the General took off his hat, swayed it gently in his hand, and bowed his powdered head:"—and again, where he and Master Simon were playing the mischief with a buxom milk-maid in a meadow, their elbowing each other now and then, and the General's shaking his shoulders, blowing up his cheeks, and breaking out into short fits of irrepressible laughter,—how perfect the portraiture! Yet, with all, the General is not a living creature; he is a mere airy puppet, a shadowy coinage of the vision, existing for the reader's mind only, in those scenes and acts in which he is specially described, and nowhere else.

Humor, as an adopted tone of style, or a permanent habit of mind, is a striking characteristic of Mr. Irving's writings: it seems, however, to be not an original, inherent, spiritual capacity, but an effect resulting from the odd, grotesque action of the fancy and taste. It will be found, almost invariably, that the humorous character of his productions, is external and visible, arising from queerness of outward form, or combination, or allusion; it is humor to the sight, and not to the soul. Quaint, droll, comic,—what you will, in the line of diverting, laughter-moving conceit,—we can scarcely admit his possession of that grand, deep, pathetic, meditative inspiration, Humor;—a faculty which seems to be the combination and the key of all our nature's sympathies; which measures the highest flights of thought, searches the deepest recesses of feeling, and sits upon the firmest seat of sense: the wisest instinct of our minds, the kindliest impulse of our hearts; a prompting always right, a guidance ever graceful; dignifying and endearing what it touches, and having relation to love rather than contempt. It would be neither fair nor practicable to compare the mirthfulness of Irving, with that of the great Cervantic mind, or with that which was the fullest, strongest, most complex action of the mighty genius of Scott; any more than to liken the simple carolings of a shepherd's reed to the multitudinous, interlinked, and infinitely complicated harmonies of one of Handel's oratorios. But taking lower and smaller parallels, the humor of Addison is intellectual, that of Goldsmith moral, and that of Irving purely fanciful. In the author of "The Spectator," the humorous seems to be the highest action of the rational; the last, and finest, and surest test of sense and argument of right. In Goldsmith, it grows out of a practical and feeling acquaintance with life, and a keen and shrewd, yet affectionate insight into the peculiarities and weaknesses of individual character, and the foibles, vanities, and innocent absurdities of domestic and social relations. In Irving, it is the humor of the picturesque and quaint. It is a ridiculing humor, founded on distortion and misrepresentation; not a genial, enjoying spirit, arising from seeing into the depths of things. In plain truth, Irving is nothing more nor less than the most delicate, graceful, and exquisite of caricaturists.

As an illustration, that humor with Mr. Irving lies in the exercise of fancy, that it exists in the outward and pictorial, and not mentally, and in ideas, we may refer to the opening chapters of Knickerbocker's History. We are told, in a late prologue, that they were intended to burlesque the pedantic lore displayed in certain American works; and the task is long and laboriously followed out. Yet how dull, vapid, and ineffective is the toil! The whole thing is a failure. It is not until we come to the second book, and the portraits of Hendrick Hudson and his mate Jewit, and the Good Vrouw, that we feel one genuine emotion of merriment, and recognize the cunning of a master.

A sense of the humorous, morally or intellectually, is a sure preservative against extravagance or bad taste; and the extent to which Mr. Irving's drollery is merely a work of the fancy, and of kin to caricature, may be seen in the numerous instances, especially in his earlier writings, in which bizarre conceptions degenerate into mere witless farce, exciting no amusement whatever. Such, we suppose, to be the account of the escape of Communipaw from the Virginia fleet, by the burghers falling to work and smoking their pipes at such a rate, as wholly to conceal the country, and the account of the origin of the name of Anthony's Nose in the Highlands. The latter story is, that as Anthony, the Governor's trumpeter, whose nose was of a very burly size, was sailing up the Hudson, he leaned over the quarter-railing of the galley, early one morning, to contemplate it in the glassy wave below.

"Just at this moment, the illustrious sun, breaking in all his splendor from behind a high bluff of the Highlands, did dart one of his most potent beams full upon the refulgent nose of the sounder of brass, the reflection of which shot straightway down, hissing hot, into the water, and killed a mighty sturgeon that was sporting beside the vessel," &c., &c.

If this is humor, we must confess our incapacity to perceive it. According to our impression, the greater part of Knickerbocker's History consists of the farcical rather than the humorous; we pronounce it infinitely droll, but we do not laugh.

In dealing with the pathetic, it is equally obvious, that Mr. Irving's power is not that of reflection, but of operating by visible images. In "The Sketch Book," under the title of Rural Funerals, there are some meditations upon the influence of death upon the affections, which have become rather famous in Elegant Extracts. They are commonplace, overstrained, affected. But turn to the story of "The Widow and her Son," and you will find that the selection of incidents, to bring out all the tender pathos of the tale, manifests a surpassing and resistless art. The first view which we have of the mother, in church:

> "A poor, decrepit old woman, bending under the weight of years and infirmities: the lingerings of decent pride were visible in her appearance. Her dress, though humble in the extreme, was scrupulously clean. Some trivial respect, too, had been awarded her, for she did not take her seat among the village poor, but sat alone on the steps of the altar."

Then the burial, when the mother had been assisted to kneel down at the head of the coffin at the grave:

> "Her withered hands were clasped, as if in prayer, but I could perceive, by a feeble rocking of the body, and a convulsive motion of the lips, that she was gazing on the last relics of her son with the yearnings of a mother's heart."

Then her first appearance in the village on the following Sunday:

> "She had made an effort to put on something like mourning for her son; and nothing could be more touching than this struggle between pious affection and utter poverty; a black ribbon or so, a faded black handkerchief, and one or two more such humble attempts to express by outward signs that grief which passes show."

These are the matchless strokes of genius, and show us that, however Mr. Irving may disappoint, when he deals with abstract reflections and thoughts, he never wanders when he follows the guidance of a visionary eye, inerrant in its truth, and unrivalable in its simple power.

The qualities which we recognize in Mr. Irving, of a mild yet lively fancy, and a refined taste, render him peculiarly well adapted to excel in narrative; and there he certainly assumes a position of especial and distinctive superiority. Walpole has remarked that simple narrative, in English, is one of the rarest and most difficult enterprises of literary art; and if the reason which he gives for it be not sound, at least the fact is verified by all experience. Gibbon was master of every form of style except this; Robertson, when he shone the most was farthest from it; Hume alone approached tolerably near to the standard, yet even in his pages we find ourselves following the progress of a philosopher's views, rather than a history of national events. Bancroft cannot narrate at all, and Prescott narrates with labor and fatigue. But Irving is always simple, direct, onward, informing, yet elegant, lively, and agreeable. The pleasantness which he diffuses over subjects the most barren or the most uncomfortable, arises chiefly from the instinctive quietness with which he seizes everything that is capable of being turned to picturesque effect, and employs it to shed light and grace upon the scene. The art of this system consists in the gentleness and fineness of the frequent rays which are thus shed abroad, and in the absence of strong, startling, and extraordinary lights. Instead of an occasional blaze diffused from prominent points, each incident, object, and interest is made mildly luminous by the lustre of a fancy almost imperceptible in its separate operation. It is by such a process that we are made to follow a troupe of adventurers across the disgusting sterilities of the north-western territories with the same delighted spirit with which we should tread the flowery vales of Cashmere, radiant with odors and ringing with the voices of birds. The unexhausted vigor, the delicate moderation, the consummate judgment with which in "Astoria" the resources of fiction are exerted to beautify the truth without distorting it, and to improve its tone without disturbing its form, are entitled to all admiration and all imitation. In some instances, in which he has allowed his pencil to leave its more brilliant touches upon the canvas, he has reached, in that work, the finest pictures that ever came from his genius. Such may be considered the narrative of the visit of Mackenzie and his companions to the village of Wish-ram, to demand the rifle of which an earlier traveller had been despoiled, and which was known to be retained as a trophy. There are no flourishes of fiction in the detail: the truth of the story is severely maintained, but the glow and splendor of poetry are given by merely supplying from general conceptions some touches of pictorial power which undoubtedly existed in the original occurrence.

"Mackenzie offered to cross the river and demand the rifle, if any one would accompany him. It was a hair-brained project, for these villages were noted for the ruffian character of their inhabitants; yet two volunteers promptly stepped forward, Alfred Seton, the clerk, and Joe de la Pierre, the cook. The trio soon reached the opposite side of the river. On landing, they freshly primed their rifles and pistols. A path winding for about a hundred yards among rocks and crags, led to the village. No notice seemed to be taken of their approach. Not a solitary being, man, woman, or child, greeted them. The very dogs, those noisy pests of an Indian town, kept silence. On entering the village a boy made his appearance, and pointed to a house of larger dimensions than the rest. They had to stoop to enter it; as soon as they had passed the threshold, the narrow passage behind them was filled by a sudden rush of Indians, who had before kept out of sight.

"Mackenzie and his companions found themselves in a rude chamber of about twenty-five feet long, and twenty wide. A bright fire was blazing at one end, near which sat the chief, about sixty years old. A large number of Indians, wrapped in buffalo robes, were squatted in rows, three deep, forming a semi-circle round three sides of the room. A single glance sufficed to show them the grim and dangerous assembly into which they had intruded, and that all retreat was cut off by the mass which blocked up the entrance.

"The chief pointed to the vacant side of the room opposite to the door, and motioned for them to take their seats. They complied. A dead pause ensued. *The grim warriors around sat like statues; each muffled in his robe, with his fierce eyes bent on the intruders.* The latter felt they were in a perilous predicament.

"'Keep your eyes on the chief while I am addressing him,' said Mackenzie to his companions. 'Should he give any sign to his band, shoot him, and make for the door.'

"Mackenzie advanced, and offered the pipe of peace to the chief, but it was refused. He then made a regular speech, explaining the object of their visit, and proposing to give in exchange for the rifle two blankets, an axe, some beads and tobacco.

"When he had done, the chief rose, began to address him in a low voice, but soon became loud and violent, and ended by working himself up into a furious passion. He upbraided the white men for their sordid conduct in passing and repassing through their neighborhood without giving them a blanket or any other article of goods, merely because they had no furs to barter in exchange; and he alluded, with menaces of vengeance, to the death of the Indians killed by the whites at the skirmish at the Falls.

"Matters were verging to a crisis. It was evident the surrounding savages were only waiting a signal from the chief to spring upon their prey. Mackenzie and his companions had gradually risen on their feet during the speech, and had brought their rifles to a horizontal position, the barrels resting in their left hands; the muzzle of Mackenzie's piece was within three feet of the speaker's heart. They cocked their rifles; *the click of the locks for a moment suffused the dark cheek of the savage,* and there was a pause. They coolly but promptly advanced to the door; the Indians fell back in awe, and suffered them to pass. *The sun was just setting as they emerged from this dangerous den.* They took the precaution to keep along the tops of the rocks as much as possible, on their way back to the canoe, and reached their camp in safety, congratulating themselves on their escape, and feeling no desire to make a second visit to the grim warriors of the Wish-ram."

"The Life and Voyages of Columbus" however, constitute the most felicitous of the more dignified efforts of Mr. Irving's pen. It is impossible that the story of the sublime old tar can ever be told in a manner more thoroughly delightful. It is a "tale to hold children from play, and old men from the chimney corner." You move upon enchanted ground, and every sight and every sound is framed for charming. But this praise implies some grave defects. The determination to make everything picturesque and entertaining is fatal to the truth of the subject. Delays, disgusts, hardships, oppressions, treacheries, and all the harsh, stern elements of the reality, instead of being exhibited in those rough, strong colors which would have kindled a manly sympathy in the reader's heart to make their rudeness welcome, are enamelled in a style of sketchy delicacy of outline and hue, that wholly betrays the genuine qualities of the subject. The rage for catching the picturesque in external effect frequently causes an utterly false notion of the moral aspect of the occasion to be rendered: the eye is fascinated and misled by the visible, material conception of what, intellectually, may be of a directly opposite nature. Thus the picture of Columbus's long and weary suit at the court of Spain, instead of being fully brought out in its uncomfortable and degrading reality, which might annoy the sensibilities of the reader, is touched up with images of romantic scenery which convert the dulness of the period into brilliant and poetic interest. These years were passed, it would seem, amid scenes of peril and adventure, following up the court in striking situations of wild, rugged, and mountainous war; attending the sovereigns at sieges of Moorish cities, and fighting himself in the dashing forays that gave a zest to the war; until at length "Columbus beheld Muley Boabdil, the elder of the two rival kings of Granada, surrender in person all his remaining possessions and his right to the crown to the Spanish sovereigns." It is indeed a very curious study to a literary artist, to observe with what diligent dexterity the historian has mixed up the figure of Columbus with the persons, scenes, occurrences of the day, with whom we associate sentiments of romantic interest; how the gloom of unsuccessful conferences is relieved by the gorgeous costumes of cardinals, and bishops, and noble dames; how the splendid trappings of royalty flit before the dazzled sight; until, at last, the period of this long attendance fills our thoughts as the most entertaining portion of Columbus's life. To the imagination and feelings of the reader the whole thing is an enchanting falsehood. It is really the feebleness and not the force of art which, unable to manage the strong contrasts that should have brought out the noble harmony of the sublime story, levels all in one insipid melody. Moreover, the dreamy, Arcadian style of the narrative causes a complete want of those definite, sharp particularities which, in a history, are indispensable; and which, after all, give an interest and an effect which all the flakes of sentiment and fancy, however accumulated, cannot supply. For example, in attempting to impress us with a notion of the frailty and slightness of the vessels in which Columbus embarked upon his awful mission of exploration, he describes two of them as "light barks not superior to river and coasting craft of more modern days;" open and without decks, &c.; but he nowhere mentions their tonnage. If he had told us that one of the vessels was of only fifteen tons, which is the fact, we should have had a far more vivid conception of the daring of this enterprise. But Mr. Irving is too nice a gentleman to deal in vulgar statistics. The consequence of this style of dainty selection and exquisite indistinctness is that we cannot determine whether we are reading a professed fiction or an intended history. The pictures lack that individuality and force which tell us that we are looking at a portrait and not at a fancy-piece. While we read we are held as by a wondering spell, but when we close the volume, the "*incredulus odi*" succeeds, and we long for a real history of the times, so that we may know how much of the fairy tale we have read is true. In the history of the siege of Granada this puzzle between truth and fiction becomes absolutely offending. We feel as if the chronicler was trifling with us. The essence of romance is poured out in such profusion as to become sickening. In attempting to throw a perfume on the flowers of natural truth he seems to have spilt the bottle of attar, and the nosegay is fairly fetid with artificial and excessive odor.

The work upon which Mr. Irving's fame as a literary creator and artist will rest in future times is, no doubt, "The Sketch Book." The variety of its materials, the refinement mingled always with natural and familiar ease, the adaptation of its topics and tone to the general sympathy, the union of Italian brilliance with Flemish fidelity in the sketches, render it justly a favorite with all. Walpole used to say, that an author's genius usually comes into flower at some period of his life. And probably there will be little difference of opinion upon the point that "The Sketch Book" is the perfect flower of all of Irving's faculties. "Bracebridge Hall" falls entirely below it. The design of that work cannot be regarded as a happy one; and objectionable as at best it is, the execution of the scheme is such as to develop new faults. In the first place, the plan or groundwork of the thing is misconceived; and the misconception springs from that want of imagination which we have spoken of. The purpose of the work is to sketch the ancient poetic manners of the English people, especially in their country life; and with a view to add the interest of a present scene to the beauty of old romance, the author supposes a character devotedly attached to all bygone customs, and passing his life in an endeavor to realize the life of the past in all the usages upon his own estate. Now, in order that such moral anachronism as Mr. Irving conceives, should be at all probable or possible, the first requisite is that the person from whom it originates should be represented as a man of ardent poetic genius, identifying himself by force of creative energy with the spirit of long departed institutions, and able, by the enthusiasm and force of his character, to infect all around him with the same illusion. Such is not Mr. Irving's Squire; and it is against all consistency, that the commonplace, feeble, vacant creature whom he introduces to us as the proprietor of the Hall, should develop from his own temper, against all surrounding influences, the beautiful elaboration of ideal existence which is exhibited to our view, and that his dependents, stewards, woodmen, and farmers, should breathe the atmosphere of his mind instead of their own actual and real consciousness. The primary and indispensable conditions of the scene are violated. We feel, therefore, in reading this work, a sense of falsity and difficulty. A vigorous imagination would have kept the author from this failure. But the literary defects of Bracebridge Hall are also striking. To refine the critical perceptions and sentiments by diligent familiarity with older models, and to reproduce the spirit of Addisonian grace, might be a worthy ambition; but to subordinate the mind and character to the local and temporary form of a particular passage,—to labor to observe, think, and speak precisely upon the example of the Spectators—to make not a rational imitation, but a mechanical mimicry—is not a very lofty or a very wise employment of genius. As far even as this design is intentionally carried out, it is not successfully done. While the endeavor to imitate Addison is palpable and displeasing, the constant intervention of phrases and even particular words, which are wholly modern and American, exposes the falsity of the counterfeit, and even gives an air of vulgarity to that which, properly used, might have had the dignity of genuineness. It will be observed that the attempt to impart an Addisonian air to the style, consists chiefly in the frequent use of certain expressions which are the accidental peculiarities of the model:—"I could not help observing"—"I am apt to find or to think"—"A very tolerable scholar," &c. But in the midst of these the constant recurrence of such words as "I noticed," and half a dozen others, which are neither Addisonian nor English, not only breaks the illusion, but converts it into an imposture. A greater difficulty, however, is that the imitation is not kept up, and in the nature of the case, could not be kept up. For, the moment that the author becomes warmed, and his mind gets into vigorous play, such is the sympathy between thought and style, that as the former grows earnest the latter becomes characteristic and genuine. This transition from the falsetto of an affected Addisonianism to the natural tones of individual truth, causes the tales,(?) fine and musical as they are, to displease by inappropriateness. Take, for instance, in the early chapters of "Bracebridge Hall," the paragraphs about family servants, and about the duties of women *after* they are married, where the author gives vent to his own serious and sober feelings and opinions upon interesting subjects. They are beautifully written, but have not a touch of the false antiquity of the rest; and this partial change of the key throws everything into discord. It is like a man who, acting a part under a false-face, thrusts out his own features from the mask whenever he has anything particularly clever to say.

Of Mr. Irving's works, generally, it may be observed, that in a grammatical point of view, the style is delicate rather than pure, and more exquisite than correct. His use of words is not exact; indeed, we constantly meet with expressions which it surprises us that a man of good education should, even in the greatest carelessness, let fall. Such phrases as the following: "the creaking of the cords seemed to *agonize her*," in "The Widow and her Son;" "he *emerged his head* out of his shell," in "Bracebridge Hall;" "whom he thought fully entitled of being classed," &c., in the same place; are among several that struck us upon our recent perusal of one or two volumes.

THE FEMALE POETS OF AMERICA. By RUFUS WILMOT GRISWOLD.

THE elevation and purity of the moral tone of a nation may be pretty exactly estimated from the social position and influence enjoyed by women. The female character, in truth, embodies and represents a special portion of the qualities of humanity; and that portion the most exalted and the least earthly. The deference paid to the sex and the control exercised by them, depend upon the extent to which those qualities have sway in the breasts of men. As natural energy and intellectual discernment are the masculine elements of the race, so those self-annihilating emotions and affections—that exquisiteness of virtuous sensibility—that secondary and transcendental consciousness—which form the spiritual in our constitution—are the dowry which Providence gave with woman, when her loftier destiny was blended into eternal unity with our kind. In the civilization of modern Europe, it would be difficult to determine whether an increased reverence for woman was a result of the new religion, or a means providentially appointed for securing its reception; so identified in their progress have been these two sentiments. From the early days of Christianity, the mother and her child became the symbol of that faith and feeling which were to humanize the world; and from that central idea, as from a germ of diviner life, the whole system of catholic virtues flowered. When, at a later period, the forces of intellectual vigor, eager to expand into a brighter existence, gushed forth into imaginative art, the maternal relation and the domestic circle became the type of that mystic power which, rising from the ruins of Judea, had pervaded the earth with its transforming energy. The Madonna—that natural apotheosis of woman—is the permanent emblem of Christianity.

The American system, as it whirls onward in its mighty and amazing progress, is manifesting several new qualities of life and power, which give promise that the social condition ultimately to be realized in this country, will differ strikingly from any that has been exhibited in former times. Not the least observable of these are the change and advancement which have been worked out in the position of that sex which, whether for good or for evil, has always wrought such memorable effects upon the world. The prominence and influence of women in their relation to society have passed into a more expanded phase of dignity, and operate in original methods and through novel channels. "*Les Races se feminisent,*" says Buffon.

This peculiarity of our age, indeed, to which we have alluded, is by no means confined to our own country. The circumstance of literary development most characteristic of the present time everywhere, is the superior distinction, relatively, which women have acquired in some of the most brilliant departments of authorship. In fiction, they seem, in every country in Europe, as well as on this side of the water, to have vindicated their claims to an equality with the other sex, and perhaps, indeed, to have supplanted them in popular favor. No northern writer has ever acquired a reputation so pervading and universal as Miss Bremer. In France, Madame Dudevant, better known as George Sand, has obtained, by her analysis of character, her mastery of the passions, and the splendid vigor of her imagination, a position of commanding superiority. In England, we have the names of Miss Ellen Pickering, Miss Howitt, Mrs. Gore, and many others: and the English muse finds among her male votaries, no utterance in tones so rich, and bold, and genuine, as those which answer to the touches of Mrs. Norton, and Miss Barrett. So in the generation just closed, Mrs. Hemans, and Mrs. Baillie, and Miss Landon, held a place scarcely subordinate to that of the great masters who then swept the lyre with a power and freedom which had not been known for two centuries. The causes of this honorable peculiarity of our own days, like most other changes in society, would probably be found to lie among influences which are so subtle as to elude inquiry. It is obvious, however, that there has been, through two centuries, a progressive advance in the relation which the female sex has held to the intellectual condicton of the race, and in their influence upon the public mind. Along with this, we think it equally clear, that there has been a gradual expansion in the literary character and calling, favorable to the display of natural and unschooled talent. Formerly, authorship was looked upon as a distinct profession, as much so, almost, as the law; it was regarded as eminently a learned profession, and as specially demanding a thorough familiarity with a certain course of classical discipline. Hence the great traditionary wonder of Shakspeare's want of education. If a

Shakspeare were to appear now, whatever wonder his genius might raise, the circumstance that he had "little Latin and less Greek" would not generally be considered as among the causes of surprise. In the modern world, literature has followed a course of development directly opposite to that which we see among the ancients: with them, it began from spontaneous inspiration, and, as it went on, became encumbered with artifice and technicalities. In modern Europe, it started from profound learning, and has gradually worked its way to liberty and nature. It is now "the free thought of the free soul." No author is now struck down by the critics at his entrance upon the field, because he has not a scholastic badge upon him; on the contrary, we court and commend, as conducing to originality, a complete ignorance of the classics, and of the earlier writers of our own tongue. Now, as from the nature of the case, however superior in other respects, women can rarely be as profoundly and systematically educated as the other sex, we look upon the ponderous and pedantic style of composition in former days, as one of the causes of the suppression of female genius, and the change which we have alluded to, as having prominently led to the noble *sortie,* which it has made of late. With all these European illustrations, however, the action of the gentle sex abroad, has been, as a usual thing, domestic, moral, invisible: among us, it has grown to be general, intellectual and obvious; this contributes largely to the force and direction of public opinion: its weight is felt in the action of the country: by a direct and palpable control, it affects the tone of the national mind and feeling. Alterations in the laws of a people are a sure sign of some antecedent modification in the circumstances of society, which they accommodate and register; and the legislation which, beginning at the East, has extended throughout most of the States of this Union, recognizing the increased independence and power of the wife, and giving protection to her interests, is one of the evidences of the social change which we allude to. Common-law principles have been broken up, because the conditions upon which those principles formed themselves have undergone variation. The extent to which women share the toils and the honors of literary production among us, is altogether unexampled in the records of any of the European states to which, with a full exhibition of them, we have alluded. Look at any department in America that you please,—except, of course, such as concern some special profession or craft, with which women necessarily are not conversant—and you will find that the proportion of works bearing feminine names upon their titles, is larger than in any other land, and in many instances exceeds that of their masculine rivals. In fiction—from its most substantial to its slightest shapes—in criticism, in politics—in the useful and in the elegant alike—those to whom it was once a rare and almost forbidden accomplishment even to read, now equal or excel that sex which formerly boasted that the pen was as exclusively its possession as the sword. The extent to which graceful forms mingle in the masquerade of the daily press, and the amount of power that thus emanates upon society from the purest sources, would scarcely be believed by any who are not initiated in the mysteries of that secret fraternity.

The workings of all this upon the character and condition of our people, cannot, we must say in passing, but be admirable. In the present day, the literary class forms the great moral estate of a nation. The press is the grand medium through which the rays of mental and political and spiritual illumination and guidance stream forth upon the world. That so large a portion of the best and purest light which our nature has garnered up from the primal beam which shone upon it in the morning of creation, mingles in that pillar of fire which conducts us through the night of doubt, and trial, and danger, is the truest augury of the grandeur and elevation of our destiny. American literature, at this moment, possesses more genuineness, chasteness, simplicity and virtue than the literature of any European country which displays the same vitality and force. The presence of womanhood, pervading its life like a religion, has reproved and cleansed its spirit. The same power has acted like a solvent upon public taste; precipitating into neglect and disfavor all coarse and gross productions, and leaving only the correct and good afloat. No authors among us, but such as have pursued upright and honest aims, and have promoted the interests of morality and refinement, have acquired a permanent reputation and popularity; and distant may the day be in which this shall be otherwise. The minds of our countrymen have been swayed towards many benignant reformations in society—schemes promotive of peace, and justice, and charity, and opposed to selfishness and violence, have been brought to bear upon the opinions and action of the people; and in all these things we may trace the operation of female sympathies, acting usually through the channels of the press. It must be observed, also, that literary habits on the part of women here, are not liable to the evils which sometimes attend them in Europe. In France and England, female authorship, being much rarer than with us, and being a good deal in opposition to the prejudices and tastes of the community, must be accompanied by a boldness of temper and a defiance of the public opinion, which reacts very injuriously upon the character of those who become subject to such an influence. But with us, the pen is so frequent and approved an ornament of hands which wear it as gracefully as they wear a bracelet or a ring, that the practice of composition does not form, to our common feelings, the faintest departure from the gentleness and delicacy of female reserve. We hail, therefore, the new work, "The Female Poets of America," with admiration, and thanks, and pride. No idea is a more favorite one with this country and with us, than that it is among the future glories of our destiny to give to the admiration of men a literature grander, richer, more magnificent in tone and spirit, than all that have yet preceded it. An omen is here before us! Poetry is, in its nature, prophetic. It is the emanation and witness of that imaginative sensibility, that anticipating apprehension, of the finer and subtler kind of souls, in whose reflective feeling, that which is not yet, is mirrored with a brilliancy and distinctness more vivid than the present and the real. It is the full-flowering, in a more delicate and vital atmosphere, of that plant of national genius which in the actual scene around, as yet exists only in the germ. It is the forward-thrown echo—

airy and musical, yet truthful and definite—of that action which is about to be evolved by the system of which it is the symbol and the signal. Now, as the most marked peculiarity of our new condition of society has been stated to be the relative position and eminence and influence of women among us, it is an evidence of the genuineness of the creative talent which has been manifested on these shores that it is so predominantly feminine. Freshly and freely have the sources of this inspiration been opened upon our domestic state; and appropriately are the fairest *primitiæ* of the poetic faculty, on this soil, offered from gentle hands. No literary annals of Europe can show an instance of the powers of the muse, so widely diffused, so variously toned, so highly cultivated, in the softer sex, as is here displayed.

Dr. Griswold has performed the duties of his undertaking with a diligence, a taste and a discrimination which we doubt whether any man in this country could have equalled. The selections are copious and judicious, and the criticisms upon them are delicate and just. A great deal of trouble has obviously been taken to obtain materials for the work, and to bring together accurate information in regard to the authors. A very large portion of the poems—and those among the best in the book—have never been printed before, having been given to the editor expressly for this collection. The work has therefore, to a great extent, the value of an original production by the combined efforts of our female poets. We purpose a series of papers on the female poets of America,* and shall have occasion therein to return and linger upon the labors of this enthusiast of the literary fame of his country. He has largely increased the field of survey, and brought into view, as entitled to permanent places in our Pantheon, persons who before were but names without embodiment. His judgments are fearless and inde-

* These papers, to which the present criticism was meant as introductory merely, were subsequently written, and are spoken of by a most competent judge as having been among the few of Mr. Wallace's perfectly finished papers, and such as he was willing to have printed. Unfortunately, however, they are not found among his MSS.—ED.

pendent, and his experience and good sense have always saved his freedom from being perverted into paradox or rashness. He seems to look, as we do, to the Occident for the birth-place of those rays that gleam "unborrowed from the sun." We are much struck with his remarks upon those youthful prodigies, Alice and Phœbe Carey:—

"In the west," says Dr. Griswold, "song gushes and flows, like the springs and rivers, more imperially than elsewhere, as they will believe who study her journals, or who read these effusions or those of Amelia Welby, the author of 'The Wife of Leon,' and other young poets, whose minds seem to be elevated by the glorious nature there, into the atmosphere where all thought takes a shape of beauty and harmony. A delicious play of fancy distinguishes much of the finest poetry of the sex; but Alice Carey evinces in many poems a genuine imagination and a creative energy that challenge peculiar praise. We have perhaps no other author so young, in whom the poetical faculty is so largely developed. Her sister writes with vigor, and a hopeful and genial spirit, and there are many felicities of expression, particularly in her later pieces. She refers more than Alice to the common experience, and has perhaps a deeper sympathy with that philosophy and those movements of the day, which look for a nearer approach to equality in culture, fortune, and social relations."

Of the delightful Grace Greenwood, another child of the forest, the editor writes thus pleasantly and happily:—

"It was from the beautiful village of New Brighton, on the Beaver river, thirty miles below Pittsburg, in a quiet valley, surrounded by the most bold and picturesque scenery, that in 1844 she wrote the first of those sprightly and brilliant letters under the signature of 'Grace Greenwood,' by which she was introduced to the literary world. They were addressed to General Morris and Mr. Willis, then editors of The New Mirror, and being published in that miscellany, the question of their authorship was discussed in the journals and in literary circles; they were attributed in turns to the most piquant and elegant of our known writers; and curiosity was in no degree lessened by intimations that they were by some Diana of the West, who, like the ancient goddess, inspired the men who saw her, with madness, and in her chosen groves and by her streams used her whip and rein with the boldness and grace of Mercury. Such secrets are not easily kept, and while the fair magazinist was visiting the Atlantic cities, in 1846, the veil was thrown aside, and she became known by her proper name. She has since been among the most industrious and successful of our authors, and has written with perhaps equal facility and felicity in every style, 'from grave to gay, from lively to severe.' Her apprehensions are sudden and powerful. The lessons of art and the secrets of experience have no mists for her quick eyes. Many-sided as Proteus, she yet by an indomitable will bends all her strong and passionate nature to the subject that is present, plucks from it whatever it has of mystery, and weaves it into the forms of her imagination, or casts it aside as the dross of a fruitless analysis. Educated in a simple condition of life, where conventionalism had no authority against truth and reason, and the healthful activity of her mind preserved by an admirable physical training and development,—all her thought is direct and honest, and her sentiment vigorous and cheerful. But the energy of her character and intelligence is not opposed to true delicacy. A feeble understanding and a nature without the elements of quick and permanent decision, on the contrary, cannot take in the noblest forms of real or ideal beauty. It is the sham delicacy that is shocked at things actual and necessary, that fills the magazines with rhymed commonplaces, that sacrifices to a prudish nicety, all individualism, and is the chief bar to esthetic cultivation and development. She looks with a poet's eye upon nature, and with a poet's soul dares and aspires for the beautiful, as it is understood by all the great intelligences whose wisdom takes the form of genius."

LETTERS ON THE STUDY AND USE OF HISTORY; WITH REFLECTIONS UPON EXILE. By the late Right Honorable HENRY ST. JOHN, Lord Viscount BOLINGBROKE.*

I AM amazed at the neglect into which the writings of this great philosopher have fallen. If there be a life in wisdom, or a soul in wit, or in sentences of magic beauty a force that makes itself to be remembered, his fame should never have passed away from the earth. There was that both in his character and in his genius which addressed posterity, rather than the present, and yet his distinction died before him. It is indeed lamentable to see to how mean an influence of prejudice his renown has been succumbed. His reputation, like his person, has been devoured by worms. I yield the profoundest homage to his greatness. Of all the lords of mind, none hath a larger state or loftier pace than he. The whole frame of his intellectual exhibition is marked by a grandness of conception, a majesty of mind, that is as rare as it is delightful; the natural high utterances of one that breathes a superior atmosphere of thought to that of ordinary men. He is the only infidel derider of man, from whose

* The criticism on Lord Bolingbroke, which follows, is extracted from the author's early diary.—ED.

writings you come exalted, ennobled, and with added vigor in the cause of virtue. The most generous believer might read Bolingbroke, and in the spirit of his sentiments find nothing alien to the high hopings of the Christian heart. He looked on man with the scowl of a demon, and on truth with the smile of a seraph. His intellect was brilliant, though disordered; splendid, though erring; bright, but blasted. The gorgeous structure of his philosophy is riven to the foundation; but genius always commands our sympathy, for, "like the temples of the gods, she is venerable even in ruins." I never read Bolingbroke without a feeling of deep melancholy; so sincere and elevated are his aspirations, so vain and errabund his theories. He often seems to feel the hollowness of the portion which he had chosen, but there abides within him a native nobility of soul, an inherent dignity of character, which forbids the vanity of regret or the weakness of a groan. We find in him none of those fretful and deep repinings, whereby Byron hourly showed that the load which he had assumed was too heavy for him, and daily crushed him to the earth; nor, on the other hand, do we see either the wild revelry of the feebler children of perdition, or that rigid calmness beneath which the arch-apostate veiled from his peers the burning anguish of his soul; but rather the sad cheerfulness and vain hopefulness of one that did not feel that all the fault was his. Towards the regions of moral truth he often turns a sightless eye; but the placid countenance tells that the blindness was not wilful. He reminds me of a benighted fisherman, who, to join his family on shore, makes his way cheerily over the ice with pole and push, and dexterous leap; not seeing that the field which he is crossing is detached from the land, and is drifting away to the solitudes of the midnight sea. Though he shivers by the flickering bonfire of deism, he utters no complaint; though he wanders through the sands of barren and irremediable error, he never quits the philosophic dignity of the flowing robe and burnished ring. His step along the paths of infidelity is like the tread of Vathek down the stairs of the hall of Eblis; for though the road is to utter and eternal perdition, the feet of a born king of men are upon it. We might liken him to a banished noble among the frosts of Siberia; noble, though banished,—though destitute, still dignified; conscious that there still remained to him an "order," from which none could degrade him, and that a star still shone upon his breast, which no monarch could strike off.

In pronouncing sentence upon the moral course of a man like St. John, we must take into account those splendid infirmities of nature which ensure for genius the fame of a conqueror, and the fate of a victim; that irrepressible ardor of spirit, which, while it kindles the intellect into a flashing fire, clouds the judgment with the fumes of excitement, and disturbs the reason with its wild impatience. His is a breast which passion has vexed with all its storms. The chords of sensibility have been swept from the highest to the lowest note by blasts of suffering. Yet, throughout all his nature there are traits of high nobility; there is visible in him none of the languor of a mind washed with debauchery, or drenched in the "sickly dews" of selfishness; "*le vice l'entrainait sans l'asservir.*" Much still "sounds man" about him. For the waywardness of his temper and the madness of his conduct, some excuse may be found in the history of his life. Soon after his entrance into public scenes, he found a rival, whose character he detested, and whose talents he despised, safely fixed in circumstances to laugh at him, and by force of dull and regular exertion pinning him to the stake of exile and contempt. He found factions using him when they needed his assistance, and turning from him in the day of his calamity. With energies that demanded action, and a heart which domestic interests could not satisfy, he was doomed to feel in the flush of early manhood, that his day had gone by forever. When I look upon him struggling under the deadly load of genius, and taking his steps, perforce unsteady, over the burning marle of statesmanship, at a time when politics swayed the hearts of men with the firmness of a principle, and the fervor of a passion, I confess that I cannot discover his failings; and before I have finished his majestic apologies for his errors, I have already forgotten what they were.

It has been his misfortune that there are few persons who

have been capable of representing him justly; for those who admired his politics were sure to abhor his philosophy. The eunuch-mind of the younger Walpole could as little taste the strong and rasping sense of the moralist, as his filial tenderness could tolerate the contemptuous energy of the politician. This variety of quality which made his character inconsistent, entered likewise into his genius, and made it copious. He partook of the best essence, and was tinged with the distinct peculiarities of many of those distinguished persons by whom he was companioned and courted. He had much of the sagacity of Swift, all of the moral purpose, mild fancy, and untrembling judgment of Pope, the severe taste of Atterbury, and the rich scholarship of Arbuthnot. I think that his power of sarcasm was by nature both stronger and more delicate than that of his poetical friend; but the latter had so educated his mind in bitterness, that he had become, like Lot's wife, a pillar of salt. His sneer is often savage, but it is never the sneer of jealousy or hate; it seems to proceed from conscientious contempt. He unites the full compass of English sense with the pointed vigor of the wits of France. His style has a corresponding breadth and liberality, and lies between the high cathedral style of Milton and the sauntering grace of Addison. He exhibits a fresh and ever-springing life of mind. Every sentence rays distinct and vivid thought. He tears down systems with the naked hand of masculine sense; and like a moral Milo, rends the aged trunks of philosophic theories with the arm of unschooled force. His sentences are not rich nor highly wrought: it is their tone, rather than their structure which gives them their weight. In every member you see the force and shaping of a serious mind. His stately tread is the accustomed princely step of one who has ever moved on marble, reposed on velvet, and breathed the air of palaces. The grave procession which rests in the spectator's mind as a passing dream of splendor, is the daily condition of his life. There is nothing dreamy or scholastic about Bolingbroke: he is always fresh with the hourly interests of life. He examines theories of metaphysics with the closeness and seriousness of one discussing measures in council. He states his system with the air of a man ready to furnish an estimate, or to embody his sentiments in resolutions; and without dreaming of comparing the magnificent moral force of the patriot with the merely intellectual vigor of the partisan, I must say, that as a stylist, as a communicator of thoughts, I prefer the well-laced sobriety of Bolingbroke to the Persian prodigality of Burke. Bolingbroke shapes his thoughts into ornament; Burke weaves decorations around his. Beauty, with one, is the form of the conception; with the other, it is the garniture of the apparel. Bolingbroke's entertainments are like the European banquets on silver plate, where what is showy, is also useful; Burke reminds us of that Asiatic prince who breakfasted his friends on stacks of roses.

THE DOCTOR, etc. In two vols. 12mo. (Two volumes in one.) Harper and Brothers. Second Edition.

[THE twenty years which have passed since that strange literary work, "THE DOCTOR," appeared, leaves but an imperfect recollection with this generation, of the interest which the question of its authorship excited. It was imputed by most persons to Hartley Coleridge, by many to Charles Lamb, and by others to different persons; some attributing it to one, and some to another. It was, in most respects, so unlike any thing which Mr. Southey had ever written, either in poetry or prose, that few would have been disposed to give it to him under any circumstances. And as he himself was known to deny the authorship, the question, so far as he was concerned, appeared to be settled. From the time that Mr. Wallace read the first twenty pages of the book, he pronounced with confidence that Southey was the author; and after finishing the first two volumes—the only ones which had then appeared—expressed the grounds of his opinion in the anonymous criticism which follows. A competent judge—Dr. Shelton Mackenzie—has said of it, that "with the sole exception of Mr. Adolphus's Letters to Richard Heber on the authorship of the Waverley Novels, it is the ablest, clearest, and most complete thing of the kind ever published." Southey himself, who had heard of it, was almost as curious to know the author of the Essay as the public had been to know the author of "The Doctor." But he still denied that "The Doctor" was his. "That such a book should be ascribed to me," he said on hearing of the Essay, and before he saw it, "I look upon as the greatest compliment that could be paid to any living author, but I shall not take credit for it, as Porson did for 'The Devil's Thoughts.' The argument proves only what is apparent from other circumstances; that the writer wishes it (for the present) to pass for mine, and that he is a skilful imitator. It is evident that he is very well acquainted with my writings; and I have reason to think that directly or indirectly he knows something of my table talk. There are, indeed, some parts which I should without hesitation filiate upon some of my friends, if it were not for a persuasion that they would not have kept the secret from me." Mr. Southey, it is known, never at any time acknowledged the book as his.

Had the third and fourth volumes appeared at the time this criticism was written, the proofs of the Laureate's authorship would have been greatly accumulated. As it is, they will probably be thought conclusive.—ED.]

The reimpression of the two first volumes of this work in England, the publication of a third volume, and the announcement of a fourth, together with the fact that one American edition has been exhausted, and that another has been demanded, indicate pretty decisively such a degree of interest in the work among the reading community of both countries, as to warrant an inquiry in regard to its source.

Excepting the letters of Junius, we do not remember any publication, in modern times, which has commanded, in any considerable degree, the popular attention, concerning which there has long been much doubt as to the author. Matthias, to the last hour of his life, denied any participation in the "Pursuits of Literature," but we imagine that there are few who entertain any doubts upon that subject. The claims of Scott to the title of "Author of Waverley," derived, in the popular estimation, very little additional force from his own formal acknowledgment at the Theatrical Fund Dinner. No one had the least hesitation about the matter before. Mr. Adolphus's admirable "Letters to Richard Heber" established, from coincidences in thought, expression, and feeling, between the poems and the novels, that the writer of both was, beyond all question, the same. Bentley says, in respect to some phrase in one of Cicero's orations, "*Ego vero Ciceronem ita scripsisse Ciceroni ipsi affirmanti non crediderem;*" and we apprehend that most of those who read those letters, would have been inclined to say, in a similar spirit, "If Scott were to say that Scott did not write 'Waverley,' I would not believe Scott himself."

Upon the same principle, we are abundantly satisfied, after a cursory comparison of "The Doctor" with the published writings of Robert Southey, that to that "most book-ful of Laureates" is to be ascribed the paternity of the singular production. As many literary journals here and in England have expressed doubts in relation to this matter, we proceed to state some of the facts upon which we ground our present opinion.

We are surprised that the name of Hartley Coleridge should have been mentioned among those of the possible authors. A slight acquaintance with his "Biographia Borealis" would have shown to any one such discordances of thinking between him and the author of "The Doctor" as to settle his pretensions at once. Hartley is an ardent whig, an admirer of the modern systems of education and politics, and a panegyrist of Brougham; while the other is a strenuous tory, a man thoroughly wrapt in the old forms of feeling, and at the opposite pole of sentiment, as to politics and the instruction of the people, from the ex-Lord Chancellor. Would Hartley Coleridge have written these passages, sneering at a father for whom it is evident, from his volumes of poems, that he bears such tender and profound affection? "A metaphysician, or as some of my contemporaries would affect to say, a psychologist." (*Doctor*, i., 76.) "Is it Coleridge? The method indeed of the book might lead to such a suspicion—but then it is intelligible throughout." (*Doctor*, ii., 86.) Would a *bachelor* have penned this sentence? "A bachelor, a single man, an imperfect individual, half only of the whole being which, by the laws of nature and of Christian polity, it was intended that man should become?" (*Doctor*, ii., 61.) Or, on the other hand, would the author of "The Doctor"—a churchman, and a conservative, indeed, in whom there is no flinching—have expressed such opinions as are contained in these passages by Hartley Coleridge? "We cannot but think that a yearly thanksgiving for the invention of printing might be very advantageously substituted for certain courtly services in the liturgy, which were always base and blasphemous, and are now utterly unmeaning." (*Biog. Borealis*, 131.) "Greek was an innovation, and liable to the same plausible and prudential objections which apply to innovations in general." (*Ibid.*, 344.) Or would this unknown—brimful and overflowing as he is with knowledge of the old English writers—have had occasion to add in a note, after quoting a short sentence from Fuller: "Such at least is Fuller's meaning and illustration. I am afraid I have not quoted his words exactly, for, to tell the truth, I know not in which of his works to look for them. But I recollect reading the sentiment in 'Lamb's selections?'" (*Biog. Borealis*, 322.) We apprehend that he who wrote "The Doctor," is not in the habit of being indebted to Lamb's nor to any one else's "selections" for his acquaintance with the old worthies. Is not this sentence more in keeping with the character of "multo-scribbling" Southey, than with that of an author who has published only two very narrowly-circulated works? "I have oftentimes had the happiness of seeing due commendations bestowed by gentle critics, unknown admirers, and partial friends upon my pen, which has been married to all amiable epithets; classical, fine, powerful, tender, touching, pathetic, strong, fanciful, daring, elegant, sublime, beautiful." (*Doctor*, i., 39.) The following passage has no propriety as coming from Hartley Coleridge, whose excursions upon Pegassus have been in a very regular way, while it exactly and most felicitously describes the poetry of Southey, which is chiefly upon the wildest subjects and in the wildest measures. "Tell me not of Pegassus! I have ridden him many a time; * * high and low, far and wide, round the earth, and about it, and over it, and under it. I know all his earth paces and his sky paces. I have tried him at a walk, at an amble, at a trot, at a canter, at a hand gallop, at a full gallop, and at full speed. I have proved him in the *manége* with single turns and the *manége* with double turns, his bounds, his curvets, his *pirouettes*, and his *pistes*, and his *croupade*, and his *balstade*, his gallop galliard, and his capriole." (*Doctor*, i., 25–6.) The writer of this book is manifestly a much older man, and a much more practiced writer, than Southey's nephew, and accustomed to deliver his opinions with far greater authority than can attach to the sentiments of one so little known.

Mr. Southey has always been distinguished for an affected use of certain uncommon words, some obsolete, some new-coined; and there is scarcely one of these verbal peculiarities which does not occur very frequently in "The Doctor." Such are, the verb "worsen" (*Southey's "Essays,"* i., 85; ii., 23; ii., 237; "*Colloquies,*" i., 46; i., 59; i., 236; ii., 273; *Doctor*, ii., 142, 186); the adjective "worser," the noun "dispatsey," (*Colloquies*, i., 18; *Doctor*, ii., 118,) and many others of a similar stamp.

Southey, in his notes to the poem of "Roderick," (and elsewhere when he uses the word,) always writes "Mussulmen" as the plural of "Mussulman," instead of the correct and general expression, "Mussulmans;" and we remember that when "Roderick" appeared, this deviation was animadverted upon by the reviewers in "The Christian Observer." As Southey, however, has continued the custom, we presume that he does it on conviction of its propriety. Now the author of "The Doctor" adopts the same unusual fashion: "The English might have been 'Mussulmen.'" (*Doctor*, i., 198.) "Remarks which are not intended for Mussulmen." (*Doctor*, i., 92. *Contents of the Interchapter.*) Throughout the work we find continued traces of Mr. Southey's personal feelings; in the high praise of the unpopular Walter Landor, and the despised Sir Egerton Brydges, both being the Laureate's particular friends, and the latter having scarcely ever been quoted by anybody else: in the sneers against Lord Byron, Mr. Jeffrey, and others who have given him occasion of offence, and whom, like the "portentous cub" of old, he has always pursued with scorn; for the warmest admirers of Mr. Southey must allow that, if he never forgets a friend, he never forgives an enemy. In the parliament of 1817, there sat a certain Mr. William Smith, who insulted Southey, by calling upon the attorney-general to prosecute him for publishing "Wat Tyler," and whose worthless carcass Southey hewed in pieces in a most terrific "Letter." Who is there now, in all England, except the author of this letter, who would have retained recollection enough and feeling enough about this Mr. Smith, to have made him the object of the sneer which we find in the second volume of "The Doctor?" And, what is remarkable, we find the same topic of reproach urged against him in Southey's "Letter" and in this book—the reproach of having the feelings of a dissenter:

"Is it Smith? which of the Smiths? * * There is Sidney, who is Joke Smith to the Edinburgh Review, and William, who is Motion Smith to the dissenters, orthodox and heterodox, in parliament, having been elected to represent them—to wit, the aforesaid dissenters—by the citizens of Norwich."—*The Doctor*, ii., 87.

"The poem may possibly have been honored with a place in Mr. William Smith's library, as it received the approbation of all the dissenting journals of the day. It is possible that *their* recommendation may have induced him to favor 'Joan of Arc' with a perusal."—*Southey's Letter to Smith.*

In the same chapter, where the author is speculating about the persons to whom his work will be attributed, we find this singular sentence about Porson: "And Professor Porson, if he were not gone where his Greek is of no use to him, would accept credit for it, though he would not claim it." (*Doctor*, ii., 85.) To explain this, it must be remembered that Southey, in conjunction with the late Mr. Coleridge, wrote a poem called "The Devil's Walk," which, while it was anonymous, Porson recited so frequently and mysteriously, that during his whole life he was supposed to be the author of it, and he never denied the honor: "he accepted credit for it, though he would not claim it."

Southey, in the early part of his career, went to London to study law, and, like most persons who do not study it profoundly, imbibed a most hearty hatred both for its theory and practice—a hatred which is constantly appearing in his writings, and which equally belongs to the author of "The Doctor."

"But no suggestions could ever have induced Daniel to choose for him the profession of the law. The very name of lawyer was to him a word of evil acceptation. He knew that laws were necessary evils; but he thought they were much greater evils than there was any necessity that they should be; and believing this to be occasioned by those who were engaged in the trade of administering them, he looked upon lawyers as the greatest pests in the country."—*The Doctor*, i., 136.

"The most upright lawyer acquires a sort of Swiss conscience for professional use; to resist a rightful claim with all the devices of legal subtlety, and all the technicalities of legal craft: I know not how he who considers this

"Law-craft, if not a twin fiend with priest-craft, is an imp of the same stock; and perhaps the worser devil of the two."—*Colloquies*, i., 108.

"He who may wish to show with what absurd perversion the forms and technicalities of law are applied to obstruct the purposes of justice, which they were designed to further, may find excellent examples in England."—*Colloquies*, i., 8.

"The worst grievance that exists—the enormous expenses, the chicanery, and the ruinous delays of the law."—*Essays*, ii., 29.

"We venture to ask whether it be absolutely necessary that so many loopholes should be left for the escape of guilt? Whether the purposes of justice are not sacrificed to the technicalities

to be his duty toward his client can reconcile it with his duty toward his neighbor."—(*The Doctor*, ii., 60.) See the whole of page 60 and page 61.

"You employ lawyers to express your meaning in a deed of conveyance, a marriage settlement, or a will; and they so smother it with words, so envelop it with technicalities, so bury it beneath redundancies of speech, that any meaning which is sought for may be picked out, to the confusion of that which you intended. You ask for justice, and you receive a nice distinction—a forced construction—a verbal criticism. By such means you are defeated and plundered in a civil cause; and in a criminal one, a slip of the pen in the indictment brings off the criminal scot free."—*The Doctor*, i., 181.

of law, which is sacrificing the end to the means? and whether the weight which is allowed to flaws and informalities in the practice of our courts, and the importance which is attached to things so utterly insignificant in themselves, be a whit more honorable to the profession of the law, than the grossest quackery is to the science of medicine."—*Essays*, ii., 177.

He goes on to give instances of criminals escaping by verbal error in the indictment.

We subjoin other coincidences in opinion, and similarities in thought and expression:

"The auxiliaries *must*, *have*, and *been*, which enabled Whitaker, of Manchester, to write whole quartos of *hypothetical history* in the potential mood."—*The Doctor*, i., 28.

"Whitaker, the hypothetical historian of Manchester."—*Vindiciæ Ecclesiæ Anglicanæ*, 225.

"Whether the children went to seek school or not, it was his wish that they should be taught their prayers, the creed, and the commandments, at home. These he thought were better learned at the mother's knees than from any other teacher."—*The Doctor*, ii., 186.

"The rudiments of religion are best learned at our mother's knees."—*Essays*, ii., 144.

"The habits of religion which a boy learns at his mother's knees."—*Colloquies*, 294.

"The child should receive from her its first spiritual food, the milk of sound doctrine."—*The Doctor*, i., 186.

"Fed with the milk of sound doctrine."—*Essays*, ii., 143.

"They must be fed with the milk of sound doctrine."—*Essays*, ii., 225.

"But he had a wise heart, and the wisdom of the heart is worth all other wisdom."—*The Doctor*, i., 62.

"The richness of his mind, and the wisdom of his heart, for in the heart it is that true wisdom has its seat."—*Vindiciæ*, 6.

"The wisdom of the heart is wanting there."—*Colloquies*, ii., 264.

"In the wisdom of the heart he was far beyond that age."—*Colloquies*, i., 102.

"A metaphysician * * if he were at all master of his art babblative."—*The Doctor*, i., 76.

"Professors of the arts babblative and scribblative."—*Colloquies*, ii., 48.

"The soporific sermons which closed the domestic religiosities of those melancholy days."—*The Doctor*, i., 69.

"A feverish state of what may better be called religiosity than religion."—*Colloquies*, ii., 102.

Both of our authors believe in ghosts, and there is some similarity in their mode of defining their belief:

"The belief in apparitions, which was all but universal a century ago, is still, and ever will be held by the great majority of mankind. Call it a prejudice if you will."

"What is a universal prejudice, says Reginald Heber, but the voice of human nature?"—*The Doctor*, ii., 180.

"That the spirits of the departed are permitted to appear only for special purposes, is what the most credulous believer in such appearances would probably admit, if he reasoned at all on the subject."—*The Doctor*, *ibid.*

"You believe then in apparitions," said my visitor.

"Even so, sir. That such things should be, is probable *a priori;* and I cannot refuse assent to the strong evidence that such things are, nor to the common consent which has prevailed among all people, every where, in all ages."—*Colloquies*, i., 11.

"My serious belief amounts to this: that preternatural impressions are sometimes communicated for wise purposes; and that departed spirits are sometimes permitted to manifest themselves."—*Colloquies*, i., 11.

In strongly advocating the culture of bogs and waste lands, Southey and the author of "The Doctor" agree:

The cultivation of bogs "is the readiest way in which useful employment can be provided for the industrious poor. And if the land so appropriated should produce nothing more than is required for the support of those employed in cultivating it, and who must otherwise be partly or wholly supported by the poor-rates, such cultivation would even then be profitable to the public."—*The Doctor*, i., 163.

"Is it fitting that this should be, while there are fifteen millions of cultivable acres lying waste? Is it possible to conceive grosser improvidence in a nation, grosser folly," etc.—*The Doctor*, i., 162.

"Give them employment in public works; bring the bogs into cultivation."—*Essays*, ii., 442.

"It will not always be the reproach of this kingdom that large tracts of land are lying waste while thousands are wanting employment, and tens of thousands owe their chief means of support to the poor-rates."—*Colloquies*, ii., 274.

"Surely it is allowable to hope that whole districts will not always be suffered to lie waste while multitudes are in want of employment and bread."—*Essays*, ii., 25. See also, *ibid.*, i., 113; ii., 29.

They accord, as well, in thinking that much may be done by individuals in relieving the grievance of the poor-laws:

"Let parishes and corporations do what is in their power for themselves.

"It should be well understood how large a part of the evil arises from

And bestir yourselves in this good work, ye who can! The supineness of the government is no excuse for you. It is in the exertions of individuals that all national reformation must begin.—*The Doctor*, i., 162.

causes which are completely within the power of the local magistrates, and how much might be accomplished by the efforts of benevolent individuals which cannot be reached by any legislative enactment."—*Essays*, ii., 116. Same sentiment in *Essays*, ii., 106.

Here are other opinions wherein the two do "marvellously agree:"

"They were plain people, who had neither manufactories to corrupt, alehouses to brutalize, nor newspapers to mislead them."—*The Doctor*, ii., 182.

"The multiplication of ale-houses is not less surely the effect and the cause of an increased and increasing depravity of manners."—*Essays*, ii., 117.

"For the laboring man, the alehouse is now a place of pure unmingled evil.—*Essays*, ii., 120.

"Your manufactories have produced a moral pestilence unknown to all preceding ages."—*Colloquies*, i., 50.

On this point see Southey, *passim*.

On the evil of newspapers. See *Essays*, i., 120, and ii., 170.

"During the summer and part of the autumn, he followed the good old usage of catechizing the children after the second lesson in the evening service. Once a week during Lent he examined all the children on a week day: the *last examination* was in Easter week, after which *each* was sent home happy with a homely *cake*, the gift of a wealthy parishoner," etc. —*The Doctor*, ii., 186–7.

"Were the children catechized in the church at stated seasons, according to the good old custom, a few trifling rewards to the children themselves, and a few marks of encouragement to those parents who deserved it, would produce greater and better effects upon both," etc.—*Essays*, ii., 144–5.

In his Essays, he supposes the case of a parish as it should be:

"The children of the other inhabitants would be examined in the elements of religion on stated days in the church, and receive from the clergyman, after the *final examination*, some little reward proportioned to their deserts; some remuneration *of that kind which is acceptable to all*, being, however, distributed to *all* who had attended regularly, without distinction, as the means of rendering attendance, a thing desired by the children themselves."—*Essays*, ii., 148.

"The dispersion of families and the consequent disruption of natural ties." —*The Doctor*, ii., 197.

"The dispersion of families and breaking up of family ties."—*Essays*, ii., 114.

"There is evil, great evil, in this disruption of natural ties," (by the separation of families.)—*Colloquies*, ii., 259.

"The disruption of natural ties."—*Vindiciæ*, 293.

"With all this expenditure, cases are continually occurring of death by starvation, either of hunger or of cold, or both together; wretches are carried before the magistrates for the offence of living in the streets, or in unfinished houses, when they had not where to hide their heads; others have been found dead by the side of lime-kilns or brick-kilns, whither they had crept to save themselves from perishing with cold."—*The Doctor*, i., 162.

"Hence those shocking instances of persons dropping down in the streets, or crawling to brick-kilns, and dying from inanition, cases which could not happen in a country where so many laws have been enacted, and such heavy imposts are raised for the relief of poverty, unless there were something radically erroneous in the system of administering that relief, something that increases the evil that it was intended to remove."—*Essays*, ii., 170.

"I say nothing of those who perish for want of sufficient food and necessary comforts, the victims of slow suffering and obscure disease; nor of those who having crept to some brick-kiln at night, in hope of preserving life by its warmth, are found there dead in the morning."—*Colloquies*, ii., 259.

"Trade itself had not then been corrupted by that ruinous spirit of competition, which, more than any other of the evils now pressing upon us, deserves to be called the curse of England in the present age."—*The Doctor*, ii., 195.

"So long as men in trade are actuated by selfishness, which is the spirit of trade, and as competition, which is the life of trade, continues unrestrained, so long will a manufacturing country be liable to the distress that arises from having overstocked its markets."—*Essays*, ii., 268.

"In the competition of trade, one ill principle sometimes counteracts another, and yet both being ill, work for ill."—*Colloquies*, ii., 246–7.

"As if scorn had been the influenza of the female mind that morning."—*The Doctor*, i., 29.

"Such preachers have never failed to appear during the prevalence of any religious influenza."—*The Doctor*, i., 25.

"The intellectual atmosphere had received its taint; and as an *influenza* beginning in Tartary travels from China, throughout the whole inhabited part of the old continent, so was this moral pestilence to run its course."—*Essays*, ii., 74.

"The moral influenza of methodism."—*Colloquies*, ii., 204.

"The soul of Hans Engelbrecht not only went to hell, but brought back from it a stench which proved to all the bystanders that it had been there."—*The Doctor*, i., 25.

"Did you ever, Sir, meet with the 'divine visions of Hans Engelbrecht?' He not only went to the place of torments, like Drithelm, and smelt the stink of the infernal pit, but brought some of the stink back with him, to convince his friends that he had been there."—*Vindiciæ*, 187.

"But let this quackery pass."—*The Doctor*, i., 187.

"But let this folly pass."—*Vindiciæ*, p. 48.

"And here Horrebow, the Natural Historian of Iceland—if Horrebow had been his biographer—would have

"With this I conclude a letter which may remind the reader of the chapter concerning owls in Horrebow's Na-

ended this chapter."—*The Doctor*, i., 229.

tural History of Iceland."—*Vindiciæ*, 57.

Both of these gentlemen revenge themselves on the bulk of Rees's Encyclopœdia by docking it of the initial *En:*

"He would have filled more volumes than Rees's Cyclopedia."—*The Doctor*, ii., 116.

"Would have filled more volumes than Dr. Rees's Cyclopœdia."—*Vindiciæ*, 101.

"Which Lord Byron is as incapable of understanding, or even believing in another, as he is of feeling it in himself."—*The Doctor*, ii., 81.

"A feeling, of which Lord Byron had no conception, would have withheld me from animadverting in that manner upon his conduct."—*Southey's second Letter concerning Lord Byron.*

Argument against Southey might be thought derivable from the sneering use of Wynn's name on page 146, vol. i.—Wynn being one of Southey's oldest and dearest friends—to whom both Madoc and the Vindiciæ are dedicated. But there is a passage in the Essays which not only affords precedent for this use of Wynn's name, but may be considered as the germ of the idea in "The Doctor." The coincidence is very striking. He is speaking of Catholic emancipation:

Speaking of the bells to be rung for the triumph of the Catholic cause: "And to commemorate the extraordinary union of sentiment which that cause has brought about between persons not otherwise remarkable for any similitude of feelings or opinions, they might unite two or more names in one bell, and thus, with a peculiar felicity of compliment, show who and who, upon this great and memorable occasion, *pulled together*. In such a case the names selected for a peal of eight tunable bells might run thus:

"1. Canning O'Connel. 2. Plunket Shiel. 3. Agustus Frederick Cobbet. 4. Williams Wynn. 5. Burdett Waithman. 6. Greenville Wood. 7. Palmerston Hume. 8. Lawless Brougham."—*The Doctor*, i., 146.

"How is the Marquis of Lansdowne to agree with his Irish tenants and with Captain Rock in this matter? Earl Gray with Joseph Hume? Mr. Grant with Mr. Doyle? Lord Plunket with Mr. O'Connel? Mr. Williams Wynn with Cobbet and Jack Lawless?" —*Essays*, ii., 370.

"The angelic Doctor, St. Thomas Aquinas, this greatest of the schoolmen."—*The Doctor*, ii. 115.

St. Thomas Aquinas, "a man whose extraordinary powers of mind few persons are competent to appreciate."—*Vindiciæ*, 329.

"An eloquent and wise and thoughtful author."—*The Doctor.*

"With the wise and the thoughtful." —*Colloquies*, ii., 173.

"Hopes scarcely less delightful than those which seemed to dawn upon mankind with the discovery of the gases, and with the commencement of the French Revolution, and in these latter days with the progress of the Bible Society."—*The Doctor*, i., 54.

"Sunday schools, which make Sunday a day of toil to teachers, and the most irksome day in the week to children."—*The Doctor*, ii., 186.

"Long before Sunday schools—whether for good or evil—were invented. Patrons and patronesses of Sunday schools, be not offended if a doubt concerning their utility be here implied! The Doctor entertained such a doubt, and the why and the wherefore shall in due time be fairly stated."—*The Doctor*, ii., 55.

"You surely do not expect that the millennium is to be brought about by the triumph of what are called liberal opinions, nor by Sunday schools, and Religious Tract Societies, nor by all the portentous bibliolatry of the age."—*Colloquies*, i., 35.

Southey was a republican in his youth, and is a tory in his manhood, and thus has contrived to get abused by both parties: and it seems, strangely enough, that the unknown "Doctor" shared the same fate:

"Your dealers in public and private scandal, whether Jacobins or Anti-Jacobins, the pimps and panders of a profligate press."—*The Doctor*, i., 41.

"All the abuse and calumny with which, from one party or the other, Anti-Jacobins or Jacobins, I have been assailed."—*Essays*, ii., 30.

"A spirit of Anti-Jacobinism was predominant, which was as unjust and as intolerant, though not quite as ferocious, as the Jacobinism of the present day."—*Essays*, ii., 10.

The peace of Utrecht galls both of them:

"Hartley, famous for his library, and infamous for the peace of Utrecht."—*The Doctor*, i., 55.

"England never had so much in her power as during the conferences at Utrecht, and never did she appear in so degraded and disgraceful a character. * * The faction which then, for its own sinister purposes, betrayed the interests of Europe."—*Essays*, ii., 66.

"Hartley, who betrayed Europe at Utrecht."—*History of the Peninsular War*, ii., 58.

"Did Lord Lauderdale know that children inevitably lacerate themselves in learning this dreadful occupation? that they are frequently crippled by it? frequently lose their lives

Chimney sweeping. "Children cannot be compelled to learn it, frightful and perilous as it is, without cruelty: it induces a peculiar and fatal disorder, so common as to be called the chimney

in it by suffocation, or by slow fire? that it induces a peculiar and dreadful disease, and that those who survive, have at the age of seventeen or eighteen to seek their living how they can in some other employment, for it is only by children that this can be carried on."—*The Doctor*, i., 90.

sweeper's disease; and the boys who escape the disease, and are neither killed by filth nor hard usage, outgrow the employment when they shoot into manhood, and find themselves adrift upon the world, without any means of getting a livelihood."—*Essays*, i., 225.

Both have noticed what I do not remember to have seen observed elsewhere—that by English writers—Swift, Sidney, and others—"Stella" is erroneously employed for a female name.

"Cleon serving for a name feminine in French, as Stella has done in English."—*The Doctor* ii., 110.

"Is Sidney the first person who used 'Stella' as a female name? He must have known it was a man's name among the Romans."—*Southey's Letters to Brydges—Brydges' Autobiog.*, ii., 282.

"The law would not allow him to marry his brother's widow; a law, be it remarked in passing, which is not sanctioned by reason, and which, instead of being in conformity with scripture, is in direct opposition to it, being in fact the mere device of a corrupt and greedy church."—*The Doctor*, i., 37.

"No extenuation can be offered for these prohibitions, which were not more unwarranted by the laws of God and man, than they were unreasonable in themselves, and vexatious in their operation."—*Vindiciæ*, 235.

He says (*ibid.*) that the object of the Romish church in making these prohibitions was to increase its revenue by the prices of permission—which explains the word "greedy."

We have thus placed in juxtaposition some passages, (and we might easily double their number,) which seem to us to afford decisive proof of proceeding from the same author. The peculiarity of the sentiments is as worthy of notice as their coincidence. On both sides a *tory* is seen condemning the peace of Utrecht, and arguing for law reform, two things which tories are not used to do: both seem to have suffered from Jacobin *and* Anti-Jacobin abuse—and where is the man, beside Southey, to whom that answers? Both condemn manufactories, ale-houses, and newspapers: both strongly argue the cultivation of waste lands, and condemn competition in trade; both, being religious men, oppose Sunday Schools and Bible Societies; both advocate catechising: both argue that the poor-laws are so administered as to enhance the evil they were designed to check, and the imagination of both has been singularly impressed with the circumstance of poor persons dying in brick-kilns; both are anxious to remove the evil of children sweeping chimneys; both ridicule phrenology; and by both authors is displayed an unlimited command and use of the stores of Italian, Spanish, and old English literature. The author of "The Doctor" quotes and praises Southey; but not more frequently, nor otherwise, than Southey does himself. In short, there are innumerable points of agreement between them —not one of discrepancy; and there are not two distinct authors, or two distinct men, living, of whom this can be said: either the "hands" or the "voice" would differ.

We add one circumstance which we think admits of no rebutter, and fixes the authorship, beyond skepticism, upon Southey. The author of "The Doctor" says, (*vol. ii., p.* 80,) "Lord Brooke, who is called the most thoughtful of poets, by the most book-ful of Laureates." *Where* does Southey give Lord Brooke this title? In a letter to Sir Egerton Brydges: "'Lord Brooke,' who is the most thoughtful of all poets." (*Autobiography of Sir Egerton Brydges, vol. ii.*, 278.)

A tolerable familiar acquaintance with Southey's writings enables us to say, with entire confidence, that he applies this phrase to our English Lycophron *no where else*. Now "The Doctor" was published early in *January*, 1834—the Autobiography of Sir Egerton, which first gave the letter to the public, not till late in *June*, 1834: so that here was the *author of "The Doctor" quoting a composition of Southey's a good half year before it was published.* "If that be not proof, speak!"

If our readers have not been able to penetrate the meaning of the words on the last page but one of "The Doctor," (*vol. ii.*,) *p.* 219., we have the satisfaction of giving them the clue. The words are composed of the first syllables of the names of the author's friends, and of the author himself:

Isdis, -	- Israel D'Israeli.
Roso, -	- Robert Southey.
Heta, -	- Henry Taylor.
Samro, -	- Samuel Rogers.
Theho, -	- Theodore Hook.
Heneco, -	- Henry Nelson Coleridge.

Thojama, -	-	Thomas James Matthias
Johofre, -	-	John Hookham Frere.
Wala, -	-	Walter Landor.
Venarchly,	-	Venerable Archdeacon Lyell.
Verevfrawra,	-	Very Rev. Francis Wrangham.

AMERICA AND THE AMERICAN PEOPLE. By FREDERICK VON RAUMER, Professor of History in the University of Berlin, &c. Translated from the German.

THE Baron Von Raumer is a very respectable man; a most eminently respectable and exemplary person; but he a little exceeds the license which respectability is allowed to possess, of being pedantic, formal, and commonplace. From what we saw of him personally, and from what we knew of his writings, we had expected that his book about America would be rather a heavy performance; but we were not prepared for any such result as this. The Baron has gone beyond all his promises, and outdone the anticipations of his best friends. We had not supposed it possible for any man to possess himself of so rare an assemblage of disqualifications for agreeable writing, of such select talents for heaviness, such acquired capacities for commonplace, such extraordinary powers of prosiness. We did not before believe that, in any one, such a variety of abilities could act together with such mutual adaptation and absolute unity of effect, for the production of one definite result,—that of what Burke would call pure, defecated, dephlegmated dulness. There is learning, observation, study, labor, in all the details; and only stolidity in the grand total. The work reminds us of nothing so much as some of those huge equations which one meets in the higher mathematics; where, after a great deal of figuration with numbers and letters, and a great deal of plus and minus, and cubing and differentiating, the whole is summed up as equal to zero. There is depth and range enough, but the informing spirit of genius and vigor moves not upon the face of the waters. The book is a Run of Cutch,—myriads of particles of fine and curious ores are borne along on a copious stream, to form at the end only an enormous mass of mud. It is surprising to us that a man can touch upon so many subjects which have drawn out all the sense and passion of a nation for years together, and been illuminated with all that is brilliant in the intelligence of a vast continent, and yet contrive to say not only nothing that is new, (which might well be excused,) but nothing that is philosophical—nothing that, in any higher sense than mere literality, is *true*, nothing that is striking, nothing that is valuable. The only original conception which we have met with in the volume, is the eulogy of President Tyler, in which, with a certain felicity of fearlessness, the writer selects the veto of the Bank bill, as the prominent topic of commendation. The only original facts which we find, consist in some *statistics of spitting:* "With watch in hand," says the Professor, "I ascertained that, on an average, in the space of *one* minute, one man spit five times, and another, (a clergyman too,) eight." We express our admiration at this dignified and interesting spectacle of a Professor of History coming a thousand miles with a choice chronometer in hand to count the number of times that our native blackguards expectorate. Seriously, was not the Baron afraid, like Coriolanus, that

> "Boys with *spits*, and girls with stones,
> Would slay him in the puny battle?"

There is but one thing in which we are not satisfied with this report; we should have been glad to have had a tabular statement of the number of separate spitments, clerical and lay, from which this average of eight to five in favor of the hierarchy was deduced, such as he has given of the length of time employed by all the students in Harvard College in going through their recitations. The Baron himself, it must be confessed, labors under no such infirmity as these subjects of his *watch* seem to have been afflicted with, an excess of *humor*.

To give a correct account of this work, we should characterize it as that of a democratic German De Tocqueville; without, however, any thing of democratic energy, any thing of German originality, or any thing of De Tocqueville's brilliance. We are struck at once with what Coleridge called the *encyclopedic* tendency of the German mind, its desire to embrace a totality of view. Like our "*ami Belier, il commence par le commencement.*" We find him, in the first paragraphs, among the remotest geological periods, describing the probable time of the upheaval of the American continent; we are then carried through a course of geography; and next through a series of mineralogical observations. We then have a judicious and rather neat abridgement of Grahame's History, running through half a dozen chapters; then an account of the political and legal constitutions of the country, which is merely the first volume of Kent's Commentaries, with additions out of the American Almanac; and then a series of discussions on Banks, Tariffs, Cities, Schools, and Religion, as vapid and worthless as last year's port entries, or weekly lists of stocks. This range of discussion belongs, we suppose, to what the cant of the hour calls the German *many-sidedness.* We are content that a treatise should have as many *sides* as its author chooses to give it, but we insist, for the sake of its readers, that it should have a few *points.* We suspect that this many-sidedness is merely one of those delusions which prevail for a time because nobody understands their signification enough to expose their want of sense. It seems to us that formal and physical extension of the field of view is sometimes confounded with expansion of intellectual conception, and a widening of the natural horizon mistaken for an increase of mental light. For ourselves, we do not perceive what connection there is between geological upheavings and social ones; nor why an account of the explosive tendencies of radicalism should be ushered in with a preface on primeval volcanoes. There is a long chapter on Slavery, which is as formal as an ancient sermon and as trashy as a modern song. There is another on currency and credit, in which the author shows that he has never comprehended the *principle* on which banking is founded: he sneers at truths which are as settled and certain in the *science* of paper credit, as the laws of gravitation are in mechanics; and utterly confuses historical order and accuracy in his account of the affair between General Jackson and the United States Bank, misapprehending motives, mistaking causes for effects, and putting consequents before the antecedents. Throughout, a certain *philosophical* character is affected by assuming a position of indifference between contending factions, and stating the views of both without inclining to either. There are certainly some cases, in which opposite parties represent different elements of the same truth, and are about equally right; both, *then*, are to be appreciated, and neither to be condemned. But there are other instances, in which, without any doubt at all, one side is entirely right, and the other side is entirely wrong; and for a man to hold his judgment *in equilibrio*, on such occasions, as this author clearly does, is merely to be absurd in a systematical manner, and to give up the approbation of men of sense for the applause of pedants and sciolists. The Baron's chapters suggest no new topics, and offer nothing fresh upon old ones. He seems to write even in ignorance of the progress which has been made by others in the philosophy of our character and institutions, so that his movement is effectually retrograde. The distinction between Federal or whig liberty and democracy, is of singular nicety and interest, and one which American and French authors have made some advance in developing; but the present author totally fails to apprehend it, and lauds Washington, Jefferson, Adams, and Jackson, as men of the same stamp, differing in the degree of their republican feelings, but not in the nature of their political views. The observations on American Art, especially those on Greenough's sublime statue, are stupid beyond any thing we could have supposed possible.

The truth is, intellect is a department of the Baron's education which has been neglected: and after all said and done, a man of inferior understanding cannot write a superior book. The Baron is a person of many kinds of knowledge, but the knowledge of the measure of his powers is not among them. In these pages "America and the American People," are (to use the quaint language of Burton's title page) "opened and cut up," geologically, physiologically, politically, and statistically,—

every way, in short, except sensibly, ably, or agreeably. After reading a recent History on a great American subject, we concluded that flippancy was the worst fault of a historian; but upon finishing Von Raumer, we are compelled to admit that dulness, when carried to such an extravagant excess, is quite as bad.

THE PROSE WORKS OF JOHN MILTON; with a Biographical Introduction. By R. W. GRISWOLD.

THE mightiest spirit, probably, that ever illustrated in literature the extent of human capacity, and the force of human will, was Milton. In regard to his character as a poet, this appears to us to be the capital consideration, that he lived in an unpoetical time. Nations have their ages, like individuals. Homer in the old world; Dante and Petrarch in Italy; in England, Chaucer, Shakspeare, Spenser, flourished at a period in the national life, when fancy and sentiment, the staple of poetry, were still predominant over pure reason,—when manners were picturesque, and common life had the spirit of a romance—when the genial infusion of new feelings into old institutions was hourly realizing brilliant effects,—above all, when language, sensitive and intensely vital, responded with music to the least skilful touch. But for a man to rise up, as Milton did, after the era of Art has fairly past—when the fine enthusiasms of national youth and hope have been checked or extinguished, and a critical spirit has established itself in every department,—when society on the one hand is frivolous, and on the other is harsh, and stern, and dry—when contemporary literature exhibits only the weakness of inanity, or the more desperate weakness of extravagance, and when language has lost its esthetic vigor;—for a man at such a time, to start aside from the mass, and laboriously educating himself into the originality and power of an early epoch, to develop from the depths of his own strenuous and teeming mind, a literary work of unrivalable magnificence and grandeur,—stamped with the force and freshness of a remote antiquity—against all models, and beyond all imitation,—this appears to us to be a thing without a parallel, and to partake of the character of a prodigy. The colossal images of the Alps are natural at sunrise: to produce them at mid-day would be the work of magic.

But if Milton, in his poetry, drew back in moody loneliness behind his contemporaries, in his philosophical writings he strides on as far before them. Indeed, after centuries of eventful experience, and of mental discipline, it is only now that the general mind may be said to have been brought up to that level of freedom and fearlessness, from which Milton's speculations begin: it is only at this day that the world is able to read Milton. There are few treatises on political or social questions, a century and a half old, which would bear to be re-printed at this time. But Milton is still above us, though no longer beyond us. What strikes us when we turn to Paradise Lost, is the immensity of imaginative conception which we there meet with: and when we open any one of the larger treatises in this collection, we are equally caught by the elevation and extent of moral view which are displayed. We are not compelled to work through laborious processes in the close atmosphere of metaphysical subtlety; we are taken up at once upon a lofty and commanding platform, bright and breezy, where the light of heaven shines upon us, and the divisions of the earth are marked out as on a map, beneath our feet. The blaze of imagination discloses the recesses of Truth, and Inspiration does the work of analysis. The circuitous caution and timid advance of the old strategy is rejected by this Napoleon of morals; and the Sierras of falsehood are carried by a charge.

Republican in all the constitution of his character—self-formed and self-reliant—hardy, conscientious and uncorrupt,—rejecting the control of others only that he might the more perfectly control himself,—Milton realized by meditation that sublimity of life which in other cases only a great course of action has inspired; and we believe that the most effective substitute for the elevating circumstances and scenes by which the august characters of our revolution were produced, might be found in a right use of the prose works of Milton.

Undoubtedly in many of Milton's papers we may find the true principles of English liberty, which are the origin of American Independence, and the safeguards of American society. There never has been any genuine freedom in the world, except that which has been developed by the constitutions of modern Europe, of which that of England has been agreed to be the best contrived and the most advanced; and it is only in so far as we maintain and enforce in this country the notion of constitutional principles and constitutional rights, that we can hope to keep alive any liberty here. We do not mean those edicts in limitation of political power which are contained in the written "constitutions" of the United States, and the several States, and which, in that form, derive their obligation from the consent and authority of the people who have established them in conventions. We refer to those fundamental, inherent and fixed principles upon which the system of Anglo-Saxon liberty is organized, and in which it subsists; rational, not conventional; existing in nature, and therefore not capable of being extinguished by agreement or force; indestructible; the true *rights of man* in political society; any wilful departure from which justifies, even politically, rebellion and revolution. One of these principles, for example, is that which recognizes a distinction between a tax law, and every other kind of law, founded upon the difference between taking property and regulating conduct; by which no law may be made which imposes a tax unequally, or without consent and without compensation. This is no formal, technical rule, which is satisfied by a literal compliance with it; it is a great essential principle of reason, justice, and practical freedom; founded in the temper of modern society, and traditionary in English politics; and when any act of legislation emanating either from the omnipotence of Parliament or the sovereignty of the people, violates this maxim, in its spirit and tendency, it is, in the just meaning of the term, *unconstitutional;* and if it be persisted in without hope of alleviation, it becomes the duty of men, as citizens, and as subjects of the law, to rebel. Lord Coke maintained the noble doctrine that "An Act of Parliament against a common right is void," but in England it is now settled that Parliament in its legislative capacity judges of its own jurisdiction, and the judiciary has only power to interpret statutes, and not to set them aside. In this country, however, we suppose it to be a general principle that the courts are to judge of the jurisdiction of the legislatures, as well in respect to those unwritten *constitutional* principles which exist of "common right," as in regard to those legal limitations which are prescribed in the written constitutions, and that when an Act is passed which, in a sound political point of view, is in contravention of the spirit of constitutional privileges and constitutional protection, as ascertained by the philosophy of modern political science, it becomes the right and duty of the judges to pronounce it void. The study of this subject becomes therefore of the first consequence to lawyers and statesmen, and in some of Milton's writings it is nobly taught. We are much obliged to Mr. Griswold for his services in putting us in possession of these handsome and convenient books. His pen possesses considerable felicity; and on this occasion he has written with unusual spirit.

MEMOIRS OF THE REIGN OF KING GEORGE THE THIRD. By HORACE WALPOLE. 2 vols. Philadelphia.

LITERATURE and history seem destined at present to be overrun with a flood of *Walpoleism.* Since we have holden our present office of usher of the Black Rod, to the sovereign Public, this, we believe, is something like the twelfth volume to which we have had the pleasure to invite attention. For a man who wrote nothing larger than a note or a tract, and nothing more dignified than a squib or a gossipping letter, and who had been in his grave twenty years when the first of this line of volumes took up its march, this, we think, will do very well. Horace Walpole died in the winter of '96–97; and five stately quarto volumes, published within a year or two of that event, seemed to form "monumental pomp" enough for one who denied and deprecated the character and name of a literary man. As for those volumes themselves, they are books of scraps: and we may describe the whole work in the terms in which Walpole himself described the front of the old Versailles, as "a lumber of littleness." It soon appeared, however, that this affluent noble, much of his literary wealth as he had given to the public in his lifetime, had still an immense estate left, which, like Mr. Thelusson, he had entailed upon a remote posterity, to be enjoyed only after a life or lives in being, and some one-and-twenty years afterwards. About 1820, a correspondence with the lively George Montague was published: then letters to Lord Hertford, and to Dr. Zouch: then appeared a series of three volumes of epistles to Sir Horace Mann, and soon after another series of four to the same dull and trifling person; to say nothing of *Ana*, Reminiscences, &c. This of which we now have the second portion, is in the English impression, a four volume work: and there is a talk of other mysterious piles of manuscripts,—of "Bag A," "Bundle B," and Cs and Ds, black with gouty hieroglyphics, and of unknown contents—which lead us to suppose that we see but the beginning of the thing. Really, if it were not for Walpole's frequent and serious protestations, posterity might be in danger of mistaking this man for an author. If it should take him for a person morbidly eager for literary distinction, it would probably make no mistake at all. Wanting courage to attempt, as much as strength to accomplish, any great work, Walpole loved "to mumble of the game he dared not bite;" and inditing prefaces, tales, biographical notes, and other small performances, writing with infinite care those things which others wrote negligently, he labored to have it thought that he wanted nothing but the inclination, to beat all the Johnsons, Goldsmiths, and Burkes of the time, at their own weapons. Gilly Williams read his character with accuracy: "*monstrari digito,*" says that shrewd and witty person, in a letter printed by Mr. Jesse, "is the end and object of all he does: for this, he wrote, he built, he planted: to this we owe his Lord

Herbert, and in future we shall owe many entertaining things." So indeed it has proved; for though the *dicier Hic est*, may be less than even an empty sound to the cold ear of Death, yet a feeling kindred to it has been the origin of these posthumous volumes. Knowing that gossip may acquire from time an interest not due to its worth, and thinking that a vast number of small works might be deemed equivalent to one great one, he devoted many hours of every day of his life, to perpetuating the anecdotes and incidents of the hour, in letters, memoirs and reminiscences. Neither gaiety nor the gout—neither the dissipation and whirl of youth, nor the solitude and chalk-stones of old age—could stay the restless diligence of a pen, which thus wrote more than almost any professed author of the times; until after about eighty years of action the "unwearied mill that turned ten thousand *letters*," at last stood still. This method of remote posthumous publication, seems to be one of the tricks of an actor who did nothing naturally, but all for notoriety.

Walpole was, undoubtedly, a man of pretty parts: his wit, though not solid, strong, nor true, was delicate and sparkling: his turns of thought are lively and neat: he described manners with a success which showed the true level of his genius: he drew characters upon a happy system, which by abusing everybody, painted many correctly. If any one is inclined to refine his taste or point his style by a close study of Walpole's letters on society, we can offer no objection: but we make a protest against his books being regarded either as *History*, or as materials for the formation of the historical judgments of the age. He was the unfittest person of that century for the difficult and responsible duties of an annallist. He had not the least regard for truth; he had no judgment; was as inquisitive, as credulous and as inaccurate as a lady's maid: and by the measure of his understanding was as incapable of appreciating what was great, as by the height of his moral sensibilities he was unwilling to believe or respect what was worthy. His vanity made him jealous of everybody; and his ill-success inclined him to malignity. He inherited all his father's animosities, and as to *his* contemporaries, wrote with the "*recentibus odiis*" fresh about him. As to his own career, the newness of his family made him jealous of all the great lords; his extreme anxiety to shine in affairs, and incapacity to do it, made him hate all the great statesmen and orators; his efforts as an author caused him to look with scornful eyes on all real literary merit: and thus, about himself and the men of his own time, he wrote with little to guide his pen, save the "*ira et studio*," which distort the picture that they animate, and discolor as much as they warm it. The present volume is but a series of outrageous libels: the wildest and most reckless charges are flung around on the right hand and the left; infamous suggestions, without the smallest probability, made against the most excellent persons of the age: unbounded contempt thrown out against the wisest and ablest writers of the country, men who have since taken their rank among the great heroes of fame. The absurdity of such an attempt to degrade, belittle and blacken everybody and everything, and the wickedness of it, can be equalled only by the cowardly and cunning baseness of reserving the publication of the trash, until all who possessed a direct knowledge of the facts perverted or an immediate interest in the persons maligned, are dead, and there no longer remains ability or disposition to confute the mass of calumny. But the reputations of the great are the heritage of the race, and honesty and truth are the concern of all men; and we venture a confident prophecy, that the high repute which Walpole justly acquired for wit and elegance, from the publication of his letters, is destined to be quite shaken by the discredit which the untruth and unfairness of his memoirs is certain to bring upon him. The fate of Archdeacon Coxe, is a warning to all future writers to place no reliance on Walpole's most confident statements about the private history of the court; and the opinions of a whole nation are a sufficient confutation of his views of men and their motives.

Of the eminent men under the Hanover dynasty, there are few whose reputation has increased more steadily, with the lapse of time, than Lord Hardwicke's: but Walpole writes of him thus: "The gloomy and revengeful temper of Hardwicke waited for an opportunity of repaying the disgrace Pitt had inflicted on their cabal. The disgrace of his country was meditated, at least effected by Lord Hardwicke, as revenge on Mr. Pitt." (ii., p. 256.) Lord Mansfield's character had probably many weaknesses, and some blemishes; but what in his career could justify such frantic outrages on common decency and common sense as this? "Lord Mansfield was by birth, education, principle, cowardice, and revenge for the public odium, a bigot to tyranny. He would have sacrificed the universe, and everything but his personal safety, to overturn the constitution and freedom of England." (ii., p. 232.) Lord Chatham figures here as a ridiculous compound of arrogance, corruption and insanity;—Wedderburne, as "that abandoned man," who had "no superior in Westminster Hall for want of principles." (ii., p. 300.) To insult Burke, the ten-times confuted lie of his having been "born a papist" is gravely affirmed (ii., p. 189); and when Burke printed his splendid "Thoughts on the present Discontents," we are told that "Mrs. Macauley, whose principles were more sound and more fixed than Burke's, and whose reasoning was more simple and more exact, published a short tract in answer." (ii., p. 251.) The extravagant absurdity of this is exceeded only by the character which he gives of Dr. Johnson—a specimen of candor, truth and dignified writing, with which we close our extracts. "With a lumber of learning and some strong parts, Johnson was an odious and mean character. By principle a Jacobite, arrogant, self-sufficient, and overbearing by nature, ungrateful through pride, and of *feminine bigotry*, he had prostituted his pen to party even in a dictionary, and had afterwards, for a pension, contradicted his own definitions. His manners were sordid, supercilious and brutal, his style ridiculously bombastic and vicious; and, in a word, with all the pedantry, he had all the gigantic littleness of a country schoolmaster." (ii., 2, p. 323.)

THE LETTERS OF THE EARL OF CHESTERFIELD, including numerous Letters now first published from the Original Manuscripts. Edited with Notes by Lord MAHON. In four vols. London, Bentley, 1845.

No sort of justice has been done by critics and historians to the great sense, high character, and noble accomplishments of the Earl of Chesterfield. In action, England, fertile of able politicians, never produced a more consummate statesman. As Lord-Lieutenant of Ireland, he carried the government in safety over the crisis of 1745; his firmness maintaining order, and his justice inspiring confidence, in a nation where the elements of discontent were more abounding and more violent than in the neighboring kingdom where the explosion actually took place. His policy has since been often appealed to by rival parties who agreed in nothing but their admiration of him; and "his name, I am assured," says Lord Mahon, "lives in the honored remembrance of the Irish people, as, perhaps, next to Ormond, the best and worthiest in their long vice-regal line." In letters, Lord Chesterfield exhibited qualities rare in kind, still rarer in their combination;—a severe sagacity that nothing eluded, a rectitude of judgment that nothing could impose on, joined to a loftiness of spirit, a gaiety of temper, and a sensibility to all the charms of grace and beauty, that make him at once an instructor and a companion. He possessed singular delicacy of observation, which, however, never became entangled in its own refinements. The consciousness of talents to shine without a rival, in politics and fashion, never led him to overvalue those pursuits, or follow them beyond the dictates of respectability, propriety, or prudence. He had a range of intelligence which enabled him to see things in the light in which others saw them, without losing the truth of his own perceptions, and a versatility of powers to play to their views without departing from his own moral standards. Few men formed juster estimates of the value of things. Common sense was his most eminent quality. Dr. Franklin himself was scarcely more rigorously practical in the tone of his judgments. Yet Chesterfield had the yet more uncommon ability to appreciate the things which he despised, to allow for influences which he heartily condemned, and to accommodate himself temporarily to establishments which he constantly and avowedly labored to overthrow. This fine discrimination between truth and convenience, between permanent ends and occasional means, which his understanding took and his self-control maintained, permitted him to be politic without impairing his virtue, and to deal with trifles without ever lowering his dignity. Familiar with the homeliest and most solid parts of prudential ethics, he was an unapproached master in all that concerns the higher and more refined applications of it. His taste was wonderfully sound; and his style, which commonly is the image of taste, though it was refined and correct, was perfectly simple, natural, and genuine; and wholly free from quaintness, affectation, and fastidiousness. Rarely has life been looked at with a more keen and distinguishing eye, or the results of moral scrutiny been fixed in colors more brilliant and true. He knew how to reconcile and unite with manliness and solidity, those refinements of sentiment and that delicacy of feeling, which are usually to be found only among the frivolous or immoral; but which are so delightful and admirable as almost to make frivolity enjoyable and vice itself endurable.

It is this thoroughly practical turn of Lord Chesterfield's character which has given rise to the popular opinion that he professed a system of loose and accommodating morals. We have read his correspondence, in one form or other, something like twenty times; and unless the impressions of a life-long familiarity are at fault, this popular opinion is a mistaken one. But the error is easily explained. Men of extreme common sense, who take up the pen, not to breathe their fancies in an airy chase of fine and flimsy sentiments, but to effect some actual result of conviction or conduct—such men as Franklin, Paley, Chesterfield—always understate their case and their argument, as much as the safety of their position will admit of: they lay the line of their requisitions as low as possible, and give, not the highest, best, or strongest reason for its adoption, but the simplest, most direct and least questionable one: they endeavor to identify the principle they are contending for, with some familiar and admitted truth of daily experience, and to associate the acceptance of it with some certain, palpable, material interest of the reader. In such cases, if we mistake for his conception of the abstract truth and right, what the author has put forward with a view only to practicability, or confound the motive which urged the writer with the reason which he has given to the reader, we make a great error. Thus Franklin, when he would persuade to early rising, appeals to the saving of coin that will be effected by using sunlight instead of lamplight: not that he was insensible to the romantic attractions of the subject, the cheering and exalting influences of the day-spring hour,—"the charm of early birds," and all the inspirations of the dawn—for his writings show that he was finely sensitive to all such suggestions; but that he wished to rest his plea upon the lowest attainable ground,—a ground absolutely certain and unassailable. So it was with Paley:—finding that a spirit of critical and utilitarian philosophy was come up, which invalidated the logic and impeached the first principles of former theologians as much as it opposed the end which those principles and logic were employed to establish, he determined to take that enemy in the rear, and to occupy its own firmest and most favorite ground. He therefore proceeded to prove that morality is, upon the whole, a very convenient thing; that, extravagant as society is, in its general statement, it is quite as useful as any thing else that we set up in its stead; and that the divinity of the Saviour and the inspiration of the Evangelists, absurd as they may be, carry fewer difficulties with them, after all, than any other theory that you can propose. This admirably sensible and sagacious way of dealing with the subject has conciliated and attracted as many cold hearts out of the church as it has offended hot heads within it, and hitherto has answered the zealots only by confuting the infidels. Chesterfield, substantially, was of the same stamp and temper as these men. Take an extreme case,—the most difficult for our argument in the whole of his book. He gives his son leave to have an intrigue with any woman of high fashion that he takes a fancy to; nay, he rather advises him to it. This is certainly very bad indeed; but, before we throw the book into the fire, let us look at the thing a moment. The Earl of Chesterfield wished to accomplish a certain practical improvement in the character and conduct of his son. The young English, with whom his residence, his years, his pursuits, placed him in association, were low and vicious in their habits and tastes. By persuasions, by entreaties, by commands, by threats,—by serious arguments and sportive raillery—he strives, without cessation, to keep this child from adopting their disgraceful style of life. In deciding on the means of effecting this result, we may imagine the Earl to debate somewhat thus with himself: "If I draw the bow too far, it infallibly breaks: if I insist on a course against which the spirit and passions of youth rebel, I destroy my own influence with the boy, and do not accomplish my purpose: if I let him see that I am not opposed to any species of his enjoyments, I gain his confidence and will be able gradually to mould him. It is a case for compromise: if he passes the evening with a lady of *ton*, he loses his virtue, it is true; but if I do not send him to such a woman, he will certainly go himself to one of a lower sort, where, besides his virtue, he will lose his character and impair his manners to boot." The whole affair thus reduces itself to a plain question in common arithmetic; the woman of fashion carries the day, or the night, by all the difference of manners and character; and the same despatch which carries out an absolute prohibition to the youth from "*s'encanaillant*" with the creatures of the opera and ballet, conveys a permission to break the seventh commandment with the gay and witty Madam So-and-so. Such is our impression of Chesterfield's system; and when we find him inviting his son to turn over the classics in the morning, and *la petite Blot* in the evening, we see in that, not the laxity of a man of the world, careless of moral distinctions, but the anxious solicitude of a parent, who, fearing the utter ruin of his son, consents to give up a part, rather than risk the loss of all. That Chesterfield recognized the principles of morality, and felt their weight as much as any of the Sorbonne, it is scarcely possible for any candid reader of the letters to doubt: his mistake lay in the means of attaining an unquestioned end; he erred in finessing in a matter where uncompromising thoroughness alone will do. For our own part, we will engage that if ten readers will go through these volumes, remembering that Chesterfield was not writing dissertations on morals, but was managing a practical task, and will compare, not their principles, sentiments, or intentions, but their actual past moral practice, with his practical standard, nine of the ten will find that his system is above theirs. As to the undecalogued part of morality, his teachings are beyond any man's criticism. In all that concerns decency, decorum, true dignity, genuine propriety, better instruction can nowhere be found; and we are disposed to think that those qualities bring virtue with them, in their midst, so that he that seeks for them will find their queen. In justice, also, to the character of Chesterfield, it should be recollected that he did not undertake the *whole* education of his son, but having put him into the hands of an exemplary clergyman of the Church, and written to him once a week to obey every thing that that gentleman told him, he felt himself at liberty to confine his own efforts to those outward and lighter matters in which alone the youth was deficient. We should be glad to enter more at large into the display of a mind and character in which we have long felt a peculiar interest, and which we cordially esteem and admire; but our limits are already exceeded.

We suppose the work will soon be printed in this country, and we trust that whatever publisher undertakes to apparel and introduce the Earl, will suffer him to appear like a gentleman. We express in advance our disapprobation of the unworthy style in which the respectability of books is degraded by the operations of more than one American publisher. Literature itself is insulted and injured, when it becomes a reproach to a gentleman or lady to have handled the vulgar pamphlets in which the finest works have been given to the world. Let then the Harpers, or whoever else reprints these volumes, take this occasion to solve the insoluble problem of the modern press, in uniting, if they must reduce the size, compression of form with distinctness and elegance, and in sparing the purse without increasing the expense of eyesight. They will be entitled to better praise than any which they have yet received, if they will inaugurate an era in popular printing, in which cheapness shall be no longer synonymous with vileness, nor those works which are addressed to the taste and are intended to delight the most refined and sensitive part of our being, be the least reputable part of the furniture of our drawing-rooms.

Spence's "Anecdotes of Books and Men."

This book, of which an American reprint is said to be contemplated by a Philadelphia publisher, is one of the most curious and entertaining volumes in our language, and it is one of the least known. It is a sizeable octavo, consisting of remarks made to Mr. Spence in conversation by Pope, Bolingbroke, Warburton, Le Sage, Lady Montague, and many other distinguished persons. It is the "Boswell" of the era of the two first Georges. The fate of this extraordinary collection is one of the most singular in literary history. In consequence of the unwillingness of the Duke of Newcastle to have it published, it remained in manuscript for about sixty years after the author's death. It was referred to by Warton for his Essay on Pope; Malone made use of it for his edition of Dryden; and it was placed at Dr. Johnson's disposal for his Lives of the Poets, who thought "the communication of it a favor worthy of public acknowledgment." After exciting infinite curiosity among literary persons for more than half a century, two editions from different manuscripts were published in the year 1820, and both may be said to have fallen still-born from the press. Curiosity seems to have been exhausted by protracted expectation.

Yet I know of no volume which contains a richer fund of wit and wisdom, and amusing lore. It presents an elegant picture of the drawing-room conversation of the gifted and accomplished men that adorned English literature and enlivened English politics in the beginning of the last century. Here we have a minute picture of the studies, tastes, and literary and domestic habits of Pope; the bold, dashing and vigorous conversation of him "whose lightning pierced the Iberian lines;" the eccentric and brilliant Earl of Peterborough; the sagacious and powerful observations of Warburton, never without a tinge of malice; the philosophical and elegant remarks of Bolingbroke, always with a touch of nobleness; and the learned, discursive and delightful anecdotes of the Chevalier Ramsay.

The author is the Rev. Joseph Spence, who wrote the Polymetis and other literary works. He was a man of considerable learning, extensive curiosity and polished taste. His death was singular. He was found drowned in his garden, in a pool which was not deep enough to cover his head as he lay extended. The wits of the time amused themselves by observing that the man who could be drowned in such a stream must have been still shallower than the water.

The chief value of the book consists in the moral and critical reflections which it contains; but as these are less interesting to general readers, I shall select only a few of the anecdotes.

Sir Godfrey Kneller, who was perhaps the vainest man that ever lived, yet an excellent painter and a pleasant wit, figures very amusingly in this volume.

"Did you never hear Sir Godfrey's dream?" said Pope one day. "No." "Why, then, I'll tell it to you. A night or two ago," said Sir Godfrey, "I had a very odd sort of dream. I dreamt that I was dead, and soon after found myself walking in a narrow path that led up between two hills, rising pretty equally on each side of it. Before me I saw a door, and a great number of people about it. I walked on toward them. As I drew nearer I could distinguish St. Peter by his keys, with some other of the apostles; they were admitting the people as they came next the door. When I had joined the company, I could see several seats, every way, at a little distance within the door. As the first, after my coming up, approached for admittance, St. Peter asked him his name and then his religion. 'I am a Roman Catholic,' replied the spirit. 'Go in, then,' says St. Peter, 'and sit down on those seats there on the right hand.' The next was a Presbyterian: he was admitted too, after the usual questions, and ordered to sit down on the seats opposite to the other. My turn came next, and as I approached, St. Peter very civilly asked me my name. I said it was Kneller. I had no sooner said so than St. Luke (who was standing just by) turned toward me, and said with a great deal of sweetness—'What! the famous Sir Godfrey Kneller from England?' 'The very same, sir,' says I, 'at your service.' On this St. Luke immediately drew near to me, embraced me, and made me a great many compliments on the art we had both of us followed in this world. He entered so far into the subject that he seemed almost to have forgot the business for which I came thither. At last, however, he recollected himself, and said: 'I beg your pardon, Sir Godfrey; I was so taken up with the pleasure of conversing with you! But, apropos, pray, sir, what religion may you be of?' 'Why, truly, sir,' says I, 'I am of no religion.' 'O, sir,' says he, 'you will be so good then as to go in and take your seat where you please.'"

"I paid Sir Godfrey a visit," said Pope, "but two days before he died. I think I never saw a scene of so much vanity in my life. He was lying in bed, and contemplating the plan he had made for his own monument. He said he should not like to lie among the rascals at Westminster; a memorial there would be sufficient, and desired me to write an epitaph for it."

The younger Richardson (in the Richardsoniana) has furnished us with another anecdote of this scene, which he had from Pope. The poet, finding his friend impatient at the thoughts of going out of the world, told him he had been a very good man, and no doubt would go to a better place. The dying artist reproved this meagre cant very humorously. "Ah! my good friend, Mr. Pope," said he, "I wish God would let me stay at Whitton."

There are in this volume some conversations of the Signora Rosalba, a painter of miniatures at Venice, all of which taste of true genius. She remarked of Sir Godfrey: "I concluded he could not be religious, because he was not *modest.*"

"As I was sitting by Sir Godfrey Kneller one day," said Pope, "whilst he was drawing a picture, he stopped and said, 'I can't do so well as I should do, unless you flatter me a little; pray flatter me, Mr. Pope! You know I love to be flattered.' I was once willing to try how far his vanity would carry him, and after considering a picture, which he had just finished, for a good while very attentively, I said to him in French, (for he had been talking for some time before in that language,) '*On lit dans les Ecritures Saintes, que le bon Dieu faisoit l'homme après son image: mais, je crois, que s'il voudroit faire un autre à présent, qu'il le feroit après l'image que voilà.*' Sir Godfrey turned around and said very gravely—'*Vous avez raison, Monsieur Pope; par Dieu, je le crois aussi.*'"

Secretary Craggs brought Dick Estcourt once to Sir Godfrey Kneller's, where he mimicked several persons whom he knew; as, Lords Godolphin, Somers, Halifax, etc. Sir Godfrey was highly delighted, took the joke and laughed heartily: then they gave him the wink, and he mimicked Sir Godfrey himself, who cried, "Nay, now you are out, man; by heaven, that is not me."

It seems, however, that when the point played upon the vanity of the artist, the latter could sometimes put teeth in his replies. When Sir Godfrey was once talking very freely about the imperfections of the world, Pope said to him, "If Sir Godfrey had been consulted, the world would have been made more perfect;" Kneller immediately turned round, and looking at the diminutive person of the bard, said, with a good-humored smile, "Without doubt, there are *some little things* in it I think I *could* have mended."

Such is the anecdote which Bowles, in the notes to his edition of Pope, gives us as the true version of a story differently related by both Walpole and Warton. He gives no authority for his form of the reply; and their account, which makes Sir Godfrey's answer a simple assent to Pope's observation, strikes me as more consistent with Sir Godfrey's character, whose vanity often trenched upon the bounds where sanity ceases and idiotcy begins. Bowles's narrative has too full-dress an air; and smells strongly of the malignity which that editor delighted to infuse into everything he wrote about that great and admirable poet. I rather incline to think that they are all versions of the story above related about the picture.

Here is an anecdote which Dr. Warburton related, and which would have made Rabelais shake with laughter in his "easy-chair." It is as capital a specimen of natural or accidental humor as history affords.

Mr. Pope was with Sir Godfrey Kneller one day when his nephew, a Guinea-trader, came in. "Nephew," said Sir Godfrey, "you have the honor of seeing the two greatest men in the world." "I don't know how great you may be," said the Guineaman, "but I don't like your looks. I have often bought a man much better than both of you together, all muscles and bones, for ten guineas."

There are several anecdotes of Kneller, in the Richardsoniana; but they display nothing but a gross, besotted vanity, that excites disgust rather than merriment. The passions are amusing only so long as they are struggling with reason; when they have extinguished it, the object excites only pity or aversion.

I add another anecdote or two from Spence.

When Sir Isaac Newton was consulted about the rise of South-Sea stock—"I cannot estimate the madness of the people," replied the geometer.

"*Sacrez-vous vos rois?*" said the Prince of Celemar to Lord Peterborough. "*Si nous les sacrons, Monsieur,*" was the reply. "*Parbleu, nous les mas-sacrons.*"

"In the coffee-house yesterday," said Swift, "I received a letter, in which there was one word which consisted of but one syllable, and that syllable of but one letter, and yet the fellow had contrived to have three false spellings in it." It was the word *eye* that was written for *I*.

Filicaja, in his sonnets, makes use of many expressions borrowed from the Psalms, and consequently not generally understood by the Italians. A gentleman of Florence, on reading some of the passages in him, (which were taken literally from David,) cried out—"Oh, are you there again with your Lombardisms!" and flung away the book as not worth the reading.

DR. ARNOLD'S LECTURES ON MODERN HISTORY, AND MISCELLANEOUS WRITINGS.

"DR. ARNOLD is justly entitled to rank among the great men of the world," says an amiable gentleman, whose lucubrations are at present before us. This is not exactly true. He was an ingenious, independent, earnest speculator,—quick to catch the suggestions of an enlightened skepticism, and fearless in following them out even to their extreme conclusions; never trusting to the dead reckoning in his political or moral course, but constantly taking new observations, on all matters of personal or social concern—generally plausible, sometimes able, always honest:—but there goes more to the making of a great man than the master of Rugby had attained. He was a man of many talents, and of many virtues, possessing some of both in extraordinary degrees; his writings deserve the studious consideration of scholars, and his character demands the sympathy and reverence of all: but that comprehension, calmness, expansion, strength and firmness, which give a nature of greatness to either mind or morals, Dr. Arnold had not. Indeed, an intellect that was marked by so many novelties of opinion, could never be of the first order; for the highest intellects, though they cast the truths of experience into new order, and furnish new demonstrations of them, yet always move parallel with the collective sense of the world, and in their spirit and conclusions are in harmony with it. Arnold loved paradox; and it was a recommendation of any view to him that it contradicted the practice of ages, or the instinct of the nation; such wisdom, we will only say, is of another stamp of greatness from that of Johnson, Burke and Mackintosh. His intelligence was of the microscopic sort; he saw the particular matter before him, with startling clearness, and an exaggerated distinctness, because the light was concentrated and the field of vision narrow. His mental apprehension was too sensitive, which made its operations fall too much into intensities. As a consequence of this, his inductions were often hurried and partial; his opinions ran into affections; and those differences which should have been taken merely as distinctions of the judgment, were held with something of the ardor and vehemence of passion. He asserted with unquestioning dogmatism; and attacked the notions of others with an intolerant and heated zeal, which, as he changed his own opinions frequently, exposed him to misunderstanding and injury. In the combination of his moral virtues there was a want of proportion. If none were absent, at least some were in excess. The materials of the moral structure were rare and admirable; the architecture faulty. Particular tones in the symphony were of a superhuman loveliness; the whole not quite harmonious. He engages by his sincerity; stirs us with his animation and eagerness; raises and refines our principles by the purity of purpose and conscious integrity of design which everywhere are apparent in his writings: but he fails to command the confidence of our minds, and we attend to his finest displays with the guarded interest and suspecting admiration which we lend to an enthusiast, rather than the respect and deference which we pay to a guide and teacher.

But the point of view in which the characteristics of Dr. Arnold strikes us as possessing most interest, consists in looking at him as a "sign of the times,"—a representative of the qualities and influences of the present century,—a time described by Carlyle, accurately enough, as "destitute of faith, and terrified at skepticism." The social and political development of nations has been hitherto carried on by the united operation of two divergent elements,—those of Order and Progress; and almost every mind has been constituted by nature for serving under the banner of one or other of these principles, the grand resultant of whose antagonist action is seen in the actual history of the world. This distinction, which is in effect that of whig and tory, runs through all time and appears in every European nation: and almost every great mind, especially among the English, may be referred to one or other of these types. But of late years, in England particularly, this distinction seems to have become confused in the politics of the country, and one new blended system to have taken the place of the two opposing, yet harmonious elements, which formerly wrought out the government. It is therefore not surprising that a corresponding anomaly should show itself in the frame or operation of the eminent minds of the time; or that an Arnold should appear in philosophy when a Peel is found on the Treasury Bench. As the opinions and sentiments of such men are not associated according to the laws which we had become familiar with in either of the other two classes, we are inclined to call them inconsistent and self-contradictory. It is true, they are metaphysically repugnant and irregular: but it does not follow that positively they are false. Dr. Arnold might be characterized, in religion, as a Kempis-Voltaire; in politics, as a Johnson-Cobbett. His theory of society was a mosaic of Toryism inlaid with Radicalism: his scheme of government was absolutism interleaved with anarchy. The principle of a church he asserted with an ardor and constancy as great as Newman's, and fought with still greater eagerness, against every practical embodiment of the principle. He maintained the union of Church and State in the abstract, and battered it down in detail. All this renders his character curious and his writings remarkable. Those who know how to read such authors may draw much instruction from his volumes. He shakes up the elements of opinion in his reader, and sets one to thinking on many subjects which one had scarcely deemed questionable before. Whether, as men now are, there is much benefit likely to flow from that, we shall not try to determine.

WILEY & PUTNAM'S LIBRARY OF CHOICE READING. Vol. xxvi.; containing selections from TAYLOR, BARROW, SOUTH, FULLER, &c. By BASIL MONTAGUE. New York, Wiley & Putnam, 161 Broadway.

THIS is a noble series of works, and we desire to commend it, specially, to the patronage of families and individuals. It seems to us to be peculiarly important, at this time, that the community should manifest a decided and active interest in favor of publications which pretend to some better merits than *mere* popularity and cheapness. We confess that we have begun to feel some concern about the ultimate results of cheap printing, specious and alluring as some of its attractions undoubtedly are. The old system of publication it has pretty completely broken up; and the channels of what was termed *the trade* have become so much disturbed, that a recurrence to it is not easily practicable. If, therefore, the new method is not to develop from itself a literature equal, or superior to the old one, in the substantial excellence of the works, or in the mechanical execution of them, the mere privilege of buying worthless volumes at a low price, will poorly compensate us for the inability to get handsome and good ones on any terms whatever. Hitherto, it must be admitted, the results have been truly melancholy; and we cannot see that matters exhibit any tendency to recover themselves; on the contrary, the declension, both in the character and the appearance of the works, has rather gone on at a more rapid rate, as the system has become more firmly established. The new style of publication is sufficiently well suited to that kind of literature, now perhaps the most abundant, whose popularity is as transient as it is rapid and universal; for the volume itself has worn out and perished, when the interest of the composition has exhaled; and the one is fit only to be cast forth from the drawing-room or the shop about the same time that the other is ejected forever from the regard and recollection of readers. But books fit to be kept, must be printed with some elegance, to allow of their preservation; a publisher, however, cannot safely make this provision for future times, unless he is allowed the benefit of the present popularity of the work. But now, a cheap edition strikes in between him and his market, and his more costly publication remains upon his shelves to await the lagging demand of those who shall be desirous of reading the work after the other impression has vanished from existence. Accordingly, all descriptions of publishers, both regulars and volunteers, have joined in one reckless race of cheapness and vulgarity for the depreciated prize of popularity. Each has succeeded enough to ruin the others, but not enough to benefit himself; and the public which was the dupe of its own short-sighted cupidity, finds at last that if it has given little, it has got less than nothing.

Wiley & Putnam's Library of Choice Reading is an honorable and laudable attempt to introduce a better state of things. The volumes are cheap, but they are printed with what would have been superior elegance even in the days of octavos and leather bindings; the moral and literary tone of the works is the highest and most unexceptionable. They consist in almost all instances of selections from those works which, though adapted to be extensively popular, are yet, in point of fact, somewhat difficult to obtain; having agreeableness enough to make them universally acceptable, and a tone of refinement and purity high enough to save them from notoriety. Some of the works are not merely salutary, but, as Bacon would say, "medicinal to the times." A man may count it among his good deeds, tending to the repose of conscience at the close of his life, to have been instrumental in giving circulation to such a book as that which comes so immediately under our notice as the twenty-sixth volume of this series—Basil Montague's Selections. We are not favorably inclined, as a general thing, to these excerpted presentations of an author now becoming quite common among us. "Distilled books," says Bacon, "like distilled waters, are flashy things;" and selections are, as commonly, vapid ones. But there is room for discrimination. To compile Beauties from Addison, Specimens of Johnson, or Selections out of Irving,—writers of short papers, in which every paragraph is a specimen of composition, every sentence a selected elegance, and every phrase beautiful—is a plain mistake. But the great authors of an earlier time—the heroic age in letters—thought that an enduring reputation could be established only by some large treatise on some vast and comprehensive topic; they likened a book to an animated being, to which form and organization are of vital consequence, or to a building, such as a cathedral, of which magnitude, proportion, and detail are of the essence. These colossal productions, though they have kept their authors' names alive, have not been able to keep themselves so. If the subject was useful, and the conclusion right, the result passed into the general sense of the world, and the process ceased to have interest; if the theme was temporary, or the deduction mistaken, every succeeding critic signalized the failure of a work in which perhaps he could not have written the feeblest section. Either way, they remain as monuments of the strength or extravagance of the human intellect, but have ceased to be a part of the living literature of the nation. Yet are they, like the tombs of the old Etruscan kings, full of rare treasures. They are abounding in all the wealth of thought and language; a majestic rhetoric rolling along, in a sounding stream, the confluent riches of wisdom and wit, learning and invention, moral prophecy and politic shrewdness. All that has permanent and present interest, for any man, in these works,—all that common readers can enjoy or that the studious book-man does, in point of fact, revert to and dwell upon, may be brought into the compass of a very few pages. Indeed, the disgust occasioned by the formal cast, and scholastic manner, and antiquated style of these writers, is so great, that to be read at all, they must be read thus, as it were, from the commonplace book of a candid and judicious scholar. Who, for example, now cares to be amazed and fatigued by the daring subtleties of "The Divine Legation?" Yet, what examples of sense and sarcasm, what precious illustrations, and what vivid eloquence might be picked out of it! How many at present, are eager to wade through the morasses of quotations from whose midst spring Taylor's fairy islands of originality, for the sake even of the fragrant flowers and golden fruit that bloom there as they bloom nowhere else? Who is willing to sit out one of Fuller's elaborated and highly-spirited entertainments, though a single dish from his profuse table would be prized as a feast-day's dinner to the daintiest modern appetite? Many could enjoy the ethics and poetry of Bacon who can make nothing of his science, and admire the copious logic of Barrow, or taste the strong sagacity and as strong humor of South, who care little for their theology. The merit of Basil Montague in this selection, consisted therefore, in perceiving the exactly fitting application of a plan which had been applied injudiciously a hundred times: this being one of the many cases in which it requires more understanding to use a conception rightly than to have originally suggested it

A collection like this, restricted to relics of antiquity, differs from Elegant Extracts, or Beauties of Popular Authors, furnished with miniature specimens of what we are daily conversant with in large, in the same way that a museum differs from a baby-house. We may add that the compilers of Anthologies might, we think, properly take a hint from Mr. Montague's example; and leaving alone Milton, Shakspeare, and Pope—geranium authors of whom every leaf is a flower—bring the process of excerpting to bear upon Lee, Blackmore, Davenant, and Drayton, writers who have five lines well worth remembering among five hundred scarce worth reading.

Montague is well known to professional persons as an eminent chancery lawyer; and recently to the public by his edition of Bacon,—in our judgment, a very respectable, but very complete failure. His powers are not great; but his reading has been extensive and curious; his taste is delicate and correct; his sympathies high and good; and his principles amiable, enlightened, and humane. His name will long be remembered from its connection with this pleasing volume, a work which will prove as useful to the morals of this age and succeeding ones, as it is honorable to the past. As we open it an atmosphere of quiet and awe seems to expand around us, filled with the lustre of purity and peace. We find ourselves on the hilltop of virtue and truth, in the presence of august intelligencies, arrayed in stainless garments and conversing together as in a cloud of heaven; and we cannot err in thinking that it is good for any one to be here. A feeling almost sad creeps over us with the reminiscences that the names of Taylor, Fuller, and Milton call up; and we are nearly ready to fly away from "the guilt and fever of city life" and professional strain, and abide always in "the still air of delightful studies."

We had intended to offer a few suggestions to the editor of this series, whoever he may be, as to the future contents of his list; but upon looking at the advertisement in the last number, where we see the names of Landor, De Quincey, and Beckford, we believe that we are anticipated as to nearly all that we should have named. In regard to Landor, we take it for granted that the editor will not overlook "The Citation and Examination of Shakspeare for Deer Stealing," nor the Dialogues of Petrarch and Boccacio, both of which, we believe, were published anonymously. Of Mr. De Quincey, we shall of course have the articles on Shakspeare, Pope, and Schiller, from the Encyclopædia, the articles in Blackwood, and a judicious selection from those in Tait. What would the editor think of "The Doctor," &c.? Only two volumes of the five were ever published in this country, and those so villainously that it is a charitable hope that not a single impression is now to be found. Has he ever fallen in with a little work called "Conversation at Cambridge" —an exquisite morsel of scholarship and genius; or another called "The Living and the Dead"—full of genuine humor, brilliant sense, and beautiful composition? We have several of Lamb's works in the series; we confess we should like to see his letters as published by Talfourd. But we have entire confidence in the resources and good judgment of the gentleman who presides over the work, and are quite sure that nothing really proper will be omitted.

A Popular and Practical Introduction to Law Studies, etc. By Samuel Warren, Esq., of the Inner Temple.

Mr. Canning said of Ward, the author of Tremaine, who wrote also on the Law of Nations, that his law books were as pleasant as novels, and his novels as dull as law books. In that instance there was more truth in the disparaging half of the remark, than it was at all necessary that there should be in any thing so witty. Those who did not relish the politics or the peculiar humor of "Ten Thousand a Year," might be disposed to think that something of the same transposition of talents had taken place in Mr. Warren's case, and that a portion of the prosiness had been let out upon the scenes which ought to have been reserved for the Studies. For our own part, however, we have always thought that work the most readable novel, and the best worth preserving, of any since the death of Scott. But whatever may be thought of the present treatise, there will be no doubt among any class of readers, that it has all the liveliness and point of a clever romance. The first edition was extensively read both here and in England; this new edition presents not merely an enlarged and improved version of the original production, but in addition, another separate work incorporated with it, of a more practical character,—exhibiting an outline of civil, criminal, and ecclesiastical law, as those distinctions exist in England,—an account of the immense changes which the legislation of the last fifteen years has made in conveyancing,—an abstract of the principles of pleading, which is none the worse of being pretty literally copied from Sergeant Stephen,—and a view of the jurisdiction and proceedings of the Spiritual Courts, a subject highly curious and interesting to American readers.

Mr. Warren's book is as good a book, we suppose, as could be made by anybody upon this plan: but we have no very high respect for the design itself. We have doubts of the practicability of thus trying to shoot between wind and water; and are inclined to think, in endeavoring to be at the same time popular and professional, the author will have to meet the fate of those who are candidates for inconsistent honors. There are many ways of making legal martinets and *petit-maitres;* there is only one way to make a lawyer, and that is, earnest, concentrated, continued hard labor; the "live-like-a-hermit and work-like-a-horse" method of Lord Eldon. And it appears to us to be more desirable that all the native difficulties, roughness, and disgusts of the thing, should be met at once; and that the student should understand, at the very threshold of the profession, that his taste and temper must be accommodated to the law, and not that the law is to be moulded to suit his temper and tastes. And if it were possible to make the preparation for the law an easy and pleasant matter, it would be, in our opinion, a very unfortunate thing. The discipline of difficulty,—the alterative and bracing influences of its severity and rigor—are the inestimable blessings which the study of the law promises to those who adopt it. To simplify it in such a way that it should require no effort, no patient research, no long, keen courses of thought, would be as injudicious as to make the exercises of the gymnasium,—the climbing of ladders, the jerking of dumb bells, or the swinging on parallel bars—light and unfatiguing: in both cases, it is in the hardness of the occupation that its value consists. The law is, and always must be, a severe, perplexing, profoundly difficult science, adapted only to great intellects, in whose constitution all the faculties have been happily developed in their fullest force and fineness, by principle, circumstances, or the power of passions; *because* the subject with which the legal mind deals is complicated of all the variety of earthly occurrences, the confusion of worldly conjunctures, the range and obliquity of human interests. Those who propose to make law simple and easy, seem to us to make a mistake as to what law means, as a profession and practical science. It is not an affair of books; it does not lie in a knowledge of certain traditions and secrets among a certain set of men, and a familiarity with some special ceremonies and rites connected with particular public tribunals. It consists in the ordering of human society, in the settlement of men's interests, the vindication of respective rights, and the adjustment of the moral relations of the community. To find out the truth of a protracted and involved course of action —to discover how far and in how many different directions the line of justice has been departed from by all parties concerned, and how, accurately and safely, the tangled error can be brought straight;—this is THE LAW; this is what the Counsellors, and the Judges, are engaged about; the definitions, rules, maxims and forms, which fill the text-books, are not the profession or practice itself, but are designed to minister to that of which they might be said to form no part whatever;—to simplify, by reducing as much as is possible to general and familiar conceptions,—to aid, by suggestions of good sense and sound logic, embodied in fixed usages and received axioms, to keep the sagacity of the professors on the alert, and impart rectitude to their judgment. Such being the case, it is plain that the real stress and pressure of this great practical profession, never can be lessened until the elements and laws of moral being are changed; and the subject of legal education resolves itself into a question whether the strain shall be diffused over years of irksome and laborious education, or be accumulated upon the occasions of practice. It appears to us, that so far from striving to coddle and intenerate the mental fibres of the young apprentice to the law, by facilitating every process, the effort should be rather to heap difficulties and trials upon that period of probation, provided, of course, that the matter is not carried to the extent of shocking and breaking down the spirit and strength. That the youthful nature is disinclined to effort, we know very well; but that any one should be disposed to humor and foster this disposition, is to us surprising. Such is the law of our imperfect condition, that labor is our greatest privilege and blessing; the true path to happiness; the appropriate development of our best power; the only source of our highest virtues. Besides this, we are inclined to think that by making preliminary study easy, one great incentive to after professional energy will be withdrawn. A long, distressing discipline of research and thought leaves a kind of fine resentment in the nature: a man is anxious to wreak the power which he feels within him, upon some high course of professional action; to justify the propriety of his long, solitary labors, to himself and others, by displaying an abundance of valuable fruits from them; to vindicate his own conscious superiority against the negligence of society, by forcing himself to distinction. In addition to this, by simplifying study, and communicating the results of knowledge, instead of imparting the means of attaining it, you take away a great part of the knowledge itself; at least, you impair the distinctness with which it is apprehended. A man never fully knows any truth, till he has discovered it, anew, for himself; nor wholly understands a conclusion till he has seen it analytically in the form of its elements. The old way of teaching boys to swim, was to plunge them souse into the river, and let them kick for their lives: now, they tie cork jackets on them, and give a great deal of instruction in hydrostatics and anatomy, beforehand. But it is easier, in every thing, to proceed from the practice to the theory, than from the theory to the practice: practice, indeed, teaches the theory, and is the only way of learning it thoroughly, but theory does not teach practice. We would give more for the few, definite, precise, and actual notions which a young man will have after working and crying over Littleton, than the mass of vague, vaporous half-shaped conceptions he will ever acquire from a book of this sort. We do not mean to disparage Mr. Warren's treatise in particular; but only the system to which it is accommodated. His work is ingenious and amusing; and in an age like this, which is at once restless, busy and inactive, and is fond of touching knowledge at a great many points, it is adapted to be generally popular.

THE LIFE OF THE REV. JOSEPH BLANCO WHITE. Written by himself; with Portions of his Correspondence. Edited by JOHN HAMILTON THOM. In three vols. London, 1845.

WE know not why these curious and instructive volumes have not yet found a publisher in this country; unless it be that they are neither fantastic enough, nor prurient enough, to be suited to the popular taste. They are the record of the life of a most amiable and excellent person, whose religious nature having once got out of poise, was never happy enough to recover its balance. Sincere, earnest, acute even to subtlety, he was able to confute all errors, but never able to settle the truth. If a man has but a touch of philosophy in him, he must read this autobiography with a profound and almost painful interest. If he is himself a wanderer, he will desire aid and guidance; if, happily, his own views are fixed, he will rise from its perusal "a sadder and a wiser man." The experience which it records, is such as probably only the nineteenth century could have rendered practicable, and which a man must have been very peculiarly situated even then to partake of. Chillingworth's variations, indeed, bear some resemblance to Blanco's; but his were merely speculative and notional, while Blanco's were actual, practical, and real. Here is a man who passes in succession through the characters of a devoted Romish priest, an atheist, an earnest clergyman of the Church of England, an Unitarian, a rationalist, an utter unbeliever in all revelation; proving the soundness of each of these systems while he is in it, and its utter falseness the instant he has left it; yet in all these changes never weakening the integrity nor sullying the sensitive purity of his moral nature, and never forfeiting the esteem and affection of those with whom he had been associated, many of them, too, the ablest and most eminent persons in the nation.

But our purpose is to refer only to Blanco White's literary character. There are in this book some small poems of White's which, in our judgment, are among the most genuine and beautiful that we have ever met with from the pen of one not professionally a poet. Of the following, Coleridge, in a letter to the author, says, that it is "the finest and most grandly conceived sonnet in our language: at least," he adds, "it is only in Milton's and in Wordsworth's sonnets that I recollect any rival to it; and this is not my judgment alone, but that of the man, κατ' εξοχην φιλοκαλον, John Hookham Frere." To us, it appears to be conceived in the temper of that profoundly meditative sentiment which we meet with only in the Greek anthology, and to be expressed with the sensuous richness of true poetry. It is a sublime composition.

SONNET ON NIGHT AND DEATH.

Mysterious Night! when our first parent knew
  Thee, from report divine, and heard thy name,
  Did he not tremble for this lovely frame,
This glorious canopy of light and blue?
Yet 'neath a curtain of translucent dew,
  Bathed in the rays of the great setting flame,
  Hesperus with the host of Heaven came,
And lo! creation widened in man's view.
Who could have thought such darkness lay concealed
  Within thy beams, Oh sun? or who could find,
Whilst fly, and leaf, and insect stood revealed,
  That to such countless orbs thou mad'st us blind?
Why do we then shun death with anxious strife?
If light can thus deceive, wherefore not life?

Another sonnet, "On hearing myself for the first time called an old man; ætat. 50," is singularly truthful and touching:

Ages have rolled within my breast, though yet
Not nigh the bourn to fleeting man assigned:
Yes: old! alas, how spent the struggling mind
Which, at the noon of life, is fain to set!
My dawn and evening have so closely met,
That men the shades of night begin to find
Darkening my brow; and heedless, not unkind,
Let the sad warning drop, without regret.
Gone youth! had I thus missed thee, nor a hope
Were left of thy return beyond the tomb,
I could curse life: but glorious is the scope
Of an immortal soul. Oh death, thy gloom,
Short, and already tinged with coming light,
Is to the Christian but a summer's night.

Poor Blanco! ere the shadows of that night gathered about him, he had reasoned himself out of all belief in a dawn beyond the darkness.

These exquisite couplets, entitled "A thought suggested by the custom of writing a few lines to be kept as a memorial of the writer," flow from the deep fountains of thoughtful feeling.

Mysterious Lines! the heart is loth to tell
The gloomy sources of your wonted spell.
Absence and Death, these are the magic springs
That turn to treasures e'en such worthless things.
But why complain? The softness that pervades
Man's truest virtues, springs beneath death's shades.
'Tis sorrow tempers joy's too dangerous glare;
Too proud would be the eye ne'er moistened by a tear.

There are some delightful letters from Southey in these volumes; learned, playful, ardent, "full of matter," as the Laureate was ever wont to be; some from Coleridge, more respectful and to the point, than was usual with that quaint enthusiast, and a copious correspondence with Dr. Channing. In a letter of the latter to Mr. Thom, after the death of Blanco White, we find this beautiful thought:—"I have sometimes observed on the beach, which I am in the habit of visiting, a solemn unceasing undertone, quite distinct from the dashings of the separate successive waves; and so in certain minds, I observe a deep undertone of truth, even when they express particular views which seem to me discordant and false. I had always this feeling about Mr. White. I could not always agree with him, but I felt that he never lost his grasp of the greatest truths."

MISCELLANEOUS SERMONS. By the Rev. SYDNEY SMITH.

IF the dignity of any mental quality were to be judged by the greatness and splendor of the faculties with which it is commonly found in company, *humor* would probably be ranked as one, the loftiest and least earthly, of our intellectual characteristics. It is the almost inseparable associate of genius, as wit is the usual attendant of talent: nay, in its finest essence, as in the instances of Cervantes, Rabelais, Sterne, and Hood, it well nigh constitutes, in itself, an inspiration. It is equally often seen in combination with strong sense and piercing logic. It is allied to pathetic sentiment; it mingles naturally and gracefully with the deepest feeling: it is akin to noble principle, and the sincerest virtue. It is as kindly, and affectionate, and good, as wit is sarcastic, and cynical, and bitter. Nor are these circumstances at all extraordinary: for humor is nothing more than the gay and cheerful outflow of that genial sympathy with the character of humanity, and the course of nature, which, when it acts creatively, gives into life the noblest conceptions of art; when it proceeds reflectively, evinces all the power of practical reason; and when it indulges its instincts in moral and social speculation, is one with love and truth. We challenge any man to go through the writings of Sydney Smith—where he will find more right feeling, common sense, and useful reflection, than in any hundred grave writers,—and say that we have spoken too highly of that which seems to be the source, support, and strength, of all his excellence.

Humor was, in truth, the guardian spirit of Sydney Smith. He was a whig; but with *none* of "the virulence and malevolence of his party." He was a low-churchman; but he felt too practically to lend his aid to subvert a church system which, created by experience, finds its justification in the ordinary workings of men's thoughts and tempers. He was a theorist, an "economist, and a calculator;" but the healthful affinity of his feelings for the truth of the actual and real, kept him safe from the perversion and hardness of that poor profession. We love Sydney Smith: nay, we doubt whether any man can read the fragment on the Irish Church, with which this volume concludes, without feeling for the author of it a respect partaking of veneration. He was a sound, and honest, and sincere man; and labored with a gay heart, but a steady purpose, for the advancement of those interests which he deemed important to his fellows. He saw what was true; he admired what was beautiful; he followed what was good. The merit of him who employs his energies in correcting "the little, nameless, unremembered" faults and wrongs of society, addresses itself to our sympathies, as far more genuine and respectable, than that of him whose sounding efforts are directed to the emancipation of races, and the civilization of savage continents. A philanthropist of the reason, and not of the imagination, he discovered the illusions of virtue as shrewdly as he laid bare the impostures of vice. He concerned himself with those matters which are nearest and most constant, and least observed in their action, and which, on those accounts, are most effective in their influence upon rational and social character. The self-deceptions of a specious piety—the excesses of fanaticism—the errors of an irrational and vain philanthropy—these were the subjects of his critical exposure, not more than the removal of prejudice, and the abatement of social abuses, was the effort of his amending hand.

We heartily wish that there were more sermons of modern times, like these of Sydney Smith. The preachers of this day display an utter ignorance of the constitution of that human nature which it is their duty, first to know, and then to elevate. They overlook the truth that, in regard to sensitive and intelligent beings, *moral suasion* must ever be the true and greatest engine of control and effect. They begin by insulting the understanding, which they propose to convince: they proceed by wakening and exasperating every dormant prejudice, which they ought to have charmed into deep repose: and they end with leaving those errors, which they attack by so mad a strategy, entrenched in pride, and fortified by passion. Their theology is of unimpeachable orthodoxy; but all the moisture of human sympathy is evaporated out of it. They distinguish subtlety; they argue irresistibly; they fulminate magnificently; but they never condescend to attract, allure, and win. The consequence is, that while the air is filled with the strife of tongues, and the city is set on fire with the rivalries of religions, that celestial presence which is the inner soul of all religion—that spirit which "vaunteth not itself, is not puffed up, doth not behave itself unseemly, seeketh not her own, rejoiceth not in iniquity but rejoiceth in the truth, beareth all things, hopeth all things, endureth all things"—has fled away from us to the mountains, and to the vallies, and to the ends of the earth. Far different is the course pursued by the prebendary of St. Paul's. He sets out by conciliating all our sympathies, and lulling all our animosities against his cause; he goes on through a rich, delightful course of moral reflection, till at last he has made all our natural tastes and inclinations in love with spiritual truth. He sets up a practical standard; he brings men to it by attracting their feelings, and keeps them there by satisfying their judgments. To the honest and good heart, which, like Naaman, the Syrian, craves some indulgence to the force of circumstances, and the necessities of its position, he says, with the indulgent wisdom of the prophet, "Go in peace." In dealing with the sins of frailty and weakness, he ever proscribes the fault without condemning the person, by administering exhortation, not reproof—"Go, and sin no more." He accomplishes more than others, because he does not attempt as much.

CRITICAL AND MISCELLANEOUS ESSAYS. By THOMAS CARLYLE.

MR. CARLYLE'S Essays and Reviewals, of which this is the first complete publication, appear to us to be the most valuable and agreeable of all his writings. They touch a great variety of important topics, are well and carefully considered, and are better adapted than the longer and formal treatises which he has of late produced, to the particular character of his powers, which we take to be critical and suggestive, rather than constructive and systematic. Mr. Carlyle has been variously estimated, according to the predispositions of those who have judged. Excellence, when it appears in a novel shape, is sometimes estimated below, often much above, its merit; rarely according to its desert. The natural eye, we know, is deceived as to the distances and magnitudes of objects, when it cannot compare them with other familiar objects; and the mind is still more prone to misconceive the proportions of those things which it cannot refer to some wonted form. So it has fared with Mr. Carlyle: he has been unjustly condemned, and he has been extravagantly praised. Not that we think he has been, upon the whole, too highly estimated by any class, were their applauses somewhat more discriminating. We should be glad to believe that there were any persons, amidst the mob of talkers about Carlyle, who were capable of valuing to excess the excellencies which he unquestionably possesses. His peculiarities they esteem too flatteringly; his greatness they scarcely appreciate at all. For ourselves, we cannot give him the rank of a first-rate intellect; we cannot approve his writings as a whole; but we admire many of his qualities as brilliant and admirable, and we think him possessed of some capacities which are as rare as they are excellent.

One of the most striking peculiarities of Mr. Carlyle's character, is his intolerance of cant in every shape; whether it be the traditionary cant of moral and political principle, or the cant of the most enlightened opinion of the time; the cant of the nation, or the cant of a noisy sect; the dogmatizing cant of the age, or the flippant cant of the hour. Now, undoubtedly, an infinite deal of sense is in solution with all these kinds of cant, and in unsettling or dissipating the strength or weakness of any one of them, the defences of truth in its fastnesses, or the supports of truth in its open marches, are to some extent enfeebled. Still it is of incalculable value to every reader to have before him an example of a writer who is laboring only to judge sincere judgments; who brings the conscience of his intellect, not its prejudices or affections, to investigate everything, in its search after truth. The influence of such an example is of salutary moral tone, and it invigorates and strengthens the intellectual temper.

Mr. Carlyle belongs, undoubtedly, to the skeptical school: his mind is naturally fertilè of "obstinate questionings" of everything. But he does not make his sword his worship; he does not mistake the method for the end. His object is truth and its repose: the means he employs are skepticism and its disorders. He obviously is endeavoring to work *through* the confusions of opinion, and *by* them, to a higher region of light and peace. Looking beyond the excitement and bustle which occupy the foreground of his mind, you clearly see the reposing figures of those great sentiments and sympathies that are akin to the eternity of changeless truth. In this respect, there is a very agreeable difference between himself and Mr. Macauley. The latter seems to think criticism, not progression, to be the chief end and final cause of all intellectual effort. Like the captain in Farquhar, to him, "Fighting for fighting's sake's sufficient cause." Mr. Carlyle is a traveller by profession: he is a fighter only by necessity. He carries a staff as well as a sword, and under his armor is the scallop shell of the pilgrim: he attacks no enemies but those that block up his march upon the high road to the hilled city, which he sees far before him; and if he lays about him manfully at times with his blade, it is only to occupy the ground with his advancing steps.

We take him to be a writer whose true function is, not to guide, instruct, or satisfy, but to rouse, and prompt, and stimulate. A strong man will be infinitely the better for reading him; a weak one might possibly be injured. His writings are like a glass of spirits: a stout man can work better and steadier after it; a feeble one is only intoxicated. There is a fearlessness, and force, and fire about him, from which a noble inspiration may be caught; but, then, there must be vigor and head to turn that inspiration to account. There is an ardor about him that communicates to the reader the flame of its own earnestness. We come from him refreshed, and stirred, and charged with enthusiasm. He may have many errors, but he has much sense; and a great intellect, when it goes wrong, benefits us more than a little one when it accidentally goes right. The faults of genius are full of good.

SKETCHES OF MODERN LITERATURE, AND EMINENT LITERARY MEN: Being a Gallery of Literary Portraits. By GEORGE GILFILLAN.

THIS production is all light and no shade. It is not the brilliance of a starry sky, but the unmitigated glare of a gas chandelier. It has not the fresh odorousness of the air blowing over rose-gardens, but the oppressive fragrance of a close and heated room, filled with flowers of the tuberous plant. Hesiod's maxim, that the half is more than the whole, is as true in litera ture as it is in morals, and even more important to be observed. On opening the book, we are saluted with a shower of wit-arrows, which occasion some little alarm, until, like Richard in his interview with Saladin in the desert, we catch one or two of them in our hand, for closer inspection, and discover that they have no heads—being merely light bits of wood, cut and painted to look like arrows. We have no respect for such writers. Such a style is not only a vice in taste, but it argues some grievous wants in respect both of intellectual and moral greatness. Those lofty and comprehensive intelligences, whose mental consciousness is in sympathy with the great spirit of truth, reduce the elements of thought to a few general principles, examine and judge with an apparent uniformity of reflection, and seem often to repeat themselves. The *brilliant point of view* of every object, and of every side of every object, cannot be reached but by one who has cut loose from those liens which consistency lays upon all the liege men of truth; and the refracted light under which a thing looks brilliant, is so opposite to the plain white light in which it is seen as it is, that a love of point and glitter, if it does not begin in insensibility to truth, will almost invariably end in leaving a man in that condition. There was a great deal of psychological profoundness in the remark of Charles Lamb about Hazlitt, of whom the present writer has frequently reminded us. Commending him one day, to an extent that called forth some expression of surprise from his companion, Lamb added, by way of gentle qualification, as if he had supposed his hearer would have taken that for granted: "It is true the man does not know the difference between right and wrong."

We never love to condemn anything having the port and countenance of a book, unless it be morally bad. We cannot charge any higher crime upon Mr. Gilfillan's performance, than being worthless, and that, as the modern world goes, may, perhaps, be negatively a virtue. A judicious prince, says Machiavelli, will from time to time, commit acts of wanton cruelty, that his subjects may appreciate how much they are indebted to him for not being constantly wanton and cruel. There have been, of late times, so many pernicious publications, that we have come to consider an author as somewhat commendable, who neither springs a mine under religion, denies the first principles of social and political order, nor melts down virtue in the fire of the passions. We shall, therefore, decline passing any sentence on Mr. Gilfillan, considering that he does not fall within that class whose discharge, according to the Edinburgh's maxim, is the condemnation of the judge. We shall be content with saying, that the best thing about this book, is the articles of De Quincy, the *soi disant* opium eater, to which it has given rise in Tait's Edinburgh Magazine.

An Author's Mind. A Bookfull of Books, or Thirty Books in One. Edited by Martin Farquhar Tupper, Esq., M. A., &c.

Mr. Martin Farquhar Tupper is one of those gentlemen of acknowledged genius, and sovereign popularity, whose merits, however, we have never been able to discover. If oddity were always originality, if quaintness and beauty were synonymous, if paradox were necessarily wisdom, we should be ready to grant that Mr. Tupper is a wise, beautiful and original thinker. But thought, after all, is an affair of mind, and though a man of genius may write what is far more brilliant than common sense ever is, yet no man can utter valuable truths on moral and prudential subjects, unless he possesses a vigorous and powerful understanding. Now Mr. Tupper's art consists in contriving, not thoughts, but things that look like thoughts; fancies, in imitation of truths. The "Proverbial Philosophy," in fact, appears to us to be one of the most curious impostures we have ever met with. When you first read one of the aphorisms, it strikes you as a sentiment of extraordinary wisdom. But look more closely at it; try to apply it; and you will find that it is merely a trick of words. What flashed upon you as a profound distinction in morals, turns out to be nothing but a verbal antithesis. What was paraded, as a kind of transcendental analogy between things not before suspected of resemblance, discovered by the "spiritual insight" of the moral seer, is in fact no more than a grave clench,—a solemn quibble,—a conceit arising not from the perfection of mind, but the imperfection of language. Those conceptions, fabricated by Fancy out of the materials that Fancy deals in, and colored by the ray of a poetic sentiment, bear the same relation to truths, that the prismatic hues of the spray of a fountain in the sunshine bear to the gems which they perhaps outshine. It dazzles and delights, but if we try to apprehend it we become bewildered; and finally discover that we were deceived by a brilliant phantom of air. You may admire Mr. Tupper; you may enjoy him; but you cannot understand him: the staple of his sentences is not stuff of the understanding. Take one of Mr. Tupper's and one of Lord Bacon's aphorisms.

They flash with an equal bravery. But try them upon the glassy surface of life. Bacon's cuts it as if it were air: Tupper's turns into a little drop of dirty water. One was a diamond, the other but an icicle; one was the commonest liquor, artificially refrigerated; the other was a crystal in form, but in its substance the pure carbon of truth. If these bright delusions which Mr. Tupper turns out to the wonder and praise of his admirers, were really *thoughts*, is it to be supposed that he could go on in this way, stringing them together, or evolving one out of the other, as a spider weaves its unending line, or as a boy blows soap bubbles from the nose of a tobacco pipe? Fancies, conceits, intellectual phantoms, may be engendered out of the mind, brooding in self-creation upon its own suggestions: but *truth* is to be mined from Nature, to be wrung from experience, to be seized as the victor's trophy on the battle-field of action and suffering. The flowers of poetry may bud spontaneously around the meditative spirit of genius, but the harvest of Truth, though to be reaped by mind, must grow out of Reality.

Having thus signalized our incapacity to appreciate the value of Mr. Tupper's productions, we need hardly be at the trouble of expressing our opinions of the particular work now before us, as all who admire the author would at once challenge us as incompetent to criticise it. To those who value Mr. Tupper, we can say with an honest conscience, that we think this volume quite equal to any that have gone before it, from the same quarter. Though we cannot discover what relation these "title-pages" bear to common sense, we have no doubt of their being equally valuable with the Proverbs; and though we have tried in vain to divine the motive of the author, in this "bookfull of books," we are satisfied that the purpose of the volume is quite as rational as that of any previous production of this singular writer.

RUBIO'S RAMBLES IN THE UNITED STATES, AND IN CANADA, during the Summer of 1845.

THIS work is one of those ill-advised productions of a bigoted, self-sufficient individual, who, having formed in his own obscure and circumscribed sphere, opinions of perfection, founded upon the satisfaction of his personal wants and conveniences, ridicules when only glanced at, and abuses when participated in by himself, every custom differing, in the minutest particular, from his self-created standard of excellence.

Rubio is a man who would condemn a whole nation because he found tough beef-steaks in the country, and because dinners were not served up after the "manner at home." How unfortunate it has been for the kindlier sentiments existing between this country and Great Britain, that men like Hamilton, Dickens and this author, should come here, and, because the English language is spoken, refuse to us the courtesies that are never withheld to any nation differing from them in that respect! The foundation of half the abuse and misrepresentation manifested towards us, arises from the absurd first principle of the majority of visitors to this country from England; they have the presumption to assume us to be English, and then to judge us by their own self-created standards of excellence, rating us soundly for every circumstance in which we differ from them. This is not the manner in which a philosophical mind would view us, or our institutions: we are as much a foreign nation towards England, as is France, or Germany: separated from Great Britain for seventy years, our manners and customs do not differ so much from theirs, as their own vary in the present time from what they were then. Thus we have individuals arriving in New York, without letters of introduction, without knowledge of localities—without even consulting a fellow-passenger—plunging, at once, like this book-maker, into a cheap boarding-house—where they find breakfast at six o'clock! and dinner at twelve! and their opinions of the manners and customs of our country are founded upon this sage experience. This first friendly impression is vented by Rubio in the following ludicrous attempt:

"The Americans are truly a vulgar, ignorant, bragging, spitting, melancholy, sickly people. Passing their lives in a high state of mental excitement, some kill themselves with drink, and some with tobacco; some are hurried to the ever yawning gates of their cemeteries by excesses in religion, or excesses in politics, excesses in commerce or excesses in speculation, or tribulation of mind induced by a combination of these causes. But calamity is not of very long life in America, for the men are soon dead, and soon forgotten. Duels and assassinations also help to thin their ranks; for strange as it may appear, it can be proved that famous as Italy, Sicily, and Spain, are for the stiletto, there are many more assassinations and stabbings in the slave States of America, than in all those countries put together. This is a melancholy truth; but, as the minds of the masters in the Southern States insensibly become degraded by the mere contact, not to say association, with beings so degraded as their slaves, the moral sense becomes blunted, they care little for assassination or for murder, and nothing for stabbing and maiming."

Thus we see a man forming, *ad captandum*, such opinions of a nation, on his first arrival in the country—seeking only to confirm the unjust and injurious sentiments he has conceived of a whole people unknown to him, and from whom he afterwards says he had "received constant civilities;" putting his prejudices and calumnies in print, to insult and goad a country naturally and proudly sensitive, where every man becomes an active participator in, and guardian of, the government of the land.

Rubio—whom we take to be some growling, half-pay British officer, of fifty or sixty years of age—misses, undoubtedly, in country hotels, the "mess table" of his regiment; and founds much of his indignation against us upon our barbarous toleration of bad cooks. He says the "castor department" of our tables is "the filthiest compound of nastiness that was ever exhibited to the disgust of an Englishman"—that he was constantly disgusted by persons jumping up from the table before a decent man could eat one plateful of his meat, and in truth, all the worst habits of the less particular portions of the people are exaggerated to the veriest absurdity, and fixed upon all grades of society as the universal customs of the nation, and one unjust, false, sweeping, and virulent condemnation is the result. Our readers will not, we hope, suppose that we intend to flatter the faults or foibles of our countrymen; we know that no people on earth are without them; but we do place our stamp of utter disapprobation upon the individual of any nation who prostitutes his pen to the base and degraded purpose of fostering injustice and prejudice by a sweeping and false condemnation of a whole people. In this instance even the apology of ignorance and misinformation, can plead no excuse for the writer—for every man, however much he may be capable of a malignant action, is quite aware of the vileness and infamy of the act he perpetrates.

We are not pleased at the re-publication of these works; they fester wounds that should be permitted to heal, and sow dissensions between nations that should be friends. At the same time that we make this remark, we cannot but express an earnest hope that we may live to see the day when Americans shall mentally acknowledge a conscientious standard of their own, and learn to treat with laughter and contempt, the petty attacks made through ignorance or envy of our institutions, and fear at our increasing power and commanding position.

UNDINE: A ROMANCE. By the Baron DE LA MOTTE FOUQUÉ.

[THE "wild, graceful, and touching Undine," to use the felicitous epithets of Mrs. Austen, has had the good fortune to unite the applauses of several of the finest and most fastidious judges of high excellence in Art, that England and Germany have produced. "It will always continue," says Menzel, "one of the most delightful creations of German poetry." "If you would have a good opinion of Fouqué," said Goethe, "read his Undine, which is really a most charming story." "Undine," said the late S. T. Coleridge, "is a most exquisite work. It shows the general want of any sense for the fine and the subtle in the public taste, that this romance made no deep impression. Undine's character before she receives a soul, is marvellously beautiful." "Mr. Coleridge's admiration of this little romance," adds his nephew Henry Taylor, "was unbounded. He read it several times in German, and once in the English translation. He said there was something in Undine even beyond Scott;—that Scott's best characters and conceptions were *composed*, by which I understood him to mean that Baillie Nicol Jarvie, for example, was made up of odd particulars, and received its individuality from the author's power of fusion, being in the result an admirable product, as Corinthian brass was said to be the conflux of the spoils of a city. But Undine, he said, was one and single in projection, and had presented to his imagination, what Scott had never done, an absolutely new idea." Sir Walter himself has also expressed his hearty admiration of the work. "Fouqué's Undine or Naïde," said he, "is ravishing. The suffering of the heroine is real, though it is the suffering of a fantastic being."

The author of this work, Friedrich, Baron de la Motte Fouqué, was born at New Brandenburg, February 12th, 1777. His grandfather, a Protestant, and belonging to one of the most ancient families of Normandy, took refuge at the Hague upon the revocation of the edict of Nantes. Henry Augustus, Baron de la Motte Fouqué, so distinguished for his military bravery and skill during the wars of Frederic the Great, and whose correspondence with Frederic is contained in the first volume of the works of that monarch, was the uncle of the subject of this notice, who published his life at Berlin, in 1825. A Protestant, and the descendant of Protestants, the character of the author of Undine seemed to embody a complete reaction against all that was revolutionary and progressive in social and political feeling. Doubtful of the result at which the troubled stream of modern civility was likely to arrive, his sympathies started back to the shadows of its source, and sought in a dreamy revival of the sentiments and fancies of the middle ages, at once the antagonist and the substitute of modern passion. His career seems to have realized in a remarkable degree, that ideal life with which he loved to invest his imagination; and to have illustrated that union of daring energy and active valor with refined emotions and high intellectual culture, which is popularly associated with the old knights of romance. He served as lieutenant in the Prussian horseguards against the French in the campaigns on the Rhine in 1794 and 1795. After this, he spent many years in literary retirement, engaged in study, and in the composition of a great variety of romances, and tales, and poems. In 1813, when Prussia rose as one man against Napoleon, in the rage of the justest retribution that ever yet trampled the destroyer to the earth, Fouqué again entered the service; but in his mind, even the enthusiasm that urged the charges of Lutzen and Leipsig seems to have been animated rather by visions of long-past national ideas which to his eye were mingling in the contest, than by the passions and interests of the passing hour. He entered the army as a captain, and had attained the rank of major, when he retired at the close of the campaign. The remainder of his life was past at or near Berlin in the quiet of literary occupation. Among other honors, he was a Knight of the Order of St. John. He enjoyed the cordial and intimate friendship of the present king of Prussia. He died at Berlin, on the 23d of January, 1843. He was thrice married, and left a daughter and two sons.

In Germany, where the vintages of wit are as sedulously discriminated and labelled as those of wine, Fouqué's writings are referred to the school of Romanticism,—a class who sought to revive in their writings the mysticism of aboriginal fiction, to restore the picturesque manners of feudal times, and call again to the scene of art the shadowy forms of northern mythology. But of all this school, Fouqué is the only one who has succeeded in bringing up this local and temporary feeling to the level of European intelligence and taste; and that, indeed, only in Undine: for while Treck, Herder and Novalis never became even national, this fine and graceful creation of Fouque has excited the warm and abiding admiration of the first minds in England and America. It has been translated into almost every European language, and a version has even been made in Russian hexameters. "The Hero of the North," a dramatic tirlogy, consisting of "Sigurd the Serpent-Killer," "Sigurd's Revenge," and "Aslauga," and founded on an ancient Scandinavian legend, is one of the most elaborate of his re-constructions. "The Magic Ring" is a tale of feudal adventures mixed up with enchantment, contrived with singular complication and skill. "Sintram and his Companions" is a tale of higher power, and of a more earnest simplicity and concentration. He has written a number of other tales, distinguished for similar characteristics of high-wrought fancy, solemn enthusiasm, and picturesque brilliance. Among his poetical works, one on occasion of the murder of Kotzebue by George Sand, and another on the death of Major Von Roder, who fell at Culm, and others referring to incidents during the war, have been admired for their fervor and boldness. His select works, in twelve volumes, with his last corrections, were published about the year 1841, under his own superintendence at Halle.—ED.]

Fairest among the forms that come smiling towards us as we enter the garden of literature, is Undine, the Water-Nymph. Grace is in all her motions, and in her aspect are celestial witcheries. Pure as dew, and soft as a gush of distant music,—gentle as a star beaming through the riven clouds,—with mystery of charms, she comes near to us, and melts down our admiration into love; but when we would take her to us as something familiar and delicious, she floats away to the far heights of Fame, and looks down on our despair with countenance of pearl-like lustre, and smile as sweet as Spring. Divine in its essence, eternal through beauty, this marvellous effluence of genius,—perfect, without precedent and beyond pursuit,—has taken its place among the perpetuities of Art, one of the contributions which the mind of man has made to the enduring things of life.

If we were asked to select, at once for comparison and contrast with some bright work of Grecian art, a specimen of Romantic composition, which, while it illustrated even to extreme all the quaint and wild peculiarities of the Teutonic style, should vindicate its inherent truth and justness, our choice would probably fall upon this beautiful production. The stuff out of which the tale is wrought is thoroughly Gothic; nay, the whole material—thought, feeling, fancy,—is very German of the Germans. Yet the execution of the work is so simple—so clear of every national or local refraction of taste, of all conventionalisms of tone, and mannerisms of impression—so pervaded by the breadth, sincerity and directness of genuine excellence—that in so delightful a result, Pericles himself might tolerate the miracle of modern art. If the classic gem paled even the lights of Nature by the intense and single ray of its far perfection, the modern picture would be found to display a variety of forms, a versatility of effects, and a richness of hue, to which the narrow faultlessness of its rival would be a stranger. Opposite in character, yet equal in impression, the master-works of the two schools might stand over one against the other, like the two gates of the day of European civility; one gleaming with the clear, cold holiness of the pale and starry morning; the other aglow with all the fiery, tumultuous tints of a gorgeous sunset. In scenic attitude, with marble grace, in statuesque distinctness, the offspring of the Grecian mind stands solitary and unsympathizing, conscious of sovereignty. The child of the Gothic soul, warm with the life of passion, and blushing with its tenderest hues, flies to our kindled bosom and seems to become a portion of ourselves. Majestic, unconciliating, unresistible, the one compels our homage; the dazzle and turbulence of the other's charms captivate our fancy before reason can act, and our judgment is floated away upon a tide of feelings. *That* is a stainless virgin, whose sanctity of chasteness reproves the admiration which it raises, and refuses to be approved except by principle: *this*, soft and condescending, fascinates even where it is frailest, and for every fault it shows, we have more than a weakness. If our duty is to the one, our delight is with the other.

In the compass of continental literature, we do not remember an instance whereby so slight a design, an effect so definite, complete and strong is brought out, or where, in so small a compass, such profusion of gifts—such lavish wealth of powers,—is displayed, as in this curious and exquisite work. Invention, poetry, humor, wit, truth, terror,—the wild, the weird,—the gay, the graceful and the grand—are blent together with interfusion, yet distinctness and harmony, of the colors of a forest in autumn. Most of the finest, and some of the highest capacities which the exigencies of Art can call for, here come into play. A fancy, at once delicate and imperious,—which at one moment sports with frolic graces and, in the next, can accumulate all the clouds of wonder,—which, in dealing with the terrible, knows how to exclude the disgusting: sentiment, deep, soft, and brilliant as the dye of the rose-leaf: the feeling wisdom of a heart schooled in the stern love of suffering and disappointment: a pathos, pure, true, not always saved from pain: the energy of thought and the fire of passion. If some fantastic quip of humor suggests to us that we toy with a plaything, instantly a thrill of awe makes us feel that we are under the mastery of a potent magician. We raise our eyes from tracing a merry gambol at our feet, and behold! from the summit of some grand image of the mind, shapes of terror and mystery are looking down upon us. The comparison of the Knight, by Undine, to the summer, which "amidst the highest splendor, puts on the flaming and thundering crown of glorious tempests," has the sublimity of Milton. The author possesses in an eminent degree that eye of composition—that power of grouping several figures in the wholeness of a single impression, which makes the narrative expand from time to time into tableaux of startling vividness; a faculty which, though not one of the highest capacities of the artist, and though often existing in the absence of most other valuable qualities, yet, when judiciously employed, contributes to very striking effects.

It must not be supposed, however, that these differing characteristics are thrown together in a jumble, or wrought into a grotesque arrangement which produces novelty at the expense of propriety, and surprises without imparting any rational pleasure. In the mind of La Motte Fouqué, the taste for the quaint is always subordinate to the love of the beautiful, and in the wildest of his swallow-like flights he ever follows the line of grace. In truth, the skill with which the varied elements of beauty and wonder are combined and made harmonious in the completeness of a splendid poetical creation, is not less extraordinary than the versatility of invention by which such materials were contrived and brought together.

In no part of this remarkable work is that instinctive fineness of contrivance which always attends the highest genius, more strikingly shown than in the delicate mastery with which the natural and ideal characters are assimilated to one another, and the real and fabulous portions of the tale so fused, as it were, together, that, without losing the distinctness of their several natures, they are brought under the unity of a single agency. The different parts are not *wrought* into a constrained connection, but *cast*, by the creative fire of imagination, into the entireness of a homogenous conception. In this respect, even "Shakspeare's magic," uncopyable as its grace and boldness may have been, is somewhat at fault. In "The Tempest," the visionary essence of Ariel sorts well enough with the highly-thoughted, passionate romance of Ferdinand and Amanda, and the bizarre humors of Stephano and Trinculo are perhaps sufficiently in tune with the grotesque being of Caliban; but the intrusion of the quotidian and familiar characters and conversation of Gonzalo, and Sebastian, and Antonio, stops the circuit of enchantment, and breaks the charm of art. In the present case, the effect which we have alluded to seems to have been attained by bringing the supernatural characters, on the one hand, as near to humanity as could be done without impairing the perfectness of their own peculiar being, and, on the other, by laying the real persons under a species of enchantment,—involving them in the mazes of a strange and mournful fate—which makes them to our eye well-nigh as weird and fearful as the higher and more mystic agents of the tale. This bewitchment, or pervasive and overpowering influence of destiny, is felt at once so strongly by the reader, that the author has not been at the pains to express it. The generous and impulsive nature of Huldbrand triumphs over it at intervals just enough to give expansion and variety to the action which is to work out the sad history of Undine. Its existence should be borne in mind in looking at the character of Bertalda, which without such reference might seem to lack the full proportions of womanly passion; as being, in the circumstances of her position, not fierce enough to be feminine. This important assimilation of the two kinds of characters that figure on the story is aided by a discreet use of the power of illusion, on the employment of which the fame of Mrs. Radcliff is founded. Thus, the Knight, at his first entrance upon the scene, is invested through the terrors of the fisherman, with certain supernatural circumstances, the halo of which does not wholly fade for us to the very end of the story; and the old fisherman himself, in that striking scene where he stretches his arms wide over the current and nods so as to make his white hairs fall over his forehead, seems to be so identified with the marvellous inhabitants of the forest, that, to the last, in our feelings, he occupies a half-way position between men and spirits. Add to this the adoption of a highly poetic style of language and illustration, which of itself informs the natural world with a degree of life and sentiment, and gently raises us on the wings of metaphor into the region of spirit; and the employment of a half-comic and mocking tone of narrative which disarms the incredulity of the reader, and causes him to believe all by making him feel that he need not believe anything. Of these effects every reader will be sensible, and it will be the pleasure of each to analyze them according to his skill; but for a single illustration of the exquisite preparation by which the specious miracles of the author's genius are introduced, and the delicate gradations of power by which fancy leads us on, from the familiar delusions of sentiment, through the natural magic of excited passion, till we come at last into the very courts of the marvellous and to all the revelry of fiction, we may refer to the opening parts of the tale. At the very commencement, the leading notion of the water and earth being animated by affections and moved by a human spirit, is lodged in our mind by merely the use of such figurative language as forms one of the commonplaces of poetry; and a little further on, the image of a snow-white gigantic man rising out of the water is familiarized to our feelings by our being given to understand, on its first appearance, that it is only an illusion of the fisherman's terror,—"a strange mistake into which his imagination had betrayed him." So, too, the apparition at the window during the marriage of Undine, which contributes so powerfully to the interest of the event, has been foreshadowed, in some sort, and thereby divested of its first honor by a similar shape: having been made to pass across the spectrum of the *mind's* eye of the shuddering Knight, as Undine, towards the close of the first chapter, begs him to narrate his adventures in the forest; "he looked towards the window, for it seemed to him, that one of the strange shapes, which had come upon him in the forest, must be there grinning in through the glass; but he discerned nothing." These considerations might by some be thought trifling, but we hesitate not to express our conviction that it is to the consummate art which is thus displayed in stealing the supernatural characters upon the scene while our attention is engaged with illusions, and darkening the air with the mists of rhetoric while they mingle in the action of the piece unobserved, that the success of this work is mainly to be attributed, and that to the neglect of such methods of conciliating our feelings to the marvels of the narrative the failure of so many tales of enchantment, in which there has been no deficiency of power, is to be ascribed. In enterprises of every sort, the difference between failure and success usually consists, not in some great matter, for that might easily be discovered or supplied, but in something of such infinitesimal littleness that it often eludes the consciousness of the creator and the enquiries of the reader.

But the triumph of the author's genius in this rare production—the central gem among many gems—is undoubtedly the character of Undine. A child, to captivate the fancy,—a woman, to move the heart—a spirit, to raise and awe the soul,—with enchanting elegance she wears the drapery of a triple grace. Her charms might fire a sage; her purity might recover a voluptuary. From the moment when we first hear her dashing water against the window of the hut, till we behold her dissolving into tears at the grave of her lover, her beautiful life is at unity with itself and in sympathy with the highest delicacy of female excellence. She might be likened to a rainbow spanning a troubled sea,—which, formed of water and sunbeams, rises from the wave in soft divinity of splendor, and mounting, for a moment, into the heavens, and diffusing round its path the lustre of peace, and joy, and hope, sinks again in the billow and leaves the darkened scene even gloomier than before. Her goodness, her loveliness, the sad disappointment of her gentle spirit, touch our feelings, irresistibly. As a conception of art, her character, before her marriage, has the freshness, lofty simplicity, and tone, of one of Shakspeare's women; afterwards, the emotion of the character is allowed to predominate over the character and subdue it, more than Shakespeare would have permitted. If any defect may be suggested in a story so finely developed, it consists, perhaps, in the means by which the death of the Knight is accomplished,—a scene which revolts rather than rends the heart, and mingles a sensation of horror with our feeling towards the nymph. We should have wished, at least, to have it shown to us that Undine acted under some irresistible compulsion, to do what was not an instinct of her nature, but an awful necessity of her position; but, had it been possible, we would have preferred that the death of the lover should have been accomplished by some other agency. But the inducements, and, so far forth, the justification, of this irregularity in the æsthetic harmony of the piece, are moral and not critical. The disturbance of that serenity of satisfaction which belongs to the perfection of art, has been caused by the impetuous force of the inner and informing thought, or truth, which is the living principle and guiding purpose of the tale. In fact, this romance, in its just intellectual conception, is an earnest and deep spiritual myth. It is a narrative, not of self-amusing fancy, but of allegorizing wisdom, in which the personages and their relations are symbolical of the sympathies and destiny of the human soul. This is the cause of the profound impression which this little work has made upon the greatest minds. The celestial life which love flashes into light within the boundless depths of our being—the immortal wrongs which are inseparable from love's existence, and which are terrible in proportion to love's intensity—the mad resentments and the blazing ruin that are engendered of love, as the red lightning from the heaven-born warmth of the summer air—these and more fatalities that make up the mournful glories of passion, are illustrated with a subtle lore in this singular production. But our design has been to consider it only in its direct and external character as a creation of art, not in its hidden indications as a philosophical revelation, and we, therefore, continue in another paper the full exposition of the enigmas that make the higher interest of the work.*

THE ROSICRUSCIAN PHILOSOPHY.

LE COMTE DE GABALIS, ou Entretiens sur les Sciences Secrétes. Paris, 1670.

WHEN Pope, in 1712, sent forth his immortal Rape of the Lock, with its machinery of sylphs,—the most brilliant work of England's most faultless poet—he said in the prefatory letter to Mrs. Arabella Fermor, that the action of the piece was raised "on a very new and odd foundation, the Rosicruscian doctrine of Spirits;" and that he had derived his knowledge of these beings from a French book, called *Le Comte de Gabalis.* This was the first occasion on which these airy creatures ever played a part in any work of fiction,—at least under their proper names; for, according to the infallible authority of the Count de Gabalis himself, the elves and fairies of the middle ages, the demons of antiquity, nay, the whole company of heathen gods and goddesses, were, in reality, nothing else but nymphs and sylphs. We are not sure whether the ingenious and candid Mr. Bowles included Pope's intrigue with the sylphs among the moral delinquencies of the poet, but it is very certain that the little bard conferred immortality upon them. It must be admitted, however, that he took a number of less warrantable liberties with them; he lowered their dignity, changed their nature in some

* This paper is unfortunately not found among the author's MSS., and is probably lost. The curious bibliographical essay which follows—remarkable, among other respects, as being one of Mr. Wallace's earliest productions, written originally at college in his 19th year—would seem to indicate that the elements of Fouqué's tale are derived from the Rosicruscian Philosophy.—ED.

degree, and misrepresented their history. Notwithstanding the unfading lustre which the various art and animated elegance of the copyist threw upon the subject, he spoilt the delicate distinctness and beauty of the original conception. Previously to their connection with him, they had been spoken of by Sir William Temple in his miscellanies: "I should as soon fall," he says, "into the study of the Rosicruscian philosophy, and expect to meet a nymph or a sylph for a wife or a mistress:" which is said to be the earliest mention that is made of these matters by any English writer. Dryden, also, in writing to Mrs. Thomas in 1699, says, "Whether sylph or nymph, I know not; those fine creatures, as your author, Count Gabalis, assures us, have a mind to be christened, and since you desire a name from me, take that of Corinna, if you please."

This French work, therefore, appears to be the source of the knowledge which English writers have acquired of these visionary personages; and although Fouqué refers to Paracelsus as the primitive and papal authority in modern days, on all questions of occult philosophy, yet as the love of the Cabala, on this particular, is presented not only with more completeness but with far greater liveliness and grace by the French author, we shall draw from him in preference to the obscurer fountains of Bombastes' wisdom. As the book alluded to is very little known,—being, in fact, as Mr. Coleridge used to say, "as good as manuscript"—we cannot bring the subject before our readers in any better or more agreeable manner than by giving a somewhat detailed account of this dainty performance. The work is written with a prodigious deal of pleasantry and wit, and shows extraordinary learning and ingenuity; so much in fact as to leave the reader still doubting—notwithstanding many satirical touches, and the mocking tone which prevails throughout, and in spite too of the author's express declaration both in the work and in a letter appended to it,—whether he was not really to some degree a believer in a scheme whose rationality and consistency he is at the pains to vindicate with such singular and careful ability. Certainly it presents not only the most beautiful, but the most plausible and connected system of spiritual exist-ences that has ever been propounded. Some portions of the book are, however, rather more free than would be quite agreeable with the decorum of modern manners.

LE COMTE DE GABALIS, *ou Entretiens sur les Sciences Secrétes*, was first published at Paris in the year 1670 (*Barbou*). The edition which I possess is that of Metz,—"*an cinq républicain*,"—which answers to the Christian date, 1797. It has no name upon the title-page, but according to *Barbier's Dictionnaire des Auteurs Anonymes et Pseudonymes*, it was written by the *Abbé Montfauçon de Villars*. The following account is given of it in Dargonne's *Melanges d'Histoire et de Litterature* (*Rotterdam*, 1700): "The author of this diverting work is the Abbé Villars, who came from Thoulouse to Paris, to make his fortune by preaching. The five dialogues of which it consists, are the result of those gay conversations in which the Abbé was engaged with a small circle of men of fine wit and humor like himself. When this book first appeared, it was universally read as innocent and amusing. But at length its consequences were perceived, and reckoned dangerous, at a time when this sort of curiosities began to gain credit. Our devout preacher was denied the pulpit, and his book forbidden to be read. It was not clear whether the author intended to be ironical, or spoke all seriously. The second volume, which he promised, would have decided the question; but the unfortunate Abbé was soon afterwards assassinated by ruffians on the road to Lyons. The laughers gave out that the gnomes and sylphs, disguised as ruffians, had shot him, as a punishment for revealing the secrets of the Cabala."

In his first conversation, the Abbé informs us that he had always entertained such strong doubts of the soundness of what are called the secret sciences, that he never would become a regular student of them: at the same time, there were so many able and eminent persons, men distinguished at the bar, or famous for military skill, who were addicted to their pursuit, that it was not reasonable wholly to despise them, at least without some examination. Accordingly, to satisfy his curiosity, and at the same time avoid the fatigue of turning over a whole library of books, he resolved to frequent the society and seek the confidence of those who were devoted to cabalistic learning, and draw as much information as he could from their conversation. For this purpose he determined to assume the character of one who was already a proficient in these sciences, and by pretending to know all, profit by the communications of those who knew something. This plan succeeded beyond his expectations, and he found that his reputation soon grew high. The philosophers whom he met had a sufficiently lofty opinion of their own proficiency, but he perceived that the attention of all those with whom he conversed was fixed with great interest upon a certain nobleman of distinguished station and learning, who resided in Germany, not far from the borders of Poland. The sage had written that he should soon pay a visit to the initiated at Paris, on his way to England, and our Abbé had the honor to be commissioned to reply to his letter, and in doing so took occasion to enclose his horoscope. His communication produced a decided impression upon the philosopher, who wrote that the Abbé should be one of the first persons he should call upon in Paris, and if the stars did not oppose it, he should speedily be admitted into the fraternity of sages. A brisk correspondence ensued; the nobleman's letters revealed extraordinary and magnificent discoveries; and the Abbé found that he was dealing with a gentleman of "very lively and very spacious imagination." One day, as he was occupied in his study with the perusal of some of these marvellous epistles, a man of stately and imposing aspect entered the room, and saluting him after a very sublime and odd fashion, presently let him know that he was his correspodent, the Count de Gabalis. He informed him that the horoscope which had been sent to him displayed so remarkable an adaptatiou for occult science, that there was no doubt the Abbé was destined to become a most illustrious philosopher, and that the hour proper for his regeneration into the higher life of wisdom had nearly arrived. The following day was fixed upon for another interview, and after some further conversation, the Count rose to take his departure. "Watch, pray, hope, and do not talk," said he, and with these words he descended to his carriage, leaving our author in doubt whether his visitor was a madman, an impostor, or a dupe.

On the following morning, at the appointed hour, the equipage of the Count was at the door, and they drove out to Ruel, as a retired and unfrequented place, proper for the mystical communications which the noble sage was about to impart. On the way, the Abbé occupied himself with studying the countenance and character of his singular acquaintance. It was a face marked by an expression of profound satisfaction, and pervaded by the dignified composure and serenity of one whose conscience was free from every stain, and whose mind dwelt habitually in the contemplation of pure and lofty truths. His conversation on politics and literature displayed great sagacity and thorough information. When they came to Ruel, the Count disdained to admire the beauties of the garden, and marched straight to the labyrinth. After some high-flown speeches about the honor and felicity which awaited the Abbé in the initiation which was soon to take place, he gravely informed his pupil that, before he could be admitted into the society of sages, it was necessary that he should take a vow of perpetual chastity. The Abbé quickly set the mind of his companion at rest upon this particular by assuring him that he had already, long since, voluntarily assumed the discipline of monastic purity, and had never yet in the whole course of his life deviated from the strictest propriety of conduct. "But," cries the Abbé, "as Solomon, who was a much wiser man than I ever expect to be, was not able with all his wisdom, to maintain his uprightness in this particular, suffer me to enquire by what methods you gentlemen preserve yourselves from the allurements of this dangerous sex; or what inconvenience would follow if in the paradise of philosophers every Adam should have his Eve?"

"You touch upon a great mystery there," replied the Count, musing within himself for a moment. "But since you detach yourself so readily from women, I will let you know one of the reasons why the sages are obliged to exact this condition from their followers, and you will then perceive how profoundly ignorant are all those who are not of our number. As soon as you are enrolled among the sons of philosophy, and have strengthened your sight with the sacred applications which will be given to you, you will instantly perceive that the elements are inhabited by creatures of the most absolute perfection, whom the sin of the unfortunate Adam has prevented his too unhappy posterity from knowing and having communication with. This vast expanse between the earth and the heavens contains inhabitants of higher dignity than birds and gnats; the infinitude of ocean was created for other guests than dolphins and whales; the depths of the earth were not made for moles alone; and the element of fire, more elevated than the other three, was not fashioned in order to remain void and useless.

"The air is filled by a countless multitude of people, of human shape, a little haughty in their aspect, but very gentle in reality; great lovers of science, subtle, officious to sages, but enemies of fools and ignorant persons. Their daughters and wives possess a kind of mannish beauty, such as is represented in the Amazons. The seas and rivers are inhabited in the same manner that the air is; the old philosophers called these people *Undines* (*Ondins*), or nymphs. Of this race the males are few, but the females very numerous; they possess the most exquisite beauty, and the daughters of men cannot be compared with them. The earth, in like manner, is filled to the centre with gnomes, a race of small stature, who act as guardians of the subterranean treasures, mines, and quarries. They are ingenious, friendly to men, and easy to command. They supply the children of the sages with all the gold that they require, and ask no recompense but the honor of being employed. The gnomides, their wives, are small, but extremely agreeable, and very quaint in their attire. As to the salamanders, the warm inhabitants of the region of fire, they also are the servants of the philosophers, but they do not seek their company with the same eagerness that the others do, and their wives and daughters are rarely seen. The latter, however, are very handsome, more so, indeed, than the females of any other order of these beings, because they are formed out of a purer element. However, I shall not at present say anything more upon the subject, for you will soon have an opportunity of seeing for yourself these various inhabitants of the elements, and can converse with them at your leisure. You will examine their costume, their diet, their customs, their police, their admirable laws. You will be charmed with the elegance of their minds as well as that of their persons: but you will be unable to repress your pity for these unhappy beings, when they inform you that their soul is mortal, and that they have no hope of enjoying, through a blissful eternity, the presence of that divine being whose existence they acknowledge, and whose attributes they religiously adore. They will tell you that, being composed of the present particles of the elements which they inhabit, and having no commixture of baser qualities, they live for a vast length of time; but what is the lapse of ages in comparison of eternity? At last, they must sink forever into the abyss of nothingness. This consideration afflicts them deeply, and we have great difficulty in consoling them under it.

"Our fathers, the philosophers, conversing with the Almighty face to face, lamented to Him the unhappy condition of these creatures; and He whose mercy is without bounds, revealed to them that it was not impossible to find a remedy for the evil. He showed them that as man, by the connection which he has formed with the Deity, has become a partaker of the divine nature, so the sylphs, the gnomes, the nymphs and the salamanders, by contracting an alliance with man, may become sharers in his immortality. Accordingly, at present, a nymph, a sylphide becomes immortal, and capable of the blessedness to which we aspire, whenever she has the good fortune to marry a sage; and a gnome or sylph ceases to be perishable when he espouses one of our daughters. These invisible beings are, therefore, constantly seeking to gain the affection of the inhabitants of the earth. The story which you read of in Jewish writers of the Sons of God loving the daughters of men, and of the giants which resulted from those nuptials, has reference, when properly understood, to the marriage of nymphs and sylphs with women; and the fables about satyrs and fairies have a similar signification. The innocent desires of the spotless creatures, so far from giving scandal to the philosophers, appear to us so just and creditable, that we have all resolved to renounce with one accord the marriage of women, and dedicate ourselves to giving immortality to nymphs and sylphides. Admire, my son, the felicity of the sages! Instead of women whose frail beauties fade after the lapse of a few days, and are succeeded by frightful wrinkles, the philosophers are the possessors of a loveliness which never fades, and to which they have the glory of imparting immortality. Judge of the affection and gratitude of these invisible mistresses, and of the ardor with which they devote themselves to please the charitable philosopher, who applies himself to the task of immortalizing them.

"The cabalist acts only according to the principles of nature; and if you see in our books strange words and signs, and fumigation, this is only to deceive the ignorant. What I shall now communicate to you, is a portion of knowledge which we impart to those who are not yet fit to be admitted into the recesses of wisdom, but from whom we would withhold the power of conversing with these elementary creatures, chiefly on account of the interest which we take in the happiness of the latter. The salamanders, as I mentioned to you, are formed out of the subtlest particles of the sphere of flame, globed together and organized by the action of the universal fire, which is so called because it is the principle of all the movements of Nature. The sylphs, in like manner, are composed of the purest atoms of the air; the nymphs of the finest grains of the water, and the gnomes of the most defecated essence of the earth. Originally, there was complete harmony between Adam and these creatures, for he being composed out of all that was purest in all the four elements, united in himself the perfections of all these beings, and was their natural king. But when the elements of his nature became foul by the contamination of guilt, this harmony was destroyed, for how could any proportion exist between a being gross and impure, and these refined and subtle essences? What remedy, then, is there for this calamity? How can this untuned lute be re-strung, and this lost sovereignty be recovered? O Nature, why will men consult thee so little? Behold the simplicity of the methods which Nature suggests for the restoration of the blessings which man has lost.

"If you desire to recover the natural and original sway of our being over the salamanders, for example, it is merely necessary to purify and exalt the element of fire within us, and to draw up the tone of that relaxed chord. For this purpose, the fire of the world must be collected in a globe of glass, by means of concave mirrors; and this is the secret which all the ancients religiously concealed, and which the divine Theophrastus revealed. There is presently formed in this globe a solar powder which is divested of all mixture of other elements; this being prepared according to art, becomes in a very short time sufficiently efficacious to exalt the fire which is within us, and to render us, if I may say so, of an ingenious nature. From that instant, all the inhabitants of the sphere of fire become our inferiors, and delighted at finding that our mutual harmony is restored, and that we have come near to them again, they treat us with the affection which they show to their own kind, with the respect that is due to the images vicegerent of their creator, and all the attention which is suggested to them by the hope of obtaining from us the gift of immortality. It is true that the salamanders, being of a subtler essence than the others, are naturally longer-lived than they are, and therefore do not seek very zealously to be espoused to the sages. But it is not so with the sylphs and gnomes or the salamanders. As they live but a short time, they have more occasion for our services, and it is easier to obtain their familiarity. It is only necessary to seal up a glass vessel, filled with conglobate air, earth, or water, and to expose it to the sun for a month, and afterwards separate the elements according to the laws of science, which is very easy in the case of water and earth. It is astonishing what magnetic virtue each of these purified elements possesses for the attraction of nymphs, sylphs, and gnomes. You have only to take the smallest possible quantity for a few days, and you will see in the atmosphere the floating republic of sylphs; the nymphs will assemble in crowds upon the shores, and the guardians of the treasures of the earth will display their riches before you.

Thus, without signs, or ceremonies, or uncouth words, we become absolute over these creatures. They exact no worship from man, for they know that he is their superior. Thus does venerable Nature teach her children to restore the elements by means of the elements. Thus is the original harmony re-established, and man regains his proper empire, and becomes master of the world, without the aid of demons, or the resources of forbidden arts."

But, notwithstanding this philanthropic devotion on the part of the sages, it would appear from the discourses of the Count, that but a small portion of these interesting creatures become immortal; this arises partly from the want of a sufficient number of philosophers for this extensive field of missionary labor, and partly because many of their subjects prefer to die rather than risk the danger of becoming miserable in the immortality which they fear may be a curse to them; which last is a suggestion of the devil. The enthusiastic Comte de Gabalis proceeds to state another advantage which results from marriage with this invisible creation, by which it would seem that the devil is cheated on the right hand as well as on the left; for as the sylphides acquire an immortal soul from their alliance with men destined to heaven, so those men who have no share in the glory of eternity, those luckless children whom the sovereign parent has neglected to provide for, and to whom perpetual existence would be but a curse—for it would seem that these cabalists have a touch of Jansenism in their philosophy—have the option of becoming mortal by forming an alliance with these elementary people. Thus the sage runs no risk on the subject of eternity; if he is predestinated to heaven, he has the pleasure, when he is released from the prison of the body, of leading to the skies the nymph or sylphide whom he has immortalized; if he is not one of the elect, his intercourse with the sylphide renders his soul mortal, and he is delivered from the horrors of the second death.

In a subsequent conversation, the Count proceeds to review with great learning and subtlety, the history of the heathen oracles. He combats the notion that the oracles were animated by diabolical influences, and displays on that subject a force of argument, a variety of illustration, which we think it would severely task the faculties of Horsley himself successfully to oppose. He confutes with ease the notion of some among the ancients, that the prophetic answers were caused by exhalations; and then gives the true explanation of the subject. The oracles in fact were sylphs, salamanders, gnomes and undines, who took pity upon the blindness of their fallen and darkened master, man. When the Deity gave up the care of the world, as a punishment for the first sin, these elementary beings took pleasure in revealing to man through the medium of oracles, all that they learned from the Deity; they exhorted mankind to live morally, and gave them those wise and salutary counsels, which are preserved in such great numbers by Plutarch and other historians. As soon as the Deity had compassion on the world, and came himself to be its teacher, these instructors withdrew. Hence the silence of the oracles. For our part, after all that we have read on the subject of oracles, we prefer the theory of the Comte de Gabalis before all the others.

The famous problem of the origin of evil is also solved by the Cabala, and the mystery of the garden of Eden cleared up. It was the intention of the Deity, it seems, that the world should be peopled by the marriage of Adam with the females of the elemental creation, and that Eve should be espoused to some husband of that race. The sin of our parents consisted in violating this command, and contracting a nuptial alliance with one another: hence a dwarfed and degraded posterity. It is observable that in the biography of nearly all the great heroes and sages of antiquity, and of many also during the early and middle ages of Christianity, it is related that one of their parents was a god, a demon, or a phantom. The Comte de Gabalis reviews these cases, and shows such persons were in fact the offspring of marriages contracted according to the original purpose of the divine will, between human and elemental beings.

The characteristics of the different orders of these viewless creatures are very finely discriminated by our author, as the reader will, as to some particulars, already have seen. One feature in their nature should not be overlooked, as it is specially connected with a part of the machinery of La Motte Fouqué's tale. The passions of the inhabitants of the air and the water, are less amiable and smooth than those of the salamanders: their jealousy, in truth, is extremely bitter. This was illustrated by an occurrence which is related by the divine Paracelsus, and which was seen by the whole city of Stauffenberg. A philosopher, who had contracted an alliance of immortality with a nymph, was so forgetful of his faith as afterwards to marry a woman. One day, as he was dining in company with his new mistress and some of her friends, the company suddenly beheld in the air the most beautiful ancle that was ever seen. The forsaken nymph was desirous of letting the friends of the bridegroom see what a great mistake he had made in preferring a woman to her. Immediately after this display, the injured nymph put the false lover to death. However, this jealousy extends only to women, and not to females of their own race, with whom the philosopher is permitted to indulge in the most unrestrained polygamy. They prefer the interest and immortality of their companions to their own private satisfaction, and they desire the sages to present to their republic as many immortal children as they can.

As to the gnomes, their relation to men is more singular than that of the others, and as their characters have been decidedly libelled by the popular writers who have spoken of them, we conceive it but fair to allow the Comte de Gabalis to vindicate the reputation of his dusky friends, by his own unquestionable statements, in the course of which he clears up some particulars in demonology, in respect to which our vulgar knowledge is pervaded with the grossest errors.

"The gnomes," says the Comte, whom he represents as a mild and benevolent race, "become terrified by the infernal howlings which the evil spirits keep up in the centre of the earth, and think it must be better to continue mortal than to run the risk of being tormented so awfully if they become immortal. These evil spirits, who are their neighbors, persuade the gnomes, naturally very friendly to man, that they will confer a great service upon any man whom they can induce to renounce his immortality.

They engage to give to any one from whom a gnome can procure such a renunciation, as much gold as he wants, or to avert some danger that awaits him, or do anything else he may desire. Thus the devil, villain that he is, by the intervention of the gnome, causes the soul of this man to become mortal, and deprives it of its right to eternal life." "Those compacts, then," said I (writes the Abbé), "of which the popular demonographies give us so many examples, are in reality not made with the devil himself?" "Certainly not," replied the Count. "Is not the Prince of this world driven out? Is he not shut up? Is he not tied? Can he mount upwards to the regions of light, and diffuse through them the thickened gloom of hades? He can do nothing against man, in his own person. He can only persuade the gnomes who are friendly to men, to convey these proposals of his to such of the human race as he most fears will be saved, in order that their soul may die with their body." "You think then that the souls of such persons die," said I. "My son, they die," replied the Count. "And are not condemned to tortures? I think then that they get off very cheaply, and that their punishment is very slight for such a crime as renouncing their baptism and despising the death of the Lord." "Do you think it a light punishment," replied the Count, "to enter into the dark abyss of nothingness? Know, that that is worse than to be condemned to tortures,—that there is a portion of mercy in the retribution which God exercises against sinners in hades,—and that it is of his grace that the fire does not consume those whom it burns.* Nothingness is a greater calamity than all these sufferings, and this is what the sages preach to the gnomes when they assemble them together to inform them what a mistake they make in choosing death rather than immortality, and nonentity in preference to a blessed eternity, which they might possess if they would ally themselves to the human race without requiring from them these profane renunciations. Some of them believe us, and we per-

* It must be admitted that the system of the Count is here somewhat contradictory; for a little before he had represented annihilation, by means of an alliance with a sylphide, as one of the privileges of those men who had been predestined to misery in a future state.

mit them to marry our ladies." "You preach sermons then to these subterranean people?" said I. "You evangelize them?" "Why not?" he replied. "Our mission is to teach them as well as the inhabitants of the fire, the air, and the water; and philosophic charity diffuses itself indifferently over all the children of God. As these people are more intelligent and enlightened than the generality of men, they are more docile and capable of discipline, and they listen to divine truth with a respect that is truly edifying." "I should think it would be extremely edifying," said I with a laugh, "to see a cabalist in a pulpit delivering a homily to those gentlemen." "You can enjoy that satisfaction, my son, whenever you will," said the Count; "if you choose, I will assemble them this evening, and preach a sermon to them at midnight." "At midnight?" cried I. "I have always heard that that was the time of the devil's Sabbath." The Count began to laugh. "You put me in mind of the innumerable fooleries," said he, "which the demonographies relate about this Sabbath. The devil, my son, has no power to sport in that way with the human race, or to make covenants with them, much less to compel them to worship him. What has given rise to the common opinion on this subject is this. The sages, as I have told you, from time to time assemble together the inhabitants of the elements to give them moral instruction and to preach to them on the mysteries of religion. On these occasions it generally happens that some gnome is reclaimed from the error of his ways, is made to understand the horrors of annihilation, and thus consents to be made immortal. We give him a lady for his wife; the marriage is celebrated on the spot, and the nuptial festivities are honored with the rejoicing that is due to the importance of such a conquest. This is the origin of those dances, and cries of joy, which Aristotle says had been heard in islands where no person was to be seen. The great Orpheus was the first who convoked these subterraneous people. At his first preachment, Sabasius, the most ancient of the gnomes, was immortalized; and it is from this Sabasius that the assemblages of this kind took their name, for as long as he lived the sages always addressed their discourse to him, as you may see in the hymns of Orpheus.

Ignorant people have taken occasion to confuse this subject extremely, to invent a thousand impertinences about it, and traduce a convocation which we hold only for the honor and glory of the Supreme Being."

The Count took leave of the Abbé, to think over the heads of the discourse which he intended to pronounce that evening to the gnomes. The next day he shows him a copy of it as he had delivered it. "*Il est merveilleux!*" exclaims the Abbé. He promised to lay it before the public, together with other conversations which he had held with this extraordinary personage. The promised volume, however, never appeared. It is odd enough, by the by, that the volume which we have just been speaking of, opens with an announcement of the death of Comte de Gabalis by apoplexy. "Ill-natured people," says the author, "will not hesitate to say that this is the fate which generally awaits those who make a bad use of the secrets of the sages, and that ever since the beatified Raymond Sully pronounced sentence upon such persons in his will, an angel has never been wanting as executioner to wring the necks of all those who indiscreetly reveal the mysteries of philosophy." It would seem from the anecdote which we have related above, that something like the catastrophe which was thus jestingly assigned to the fictitious Count, speedily overtook the Abbé de Villars himself.

THE LEGAL RIGHTS OF WOMAN: Being remarks in favor of a Legislative creation of independence of property in Married Life, and allowing the Elective Franchise to both sexes. By a member of the Society of Friends. Pamphlet. pp. 40. 1848.

THE political philosophy of this age appears to us to be characterized rather by sensibility in the benevolent ends which it proposes, than by wisdom in the means which it employs for arriving at them. Its capital fault is, that it legislates *directly* to its objects, in matters in which direct legislation, by human power, is impotent; instead of studying the laws which Nature, or rather, a fore-planning, creative Providence has given to the social relations of humanity, and through them, *mediately*, and often remotely producing the results which it sees to be desirable, or rather so arranging the subjects to be influenced, according to the laws of nature, that the inherent forces in man's constitution shall themselves work out the best effects which Providence has permitted them to reach. In political subjects, man has yet to learn the lesson of his own utter impotency, and till then, he will never know the secret of his boundless, his magnificent capacity to control. In material science this discovery has been made, and it is the origin of the sublime mastery which human intelligence has acquired in physics. Bacon, the inspired of intellect—the poet and the prophet of the truth of things sensible—ascertained that the extent of man's power over the outward world is to change the relative distances in space, of material bodies, and that all the rest is wrought out by nature herself; and this revelation, by leading all science to investigate the laws of that all-operating nature, and all art to act in subordination to them, exalted man into a higher order of beings, gave the continuing energies of creation to him in commission, and in regard to visible existence, might not irreverently be said to have put all things under his feet. That there are such fixed laws in the moral world, however difficult fully to be discovered, has been felt with the fervor of inspiration, though dimly seen, by some great master-spirits of social science, such as Vico and Burke; but has never been dreamt of by that insane metaphysical philosophy which rules the popular legislation of this country, and which, in the last century, justly moved the statesman of Beaconsfield, intellectually, to the intensest contempt, and morally to a mingled disgust, detestation and terror. That woman, in the relation of married life, as that relation has existed hitherto, is to some extent necessarily exposed to hardships and sufferings, and that, according to the very principle of that relation, her happiness is to a fearful extent dependent upon her husband, is a fact of universal experience. But what will you do—since it is agreed that the world is so imperfect that unless we mend it thoroughly, we shall be disgraced by being seen abroad in it? The metaphysical philosophy will remedy the so-called evil by abolishing the principle of the common law which merges the existence of the wife, legally, in that of the husband, and by giving her an independent position and plenary rights. The maxim of the common law, in our opinion, was not a theory or plan contrived by men for disposing of a subject over which they had unlimited control, but was meant to be an expression of the truth of facts as they exist in life, and an accommodation of the action of human law to the state of things as is established by the divine law; not the proclamation of that which ought to be, but the recognition of that which is. Now this popular system, which promises by convulsing to reform the world, recasts the whole relation, and brings the parties together on the footing of independent partners in the trade and business of life, capable of determining and prescribing the terms and conditions of the union, according to their sovereign will. We do not think thus of marriage. We are of opinion that it is a state entirely of natural relation, and not of voluntary human contrivance; that it results, in a certain definite form, from instincts and tendencies in man, delicate and impalpable, yet irresistible and eternal: and that the relative position of the parties, as a resultant from natural and organic causes, is fixed as absolutely and unchangeably as the mutual dependency of parts of the organization of an individual being. From all these appointments and provisions established in the natures of things, the great law results, that the wife and the husband become one in marriage, neither strictly being subordinated to the other, but both being merged into the unity of a new moral existence. This transformation of persons is not notional and fictitious; it is a divine reality. Who does not remember, and who did not admire, the beautiful lecture of Mr. Dana upon "Woman?" The intellectual merit of that discourse consisted in apprehending,—as the central germ of truth upon the subject, and in developing through its manifold branchings,—the law of the inherent moral difference of the sexes. According to this fine conception, characters, thoughts, passions, sentiments, and all things within, have their sexes. The nature, sphere and duty of the several parties stand together in a relation of beautiful antagonism, one being the complement of the other, in such wise that permanent diversity is the only harmony, and similarity is discord and error. Certainly, the only true education and advancement of woman consist in development according to the organic principle of her moral being; and as that is one of polar oppositeness to man's, her refinement is soiled, her dignity impaired and her power diminished, by every attempt to approximate her to man's character, talents or employments. It is only as woman is thoroughly womanly in her sphere of action, in the subjects of her interest, and in her modes of feeling, that she can enjoy that controlling influence over man, and exert that elevating, purifying and refining action upon society, which is the glory of her sex and the blessedness of the other.

Now the office of human government in the matter is this: to ascertain the normal relation of the parties in married life, as it is constituted by abiding natural causes, and, in conformity with that relation, to regulate those things over which it has control, in such a way as to preserve that relation always from violation and disturbance. But how can there be found in distinctness and in independence, an advancement of that comfort, whose very life consists in union and identity? That protection should be given to the wife against the husband's misfortunes, is most proper. It is a protection not more to her than to him; indeed, more to him than to her. It assumes, acknowledges, and maintains their essential unity. And special cases may suggest themselves where, by those forms of legal settlements, perfectly familiar to us all, special evils should be controlled. But why as an organic law should there be sought in protection against *the husband*, a promotion of her honor and true dignity whose only safety is through him and in him? In attempting to get her happiness, in that relation, free from some of the accidents which undoubtedly do attend it, you destroy the very being of that happiness, because you interfere with the conditions of its existence. Now, if the common law neglected some matters of detail, in relation to property, which might have been more wisely regulated, it always received and maintained the great principle of moral and social unity in married life: the modern system, in endeavoring to prevent certain possible, but after all, very raic, evils of detail, fatally wounds the essential and true principle. A system of society reconstructed upon the plan of this metaphysical school of politics—which is not a new school, and in advance of the times, but is the exploded folly of all the schools, thrown behind it by the sense and practice of every age—would be in opposition to all the laws of Providence, and would be as enduring and effective as an engine whose construction was in direct antagonism to the laws of mechanics. Let no legislator attempt to be more powerful than Nature, or wiser than Truth, or better than God.

TRIPPINGS IN AUTHOR-LAND. By FANNY FORESTER.

[*Extract from the Author's Diary.* "January 1, 1846. I went this morning to St. Peter's Church; afterwards paid some visits; Mr. Chauncey, my uncle, Miss Fanny Forester. This last one, whose true name is the unimpressive one of *Chubbuck*, is a person of very considerable interest. Her talent, as a writer of light fictions, I rate highly. There is a delicacy and genuineness in her character which render her quite engaging in social intercourse. While we were talking about something, she suddenly cried out, 'Oh, Mr. Wallace, I must show you a notice of my book,' and forthwith ran up stairs and brought down a newspaper containing an extract from 'The Gospel Messenger,' in which her 'Trippings in Author-land,' were spoken of with the most vulgar, stupid and brutal contempt. She laughed, but really, I believe, was deeply wounded. If I can find any proper place I will cuff this reverend booby over the mazard, in the way that his insolent coarseness deserves."]

THE future historian of letters will surely note, as a distinction of these times, the remarkable and great extent to which every department of literary effort, during thirty years past, has been illustrated and adorned by feminine talents. The earlier records instances of *learned* ladies—a very respectable guild, but not the less, occasionally, a little tedious, for being at all times vehemently dignified in manner and topics; and some examples of an extremely opposite class of performers, chiefly in fiction and the drama, who by extravagance of invention and freedom of allusions, sought to supply the absence of that delicacy, with whose departure from female sentiment, every true excellence takes its eternal leave. It was about the beginning of this century that, for the first time in the annals of any nation, a first-rate reputation, upon a great scale, in the highest regions of intellectual exertion, was deserved and obtained by one of the gentler sex. Then, for the first time, the mind of Europe bowed and yielded, not with respect only, but with awe and wonder, to the leading vigor, the brilliant energy, and copious fervor of a woman's understanding; for Madame De Stael is as much an *authority* in the philosophy of politics, and of its kindred social concerns, as she is an idol and a worship in the more glittering scenes of imaginative art. Nor was she a luminary with whose going down the day is ended; but rather was a sort of Hesperus, to lead in a beaming throng, in whose various lustre the rays still separately shine, of that brightness whose solid and thick splendors will perhaps never again be admired in union, as they were admired in her. At this moment, fully one-half of those who hold the popular attention in England, are of that sex whose acknowledged abilities we had formerly been wont to find displayed by conversation rather than by the pen. In this country, probably, the proportion is still larger. In every direction, on every class of subjects, in every kind of style, we meet with that sparkling freshness of sentiment, that animated ease, and interest without effort, that innate justness of reflection and fine preciseness of apprehension which are the special and uncommunicable charms of feminine genius. Amongst all this bright company of native authoresses, there is none whose displays we always follow with a more gratified interest, or of whose future distinction we take a more confident omen, than the lady who relunctantly "suffers herself to be desired" under the name of Fanny Forester.

She possesses many talents; and an assemblage of lesser accomplishments, which, in her, seem to be so genuine and instinctive that they might almost be mistaken for natural talents. The movements of her mind have a quiet, soft brightness, that seems to shine for itself rather than for others, and to be spontaneous, more than exerted; glowing, apparently, without design, and almost in despite of consciousness. Her powers of reasoning are strong; her feelings prompt and abounding; her sense of humor, quick and various—but these, and other faculties, are subordinated, in their exercise, to a *delicacy* of character and taste, ethereal almost in sensibility, and timorous, even painfully, of every offence against refinement—the deepest, surest fascination that can belong to a woman; beautiful in the errors it may lead to, and most enchanting, perhaps, when it is most in excess; whose power is as enduring as the pleasure which it imparts is pure and exquisite. But there are secondary qualities, going to the manner, rather than to the nature or degree of that capacity which we desire to define as constituting a great and splendid faculty in this gentle and modest person. We regard her as possessing talents for *narrative* of a very high and rare order—talents which place her in the front rank of writers of domestic fiction on either side of the water.

All that is comprehended in the assertion of this power, might not, perhaps, be very easily or briefly defined. "It is difficult," says Horace Walpole, "in English, *to relate,* without falling too low, or rising too high; a fault obviously occasioned by the little care taken to speak pure language in common conversation." The defect, however, lies far deeper than this; and even so far as it is an affair of style, the analysis of the difficulty will be found, as all other matters of style are, only among the very elements of mental and moral speculation. A fiction of familiar life, perfectly executed, appears to involve the harmonious operation of a greater number of diversified powers than any other kind of literary effort whatever, more even than the drama: an opinion that will hardly be deemed extravagant, if we are considered right in thinking that the task was scarcely ever accomplished with absolute felicity, except by Sir Walter Scott, and Miss Austen. To develop a scene by means of all its characteristic particulars—to unfold an action by the description of those circumstances of it that would be present to the consciousness of any one who was a partaker in it, and which, in an æsthetic point of view, may be said to constitute the *identity* of the transaction—this is the faculty we are alluding to; which we surely cannot err in deeming uncommon in its kind and exalted in its comparative value. To note all the elements of a scene—to select and order them—to choose among the indefinite number of methods—direct or associative—descriptive, suggestive, or inferential—by which notions may be conveyed to the reader—to play at once, and harmoniously, upon the mind, the fancy and the feelings, for the production of one rich symphony of imaginative effect—this, truly, might be thought to be even beyond all attainment. Indeed, the problem is beyond intellectual solution, and can be accomplished only by genius; using intellect for the measure of that power within us which analyzes, and acts because it understands, and giving the name of genius to that part of our understanding which apprehends rationally beyond where it can analyze, and moves correctly from an instinct of right, and an involuntary and natural sympathy with truth and beauty. But the more familiar and acquired capacities which this divine faculty may use as its instruments for the construction of moral fictions, will be found to exhaust the farthest reach of mental accomplishment. An originative and brilliant fancy—a nice perception—a vigorous ideality—sense, tact, and judgment—these, in their best conditions, are of constant requirement; but the finest effects can be imparted to a tale of incidents, only by that correct acquaintance with character, in its individual varieties, and with human nature at large, to which much experience and much reflection must have contributed.

Such masterly touches as these it is—partaking of a nature of greatness—which impart to the narratives of this engaging person their rare effectiveness.

We are struck with the marked and increasing superiority of the later compositions of this lady over her earlier ones. The capacity to improve is one of the most certain marks of the higher order of minds; and we are accustomed, in everything, to look for it, as a distinguishing test of a real and abiding power in opposition to the mere talent to flash and dazzle. "The Bank Note," which is one of her latest productions, is contrived and conducted with genuine ability; it is a successful attempt to portray a very common, but very complext, puzzling character, kindred in some respects to the "Chloe" of the poet, and to impart interest to a train of occurrences extremely simple and ordinary, but of deep moral interest. We are desirous to see the fine and varied faculties which this lady unquestionably possesses, executed upon some extensive and sustained work of fiction, upon which all her powers may be fully concentrated and tasked. She lingers below her destiny in being contented with even the greatest popularity; the native and true atmosphere of her renown is in the regions of fame.

REMARKS ON THE PAST, and its Legacies to American Society. "Westward the course of Empire takes its way." By J. D. NOURSE, Louisville, Ky.

WE have rarely been surprised into the pleasure of so high an admiration as has been inspired by the perusal of this work. We have been debtors to it for one of the rarest and most intimate gratifications that we ever experience;—that of having all our intellectual and moral faculties thoroughly *breathed* by a vigorous thinker—of wrestling with a great mind, in generous contest, until it gives us the blessing of its inspiration. Mr. Nourse's little volume has stirred the depths of our nature with a genial agitation of pleasure and improvement; and if the tumult of admiration which it has left behind should disturb our discrimination of the qualities which have contributed to our enjoyment, or our estimate of the exact comparative value of the work as a contribution to philosophy, our very inability or indisposition to distinguish or decide with judicial coldness, will be the most genuine evidence and measure of a peculiar and superior excellence.

It gives us satisfaction to send to Mr. Nourse, across the interval of half a continent, the greeting of our appreciation and respect; and we shall feel that we perform the least questionable duty of our office, in diffusing the reputation of one who has cultivated, with such ability, that noble literary art, which, after the ignoble contests of gain have been forgotten, and the frivolities of fashionable extravagance have perished, remains forever the pride, and boast, and ornament of a nation.

Mr. Nourse not only belongs to the ranks of genius, but is entitled to take his place in that higher order of creative minds, in which the capacity of great, sustained, and just thought coexists with the glow of fancy and the fire of passion. That mental energy which develops itself into luxuriant forms of beauty, is apt to turn upon a centre within itself, and its conceptions have a personal and individuated character:—for those high, and combined, and continuing processes of ratiocination, by which the avenues of wisdom are opened, and speculation is sent along the line of abstract and essential truth, we commonly look to those severer minds in which a devotion to science has absorbed the intellectual essence which else would have flowered into poetic illustration. When these two characters are brought into union—when we meet with an inspiration so abounding, and a literary accomplishment so complete and harmonious, that while Thought is moving onward in its high and grand orbit of philosophic reason, Imagination is circling its progress with the graces of art, and the ardors of emotion are breathing before it—we recognize the first class of great and comprehensive intelligences. To reduce a subject into the exact form of science, and then to charge this form with the vital warmth and color of poetry, is to accomplish the loftiest task of genius, and to exhibit the richest forces of human understanding. Nothing gives us a more essential delight, than to meet with an author whose production addresses our *whole* nature at once, and while it exercises and impresses our intellect, kindles our feelings and enchants our fancy.

The Philosophy of History—under that majestic conception in which it has presented itself to the most profound and comprehensive thinkers of modern Europe as the grand *ensemble* of the laws, and tendencies, and influences, and characteristics, and circumstances of human development, as exhibited in the past—is the dignified theme which the author has chosen for the display of his powers of analysis and illustration. It is the great subject of study in this age; and worthy to engage every interest and faculty of cultivated minds. In his general manner of apprehending the subject, and in the fundamental principles from which he takes his departure, Mr. Nourse is fairly up to the level of the foremost inquirers in this science in Europe. He has thoroughly appreciated their teachings, and appropriated what is valuable in them. But he brings to the work powers capable of advancing the march of philosophy, and shedding light over many obscure parts of the field. We have met with many views of entire originality; wherever we find an opinion expressed upon any incidental subject, it is marked by the discrimination and strength of a powerful mind: and when suggestions from the writings of others have been adopted, they are recast in the depths of an ardent reflection, and given forth with fresh beauty, and in a new form.

We give a few observations, conceived in a spirit of wise and high-toned philosophy, explaining the title of the work, and showing the noble practical interest towards which the inquiry tends:

"Contempt for the past, especially in relation to *civil* concerns, is an error to which, from obvious causes, American society is peculiarly exposed, and which it therefore becomes the duty of the American writer to combat. We are in little danger of falling into that opposite extreme, which in Europe takes the form of high conservatism, and with desperate perverseness throws itself into direct opposition to the resistless tendencies of modern society. From the nature of the case, toryism can never take deep root in American soil, and it is idle to aim our blows at an imaginary foe, while a real and portentous tendency threatens the extinction of all reverence for the past, and with it all that ennobling class of emotions, which are allied to such reverence as their parent stock. * * * Some are absurd enough to contend for what they call an American education, which shall cut us off from the past, and cancel all our obligations to the old world. But no nation ever became great by this process, nor ever will. We must recollect that if we can see a little further than those who have gone before us, we stand upon a mental pyramid piled up by the labors of countless generations; that it is our business to carry it still farther towards heaven, not to look down with scorn upon the great works of our predecessors, or become little in the contemplation of our own greatness. Other nations may still have remnants of old abuses to demolish; *our* task is not to destroy, but to preserve and build up. We have nothing to spare of the legacies of the past. * * * The human mind can entertain but one passion at a time, sufficiently overruling and intense to effect great changes in society; and revolutionary ardor has been so busy with the work of demolition, that it is not wonderful that many should turn their backs upon the past, forgetful of its greatness, and of their obligations to it, and look forward to the future with boundless hopes and chimerical schemes for the radical regeneration of society. Yet there is nothing more certain, than that no moral or political organization, wholly severed from the past, can live. We may repair dilapidated institutions, from time to time, and adapt them to the new exigencies of society; but we must preserve the old foundations, the great *principles*, or our structure will not stand the test of time and experience. It is the order of Providence, that the new should be evolved from the old in such a manner, that the life and soul of one should be gradually transfused into the other. Great revolutions may seem to interrupt this order for a time, but after the earthquake has rolled away, the stream resumes its former channel, only clearer, broader, freer from obstructions than before."

Mr. Nourse belongs to that young and glorious school of nature and freedom, which has succeeded to the perverse and malignant skepticism of the last age. His mind seems to be thoroughly delivered from the wretched metaphysics which enslaved the politics and morals of the day just gone by; those narrowing prejudices of parties, sects and schools, which prevailed so generally as to suggest to an observer, that thought, instead of being the freest and boldest thing in the universe, is the most enfettered and cowardly. The disposition to believe—the tendency to recognize a wisdom in the movements of the world at large—a readiness to submit individual thought to the higher and grander sagacity that dwells in society, and is evolved by experience—the habitudes of sympathy, and love, and reverence —which have ever been the characteristics of the great, guiding spirits of the race—of Plato, Cicero, Bacon and Burke—are the fine attributes of this new, vigorous class of thinkers,—among the foremost of whom we confidently place the author of the present volume. He has perceived and explored the characteristics of that higher, broader, and deeper sense that breathes from the providential development of nations, and his pen moves with the energy of consciousness and genuine sense. The West may well be proud of a man whom the East would gladly select as a representative to Europe of what America can do in philosophy.

The most important element in modern civilization, according to Mr. Nourse, is Christianity: and the following remarks in relation to the nature of the *Evidences* of Christianity are conceived in the spirit of a profound philosophy; worthy of the mind of Butler. After removing some of the metaphysical objections to miracles, he proceeds:—

"But the truth is, that much more importance has been attached to the argument from miracles than it deserves. The miracles ascribed to Christ and his apostles, however conclusive to those who witnessed them, are no evidence to us, until *by other means*, we have established the truth of the writings which record them—that is to say, until we have proved all that we wish to prove. They cannot weigh a feather with any clear-headed inquirer, who does not find in Christianity a supply of his own moral wants, the proper and wholesome food of his own spiritual nature, and the source of countless blessings to society. A syllogism may suffice for a single barren proposition; a vast system of life-giving truth, like Christianity, draws to its support a variety of independent, but mutually corrobating testimonies. Combining the early monuments of Christianity, and the evidence which may be drawn from the history of the Christian civilization, with those convictions that spring up in every healthy soul, when its higher faculties are roused into activity, we have an edifice which may defy the assaults of skeptical philosophy.

"One mind will attach greater weight to one portion of this converging evidence; another to another, according to mental constitution, or early habits of thinking. It is probable that, for the majority of enlightened believers at the present day, the keystone of the arch which spans the gulf between earth and heaven, is that sort of persuasion in which deep feeling has a much larger share than cold logic.

"The most indubitable miracle of early Christianity was the heroic self-devotion of its first propagators. The Apostle of the Gentiles, of all mere men the sublimest example of moral heroism, travelled from place to place, supporting himself and his companions by the labor of his own hands, and preaching the truth without fee or reward; well assured, that in whatever city he entered, bonds and afflictions awaited him. He fought with wild beasts at Ephesus; he braved the cruelty of the Pagans and the hatred of his own countrymen; he stood undazzled amid the classic glories of Athens and the wonders of Grecian art, and proclaimed the new doctrine, unmoved by the sneers of the gayest, the most refined, the most intellectual people on earth. Dragged in chains before the proconsuls of Asia, he made them tremble on their judgment-seats: he planted the cross upon the seven hills, at the very gates of the vast palaces of those terrible Cæsars, who made the world tremble from the borders of Ethiopia to the shores of the German Ocean; and crowned his glorious life by a painful death amidst the ferocious sports of the amphitheatre!"

The function of the olden nations, in Mr. Nourse's view, was to prepare the race for the introduction and diffusion of Christianity. "To the Hebrews," he considers, "was allotted the custody of moral and religious truth; to the Greeks, the empire of reason and imagination; to the iron Romans, the power of arms, by which, with their own civil institutions, and the arts, literature and religion of the other two nations, they were to lay a broad and deep foundation for the Christian civilization. Upon that foundation, the free Germans were to build the modern world." Each of these departments of partial civilization is traced with great interest and beauty in the first chapter of the work, till they come together at the Christian era. As an illustration of the vivid and various sympathy of the author's mind, which combines the love and power of art with the insight of philosophic judgment, and recognizes the creative energy of imagination and sentiment as permanent and indispensable parts of our being, both individually and socially, we extract passages relating to the dignity of Poetry, the poetical capacities of real life, and the artistic resources of the present time:

"It is a remarkable fact, that in the earliest periods of civilization, in the robust and fervid youth of great nations, Poetry, that divine melody of thought and words, is always the first language of the newly awakened intellect. As civilization advances, and the cold abstractions of science take the life-like creations of the imagination, Poetry withdraws more and more from the domain of the understanding. But though a high state of intellectual cultivation more clearly defines the respective boundaries of science and poetry, it is by no means necessarily unfavorable to the latter, as many have supposed. Poetry, more and more hemmed in by reality, finds in reality new and inexhaustible resources.

"The vulgar and trivial details of actual life are apt to blunt our perceptions of its greatness. The bright dreams of youth, and the thoughtful sadness of maturer years; the deep communings of the soul with nature and with God; the fond loyalty which cherishes the memories of heroes and great benefactors of mankind; self-sacrificing patriotism which attaches to the idea of country an infinite import, and sacred obligations; rapt devotion, whether it recognize the Divine Presence in the Gothic Cathedral, amid the forest aisles, or on the sounding sea-shore;—what are all these things, but the rising undulations of that deepest part of our mysterious nature, in which are the fountains of poetry and religion?

"If we imagine a rational creature, upon a level with the highest of our species, to reach the maturity of his powers in another state of being, and then to have all his perceptions and sensibilities suddenly opened upon this world, in any of its brightest or most fearful aspects, what deep thoughts, what childish wonder, love or awe would fill his whole soul! The poetical temperament preserves in a greater or less degree this child-like freshness, which custom withers in other men; and by mysterious affinities, it draws to itself the poetry of life and nature from the alloy of commonplace ingredients. It is unquestionably the greatest triumph of art to idealize the present; for distance either in time or space renders the materials of poetry more pliant. Through the same mists that conceal from us the vulgar and trivial details, the grander features of the scene loom up into shapes of beauty or terror.

"Consciously or unconsciously, the poetical temperament links every thing finite and perishable with the infinite and imperishable, and our little life here with the boundless and everlasting existence that awaits us. Whatever form poetry may take, and whatever may be the nature of the materials which it draws from the actual world, its essential inspiration is the ineradicable desire of the human soul, for a wider, a more beautiful, a more powerful existence than the present.

"When the poet is destitute of religious faith, the mighty cravings of his soul, and a vivid sense of the frightful discrepancy between the aspirations and the supposed destiny of man, may eat into his heart, tear asunder his whole nature, and fever it into despair, madness, or suicide. A happier creed may overarch life with the rainbow of hope, and pour over nature the light of eternity. In either case, the poet filled with the ideal, and with that infinite love and awe which only the ideal can inspire, becomes the unconscious prophet of deeper and mightier truths than the boasted deductions of science. Even in science, no great thing was ever done by a man who had not a spice of poetry in him. As will appear more fully in the progress of our inquiry, those branches of art and literature which strive to embody the aspirations of man in forms of ideal beauty or power, have performed a very important part in human culture.

"Indeed, the history of Christianity itself, including the life and death of its Divine Founder, the moral heroism of its martyrs and apostles, and the long warfare which it has waged against ignorance, sin and misery, is a mighty epic, of which God is the author; and the refinements of chivalry, the triumphs of art, and the glories of science, are the episodes. Religion has directly or indirectly been the source of that poetry of action, which has shed a never-dying glory over the great and stirring periods of modern history. It is obvious that we use the term Poetry in its general sense of passionate recognition of all beautiful, glorious, and sublime things, manifested, not only in verse, painting, sculpture, architecture, but anything which ennobles man, embellishes life, or refines society, provided it can be embodied in sensible forms, or associated with images more or less distinct. Not only the greatest works of art, but the finest traits and noblest triumphs of civilization, are manifestations of that divine and perennial spirit of Poetry, without which life would be a poor, despicable round of sordid cares and animal gratifications."

A passage which occurs in the writer's appreciation of the peculiar character of Roman civilization, is profound and just:

"He who sees no Divinity in the affairs of men, who recognizes no Providential guidance of nations, will refer the peculiar manifestations of a people to organization, to institutions, to mere external and mechanical causes. But among a people who enjoy any considerable share of freedom, institutions and other external circumstances are rather the effects than the causes of national peculiarities. The truth lies in the middle, between the opposite extremes of the mechanical and dynamical theories, or rather is made up of both. Individual and national peculiarities are the compound results of inscrutable impulses arising in the mysterious depths of spiritual being, and of internal circumstances, acting and reacting in such a manner, that it is impossible to assign to each class of causes their intuitive shares in the product."

His conception of the grand elements and laws by whose action history is evolved, is marked by the finest strength, and fearlessness, and truth.

"Why the Omnipotent," he remarks, "has permitted the original perfection of his own workmanship to be overthrown, and what is the nature of that disturbing force which has brought *discord*, and with it death and sorrow, into the world, are questions which must return upon the thinking minds of each successive generation, in all their original perplexity, because they admit of no satisfactory answer in the present state of being. So far as the Divine counsels can be deciphered from the facts of history, nothing is clearer than that man was not destined for the tame and regular manifestation of a few genial impulses held in perfect equilibrium by the limiting properties of his nature, but rather for a vast, tempestuous existence, resulting from the *polarity* of powerful passions and antagonistic tendencies. Everywhere, in the physical and moral world, we find strife and antagonism, inordinate activity of forces followed by the reaction of others which had been for a time repressed."

In a similar spirit is a passage about the Crusades introductory to an acute and able summary of the benefits which they conferred on European society. It is as fine a specimen of fearless thought and noble feeling as we recollect to have met with:

"Chivalry reached its perfection when to the poetry of love it added that poetry of devotion which gave rise to the Crusades. What avail the endless tirades upon the folly and absurdity of the Crusades? Are the worship of gold, the enterprises of commercial ambition, the lust of territorial aggrandizement, which now embroil nations, a whit more respectable than the poetical devotion which carried the chivalry of Europe to the sepulchre of Christ? Why suffer the enterprises of sordid and earth-born selfishness to pass with perhaps a gentle expression of disapprobation, and exhaust the vocabulary of contempt upon the offspring of great and generous emotions? No doubt, that inundation of fiery valor which Europe poured upon Asia, was turbid enough with profligacy seeking to expiate a life of guilt by a martial pilgrimage to the cradle of religion, and with vague hopes of reckless adventurers to repair their fortunes and gratify their passions in the opulent and voluptuous East. What of all that? Similar facts may be affirmed of every large body of men that ever assembled on earth; the solemn homilies of conscientious and respectable persons upon the folly and wickedness of others, are to the last degree wearisome and unprofitable. It is not in this manner that the historical philosopher contemplates the great movements of society. The Crusaders were not so foolish; and those wars have not been so barren of beneficial results as some short-sighted persons imagine.

"It is difficult to obtain a clear insight into the thoughts and feelings of those 'fervent days of old,' when religious faith, instead of being a moral probability floating in a medium of metaphysical abstraction, and *patronized* by politicians as an useful auxiliary to law in the preservation of social order, was a warm and life-like reality, glowing in the hearts, and living in the daily business of men, and affording the most powerful incentives to action. In modern times, the poetry of devotion has been so much sobered by motives belonging to the present state of being, that it is hard to tell whether the chief sources of our prudential morality are in earth or heaven. Yet there is no reason why the self-complacent shrewdness of this rather barren and prosaic age of transition, should be particularly lavish of pity or contempt upon half-enlightened, but still glorious, manifestations of those high properties of our nature, which distinguish us from the beasts that perish. The chivalric, like the heroic ages, exhibit striking contrasts of strong lights and deep shadows. The conduct of men who are guided by cool calculations of profit and loss, will in general have an even tenor, seldom sinking into crime, seldom rising into heroic virtue. But ages of faith, which are also ages of fervent and overmastering impulses, are productive of splendid virtues and dreadful crimes, and show many examples of those powerful but irregular natures which are great alike in their evil and their good. The Crusades were an universal sifting and shaking up of the chaotic elements of society. To contemporaries they may have appeared, as the French Revolution did to persons now living, an aimless tempest of human passions. In such cases we observe nothing at first but the eddying of hosts, the shock of arms, the clouds of dust, and garments rolled in blood. But when the uproar has ceased, and the clouds have rolled away, a new world is disclosed, and we find that many time-honored abuses, old institutions and inveterate prejudices have passed away forever."

This is the spirit and the power in which great historical inquiries should be approached.

In the chapter entitled "Night and Morning," Mr. Nourse traces with consummate ingenuity and ability, the progressive evolution of that various and complicated social system which is now illustrated in Europe. Starting from the period when, to use his own striking language, "that free and ethereal essence, which had hitherto bound Christian societies together, warming each heart with fire from heaven, began to *crystalize* into a *church*, with an organization strong enough to withstand the storms that were about to burst upon the empire, and shelter from their fury some remnants of ancient civilization," he proceeds to appreciate the effect of each great occurrence in the next fifteen hundred years, in developing those institutions and that liberty which now form the chracteristics of Europe.

We must conclude our extracts at present by a few sentences respecting thė influence of woman during the middle ages, in educating and refining society.

"The remarks in our former discourse, in relation to the unobtrusiveness of the greatest and most durable power, apply with peculiar force to the contributions of woman to the progress of society. Even philosophic historians have been far from doing justice to female influence, because from the nature of the case, their attention is chiefly devoted to the intrigues of courts, the movements of armies, the doings of politicians, the bubbles and commotions of the surface of society. But kings, heroes, statesmen, were all children once; and no one need be told that in the quiet shades of domestic life we must look for the springs of that mighty stream which bears upon its troubled surface, warriors and statesmen, courts and armies, republics and dynasties, and all the multiform institutions and transactions of civil society.

"The noblest civilization tends to bring the two sexes nearer together in regard to their moral and intellectual character. The highest order of genius has been justly said to combine the peculiarities of both sexes; the vigorous understanding, the force of imagination, the energy of will, that distinguish the one, with the quick perception, the intuitive tact, the tenderness and sensibility of the other. . . Aside from speculation, the peculiar properties of woman's moral and intellectual structure, are precisely such as are adapted, whenever her social position commands respect, and favors the development of her powers, to smooth the asperities of man, to refine and elevate his sentiments, and to entwine his rugged strength with the foliage and flowers of tenderness and fancy. There is nothing which so calls into action the finest feelings of his nature, as the sense of being leaned upon, aud being looked up to as a guardian, by a being so graceful in her timidity, so beautiful in her helplessness, provided her virtue commands his respect; for, if she be not pure, if she revere not herself, she may have the protection, but never the sincere homage, of chivalry; and the elegance which she diffuses over society, only renders vice more attractive by divesting it of its grossness."

Extracts of this kind, however, convey no just notion of the great powers of expanded and sustained thought which this author exhibits; but his exuberance of creative vigor frequently overflows into rich forms of beautiful conception, as pure and glittering as amber.

LITERARY PORTRAITS.

GEORGE P. MORRIS.

THE distinction with which the name of General Morris is now associated in a permanent connection with what is least factitious or fugitive in American Art, is admitted and known; but the class of young men of letters in this country, at present, can hardly appreciate the extent to which they, and the profession to which they belong, are indebted to his animated exertions, his varied talents, his admirable resources of temper, during a period of twenty years, and at a time when the character of American litertature, both at home and abroad, was yet to be formed. The first great service which the literary taste of this country received, was rendered by Dennie; a remarkable man; qualified by nature and attainments to be a leader in new circumstances; fit to take part in the formation of a national literature; as a vindicator of independence in thought, able to establish freedom without disturbing the obligations of law; as a conservative in taste, skilful to keep the tone of the great models with which his studies were familiar, without copying their style; by both capacities successful in developing the one, unchangeable spirit of Art, under a new form and with new effects. In this office of field-marshal of our native forces, General Morris succeeded him under increased advantages, in some respects with higher powers, in a different, and certainly a vastly more extended sphere of influence. The manifold and lasting benefits which, as Editor of "The Mirror," Mr. Morris conferred on art and artists of every kind, by his tact, his liberality, the superiority of his judgment, and the vigor of his abilities;

by the perseverance and address with which he disciplined a corps of youthful writers in the presence of a constant and heavy fire from the batteries of foreign criticism; by the rare combination, so valuable in dealing with the numerous aspirants in authorship with whom his position brought him in contact, of a quick, true eye to discern in the modesty of some nameless manuscript the future promises of a power hardly yet conscious of itself, a discretion to guide by sound advice, and a generosity to aid with the most important kind of assistance; the fine and open temper which his example tended to inspire into the relations of literary men with one another throughout the land; and more than all, perhaps, by the harmony and union, of such inappreciable value, especially in the beginning of national effort, between the several sister arts of writing, music, painting and dramatic exhibition, which the singular variety and discursiveness of his intellectual sympathies led him constantly to maintain and vindicate; these, in the multiplicity of their operation, and the full power of their joint effect, can be perfectly understood only by those who possessed a contemporaneous knowledge of the circumstances, and who, remembering the state of things at the commencement of the period alluded to, and observing what existed at the end of it, are able to look back over the whole interval, and see to what influences and what persons the extraordinary change which has taken place, is to be referred. If, at this moment, the literary genius of America, renewed in youth, and quivering like the eagle's limbs with excess of vigor, seems about to make a new flight, from a higher vantage-ground, into loftier depths of airy distance, the capacity to take that flight must, to a great degree, be ascribed to those two persons whom we have named; without whose services the brighter era which appears now to be dawning, might yet be distant and doubtful.

Besides these particulars of past effort, which ought to make his countrymen love the reputation of the subject of this notice, we regret that our limits forbid us to speak at large of those more intimate qualities of personal value, which, in our judgment, form the genuine lustre of one who, admirable for other attainments, is to be imitated in these.

To us it is an instinctive feeling that a wrong is done to the proper grandeur of our complex nature—that a violence is offered to the higher consciousness of our immortal being,—whenever an intellectual quality is extolled to the neglect of a moral one. Moral excellence is the most real genius; and a temper to cope and calmly baffle the multitudinous assaults of the spiritual enmity of active life, is a talent which outshines all praise of mental endowments. Unhappily, the biography of literary creators affords few occasions in which a feeling of this kind can be indulged and gratified: that sensibility of mental apprehension which is the fame of the author, is usually attended by a susceptibility of passionate impression which is the fate of the man; and earth and sense delight to wreak their destructive vengeances upon the spiritual nature of him, of whose intellectual being they are the slaves and the sport. In the present instance, we are concerned with a character,—*totus, teres, atque rotundus;* which may be looked upon, from every side, with an equal satisfaction. Search the wide world over, and you shall not find among the literary men of any nation, one on whom the dignity of a free and manly spirit sits with a grace more native and familiar,—whose spontaneous sentiments have a truer tone of nobleness,—the course of whose usual feelings is more expanded and honorable,—whose acts, whether common and daily, or deliberate and much-considered, are wont at all times to be more beautifully impressed with those marks of sincerity, of modesty, and of justice, which form the very seal of worth in conduct. Those jealousies, and littlenesses, and envyings, which prey upon the spirits of many men, as the vulture on the heart of the chained Prometheus,—and whose fierce besetment they who *will* be magnanimous, have to fight off, as one drives away the eagles from their prey, with voice and gestures—seem never to assail him. It is the happiness of his nature to have *that* only absolute deliverance from evil which is implied in being rendered insensible to temptation. While the duty which is laid upon us, in this paper, mainly is to open and set forth his poetic praises and claim the laurel for his literary merits; when the crown of song is to be conferred upon him, we shall interpose to beg that the chaplet may be accompanied by some mark, or some inscription which shall declare,

"This is the reward of moral excellence."

For the success of our special purpose, in this notice, which is to consider and make apparent the specific character which belongs to General Morris as a literary artist and a poetic creator, to explain his claims to that title which the common voice of the country has given to him,—of THE SONG-WRITER OF AMERICA—it would have probably been more judicious had we kept out of view the matters of which we have just spoken. It is recorded of a Grecian painter, that having completed the picture of a sleeping nymph, he added on the foreground the figure of a satyr gazing in amazement upon her beauty; but finding that the secondary form attracted universal praise, he erased it, as diverting applause from that which he desired to have regarded as the principal monument of his skill. There is in this anecdote a double wisdom; the world is as little willing to yield to a twofold superiority as it is able to appreciate two distinct objects at once.

In a review of literary reputations, perhaps nothing is fitted to raise more surprise than the obvious inequality in the extent and greatness of the labors to which an equal reward of fame has been allotted. The abounding energy and picturesque variety of Homer are illustrated in eight-and-forty books: the remains of Sappho might be written on the surface of a leaf of the *laurus nobilis*. Yet if the one expands before us with the magnificent extent, the diversified surface, the endless decorations of the earth itself, the other hangs on high, like a lone, clear star—small but intense—flashing upon us through the night of ages, invested with circumstances of divinity not less unquestionable than those that attend the venerable majesty of the Ancient of Song. The rich and roseate light that shines around the name of Mimnermus, is shed from some dozen or twenty lines: the immortality of Tyrtœus rests upon a stanza or two, which have floated to us with their precious freight, over the sea of centuries, and will float on, unsubmergible by all the waves of Time. The soul of Simonides lives to us in a single couplet; but that is very stuff of Eternity, which neither fire will assoil, nor tempests peril, nor the wrath of years impair. The Infinite has no degrees; wherever the world sees in any human spirit the fire of the Everlasting, it bows with equal awe, whether that fire is displayed by only an occasional flash, or by a prolonged and diffusive blaze. There is a certain tone which, hear it when we may, and where we may, we know to be the accent of the gods: and whether its quality be shown in a single utterance, or its volume displayed in a thousand bursts of music, we surround the band of spirits whom we there detect in their mortal disguise, with equal ceremonies of respect and worship, hailing them alike as seraphs of a brighter sphere—sons of the morning. This is natural, and it is reasonable. Genius is not a degree of other qualities, nor is it a particular way or extent of displaying such qualities; it is a faculty by itself; it is a manner, of which we may judge with the same certainty from one exhibition, as from many. The praise of a poet, therefore, is to be determined not by the nature of the work which he undertakes, but by the kind of mastery which he shows; not by the breadth of surface over which he toils, but by the perfectness of the result which he attains. Mr. Wordsworth has vindicated the capacity of the sonnet to be a casket of the richest gems of fame. We have no doubt that the song may give evidence of a genius which shall deserve to be ranked with the constructor of an epic. "Scorn not the *Song*." We would go so far, indeed, as to say that success in the song imports, necessarily, a more inborn and genuine gift of poetic conception, than the same proportion of success in other less simple modes of art. There are some sorts of composition which may be wrought out of eager feeling and the foam of excited passions; and which are therefore to a large extent within the reach of earnest sensibilities and an ambitious will; others are the spontaneous outflow of the heart, to whose perfection, turbulence and effort are fatal. Of the latter kind is the song. While the ode allows of exertion and strain, what is done in it must be accomplished by native and inherent strength.

Speaking with that confidence which may not improperly be

assumed by one who, having looked with some care at the foundations of the opinion which he expresses, supposes himself able, if called upon by a denial, to furnish such demonstration of its truth as the nature of the matter allows of, we say that, in our judgment, there is no professed writer of songs, in this day, who has conceived the true character of this delicate and peculiar creation of art, with greater precision and justness than Mr. Morris, or been more felicitous than he in dealing with the subtle and multiform difficulties that beset its execution. It is well understood by those whose thoughts are used to be conversant with the suggestions of a deeper analysis than belongs to popular criticism, that the forms of literary art are not indefinite in number, variable in their characteristics, or determined by the casual taste or arbitrary will of authors: they exist in nature; they are dependent upon those fixed laws of intellectual being, of spiritual affection, and moral choice, which constitute the rationality of man. And the actual, positive merit of a poetical production—that real merit, which consists in native vitality, in inherent capacity to live—does not lie in the glitter or costliness of the decorations with which it is invested—nor in the force with which it is made to spring from the mind of its creator into the minds of others—nor yet in the scale of magnitude upon which the ideas belonging to the subject are illustrated in the work; but rather, as we suppose, obviously, and in all cases, upon the integrity and truth with which the particular form that has been contemplated by the artist, is brought out, and the distinctness with which that one specific impression which is appropriate to it, is attained. This is the kind of excellence which we ascribe to Mr. Morris; an excellence of a lofty order; genuine, sincere, and incapable of question; more valuable in this class of composition than in any other, because both more important and more difficult. For the song appears to us to possess a definiteness peculiarly jealous and exclusive; to be less flexible in character and to permit less variety of tone than most other classes of composition. If a man shall say, "I will put more force into my song than your model allows, I will charge it with greater variety of impressions," it is well; if he is skilful, he may make something that is very valuable. But in so far as his work is more than a song, it is not a song. In all works of Art—wherever form is concerned—excess is error.

The just notion and office of the modern song, as we think of it, is to be the embodiment and expression, in beauty, of some one of those sentiments or thoughts, gay, moral, pensive, joyous, or melancholy, which are as natural and appropriate, in particular circumstances, or to certain occasions, as the odor to the flower; rising at such seasons, into the minds of all classes of persons, instinctive and unbidden, yet in obedience to some law of association which it is the gift of the poet to apprehend. Its graceful purpose is to exhibit an incident in the substance of an emotion, to communicate wisdom in the form of sentiment; it is the refracted gleam of some wandering ray from the fair orb of moral truth, which, glancing against some occurrence in common life, is surprised into a smile of quick-darting, many-colored beauty; it is the airy ripple that is thrown up when the current of feeling in human hearts accidentally encounters the current of thought, and bubbles forth with a gentle fret of sparkling foam. Self-evolved, almost, and obedient in its development and shaping to some inward spirit of beauty which appears to possess and control its course, it might almost seem that, in the outgoing loveliness of such productions, sentiment, made substantial in language, floated abroad in natural self-delivery; as that heat which is not yet flame, gives itself forth in blue wreaths of vaporous grace, which unfold their delicateness for a moment upon the tranquil air, and then vanish away. It is not an artificial structure built up by intellect after a model foreshaped by fancy, or foreshadowed by the instincts of the passions; it is a simple emotion, crystalled into beauty by passing for a moment through the cooler air of the mind; it is merely an effluence of creative vigor; a graceful feeling thickened into words. Its proper dwelling is in the atmosphere of the sentiments, not the passions; it will not, indeed, repel the sympathy of deeper feelings, but knows them rather under the form of the flower that floats upon the surface of meditation, than of the deeper root that lies beneath its stream. And this is the grievous fault of nearly all Lord Byron's melodies; that he pierces too profoundly, and passes below the region of grace, charging his lyre with far more vehemence of passion than its slight strings are meant to bear. The beauty which belongs to this production, should be in the form of the thought rather than the fashion of the setting: that genuineness and simplicity of character which constitute almost its essence, are destroyed by any appearance of the cold artifices of construction, palpable springes set for our admiration, whereby the beginning is obviously arranged in reference to a particular ending. This is the short-reaching power of Moore—guilty, by design, of that departure from simplicity, by which he fascinated one generation at the expense of being forgotten by another. The song, while it is general in its impression, should be particular in its occasion; not an abstraction of the mind, but a definite feeling, special to some certain set of circumstances. Rising from out the surface of daily experience, like the watery issuings of a fountain, it throws itself upward for a moment, then descends in a soft, glittering shower to the level whence it rose. Herein resides the chief defect of Bayly's songs; that they are too general and vague—a species of pattern songs—being embodiments of some general feeling, or reflection, but lacking that sufficient reference to some season or occurrence which would justify their appearing, and take away from them the aspect of pretension and display!

Let us speak at greater length of Moore. He is a person of acknowledged brilliance and unquestionable ingenuity: he possesses that fertility of invention and exhaustless play of fancy, which are the usual endowment of his countrymen, and which, in another field of display, have stamped upon the oratory of the language, the features of a national characteristic. But his taste is vicious, even to an advanced stage of disease; and he farther corrupted it by indulging his youthful appetency upon the luscious banquets of those amatory poets, sophists, and letter-writers, who were engendered of the soft decay of Greek civility, and whom the scholar fears even to touch with a momentary attention. He must have studied the costume of the heralds at a coronation: as his model of decorous elegance, he might seem to have had his eye upon the Lord Mayor's state-coach, to which type, in some of his works, he has certainly approached with singular felicity of imitation. Unhappily for the fate of his name in the hands of succeeding critics, he directed this superabundance of powers to a department of effort which enacts, before all other things, as an indispensable prerequisite to anything like valuable success, a taste, keen, severe, relentless in rejection; in which, judgment is more than force, and discretion better than wealth; where, in the eye of a just criticism, barrenness is a paler fault than superfluity. He invested his talents in that cheaply-splendid finery of spurious feeling, that glittering varnish of unreal fancy, which made the fortune of his reputation in this age, but will assuredly play the bankrupt with it in the next. Those tricks of words—that clinking jugglery of sounds—those faded extravagances of "diamonds of thought," and "roses of feeling," of bowers and zephyrs of cupids—which once ravished the imagination of the youth of our land,—to us now are spangles looked at by daylight; they are those strongly-scented flowers which enchant us at night, to disgust in the morning. Mr. Moore's conception of greatness does not consist in some one, simple, broad, and majestic effect, but, as Walpole described the old Versailles, in "a lumber of littleness." In short, Moore thought that he was elegant when in truth he was flaunting, and *feared* he might be Asiatic, while he was only Irish.

The only satisfactory method of criticism is by means of clinical lectures; and we feel regret that our limits do not suffer us—to any great degree—to illustrate what we deem the vigorous simplicity, and genuine grace of Mr. Morris, by that mode of exposition. We must introduce a few cases, however, to show what we have been meaning in the remarks which we made above, upon the proper character of the song. The ballad of "Woodman, Spare that Tree,"—one of those accidents of genius which, however, never happen but to consummate artists—is so familiar to every mind and heart, as to resent citation. Take, then, "My Mother's Bible." We know of no similar production in a truer taste, in a purer style, or more distinctly marked with the character of a good school of composition.

This book is all that's left me now!—
  Tears will unbidden start—
With faltering lip and throbbing brow,
  I press it to my heart.
For many generations past,
  Here is our family tree;
My mother's hands this Bible clasp'd;
  She, dying, gave it me.

Ah! well do I remember those
  Whose names these records bear
Who round the hearth-stone used to close
  After the evening prayer,
And speak of what these pages said,
  In tones my heart would thrill!
Though they are with the silent dead,
  Here are they living still!

My father read this holy book
  To brothers, sisters dear;
How calm was my poor mother's look,
  Who lean'd God's word to hear!
Her angel face—I see it yet!
  What thronging memories come!
Again that little group is met
  Within the halls of home!

Thou truest friend man ever knew,
  Thy constancy I've tried;
Where all were false I found thee true,
  My counsellor and guide.
The mines of earth no treasures give
  That could this volume buy:
In teaching me the way to live,
  It taught me how to die.

Or take "We were Boys together." In manly pathos, in tenderness and truth, where shall it be excelled?

We were boys together,
  And never can forget
The school-house on the heather,
  In childhood where we met—

The humble home, to memory dear;
  Its sorrows and its joys,
Where woke the transient smile or tear
  When you and I were boys.

We were youths together,
  And castles built in air;
Your heart was like a feather,
  And mine weigh'd down with care.
To you came wealth with manhood's prime,
  To me it brought alloys
Foreshadow'd in the primrose time
  When you and I were boys.

We're old men together;
  The friends we loved of yore,
With leaves of autumn weather,
  Are gone forever more.
How blest to age the impulse given—
  The hope time ne'er destroys—
Which led our thoughts from earth to heaven,
  When you and I were boys!

"The Miniature" possesses the captivating elegance of Voiture.

William was holding in his hand
  The likeness of his wife—
Fresh as if touch'd by fairy wand,
  With beauty, grace and life.
He almost thought it spoke—he gazed
  Upon the treasure still;
Absorb'd, delighted and amazed,
  He view'd the artist's skill.

"This picture is yourself, dear Jane;
  'Tis drawn to nature true;
I've kissed it o'er and o'er again,
  It is so much like you."
"And has it kissed you back, my dear?"
  "Why—no—my love?" said he.
"Then, William, it is very clear,
  'Tis not at all *like me!*"

"Where Hudson's Wave" is a glorious burst of poetry, modulated into refinement by the hand of a master.

Where Hudson's wave o'er silvery sands
  Winds through the hills afar,
Old Cronest like a monarch stands,
  Crown'd with a single star!
And there, amid the billowy swells
  Of rock-ribb'd, cloud-capt earth,
My fair and gentle Ida dwells,
  A nymph of mountain birth.

The snow-flake that the cliff receives,
  The diamonds of the showers,
Spring's tender blossoms, buds, and leaves,
  The sisterhood of flowers,
Morn's early beam, eve's balmy breeze,
  Her purity define;
But Ida's dearer far than these
  To this fond breast of mine.

My heart is on the hills. The shades
  Of night are on my brow:
Ye pleasant haunts and quiet glades,
  My soul is with you now!
I bless the star-crown'd highlands where
  My Ida's footsteps roam—
Oh! for a falcon's wing to bear
  Me onward to my home.

Where will you find a nautical song, seemingly more spontaneous in its genial outbreak, really more careful in its construction, than "Land-ho!"

Up, up with the signal! The land is in sight!
We'll be happy, if never again, boys, to-night!
The cold, cheerless ocean in safety we've passed,
And the warm genial earth glads our vision at last.
In the land of the stranger true hearts we shall find,
To soothe us in absence of those left behind.
Land!—land-ho! All hearts glow with joy at the sight!
We'll be happy, if never again, boys, to-night!

The signal is waving! Till morn we'll remain,
Then part in the hope to meet one day again
Round the hearth-stone of home in the land of our birth,
The holiest spot on the face of the earth!
Dear country! our thoughts are as constant to thee,
As the steel to the star, or the stream to the sea.
Ho!—land-ho! We near it—we bound at the sight
Then be happy, if never again, boys, to-night!

The signal is answer'd! The foam-sparkles rise
Like tears from the fountain of joy to the eyes!
May rain-drops that fall from the storm-clouds of care,
Melt away in the sun-beaming smiles of the fair!
One health, as chime gaily the nautical bells,
To woman—God bless her!—wherever she dwells!
THE PILOT'S ON BOARD!—and, thank Heaven, all's right!
So be happy, if never again, boys, to-night!

How full of the joyous madness of absolute independence, yet made harmonious by instinctive grace, is "Life in the West!"

Ho! brothers—come hither and list to my story—
Merry and brief will the narrative be:
Here, like a monarch, I reign in my glory—
Master am I, boys, of all that I see,
Where once frown'd a forest a garden is smiling—
The meadow and moorland are marshes no more;
And there curls the smoke of my cottage, beguiling
The children who cluster like grapes at the door.
Then enter, boys; cheerly, boys, enter and rest;
The land of the heart is the land of the west.
Oho, boys!—oho, boys!—oho!

Talk not of the town, boys—give me the broad prairie,
Where man like the wind roams impulsive and free;
Behold how its beautiful colors all vary,
Like those of the clouds, or the deep-rolling sea.
A life in the woods, boys, is even as changing;
With proud independence we season our cheer,
And those who the world are for happiness ranging,
Won't find it at all, if they don't find it here.
Then enter, boys; cheerly, boys, enter and rest;
I'll show you the life, boys, we live in the west.
Oho, boys!—oho, boys!—oho!

Here, brothers, secure from all turmoil and danger,
We reap what we sow, for the soil is our own;
We spread hospitality's board for the stranger,
And care not a fig for the king on his throne.
We never know want, for we live by our labor,
And in it contentment and happiness find;
We do what we can for a friend or a neighbor,
And die, boys, in peace and good-will to mankind.
Then enter, boys; cheerly, boys, enter and rest;
You know how we live, boys, and die in the west!
Oho, boys!—oho, boys!—oho!

That the same heart whose wild pulse is thrilled by the adventurous interests of the huntsman and the wanderer, can beat in unison with the gentlest truth of deep devotion, is shown in "When other Friends are round Thee."

When other friends are round thee,
  And other hearts are thine,
When other bays have crown'd thee,
  More fresh and green than mine,
Then think how sad and lonely
  This doating heart will be,
Which, while it throbs, throbs only,
  Beloved one, for thee!

Yet do not think I doubt thee,
  I know thy truth remains;
I would not live without thee,
  For all the world contains.
Thou art the star that guides me
  Along life's changing sea;
And whate'er fate betides me,
  This heart still turns to thee.

"I Love the Night" has the voluptuous elegance of the Spanish models.

I love the night when the moon streams bright
  On flowers that drink the dew,
When cascades shout as the stars peep out,
  From boundless fields of blue;
But dearer far than moon or star,
  Or flowers of gaudy hue,
Or murmuring trills of mountain rills,
  I love, I love, love—you!

I love to stray at the close of day,
  Through groves of linden trees,
When gushing notes from song-birds' throats,
  Are vocal in the breeze.
I love the night—the glorious night!
  When hearts beat warm and true;
But far above the night I love,
  I love, I love, love—you!

Were we to meet the lines "Oh, Think of Me!" in an Anthology, we should suppose they were Suckling's—so admirably is the tone of feeling kept down to the limit of probable sincerity

—which is a characteristic that the cavalier style of courting never loses.

Oh, think of me, my own beloved,
  Whatever cares beset thee!
And when thou hast the falsehood proved,
  Of those with smiles who met thee:
While o'er the sea, think, love, of me,
  Who never can forget thee;
Let memory trace the trysting-place,
  Where I with tears regret thee.

Bright as yon star, within my mind,
  A hand unseen hath set thee;
There hath thine image been enshrined,
  Since first, dear love, I met thee;
So in thy breast I fain would rest,
  If, haply, fate would let me—
And live or die, wert thou but nigh,
  To love or to regret me!

"The Star of Love" might stand as a selected specimen of all that is most exquisite in the songs of the *Trouveurs*.

The star of love now shines above,
  Cool zephyrs crisp the sea;
Among the leaves the wind-harp weaves
  Its serenade for thee.
The star, the breeze, the wave, the trees,
  Their minstrelsy unite,
But all are drear till thou appear
  To decorate the night.

The light of noon streams from the moon,
  Though with a milder ray;
O'er hill and grove, like woman's love,
  It cheers us on our way.
Thus all that's bright, the moon, the night,
  The heavens, the earth, the sea,
Exert their powers to bless the hours
  We dedicate to thee.

"The Seasons of Love" is a charming effusion of gay, yet thoughtful sentiment.

The spring-time of love
  Is both happy and gay,
For joy sprinkles blossoms
  And balm in our way;

The sky, earth, and ocean
  In beauty repose,
And all the bright future
  Is *couleur de rose.*

The summer of love
  Is the bloom of the heart,
When hill, grove, and valley
  Their music impart,
And the pure glow of heaven
  Is seen in fond eyes,
As lakes show the rainbow
  That's hung in the skies.

The autumn of love
  Is the season of cheer—
Life's mild Indian Summer,
  The smile of the year;
Which comes when the golden
  Ripe harvest is stored,
And yields its own blessings—
  Repose and reward.

The winter of love
  Is the beam that we win
While the storm scowls without,
  From the sunshine within.
Love's reign is eternal,
  The heart is his throne,
And he has all seasons
  Of life for his own.

The song, "I Never Have Been False to Thee," is, of itself, sufficient to establish General Morris's fame as a great poet—as a *potens magister affectuum*—and as a literary creator of a high order. It is a thoroughly fresh and affective poem on a subject as hackneyed as the highway; it is as deep as truth itself, yet light as the movement of a dance.

I never have been false to thee!
  The heart I gave thee still is thine;
Though thou hast been untrue to me,
  And I no more may call thee mine!
I've loved, as woman ever loves,
  With constant soul in good or ill;
Thou'st proved, as man too often proves,
  A rover—but I love thee still!

Yet think not that my spirit stoops
To bind thee captive in my train!
Love's not a flower, at sunset droops,
But smiles when comes her god again!
Thy words, which fall unheeded now,
Could once my heart-strings madly thrill!
Love's golden chain and burning vow
Are broken—but I love thee still!

Once what a heaven of bliss was ours,
When love dispell'd the clouds of care,
And time went by with birds and flowers,
While song and incense fill'd the air!
The past is mine—the present thine—
Should thoughts of me thy future fill,
Think what a destiny is mine,
To lose but love thee, false one, still!

We had almost forgotten, what the world will never forget, the matchless softness and transparent delicacy of "Near the Lake." Those lines, of themselves, unconsciously, court "the soft promoter of the poet's strain," and almost seem about to break into music.

Near the lake where drooped the willow,
Long time ago!
Where the rock threw back the billow,
Brighter than snow;
Dwelt a maid, beloved and cherished,
By high and low;
But with autumn's leaf she perished,
Long time ago!

Rock and tree and flowing water,
Long time ago!
Bee and bird and blossom taught her
Love's spell to know!
While to my fond words she listen'd,
Murmuring low,
Tenderly her dove-eyes glisten'd,
Long time ago!

Mingled were our hearts forever!
Long time ago!
Can I now forget her? Never!
No, lost one, no!
To her grave these tears are given,

Ever to flow;
She's the star I missed from heaven,
Long time ago!

It is agreeable to find that, instead of being seduced into a false style by the excessive popularity which many of his songs have acquired, General Morris's later efforts are in a style even more truly classic than his earlier ones, and show a decided advance, both in power and ease. "The Rock of the Pilgrims," and the "Indian Songs," of which last we have room only for one verse, are a very clear evidence of this:

A rock in the wilderness welcomed our sires,
From bondage far over the dark-rolling sea,
On that holy altar they kindled the fires,
Jehovah, which glow in our bosoms for thee.
Thy blessings descended in sunshine and shower,
Or rose from the soil that was sown by thy hand;
The mountain and valley rejoiced in thy power,
And heaven encircled and smiled on the land.

The Pilgrims of old an example have given
Of mild resignation, devotion, and love,
Which beams like a star in the blue vault of heaven;
A beacon-light hung in their mansion above.
In church and cathedral we kneel in our prayer—
Their temple and chapel were valley and hill—
But God is the same in the aisle or the air,
And He is the Rock that we lean upon still.

BEFORE THE BATTLE.

They come!—be firm! In silence rally!
The long-knives our retreat have found!
Hark!—their tramp is in the valley,
And they hem the forest round!
The burthened boughs with pale scouts quiver,
The echoing hills tumultuous ring,
While across the eddying river
Their barks, like foaming war-steeds, spring!
The bloodhounds darken land and water!
They come—like buffaloes for slaughter!

We would willingly go on with our extracts, as there are several which have equal claims with these upon our notice, but—

claudite jam rivos. Such are the compositions, original in style, natural in spirit, beautiful with the charm of almost faultless execution, which may challenge for their author the title of the Laureate of America.

The life that is devoted to letters—says Dr. Johnson—passes silently away and is but little diversified by events. The particulars of General Morris's personal history are soon told. He was born in the second year of the present century. The brilliance of some youthful efforts in connection with the daily press displayed his fitness to take a leading part in the literary action of the country; and accordingly, in 1822, he became the Editor of "The New York Mirror." The storm of financial embarrassment which, about the years 1837 and 1838, rode over the whole country, prostrating every interest, and wasting all classes, visited even the poet and the editor. The "New York Mirror" passed out of his hands; and in 1843, its existence came to an end. In 1844, "The New Mirror" was established by the original proprietor, in conjunction with his friend Mr. Willis; and this has recently been changed into "The Evening Mirror," a daily gazette of much spirit, elegance, and popularity. "The Mirror Library," under the same control, presents far the best selection of *belles-lettres* that can be found in this country or in England. It is about to re-commence its issues under improved advantages. In the beginning of the present year (1845.—ED.), the professional *corps* of singers and musicians in New York, as a testimony of esteem to General Morris, gave him a complimentary concert—a valuable token of their respect—appropriate and deserved—which enabled the most distinguished persons in the city of his birth to exhibit, by their presence, the interest and regard which they had for him. It was understood that the profits of that concert had a vital connection with General Morris's continuing to be the possessor of the modest and beautiful seat of "Under Cliff," on the Hudson—the residence of his family—the birthplace of most of them, and the cherished home and seat of his affections. Upon that subject, it is not our warrant to speak; nor indeed have we the power to speak with accuracy. Should it be as is reported, that a "damp" has "fallen around the path" of this sweet poet and amiable man, we are sure that the people of this nation will be prompt to dispel, by offers more truly voluntary than the "aids" and "benevolences" of royal ages, all discomfort from the evening of his days, and, "in recompense" of many an hour of the purest pleasure, and many an abiding sentiment of truth and goodness, for which they are his debtors, to

"Give the tribute, Glory need not ask."*

* The concluding sentences of this short sketch of "The Song-Writer of America," written by Mr. Wallace in 1845, as an office of pleasure and a voluntary offering of regard for one whom he affectionately loved, leaves a painful interest in respect to the gifted subject of it, which it is a high gratification to be able in 1856 to dispel. The great merit and uncommon success of General Morris's present literary enterprise, "The Home Journal," which, with his friend Mr. Willis, he undertook eleven years ago, soon after the preceding sketch was written, and with him has since continued—and the constant income from his published "Songs," enabled this generous man to rise successfully above the "damp," to which Mr. Wallace in 1845 so delicately alludes: and he has been for many years past in a full enjoyment of that independence so dear to an honorable man; made yet more dear, as the reward of his own genius and his own labors.

A song is written that it may be sung: and the popularity of General Morris's writings with such composers as Bishop, Horn, Gilfert, Knight, De Begnis, Wallace, and with artists like Braham, Malibran, Mrs. Wood, Jenny Lind, and others of later fame, may be referred to as a proof how essentially lyric is his genius: and how certain therefore to command the applause of nations. Mr. C. E. Horn declared that the poet met him more than half way; that his lines were always musical, and might be said to sing themselves. Braham pronounced this author "the best lyrist of the age;"—whose songs he most liked to sing. He said that he had sung "The Miniature" some two hundred times in public and never without an *encore;* and that on some occasions in Canada and elsewhere, he had been requested to repeat it three and four times at the same concert. Indeed, few literary efforts of our time have had an admiration which has been so little local or deciduous. General Morris's fame as "The Song-Writer of America" belongs to two hemispheres, and is greater now than it has ever been before. "You ask me," says a recent letter from an English gentleman, now representing in the House of Commons one of the most ancient of the English boroughs, "whether I have seen Gen. Morris's last song, 'Jenny Marsh of Cherry Valley.' You can hardly know, when you put such a question, the place he has built himself in the hearts of all classes here. His many songs and ballads are household words in every home in England, and have a dear old chair by every circle in which kindly friends are gathered; and parents smile with pleasure to see brothers and sisters join their voices in the evening song, and twine closer those loving chords—the tenderest of the human heart. It is no mean reward to feel that the child of

RUFUS WILMOT GRISWOLD.

MANKIND, generally, are not predisposed to give any one credit for possessing, at the same time, great intellectual force and eminent personal disinterestedness. If it be not the law, it

one's brain has a chair in such circles, and that the love for the child passes in hundreds of hearts into love for its unseen parent. After all, what are all the throat-warblings in the world to one such heart-song as 'My Mother's Bible?' It possesses the true test of genius, touching with sympathy the human heart, equally in the palace and the cottage. As an instance of the effect of one of his songs, I will mention a scene in the House of Commons—at which I was present.

"It was just about the hour, near twelve, when the dandies turn in from The Coventry Club, or some Belgravian rout, when, except three or four of the first men in the House, no one would be endured, and no one is listened to, unless, perhaps, a buffo like Col. Sibthorp, or a Rabelasian wit like Henry Drummond, or a flashing hussar of debate like Osborne, who rushes in every sentence at some opposition foe and levels him with his lance. The hour of twelve is death to bores. They dare not cross its threshold. At the back of the Whig benches an old man arose, tall and silvered. From his dress of top boots and drab breeches and blue coat with gilt buttons, one would have fancied he had been dug up from some reign of the Georges, had not the fresh bloom on his cheek, caught in many a hunting morning, and his hale, hearty look proclaimed 'the fine, old English gentleman.' This was Caley of Yorkshire. At first the dandies stared, and were inclined to chastise such unusual audacity in invading an hour sacred to Peel, Stanly, Russell, Gladstone, and D'Israeli. But somehow the genial, kindly presence of the man, and the good old garments he wore, to which even *blasé* young England softened, saved him, and the House relapsed into listlessness. But listlessness soon grew into interest when, after a most earnest and touching appeal to the Premier to save the old glory, and old customs and old peasantry of England, he repeated, with a manly, touching pathos, the song of 'Woodman, Spare that Tree.' I cannot well describe the effect which these beautiful words, which do honor to the head and heart of their author, produced. The House was perfectly still when the old man sat down. Sir Robert Peel, against one of whose measures Mr. Caley's appeal had been made, felt it, and when he rose his voice faltered. 'I admit,' he said, 'the touching beauty of that ballad, but I deny its application to any measure of mine.' It was some time before the sensation subsided, but after it did so groups gathered around Osborne and D'Israeli, to listen to a personal description of the author, who was familiar to them from the picturings of Willis and others. Morris is now as well known to many of us as if we had looked into his kindly face, or felt the warm pressure of his hand."

The striking incident at a fashionable concert in France is more recent and perhaps less well known; where, after this same ballad—which has made the

is too often an untoward fact of this imperfect frame of ours, that vivid creative capacity is accompanied by an absorbing self-consciousness, which, like an elliptical mirror, concentrates

tour of Europe, and been translated into as many languages as The Vatican can interpret—had been very effectively sung by an artist of high reputation, a tall and elegant man, rising in the midst of the concert room, which was hushed into the stillness of emotion, and walking some distance up the passage-way till he caught the singer's eye, addressed him, in the breathless interest of the house,—"And pray, Sir, can you tell us if the woodman *did* spare that tree?" The answer, "He did, Sir. I give you my honor," dispelled an anxiety which could not have been greater had it been real, and gave free breath to the delighted assembly.

While the "Songs" of General Morris have given so much honor to the country abroad, and are undoubtedly the foundation upon which his permanent reputation will rest, "The Home Journal," whose many thousand copies now carry the most engaging literature of our country to its extremest ends, has made his genius an article of weekly necessity at home, among all who love the arts, who aspire to be informed upon the selecter topics of fashionable interest, or who regard with attention that lighter literature of our country which exercises not the least important influence on its destinies.

So fine an analysis of General Morris's special powers as a Song-Writer, has been lately given by an intelligent critic, that any notice of them, to be complete, should not fail to embrace it.

"If there is any literary work," says Dr. Griswold in his "Poets and Poetry of America," "which calls for a special gift of nature, perhaps it is the song. In terms of a sounder theory I may say that its successful accomplishment, beyond almost any other composition, demands an intelligent insight into the principles upon which its effect depends, and a capacity, if not to combine with imposing strength, yet to select with the nicest judgment. Other productions often gratify, long and highly, in spite of considerable defects, while the song, to succeed at all, must be nearly perfect. It implies a taste delicately skilled in the fine influences of language. It has often shunned the diligence of men who have done greater things. Starting from some common perception, by almost a crystalline process of accretion it should grow up into a poem. Its first note should find the hearer in sympathy with it and its last should leave him moved and wondering. Throughout, it must have an affinity to some one fixed idea. Its propriety is, not so much to give expression to a feeling existing in the bosom of the author, as to reproduce that feeling in the heart of the listener: the tone of the composition ought, therefore, to be, as much as is possible, below the force of the feeling which it would inspire. It should be simple, entire, and glowing.

"The distinction and difficulty of the song are illustrated by the genius of Jonson, Marlowe, and Dryden; by the fame of Moore, and the failure of Byron. Several of the songs of Morris, whether judged of by their success or by the application of any rules of criticism, are nearly faultless. They are in a

upon a focus within its own compass all the lustre that it snatches from life and nature; so that at last we come unhappily to doubt the power, if we do not perceive the infirmity. A writer, of the least questionable ability, if he be unlucky enough early to grow distinguished for literary philanthropy, for generous zeal in bringing the productions of others to the light of popular approval, for patriotic devotedness to the honor of his country, as founded upon the works of his contemporaries, will assuredly be misunderstood, at least for a season. His readiness to do everything for others will be taken for an argument of incapacity to do much for himself. But Time—in whose airy train, if passions and prejudices revel at the commencement, and false opinions crowd about the middle part, Justice ever walks slow and late, bringing up the close—will dispense a retribution that is not by measure; and the reputation, which

very chaste style of art. They have the simplicity which is the characteristic of the classic models, and the purity which was once deemed an indispensable quality in the lyric poet. They are marked by neatness of language; free from every thing affected, or finical; a natural elegance of sentiment, and a correct moral purpose. His best effusions have few marks of imitation. They are like each other; but no English song can be named from which in character and tone they are not different.—'The Chieftain's Daughter' is an example of the narrative song in which the whole story is told in a few lines, without omission and without redundancy. 'When other Friends are round Thee' is a beautiful expression of affection. 'Land Ho!' is an exceedingly spirited and joyous nautical piece; and in 'Near the Lake,' the very delicate effect which the author has contemplated, is attained with remarkable precision.

"In sentiment, as in sound, there are certain natural melodies, which seem to be discovered rather than contrived, and which, as they are evolved from time to time by the felicity or skill of successive artists, are sure to be received with unbounded popularity. The higher and more elaborate productions of genius are best appreciated by the thoughtful analysis of a single critic: but the appropriate test of the merit of these simple, apparently almost spontaneous effusions, is the response which they meet with from the common heart of man. The melodies of Mozart and Auber doubtless enchanted their ears who first heard them played by the composers; but we know them to be founded in the enduring truth of art, only because they have made themselves a home in the streets of every city of Europe and America, and after long experience, have been found to be among the natural formulas by which gaiety and melancholy express themselves in every rank and in every land. The song of 'Woodman, spare that Tree,' has touched one of those chords of pervading nature which fraternize multitudes of differing nations."—ED.

began in self-oblivion, will ultimately be all the more potent for having first been pure.

To no man of our time is the literary character of this country under more honorable obligation, for confidence imparted at home, and consequence acquired abroad, than to the person whose name is placed at the beginning of this article. To no one will those writers, personally, almost without an exception, be so prompt to profess their indebtedness for manifold acts of disinterested benefit, rendered in a spirit, and with an ease and an ability, which made the intervention as valuable and as delightful to one party, as it was meritorious and graceful in the other. But the merit has been won at a great personal loss. Dr. Griswold would have been thought entitled to more respect as an author, if he had displayed less benevolence as an editor. The praise which is not claimed is slowly yielded; and the advocate who comes forward in the cause of another, is not supposed to have pretensions of his own. A candidate without rivalry, and a competitor unconscious of jealousy, is a character so new to literary history, that it is hardly to be expected that it should be at once appreciated. Dr. Griswold's critical surveys exhibit intellectual capacities of a very high order of subtlety and force, and a skill in composition singularly felicitous; they leave to no one of his years in the country a title to take rank before him in energetic originality of thought and language; and to the discriminating mind they demonstrate his ability, by the judicious concentration of effort upon some single subject of adequate scope, to rise to the first degree of excellence in any department. Nevertheless, had the exercise of these talents been dissociated from a generosity of purpose; had they been directed to the construction of a mansion of repute for their possessor, out of the demolished houses of others' fame, instead of being employed to adorn and beautify the Pantheon of public and national distinction, by materials furnished from the artist's own treasures, doubtless the personal admiration won would have been far greater. The echoes of success would have borne to our ears the reverberations of a single name, instead of voicing the mingled glory of a throng, in which his praise who waked the long response is scarce distinguishable. But we must not impair the dignity of an honorable reputation by regret or complaint. The qualities by which the general interest is aided, and the common good advanced, take their place, in every right judgment, so much above that class of powers by which individual eminence is vindicated; it is so much nobler and greater to diffuse the rays of renown than to appropriate them; that we would counsel the friends of Dr. Griswold to value his reputation as the *author* of The Prose Writers of America, before the most fortunate endeavor to outrival the brightest subject of its page.

Every American concerned for the literary celebrity of his country is bound to bear respect to the author of "The Poets and Poetry," and "The Prose Writers of America." The effect which these works have had, is obvious to the most careless examination. We note a decided alteration since the date of their publication, not only in the increased deference with which our productions are regarded by British writers, but in the firmer countenance, the added energy, the deeper thoroughness of tone assumed and exerted by the press among us. Dr. Griswold at once challenged for his subject the very loftiest position, and did it in tones of such distinctness, decision and emphasis, as startled attention on every side, and implied not only great confidence in the correctness of his opinions, but something of moral heroism in braving the doubts and denials with which such claims were at first received. But he made good every pretension that he had advanced, and he is now followed by troops of persons, of whom not one would have dared to precede him, and but few would have been willing to stand beside him in the beginning. This presentation of the claims of American genius and accomplishment in letters, under such advantages of aggregation, arrangement and illustration, as immediately to advance them into the line of equality with all our glories, is connected, enduringly, with the name of Dr. Griswold. From several causes, not very difficult to appreciate, it had happened that the literary efforts of this country, in verse and prose alike, have been scattered, occasional, fragmentary, local; impulsive more than systematic; the work of amateurs rather than professors. The wandering rays that struggled with "ineffectual beam," from a thousand divided sources, were now brought into focal unity, with an effect not merely augmented in degree, but unexpected in nature and kind. *Si non singula placent, juncta juvant.* It was thus demonstrated that America had produced not only a poetry and romance, but a philosophy, a theology, a scholarship, and a criticism, fairly entitled to constitute a national school. Something more than research the most extensive, memory the readiest, discrimination the most just, and taste and tact the most delicate, were needed for this success. A "reconciling ray" of creative intelligence alone could give order, relation, composition and singleness of tone, to elements in many cases apparently impracticable. In hands less than masterly, the thing would have been a shapeless, discordant mass, without interest, and without effect. The combining eye, which caught the rich impression of the completed architecture, in the inexpressive and inharmonious variety of the separate material, partook of poetic ardor, and the skill which accomplished what the mind foresaw, was an artist faculty of not a common kind.

Upon the subject of American literature, Dr. Griswold is an enthusiast, with all the qualities which render enthusiasm engaging, and even admirable; generous, indefatigable, self-sacrificing, successful. Apparently, he takes as much pleasure in establishing another's distinction as he could feel if the victory were his own; and he seems to feel that a personal triumph is won, whenever the lettered fame of the country is elevated. Under a light, variable, complying manner, he conceals strongly determined points of character. There is great intensity and continuance in his nature. Beneath a superficial excitability and impulsiveness, the instincts of his deeper being move firmly onward, undeviating and unresisting, through that sphere of mental interest to which he seems to have been predestinated. To inform himself of the history, peculiarities and achievements of American effort in every form, in the past and in the present, to assimilate all this information into union with his own thoughts and views, and to organize the whole into grand and imposing views of national power, is the occupation always going on, by a kind of involuntary process, almost in the unconscious operation of this ever-active, ever-inquiring mind. This is the main pursuit of his life; all else is the by-play of his powers. It is this which gives permanence, and consistency, and unity to his character, amid the infinite multiplicity of concerns which engage his less profound attention. This imparts dignity, and the aspect even of greatness, to a mental career which, unless steadied by such a controlling passion and principle of the thought, might be frittered and frivolized by the multitudinous petty excitements to which it is subject. Whatever "quick whirls and eddies of the mind" may gyrate and gurgle on the surface, the under-current ever moves composedly onward through its direct and natural channel, and in due time deposits in glittering masses the golden particles which it had swept along with it.

With characteristics, and talents, and habits such as these, it is not surprising that his lore, on all matters connected with national history, biography, and literature, is immense. He is, without doubt, upon the whole American subject, the most learned authority in the world. For ourselves, we can say that there are certain departments in this field, more especially connected with Revolutionary personages and occurrences, which have been to us a kind of *specialité* in study; but we have not yet found the topic upon which Dr. Griswold did not know all that we know, and a little more. The system upon which all this erudition is stored and distributed, in his recollection, is deserving of imitation. There is nothing of the confusion, the chaotic agglomeration, which marks the lettered collections of the "*helluo librorum;*" all is orderly, rational, connected. With great discretion he has especially cultivated that sort of information which consists, not so much in a treasury of facts laid away in the memory, as in familiarity with the sources of knowledge. It has been his practice to cultivate that style of research which the acute good sense of Dr. Johnson commended in Gilbert Walmesly, and the advantages which all scholars are aware of—that where he does not possess the knowledge, he can at least tell where to find it. Ask Dr. Griswold as to an event or a character, somewhat recondite or controverted, and if he is not prepared to give you an exact and minute detail of the case, he will indicate, with promptness and precision, the avenues through which all the learning on the subject is to be reached; he will refer you to a letter in the middle of one book, an anecdote in the appendix of another, a disquisition buried in some series of a dozen volumes, by the combination of which a full view of what you are in search of will be reached; and he will furnish a just estimate of the comparative reliability of different authorities, and all that apparatus of study which is so satisfactory to the inquirer. His mind, in this respect, might not so truly be called a book as an index, by means of which many books may be consulted.

Doctor Griswold's life of mind is extraordinary. The energy and activity of his thoughts and efforts seem rather to be stimulated into higher force by the accumulation of toils. He cannot draw comfortable breath except in a whirlwind of occupation. To one who becomes slightly acquainted with him, and for the first time gets a glimpse into the many-roomed workshop of his mind, it is a matter of unfeigned astonishment to behold the all but limitless diversity of incompatible pursuits which this remarkable person is carrying on at the same time. As he becomes more extensively observed, and more thoroughly known, this early surprise gives way to a more permanent admiration at the distinctness with which these several employments are followed, and the unpausing onwardness with which each is carried forward duly to its conclusion. The taking up of a new project is no reason with him for abandoning or slighting an old one. It is a characteristic with him to finish everything that he undertakes. He does not deal in unexecuted suggestions or unterminated enterprises; every undertaking in his hands, soon sees its practical and final completion. Napoleon himself was not more habitually intent upon snatching the fruits of toil. Accordingly, in a brief life, he has accomplished a vast deal. As collector and editor, he has done in months what any other man would have required years for. As an original author, he has written thrice as much, perhaps, as any of his contemporaries. Much was transitory, and has passed away; much remains, and will long be valued. Yet with all this prodigiousness of employment, he always seems to be at leisure. In the morning, at noon, and in the evening, he is ready for anything that his friends may propose; is always much at their service. A stranger who should be introduced to him, without a knowledge of his character or history, and should observe the eager force and earnest ability with which he threw himself into the trifles of the moment, would set him down, probably, for a gentleman of fortune and leisure, who lived chiefly in the drawing-room, whose mind habitually wanted occupation, had not enough for its energies, and was rather running to waste from what he himself has described as the "luxuriance of intelligence unemployed." Such a one might be surprised to learn that his gay and careless acquaintance had just published a large octavo volume, after three months' consideration, of which a dozen people, under any division of labor, might have been in gestation for as many lustrums; was carrying two or three more through the press; a monthly magazine; wrote the literary articles of one or two journals, and devoted twelve hours every day to the preparation of a great biographical dictionary—the *maximum opus* of his life.

It would be unjust to pass by the personal relation in which Dr. Griswold has always stood to the other authors of his country; the system of friendly assistance which he makes it his duty to maintain to all who, in any sort, may profit by his kindness. He seems to possess an ardent and chivalrous love for the literary fame of his countrymen. He is ever ready to give any assistance that may be required in bringing out their works; and his acquaintance with the subject of publication in all its branches, and all its details, enables him to render aid that is of priceless value to the shy, nervous, secluded man of genius. "A virgin tragedy, an orphan muse," possess irresistible claims upon his philanthropy. If the time and talents of a skilful editor, who will labor *gratuitously*, in some benevolent undertaking toward the works of some defunct, are needed, Dr.

20*

Griswold is counted upon with ready confidence. The case of the late Edgar Allen Poe is an illustration of this matter, very honorable to the subject of our notice. There was nothing in the private relations of the parties to render it at all natural or probable that Mr. Poe should have left a request that Dr. Griswold would be the editor of his writings; but he knew the generous spirit and admirable capacity of the person whose regard he invoked, and felt assured that he would do in the best manner what probably no other would do at all. Services such as he is constantly rendering, give him a title to the gratitude, not merely of that large number of authors who have been immediately obliged by his courtesy, but of the country at large, which has derived from his efforts benefits which it knows not of, and which ought to admire abilities so unselfishly exerted.* No one living has conferred such important favors upon the whole class of American authors, prose and poetical; and should he be withdrawn from the sphere which he fills with peculiar advantages, there is scarcely a considerable writer, from one end of the States to the other, who would not feel that he had sustained the loss of an invaluable ally. And it is not only his personal exertions that have thus been disinterestedly given to American letters, but his purse has ever been freely open for the promotion of the same class of interests. Many a struggling young adventurer in the fields of authorship has owed to his generous hand the means of prosecuting and attaining his favorite aims. But the grace of such acts consists in their secrecy, and as the author of them has never divulged them, we cannot

* The writers of the country have not been unwilling to display their regard for him in ways the most suitable and graceful. Bayard Taylor dedicates to him his first book, "Ximena and other Poems," as "an expression of gratitude for the kind encouragement shown the author." The Rev. James Watson inscribes to him a volume of "Discourses, as the first fruits of a mental and moral culture for which the author is chiefly indebted to him." The lamented Mrs. Osgood addressed to him the splendid edition of her works as a "Souvenir of admiration for his genius, of respect for his generous character, and of gratitude for his valuable literary counsels;" and we might quote perhaps a dozen similar tributes from C. F. Hoffman, W. H. C. Hosmer, and other authors, illustrating the same feelings and opinions.

venture to refer to such as have transpired to us from other sources. The younger, less-favored class of American authors, will never have a warmer friend, or, to use an old word, without the invidious sense which of old it may have borne, a more liberal *patron*, than he of whom we write.

The *boast* of heraldry, and the *pomp* of power, alike have vanished from an era of republican maxims; yet the rational interest of the one, and the substantial value of the other, have survived the change of forms, and sentiments, and institutions. Nowhere are genealogies explored and esteemed more, than among the descendants of the Puritans; and New England, we believe, is the only community which exhibits a society, and a periodical journal, devoted to the single purpose of tracing and recording pedigrees. It is wise, and it is natural; and like all of "Nature's wisdom," it finds its vindication equally in the instincts of the feelings, and in the conclusions of lengthened observation. Struck by an historic name, awaking associations with the fame of judges, governors, and other worthies of the republic, we made application to a member of the family, for some details upon the subject. He has politely responded to our call, with a greater profusion of lore than we shall at present communicate to the public.

The family of Griswold—which has included many eminent persons in the annals of the colony and of the state of Connecticut—is descended from George Griswold, called, in his epitaph, *Armiger*, of Kenilworth, in Warwickshire, England, and for several years, during the life of his father, Francis Griswold, described as of Lyme Regis, in Dorsetshire, where he was married. Of the ancestors of George Griswold, several had been in Parliament, and one, Philip Griswold (A. D. 1391—1460), was honorably distinguished in arms in the reigns of the Fifth and Sixth Henries. The sons of George Griswold, with a single exception, emigrated to New England. Edward, whose name appears for some reason to have been changed from Francis, was one of the first settlers of Windsor, in the year 1630. Matthew also established himself originally in the same place, but after marrying a daughter of the first Henry Wolcott, he bought and occupied the place known as Black Hall, in Lyme, then Saybrook. Others of the family advanced farther into the interior, and are represented by the descendants of the settlers of Norwich, Killingworth, (a corruption of Kenilworth,) Griswold, and other towns of which they were the founders. Rufus Wilmot Griswold is of the ninth generation from George Griswold, of Kenilworth, in England; and on the mother's side is descended in the eighth degree from Thomas Mayhew, the first Governor of Martha's Vineyard. He was born in Rutland county, Vermont, on the 15th of February, 1815.

Much of the early life of Dr. Griswold was spent in voyaging about the world; and before he was twenty years of age he had seen the most interesting portions of his own country, and of southern and central Europe. Relinquishing travel, which had grown distasteful from indulgence, he suddenly married, and entered upon the fascinating but dangerous career of a man of letters by profession. *Quodcunque amat, valde amat,* is the character of his temperament, and he pursued this exciting occupation with earnest and enthusiastic assiduity. He had studied divinity, and has professed at all times to regard it as his vocation; but "once a mortgage, always a mortgage" is as applicable to the liens of authorship as to those of debts; and after nine or ten years passed chiefly in journalism and literary creation, it is not probable that he will ever wholly abandon the press for the pulpit.* There is no well-authenticated instance, we believe, on record, of a man who, for his own or his father's sin, has once been "dipped in ink" of printers, either curing himself or being cured radically of that tatter of the

* Mr. E. P. Whipple, probably the most thoroughly accomplished of all our critics, observes in a recent sketch of Dr. Griswold: "His acquirements in theology are very extensive. In his doctrinal notions he is inflexibly orthodox, and entertains some dogmas of peculiar grimness. Those who have never disputed with him on 'fixed fate, free will, foreknowledge absolute,' can hardly form a conception of his innate force of character. On these subjects he is a sort of cross between Descartes and John Calvin. In theology he is all muscle and bone. His sermons are his finest compositions, and he delivers them from the pulpit with taste and eloquence."

love of approbation which the dusky immersion always leaves behind it.

Dr. Griswold's first habits of writing were formed under the suggestive culture of an elder brother, Mr. Heman Griswold, a highly accomplished and much respected merchant of Troy, in whose house he passed the winter of 1830. From that period, his fifteenth year, he has been a practised writer; though he considers himself as having produced nothing, before twenty-two, which he would now be willing to acknowledge. For a short time he turned his attention to politics, and conducted a political journal in the country. After this he was associated with Mr. Horace Greeley, in editing "The New-Yorker," and with Park Benjamin and Epes Sargent in "The Brother Jonathan" and "The New World"—enterprises eminently successful, which influenced in various respects, and in an important degree, the character of the literary and newspaper press. In 1842–3, he was the editor of "Graham's Magazine;" and by the attraction of his name, and the liberal policy which he induced Mr. Graham to adopt, was enabled to bring into its list of contributors a better corps of writers, perhaps, than has ever before or since been boasted by such a work. Among these were Richard Henry Dana, Washington Allston, Cooper, Bryant, Longfellow, Hoffman, Willis, and others. While he was editor, the circulation of the Magazine increased from seventeen thousand to twenty-nine thousand.

He has published a large number of volumes anonymously. One of these is a collection of his verses, and two others constitute a novel. He has also brought out anonymously, partly or entirely written by himself, six or eight works on history and biography, which, though they have satisfied the critics and the publishers, appear, from being unacknowledged, not to have satisfied their author. He has printed, at sundry times, seven discourses on subjects of history and philosophy, and a volume of sermons. In reviews, magazines and newspapers he has written largely; enough to fill a dozen octavo volumes. In 1844 he published "Curiosities of American Literature." We are indebted to him, moreover, for an edition of The Prose

Works of Milton, preceded by an eloquent and valuable Life, published in 1846. This was the first American reprint of Milton's prose, and was a voluntary contribution by the editor to the fortunes of a worthy and interesting man of genius, the Rev. Herman Hooker, D. D., then struggling to establish himself as a publisher, and now well known as one of the most liberal and extensive in Philadelphia.

Dr. Griswold's position as a man of letters, however, is chiefly owing to his biographies and literary histories and disquisitions, in "The Poets and Poetry of America," 1842; "The Poets and Poetry of England in the Nineteenth Century," 1844; "The Prose Writers of America," 1846, and "The Female Poets of America," 1848.

For the difficult office of determining, and representing and portraying the respective merits of the authors of America, in which he has risen to an easy supremacy, and which now by common consent has been delegated to his hands, he undoubtedly has many rare qualifications. The mental attribute which he possesses in the most distinguishing degree, and to which his success is largely owing, is *judgment.* To say that he excels by that attribute is to award perhaps the highest praise that could be bestowed. The loftiest and rarest quality of the mind is judgment. It is above invention; it is beyond eloquence; it is more than logic. In every employment and every condition of life, private and public, deliberative and executive, the ascendancy of judgment over talent, wit, passion, imagination, learning, is evinced at once by the rarity of the endowment, and by the superiority which it is certain to confer upon its possessor. As a comparative critic, his opinions are always entitled to weight. Sensitive to the finest indications of literary promise; apt to detect essential merit, under whatever guise of oddity, or affectation, or bad taste; acute in perception, and comprehensive in sympathy; he holds aloft, firmly and steadily, the scale of just decision, and reports the result without prepossession and without timidity. He possesses a rapid and sure *coup d'œil.* He surveys the merits of a volume with a scrutiny as piercing as it is brief, and arrives promptly at a result which will commonly be found to stand the test of prolonged examination. His sagacity has been so often displayed and approved, that there is probably no one among us whose opinion on a question of literary merit would have greater influence with the judicious minds of the country. His shrewdness in prognosticating the popular taste is not less acute, and his perception of what is likely to be successful is as accurate as his appreciation of what is really meritorious.

The literary abilities displayed in the original portion of these works are entitled to very high rank, and are undoubtedly the sufficient cause of their popularity and permanence. Dr. Griswold's style is fresh, brilliant, delicate, perhaps over-delicate, but never feeble, and rarely morbid. With unerring accuracy, he always indicates the strong points of his subject; yet he indicates rather than seizes them. The outlines of truth are always traced with nicety and precision; yet are they traced rather than channelled. His coloring is refined, soft, suggestive; dealing in half tints, or mixed hues, more usually than in simple and contrasted colors. His perceptions are keenly intelligent, and full of vitality and vividness; but they are too mercurial, fugitive and hásty; they want fixity, persistency and prolongation. He touches some rich element of truth or beauty, but he does not linger upon it to develop and unfold its deep and full resources; he merely touches it, and is off in search of some remote conception, which he will strike and bound away from, like a glancing sunbeam. A discussion by him, therefore, is a series of gentle and delightful flashes, not a steady and prolonged blaze. The fault lies more in the school than in the performer. If he uses water-colors rather than oils, it is because the style is in mode, and not because the genius of the artist could not glow upon canvas as well as glitter upon paper.

But moral qualities of a very unusual and very elevated sort were needed for an undertaking like the one which we speak of, and it is here that Dr. Griswold's character rises to excellence. From partiality, from prejudice, from the bias of anger and the warp of affection, his nature seems to be wholly free. A writer so void of literary jealousy never was created upon the earth. He comes to his work, too, without any of those inveterate predilections or antipathies of taste which most men, as highly educated, contract. His views are not moulded in the forms of any systems, classes, or modes of criticism. His candor, sincerity, and utter fearlessness in avowing his genuine convictions are of inestimable value; and there is not only a perfect honesty in his mind, but a thorough freedom even from unintended predispositions and unconscious obliquities. Even where he cannot enjoy he appreciates, and he points out and expounds, for the participation of others, that which perhaps to himself may afford no pleasure. With some of the people in these volumes, his relations are those of affectionate intimacy; with others they are decidedly hostile; yet cavil itself might be defied to show an instance in which he has overvalued the merits of a friend or done unfairness to the titles of an enemy.

But while we affirm that the author of these volumes has displayed in them remarkable qualities of mind and accomplishment, we admit at the same time that what he has yet done is not worthy of the capacity which he certainly possesses. Our settled judgment is, that Dr. Griswold is a man of very superior and uncommon talents, and that he is destined to achieve much that shall be far beyond the line of his heretofore endeavors. We consider ourselves to be accurately acquainted with his nature; we have seen him closely at sundry times, and in various emergencies; with a severe, rather than a partial eye, we have explored and measured a character which interested our scrutiny. We are satisfied that neither the public nor Dr. Griswold himself has formed a just and adequate appreciation of the original and commanding abilities which he has. If opinion has fallen below his performances, they again are below his powers. His own great infirmity—if so interesting a peculiarity may thus be called—consists in a want of mental self-reliance; an absence of deep, broad confidence in his own inherent strength. And that perhaps has betrayed the judgment of the public; for the latter is usually not disposed to take a man at a higher rate than he asks for himself. The community recognizes him as an acute, searching, and correct critic; as a profound bibliographer and annalist; and as master of a bright, pointed, and discursive style, light enough to lend grace to the airiest topics, and vigorous enough to dash at the weightiest. Dr. Griswold is more than all that. He is a man of genius; abounding in the resources of inventive thought; gifted, evidently and copiously, with "the vision and the faculty divine," which give to the world more than they gain from it, and glorify all that they perceive.

There is a class of minds, whose dynamical condition is not quite accordant with their statical condition; who, in what they do, never perfectly represent what they are. Studied in themselves, they interest and impress; followed in their works, they disappoint. Endowed, unmistakably, with the characteristics of superiority, whenever they put themselves in action, some unlucky element mixes itself up with the operation, some trick of weakness displays itself, some false bias, some fatal affinity comes athwart the effort, to make it miscarry, and the movement which commenced from genius concludes in commonplace. The fault lies rather in the temperament than in the talent.

In Dr. Griswold's case, the misfortune, hitherto, has been that his interest in literary subjects has been so irritable, and his energy sprang with such instantness to seize every scheme which flashed before him, that the strong and firm capacities of his intellectual being have not had opportunity calmly and consistently to develop themselves. But within and beneath the volatile curiosity which is engrossed by externality, and almost entirely detached from it, is a deep, subtle, intensely-vital sensibility, which is a fund of creative affluence, and which, when fully worked out by the owner, will yield magnificent results. Separated from the electrical excitability of the upper and outer surface of the character, there lies a large substratum, whose action possesses a galvanic power and exhaustlessness. Hitherto, he seems not to have been able to master, and get the management and use of his genius. With the power, he possesses much of the impatience of that nervous temperament, which, when controlled, is inspiration and energy, but when unsubjected, is distraction and weakness. Time, which sometimes builds up a character, by a process of breaking down its infirmities, will advance this person into a higher sphere of effort and distinction. When he has worked out and off the too fertile alluvian, whose rapid fertility has misled him as to the true wealth of his own being, he will discern the genuine treasures with which nature has endowed him, and will address himself to the duty which rests upon the depository of such resources. Of late, we have witnessed a decided increase in the force and freedom with which his native inspiration of thought throws itself abroad. What a profound, complete and exquisite estimate of the character of Poe, is that which has recently been copied through the papers! Yet it was thrown off within a few hours after the intelligence of his death reached the city by telegraph.

Dr. Griswold possesses remarkable powers of conversation. At a dinner-table of literary men, and men of the world, few will equal him in the original, rapid, brilliant flow of his remarks. Such a scene is well suited to display the variety of his powers, and almost unlimited resources of his information. When animated by the presence of a company which commands his respect, and kindles his ambition, he seems to rise to a higher grade of faculties, to be gifted with new powers of memory, and to be furnished with unfailing supplies of appropriate and eloquent language. At such times, his discourse has the readiness, the fluency, and the correctness of written composition. With a mind quickly susceptible to every suggestion of enlightened curiosity, he catches any topic which you may present, glances with swift yet natural transition from the thing before him to something a thousand leagues away from him; enters, if invited, upon a critical discussion of some doubtful and difficult subject in literary history, gives you new, particular, and exact views of it; or discusses the topics of the day with a vivid interest, and such interior knowledge as might seem attainable only by one habitually behind the scenes in all places. At the least, he always keeps his company awake, and if a little given to paradox, he is not the less on that account a very lively and very agreeable companion.

His social virtues are excellent. He is a firm, devoted friend.

He will go through fire and water to serve those whom he respects and values. As an enemy, he is dignified and not at all vindictive. In many instances he has treated with noble magnanimity, those who did him grievous wrong. When the confidence of his mind is given, he displays a chivalrous fidelity and loyalty. As The Quarterly once said of Dr. Parr, he would never think of cutting an old friend merely because he happened to be going to Botany Bay. When the town lays a man down, Dr. Griswold is disposed to take him up with increased ardor. He has a sort of Coriolanus-passion for unpopularity in a good cause. These are the peculiarities of a noble nature; and if they provoke the impertinence of the *canaille* of scribblers, they attract and interest the sympathies of gentlemen.

FRAGMENTAL LITERARY DISQUISITIONS.

[This and the remaining series bearing the same title, are fragments. They were written in 1837, and designed as contributions to a work which a young college friend of the author had in contemplation. In reference to some observations in them, it must be remembered that they belong to a date nearly twenty years ago: although it may not be necessary, for any evidence of immaturity that they exhibit, to remark that they are the production of a boy just then twenty years old.—Ed.]

A DIALOGUE BY THE SEA.

The Ocean—Moral Reflections—Disquisition upon Pope—Pope and Byron Contrasted—Nature not always best described by those most familiar with her.

> As budding branches round a tree,—
> Thoughts cling, with feelings fraught,
> Around the silence of the sea,
> Itself a feeling thought.—Meade.

The sun had just set, and the evening breeze was freshening from the waters, when I went out to pay my respects to the ocean. Upon the whole, perhaps, I would as lief have gone alone, but encountering accidentally on my way a person whom I had formerly known well and esteemed very highly, I proposed to him to join my ramble. He assented and we went forward together.

Robert Courteney was one of my earliest acquaintances at school, and without any very tender feelings upon either side, there existed a tolerably warm friendship between us during the whole period of our connection as fellow-students. From some poetical compositions of his which I had seen, the production of his youngest years, I had formed a high opinion of his genius; and I was accustomed to think of him, when in subsequent days my memory recurred to our former acquaintance, as one who, if occasion were propitious, would probably be distinguished in after life. He was one of those persons that we occasionally meet with, who seem formed for pre-eminence, and to have that pre-eminence yielded by all; one whose frank and cordial character excited so warm a personal regard and interest, that in admitting or asserting his claims to superiority, each seemed to be gratifying his own private pride. He was undoubtedly the most admired of all who were at the school while I remained there; and his perfectly good temper and constant readiness to engage in amusement rendered him also the most popular. To tasks requiring either original genius, or acquired learning, he seemed equally fitted; he appeared to reach by a certain instinct of mind, that familiarity with difficult and unusual subjects, which others by the most plodding diligence, less successfully attained. With decided and unquestionable poetical powers, he united none of that moodiness of feeling and that lawlessness of passion, which the history of Lord Byron, and the theories of Mr. Moore, have taught the world to consider indispensable attributes of the poetical character. If the practice of one member of a profession could have justified a doubt of the necessity of those qualities which are usually demanded from the rest, I might have believed from the evidence which he afforded me, that one might still be a bard without ceasing to be a man of honor, of principle, and of decency, and that, after all, there was no such inevitable divorcement between the writing of verses and the performance of the reasonable duties of life.

We presently reached a retired part of the beach, where the broad expanse of the waters extended before the eye in all their silent majesty. The sentinel surges gleamed far along the shore like a white-plumed triple line of soldiers, to guard the rest of the deep.

"It is a glad and glorious pastime to the spirit," said my companion, "to look upon this type and token of Almighty power—to wrestle with the living thoughts which dwell like things amid the stir and strife of these eternal waters—to encounter the breathlessness of awe which comes upon the soul as we inhale at a glance the vastness of the scene. Upon the face of the deep, the spirit of eternity still is brooding: as we pause before this wide unbarriered space, and our naked mind stands bold against the unveiled, eternal universe, a silent thought of homage swells through the endless space; and that thought is God. The ocean is the material image of the Almighty. What attribute of Deity is not here substantial? Power, of an infinite fulness;—beauty, of that particular pervadingness of essence, that rain and tempest, and the winds evolve and not efface it;—life, abstract and indestructible, that never wearies and that never wastes—whose days know not repose, and upon whose bosom the cloud of nightly slumber never weighs. If the dancing water-brook should cease to chant his praises who inspired its gladness,—or if the infuriate storm-blast, as it gnashes through the forest, should burst from its bands, and disown its Maker;—if men should ever gaze upon the western sun, and forget whose countenance its brightness mirrors, or rest upon the mountain turf, nor own from whose omnipotence the strength of the hills has sprung;—if the knowledge of the Infinite One shall ever pass away from the earth, the roar of the ocean will thunder it back. It was the sublime intention of Nicholas Ferrar that a perpetual chant or solemn service of music should be established at Little Gidding, to be sustained by generation after generation, and continued to the end of time without the interruption of a moment. He wished that, whatever might be the condition of men or the character of the times, the voice of praise might ever be ascending; that it should rise amid the roar of contest, like a smiling lotus through a tangled ruin, and be the blended harmony of all the thoughts of peace; that the ancestor and his descendant might unite in the same song of thanksgiving, and century be bound to century by an all-embracing stream of worship. What the saint designed, the sea performs. There are times perhaps in which from human lips throughout the broad extent of the earth, no sound of prayer or praise is heard; but the listening seraph who looks out from the windows of heaven, hears the organ of the waters peal everlastingly. It is not without an influence which may be termed holy,—for its beginning is fear and its effect is cleansing,—that we muse within this great cathedral of the sky-roofed deep. When first seen by man, it gives him a thought and a disturbance which, though nothing can have ever before started such emotions within him, seem strangely familiar to his feelings. And when we claim instinctive brotherhood with that which stretches back, like a broad sheet of light, to the first moment that the gush of sunbeams flowed down upon the waves, and forwards till the depth of the heavens shall be opened, we realize one of those moments of existence in which man feels his immortality and trembles at it. There are thoughts of mystery and dreams of magic floating around this scene; and there are those who have feasted on them till they have become maddened, and their life has turned to parching thirst for the fulness of these unearthly sentiments. But such thoughts are the food of heaven; and while I would labor for their recognition as the proof of heaven, I would postpone their enjoyment to another life, and abide in hope till the veil of the flesh which dims them, is withdrawn."

"There are," said I, "many faculties of the heart whose true sphere of exercise is not in this world, and which bear in the fact of their being, unequivocal testimony that the intellectual frame, wherein they are lodged, is destined for employment in another field of existence. And you have indicated truly the use which should be made of them: we should question them of their secret, elicit from them the truth which they have to impart, and then dismiss them to be more fully developed in the due revolution of time. And I cannot help thinking that much of the scheme of practical Christianity has the same prospective reference. We do wrong in supposing that to the earth only, or even chiefly, is confined the application of the requisitions of the Scriptures; that this globe is the only acting theatre of man, and that the future is but a scene of calm and impassive enjoyment. Our preachers err in limiting to this small arena a struggle and an endeavor which will last through eternity,—in confining within mundane limits, a mystery which fills immensity. Instead of a blessing to man it were a mockery of his helplessness, to expect him to attain the full measure of that perfection, than which no more belongs to consummate purity: to demand of him to familiarize to his bosom and to expound by his conduct a system before whose unfathomable obscurity angel and archangel bow in humility; to comprehend which, cherubic wisdom must pray for added intelligence; to fulfil which, seraphic ardor is not too sufficient. My opinion is, that those commands which are enjoined upon us here, are intended in their completeness to apply to our conduct in future worlds, when by cumulative energy through successive stages we shall arrive at a moral vigor in some measure adequate to the task. And in the very mode of the exposition of these matters in the Scriptures, I read a confirmation of this opinion; for the doctrine of faith is therein fully and satisfactorily laid open, but the precepts, of practice are imperfectly and in many cases impracticably developed; giving glimpses, as it were, of that complete scheme, whose revelation is reserved for other spheres. For spiritual existence in the great archipelago of worlds that fills the ocean of infinity is not independent, but successive,—death being but a 'a sleep and a forgetting,'—birth, an awaking with extended power. The great sacrifice which was exhibited in our own globe two thousand years ago, believe me, was not confined to it. It was a divine immolation for total sin on the great altar of the universe, and its manifestation was simultaneous throughout the whole array of planets; to each there was a darkening of the sun; in each a rending of the veil in an old temple of superstition. Those who have been cast on these shores prior to the revelation of atonement, will learn the healing truth in some future abode of their souls. It would require a mighty argument to convince me, that I have not lived before this; it would require an almighty one to persuade me, that I shall not live hereafter. Meanwhile, whatever may be our future lot, there are incumbent upon us, here, momentous duties as members of society. Let us, therefore, secure of the developments of future time, lay aside the pursuit of these unprofitable speculations which the contemplation of nature forces on our mind, and, girding ourselves to the task before us, actively meet the exigencies of life, and calmly 'wait the great teacher, Death.'"

"I have always consented," said Courteney, "to the maxim of the great moral poet, that the proper study of mankind is man: and I hold that communion with nature is only valuable to freshen and relieve the spirit, and to strengthen the heart to pursue the study. Deeply, as from long acquaintance, I am attached to the solitary haunts where nature reveals herself to her votaries in majestic loveliness, and familiar as I am with the charms of those fair spirits who preside over lake, and stream, and mountain, I must still, in the sobriety of reasoning judgment, confess that those poets, who, like Shelley and Hemans, linger forever beneath the cope of air, and weave not one valuable moral reflection, not one maxim of prudence, among their verses, are not my most cherished favorites. The light which they dispense may be 'light from Heaven,' but it is not *for* Earth: it is all thrown upon the by-paths of romance and the groves of sentiment, not a ray illuminating the high road of human conduct,—that path of action which, while we are men, must be the chief field of our footsteps. They render *that* the essence which, in reason, is but the accident of life; they make that the substance of our business which should, in truth, be but the gilding of our leisure. It is indeed of advantage to retire occasionally from pursuing the reality of virtue to dally with its romance; but these writers make the argument of the volume of what affords but matter for a parenthesis. When the recess of evening brings repose from labor, the reveries of the fireside are in place; but it is worse than idle to linger dreaming in the twilight of the valleys, when midday duties await us on the plain."

"You are of course, then," said I, "an admirer of Pope?"

"So much so that, with the exception of a few of his avowed followers, who have caught something of his spirit, I question whether there has been any true poetry since his days. Ah! my friend, when I see the age about to crown with the title of

Immortal, a poet whose greatest productions are Hymns to a Butterfly, and whose most elevated occupation is the 'sentimental ogling of a tulip,' I fear that we are in the sad condition of the degenerate Israelites; having abandoned the God of our fathers, and gone a-hunting after strange idols. The old Egyptian plague is renewed among us, and grasshoppers and locusts have gotten into the king's chamber. The community of letters has indeed become a republic; all are now equal in insignificance. And the extinction of monarchy in song, like that of the political monarchy of France, is followed by a rabble of daily aspirants, whose fame is as brief as their popularity was vehement."

"I am afraid," said I, "that your simile extends its application to your disadvantage. If the judges will not admit Byron into the line of legitimate 'kings,' the people will crown him by the title of 'emperor.'"

"I would rather," replied Courteney, "subscribe to Byron's opinion of Pope, than the people's opinion of Byron. Of the poets now in vogue, you must unman yourself to read one-half, and unchristianize yourself to admire the other. Aristides, being guilty of no other crime than the crime of being just, was banished upon that charge; and Pope, in the dearth of fault, is condemned because he is 'moral.' The ostracists of Pope talk much of the necessity of 'invention' to constitute a true poet, and descant much on the importance of 'imaginative' topics; but it is yet to be proved that a subject rises in poetical value in proportion as it sinks in every other value. How can it affect the beauty of the structure that its foundations rest upon a rock? Are the garlands of Fancy the less lovely, or is their odor the less fragrant, because they are entwined around the sceptre of Truth? Is the splendid Pharos that, sublimely silent, gazes o'er the deep, the less picturesque, because its main purpose is utility? Is the architecture of the Doric portico at Athens the less exquisite in its impression, because it was built for a market-place? Those critics must be arrant poetical Calvinists, who deem so vilely of their own species as to deny it to be a worthy topic of the poet's pen. What subject can be more interesting than the conduct of man? more various than the nature of man?

more sublime than the duties of man? I admit then to Byron the title of Poet of the Ocean,—to Hemans, of Poet of the Lily; I admit not—I demand for Pope the title of the Poet of MAN."

"It was the sincerity of an honest freedom," said I; "the consciousness that he battled singly for the right—that with a magic transformation made the pen of Pope, as Paulus Jovius said of his own, sometimes a pen of gold and sometimes a pen of iron, and caused his couplets to flow around the land with a might of sarcasm unwithstood. Conservative in all his feelings, he yet hated cant with a fierce defiance; anxious to impress his age, he yet conciliated no sect and truckled to no party. Buying no voices and leaguing with no confederates, he stretched forth his hand in the name of truth, and in that name he wrought his miracles;—'alone he did it.' Such a man has no need to concern himself about popularity; he creates it, as the sun creates the day."

"While Pope, in action, wandered into no enormous vices," said Courteney, "he proposed in theory no extravagant standard of virtue: his precepts were guarded, as Mackintosh finely says of Paley, 'by a constant reference to convenience and practice.' How opposite to this is the modern school of teachers! Look at Shelley complaining of wrong and tyranny, and eulogising purity and heavenly love, and then marrying two wives and leaving one of them to die of a broken heart. Look at Coleridge,—who together with Wordsworth is essentially of the same tribe,—writing songs 'that bid the heavens be mute,' and leaving his wife to the charity of Mr. Southey, who is about the only literary man of our time who is not ashamed to do his duty, and is upon the whole the most perfect character of his age. This poetical *fanfaronade* about virtue and affection, is disgusting in the mouths of these worthless vagabonds:

'Remember
How easier far devout enthusiasm is
Than a good action; and how willingly
Our indolence takes up with pious rapture,
Though at the time unconscious of its end,
Only to save the toil of useful deeds.'"

"Pope," said I, "has certainly done as much to exalt the dignity of humanity by his life, as to improve the behavior of men by his writings,—an article of commendation which can be extended to but few of his brethren. That tissue of putative meanness which was woven by the unnumbered foes which his genius had created, and which Johnson was not unwilling to extend, Roscoe has blown away like the filmly gossamer of the morning; and presented us instead, with a story as touching to our feelings and as honorable to our common nature as any other with which I am acquainted."

"Sir," cried my companion, warming with enthusiasm as his mind dwelt upon the character of his favorite poet, "the hand of Biography does not present us with a finer or more generous instance of a man giving himself up solely and without reserve to high literary ambition;—with the solemnity of an Hamilcar dedication, consecrating himself at the altar of fame; bringing to it the tender blossoms of his early boyhood,—to it, the ripened fruitage of his elder years. Withdrawing himself from the world, and nursing in solitutude the fire of his heart, *that* youthful ardor which in most cases is suffered to play objectless like the ground-fire of the tropics, was by him concentered on a single object. With no vices, with few foibles; free from domestic cares, and safe from all political disturbance; wasting not a moment on the transitory,—he dwelt apart in his beautiful villa, looking out upon man as from the window of a castle, and sketching his character and his destiny with the calmness and fidelity of a superior nature; in youth creating richly, in manhood refining slowly; living out his sad and shattered age with no other purpose before him than

'To better his life and better his lay,
To virtue's improvement and vice's decay.'

Justly might he have exclaimed, '*quantum alii tribuunt tempestivis conviviis, quantum aleæ, quantum pilæ; tantum mihi egomet ad hæc studia recolenda sumpsi.*'"

"But might not the individual to whom those words were self-applied, contest the claim of Pope to superior devotion to lofty fame?"

"I think not. The part which Cicero took in public life; his military longings; his labors as an advocate and prosecutor; his occupations as a quæstor and consul, to all of which he looked for merely temporary distinction, would remove him from the comparison. Besides, you see clearly that to present duties, Cicero gave the preference in his own mind, and the time which he dedicated to labor for immortality was fragmentary, not continuous; snatched, not assigned. It is true that, in the midst of popular applause and judicial approbation; amid the tumults of official triumph and the distractions of private luxury—the still small voice of eternal aspiration reached and stung his inmost soul: but it was occasional, like the dim vistas which ever and anon open and close upon the eye of one who wanders through a forest. But Pope stood with his face full-turned upon the future, his eye resting nowhere short of the remotest posterity; knowing well that the incense of fame is the smoke of sacrifice, and that the diadem of genius is the martyr's crown. His was the sole glorious task to conquer immortality; unambitious to light an earthly lamp which might attract the sidelong glance of the passing traveller, or kindle a transitory fire which might draw together the idle and the vain, but emulous to plant a star in the eternal heavens, which though so distant that the first rays which reached the world might shine upon his grave, yet which, when seen, should be seen forever, and living on in still-abiding lustre, become a fadeless portion of the very frame of nature."

"The change," said I, "which has come over the whole character of English poetry within half a century, and has extended so deeply as to have transformed the principles of criticism, has not yet met with satisfactory analysis. 'Poetry,' says Johnson, 'has rarely been worse employed than in dignifying the amorous ravings of a love-sick girl:'—what a revolution in taste and opinion does the date of that remark exhibit!"

"And, stranger than all," said Courteney, "the verses upon which that bitter sentence was pronounced, have been repeatedly quoted as the sole evidence that Pope was a true poet. If the definition of poetry by the king of poets be adopted, Byron and Wordsworth and Hemans would fare badly. 'A poem,' says Milton, speaking by the mouth of his nephew, Phillips, 'is an illustration or embodiment of some important *moral* truth, *not drawn from individuality,* but created by the imagination, by combining, with taste and judgment, ingredients selected from the stores of fancy.' Had a description been framed with the express object of commending Pope and excluding Byron, it could not have been more scrupulously pointed. You cannot discover in the noble poet, a single notion or feeling which is general in its nature, or true upon universal application. The ability to rise above idiosyncrasy—to project general consciousness into imagined circumstance—so to expand the particular, and peculiarise the common, that any given sentiment shall be universal in reach and individual in impression—to widen views into principles, and point axioms into personalities, so that all shall embrace and each indentify—this, the keystone of poetic power, was utterly wanting in him. If Byron seems to have penetrated more deeply into the human heart than Pope, it is because the one digged so narrowly that the smallness of the extent assisted the depth, and the other opened so expansively that the wideness of the labor seemed to level the profundity. The brilliance of Byron's flashes proceeds from the ray being broken: Pope's light is the white light of unrefracted truth. To present a thought which shall be purely, precisely, and perfectly just, requires so many modifications, flattenings and smoothings down of the first bold impression, that most artists have been deterred from the undertaking; and in the hands of the few who have attempted it, the work has commonly slid into the vague and the commonplace. Pope with unequalled felicity has united truth and power. Search the rolls of poetry from Orpheus to the newest-born, and of philosophy from the first who ever guessed to the latest who has ever reasoned; explore the enigmatic revelations of the dark-thoughted Brooke, and the lucid demonstrations of the mastiff-minded Hobbes, and find, if you can, a passage so profoundly affecting and so exquisitely unerroneous; so full of dignified pathos, and so instinct with majestic wisdom—as his description of the state of man:

'Born but to die, and reasoning but to err:
Great lord of all things, yet a prey to all;
Sole judge of truth, in endless error hurl'd;
The glory, jest, and riddle of the world!'

Think of these words amid the din of worldly business; think of them in the ardor of studious toil; think of them in the silence of your midnight chamber—and they shall seem to you the utterings of a prophet's voice."

"Bolingbroke," said I, "somewhere remarks, that we might give to certain learned plodders, as chronologists and annalists, the praise which their eminence challenges, if we could persuade ourselves that they could have succeeded as well in anything else; and the thought, though false, is natural and common. If Pope's claim to reward for the philosophic be contested, as it often is, on the ground that he wanted powers for the pathetic, the confutation of the doubt is complete in a single stanza. There is not in the wide compass of our literature a more moving passage than that in which this poet, so morbidly unegotistic, turns from the attack on the miserable detractors of his time to make one allusion to his cherished mother. The man who could write thus avoided the pathetic for a reason."

"A far deeper pathos than the pathos of sentiment," said Courteney, "is the pathos of wisdom. Lord Byron's appeals to the heart are about as elevated in their character and managed with about as much artistic skill as those which form the tale of the last beggar who was wrecked on the coast of Barbary. There is more of the very heart and soul of genuine pathos in one of Sir Thomas Browne's magnificent sneers, or in Goldsmith's anticipation of the fate of England, than in a thousand dyspeptic Laras and costive Giaours. But whatever may be the defects of Byron's poetry, considered merely as poetry, his real faults are of another description: it is not the want of genius that I discern, but the want of generosity that I lament. Who is there that, fascinated as he might be by the novelty of the thoughts; the beauty of the images; and the splendor of the diction, is not disgusted by the peevish and unmanly complaint; the paltry protrusion of self; the miserable vanity and personality; and the total want of dignity, elevation, and independence? A misanthrope must be a man of a narrow soul: it must be a small mind, which, when irritated by ill-treatment, finds a satisfaction in the impotent revenge of hate. No admiration to which the genius of Byron might prompt me, could ever check the repulsive scorn which is stirred within me by the sight of one thus having 'his eyes forever on himself,' and coming before the world only to tell it how keen are his sensibilities and how painful his indigestions; that he has not loved the world, and that Wordsworth is his aversion: never will I so far debase my own inward dignity as to listen to these wretched egotisms of another, much less will I dwell upon and applaud the miserable petulant outbreakings of a disappointed and jealous lordling. I respect myself too highly to treasure up what despicable inuendoes against others, or ridiculous mystifications about himself, any other may descend to, to gratify diseased ambition, or soothe his fretted vanity. No! let *me* dwell among *manly* poets; among those exalted older spirits from whose hymnings one rises rebuked, chastened and purified, and learns to 'venerate himself as MAN:' messengers who forgot not their mission, but made their heaven-descended genius parent of heaven-ascending graces; whom you read with a free soul, and an expansion of mind like that bred by the wide ocean-scene we now survey, and whom we lay down in a better frame of feeling than we took up; in better obedience of God's great laws; in better love of our fellows; and far better appreciation of our own state and value. The transition from the morbid and self-dissecting poets of our times; the stove-room and hot-house species—to the clear and trumpet-voiced minstrels of an age gone by; Spenser, Dryden and Thomson—is like the passage from yonder heated and dizzy billiard-room to this clear, freshening, bracing air. To them and to it we turn as to exhaustless sources of high impression: from it and from them we return as from baths of the soul, nerved with gladness and springing with enthusiasm. For to nature and to those kings of song only, it belongs to ever fascinate with never changing: we look to the moon with not the less joy, because we know that we shall see but what we have seen from infancy, and read Milton with interest undiminished by life-long familiarity. Those great intelligences of young time, are commensurate with nature and similar to her; their uniformity is like the uniformity of the heavens, the necessary oneness of complete perfection; for when part has reached the summit, how can the rest differ but by descending? What variation can there be, but the variation of inferiority? The sun varies not, nor does Homer: his monotony is the level line which is pencilled on the sky, by the highest ridge of the high-looming hills. The mind loves to seize on some great watch-towers upon the shores of thought, and brace itself against a rock in the absorbing ocean. The intellect would craze with illimitation, if there were not in the wide view some eternal bounds of power, like Dante and Shakspeare."

Thus talked we by the banks of the sea, through the calmness of twilight, till the moon shone clearly and the power of its light proved the presence of darkness. "Well," said Courteney, turning to me after a pause, "if you wish to catch inspiration or a cold any longer from this scene, I see no reason why you may not; but I, you know, am a poet, and it will never do for me to study nature too long."

"But is not that your very business and profession?"

"Fudge! Take my word for it, that those who have best described nature have known least about her, and the noblest sonnets to the moon have been penned in the presence of a sea-coal fire, with shutters closed and curtains drawn. When we gaze corporeally upon the earth or sky, feeling chokes intellect, and sense stifles imagination; and thus the right hand and the left of the poet are paralyzed. Nature presents a thought too big to pass through the channel of expression, and the reason must grasp and wring it, e'er the drops of Castalia will trickle from the cloud; yet the reason is dashed by the tyranny of vision. It is this incumbency of one vast idea which renders the inhabitants of mountainous countries idiots. We become great, not by putting impressions into the mind, but by drawing them out; they are all in there. For the infant soul was nursed in the bosom of God; and the point where all the converging and diverging rays of thought and feeling meet, is God; she therefore containeth in herself all consciousness of truth and all sentiment of nature in like manner as the centre containeth the circumference. But timid are these inward emotions, and slighter than the amethystine air-curls of the spirit that sleeps in the shade of the rose-down; and, therefore, when the armed ideas of externality troop rudely near, they lurk within and pretend themselves dead; but when the moon-crowned midnight of mental quietude circles the soul with its still white drapery, then step they forth lightly, slowly, falteringly, like the fear-vestured lady from a sentinelled camp to meet her hostile lover; and ever by the day, sleeping in their caverns, lulled by the music of the heart, dream they audibly, and we may hear them dream, and 'tis that hearing which doth make us poets. Come, won't you take a game of billiards?"

"Certainly," said I; "we should take the poetry and prose of life together, like bread and cheese."

A DINNER-PARTY DIALOGUE.

A scientific Treatise upon dining—A dinner-party—Company assembles—Philosophy of dining—Various topics discussed—Roman dinners—Grecian dinners—Characteristics of the Northern and Southern nations of Europe—Proper age of a cook—Roscoe—Politian—Johnson—Parr—Warburton—Webster — Byron — Bulwer—Sir Egerton Brydges—Coleridge—Southey—The moral tone of true Genius.

Feasting hereon, we will philosophise.—SHELLEY.

A FEW weeks after the conversation with Courteney, which I have already given, I accepted an invitation to dine with a gentleman who held among his equals meridian distinction in that meridian art. Mr. Benton was one who had meditated with that earnest and chastised devotion which so great and elevated a subject demands, on the best mode of dining; and it is paying but a merited compliment to the genius and study of this good man, to declare that he understood the subject better, and practised it with more success than any person

I have ever met with. At various times I have been favored with his views upon this interesting subject; for, though not obtrusive in his proselytism as most discoverers are, Mr. Benton was always glad when an opportunity occurred of disseminating correct notions on this important topic, and he had none of that selfishness which might impel him to conceal from mankind what is necessarily never alien to humanity. But that timidity which is the fatal Cleopatra of genius, that proud resilience from the homage of the vulgar, which makes greatness splendid and impracticable, kept him always from appearing before the public. "He died and made no sign;" and the sauntering traveller as he steps carelessly over his modest grave, little knows that he treads above the remains of one whose genius the shade of Lucullus might venerate, and before whose labors the star of Orleans might dim its glories.

When I have sometimes expressed to him the sense which I entertained of his valuable researches, and the hope which I cherished that he would not suffer his discoveries to perish with him, "I confess that I have sometimes thought," he would reply, "that what you are pleased to call my discoveries are not altogether without value, nor without interest; as, indeed, nothing can be that regards a science which, to say the least of it, is indispensable. My regard for the welfare and melioration of my fellow-creatures, has sometimes impelled me to wish that an easy and safe method presented itself of conveying to the world at large, some suggestions which the kindness of my friends has induced me to fancy not entirely valueless, and to perform that duty which every one owes to his race, by handing down to posterity what might be a 'possession for everlasting' of culinary metaphysics. I have sometimes thought of publication, and indeed, I have employed some occasional hours in a few past years in the composition of a small volume on the subject of cookery; but independently on the reluctance which I feel to intrude upon the grave world a book which must necessarily be ungraceful in style, and insufficiently supplied with learning,—which, at least, from my want of familiarity with the pen, would lack that melody of words and harmony of sentences, that Ciceronian charm of aptly-balanced language, which would be required in treating of this, the first and most finished of the fine arts,—independently on this personal objection, which my vanity will not attempt to deem slight, there is a greater one inherent in the attempt itself; I mean the combat which in its tender veal-like infancy it must sustain with those butchering critics and reviewers who ever stand at the gate of knowledge, pen (knife) in hand; for these gentlemen rudely, gracelessly, and unreasonably oppugning and running counter to the precept of the immortal Louis Eustache Ude, to whom be honor, long life, and the gratitude of grateful men!"

"Amen, and amen!" cried I.

"Opposing, I say, that precept of HIS, which forbids us to slay a calf in its tender youth, but to sheathe the knife till his beef-hood shall be attained; they rush savagely upon a scarce-fledged writer, and kill, serve him up with a *garni* of *sauce*, before he has grown robust by age. Whether it be, as Goethe conjectured, that by some personal misconstruction of mind; by a peculiar obliquity in their moral constitution; by the frame of their mental powers; by the very condition of their existence—these people are prevented from telling the truth, certain it is that such a thing as a generous and genial criticism is as rare as half-boiled beef. To me, much reflecting upon these matters, it has appeared that the evil arises ,from the unfortunate position of these anti-authors: for authors and professional critics hold much the same relation to one another that England does to France; a relation, according to Mr. Fox, of national enmity. They have adopted the lying maxim, that ridicule is the test of truth, where, in fact, it is the greatest enemy truth has ever had; being much such a test as proving a sword upon a stone, trying a liquid by evaporation, or searching for vitality with a scalpel; whatever may be the result, the object examined is destroyed forever. They have let in the laughers into the gardens of Philosophy; the baying hounds into the still coverts of the ruminating stag. And they are sure to be supported by the populace, for the populace loves to demolish; I never heard of a mob assembled to construct. The more I consider this affair of laughing, the more absurd and unworthy it appears to me. But the reviewers can do nothing else, being like those tormented spirits, the ghosts of scoffers, described in an ancient legend, who are condemned to expiate their sins by grinning painfully through all eternity. Similar is the critic's destiny; for, humanity and the fresh feelings of unshackled sympathy being dead within them, they become even as dead men, and, like skeletons, deriding humanity; and they thrust forward their ever-grinning visages into the Egyptian feast of literature, and humble their author by the claim of fraternity."

Unfortunately, Mr. Benton could not look with such tranquil philosophy on these things, as Sterne* did, and the world lost forever the benefit of his meditations. His best and most honorable "works," however, were such as could not well be communicated to the world, in substance, nor could the world give them a tribute meet for their desert. One of these I was about to allude to, when interrupted by this digression.

I arrived at the house before any of the company were assembled. Soon after I had reached the drawing-room, a venerable but most cheerful-looking man, whom I knew at once to be an ecclesiastic, entered, and with an uncertain step, something between a trip and a totter, made his way to the host and bowed with entire simplicity, but with the air of a man perfectly accustomed to the great world. He was short in stature, and his feet were the smallest I ever saw; his person was firm, and face unwrinkled, although, to judge by his total baldness, "his eightieth year was nigh." His figure was a good deal bent, but apparently more from study than age; and his head generally rested on his breast, but was very frequently thrown up with a mild impatience, or forward with a kind of restless nod. He had a habit of drawing in the air between his teeth every few moments with a curious noise; an action which he incessantly displayed when another was speaking, together with many other

* "As we rode along the valley," says Sterne in one of his letters from France, "we saw a herd of asses on the top of one of the mountains. How they viewed and *reviewed* us!"

of the innumerable tricks of a nervous man. Mr. Benton named him to me as Dr. Gauden.

"Sir," growled the doctor, with great urbanity, mumbling and biting his words as he spoke, "I'm very happy to make your acquaintance. I knew your grandfather very well, very well, indeed;" throwing up his head and muttering almost to himself, "ah! ah! so it is! dead and gone!" then turning his back on me and limping off to a chair, he continued soliloquising with an alternate nod and toss of the head: "ah! as Varro says, '*vetustas non pauca depravat, multa tollit. Quem puerum vidisti formosum nunc vides deformem senectu. Tertium seculum non vidit eum hominum, quem vidit primum.*'"

Dr. Gauden had been educated for the Catholic priesthood at one of the old colleges of France, which have formed for many years the noble nursing-mothers of the Romish clergy of Protestant countries. There he had been thoroughly imbued with ancient lore, and taught to know the ancient writers and the fathers as familiarly as the divines and classics of his native tongue. When, in later years, he departed from the church of his fathers, he took with him all the tastes and habits which he had formed in its bosom; and though becoming an active Protestant clergyman, "the scent of the *cloister* had clung to him still."

Testa recens
Quo semel est imbuta, diu servabit odorem.

He lived entirely among the old, illustrious authors; for modern books, he said, only repeated one another. He fed his mind upon the golden pages of Tertullian and Chrysostom, of Cicero and Plato, for it was the aliment to which it had been accustomed. His memory was "rich with the spoils of time;" and his conversation abounded with choice fragments of Pagan and Christian eloquence. His quotations had nothing of pedantic in their frequency, but seemed to be the natural overflowing of a full mind. If he wove into his common discourse, a "thread or two drawn from the coat of an apostle," or gave his hearers "a smack of Augustin or a sprig of Basil," all knew that the display was not an exhibition of vanity: ignorance was not alarmed, and taste was not offended.

A few minutes after, Mr. Rolle entered the room; a man of singularly feeble and delicate frame, and a countenance full of feeling and poetry; a vague, uncertain smile played constantly about his mouth, indicating one whose thoughts mostly floated in some inner sphere of sentiment and rarely appreciated the reality of the real things around him; an impression which was assisted by the dreamy stare of his large, moist, gray eye. He entered the room in an amusing state of excitement, and, trembling with emotion, addressed his host in broken and almost tearful accents

"My dear Mr. Benton, could not you have dinner postponed for a little while until I recover my composure? You see how excessively I am excited: I cannot appear at the table with any propriety."

"Do not concern yourself about that, my dear sir," said Mr Benton. "The company consists of your own particular friends, and I am sure that they will excuse any disorder in youı manner."

"Oh!" replied the other, "it is not for them that I care; it is for myself. How can I enjoy my dinner in such a state of embarrassment? How can I come with agitated nerves and an excited mind to a task which above all others requires 'the conscience pure, the easy mind,'—a reason undisturbed by passion, senses cool, critical and keen in nice detection,—a body and a spirit perfectly at rest, like the stone beneath the Ægis of wisdom? Couldn't you put off your dinner till to-morrow? I am sure these gentlemen would as leave come to-morrow."

"My dear friend," said Benton, laughing heartily, while Rolle stood the picture of humorous perplexity, "you shall dine with me both to-day and to-morrow; and to secure you the degree of coolness necessary to the free and full exercise of your unrivalled powers of analysis, you shall be brought here to-morrow, like a salmon, in an ice-basket. Meanwhile, as a dinner is not like a debate, a matter which may be adjourned, I hope that if you sit down in that corner and take out your wrist-buttons, and suffer me to fan you gently, you may at length be recovered into a tolerable condition for dining. But what has been the cause of this terrible disturbance? Have you been waylaid? Have you been fired at? Have you been robbed?"

"Worse, worse!" replied the other. "Sit down and I will tell you about it: but do not look so strongly at me, for it excites me more; look naturally. The event which has so much discomposed me, is this: I was coming here when I met, two corners off, a servant-boy, with two magnificent rock-fishes—a rarity in these times, more golden than gold. They were fishes like those described in Athenæus, ἀθανάτοισι ϑέοισι φυὴν καὶ εἶδος ὁίμοιαι, 'in shape and nature like the immortal gods.' The wretch, to whose care some malignant demon had entrusted these spoils of Neptune, instead of carrying them with cautious solemnity, as the charge demanded, went swinging them both in one hand, with utter carelessness, and bruising them by striking them against one another. Instantly I perceived this barbarous and atrocious conduct, I rushed across the street, and seizing the boy, demanded to know by what infatuation he was possessed to treat those fishes in such a manner. He replied, insolently, that the fishes were his master's, and that if the latter knew how he carried them he would have no objection. I told him that I should go with him to his master and see whether he allowed such animals to be destroyed in that manner, and that if *he* did not resent it, I should punish him myself for such a public outrage. Hereupon the boy fled, leaving me alone with the precious prizes: upon examining them I found one of them utterly ruined by the bruises it had got. *Hinc illæ lachrymæ:* and judge thou if there be not cause. The other, I thank God, is safe."

"And where is it?" cried Benton, with some curiosity.

"In my hat in the entry," replied Rolle, in a whisper. "Come and dine with me alone to-morrow at ten, and we will eat it."

This conversation, which gave me a glimpse of that most curious of all characters, a sentimental *gourmand*, was interrupted by the entrance of a gentleman of Herculean proportions, oddly habited in a scarlet hunting-jacket, loose pantaloons, and a colored neckcloth loosely tied about his neck. His face had a fine, frank, but firm expression; and his large, keen eye denoted high intelligence. His manners were natural and unrestrained—the behavior of a man who lived, not against, but above, the usage of the world; and was directed to such conduct by his strong love of perfect freedom, and supported in it by the calm consciousness of powers and a reputation which would protect him against remark. Such a style of address adopted by a man of fresh and rich intellect and tempered by native delicacy and refined taste, renders intercourse delightful. It is a high relief to escape from the wearisome mistrust and the unworthy egotism of artificial manners, and from the confinement of small talk which good breeding imposes, because all may not be capable of *large talk:* you have the keen pleasure of freely coping a generous intellect, together with the gentle gratification of being, as habitual vanity suggests, in one respect *above* your companion. There was an odd mixture of rudeness and refinement in the character of Mr. Wilkins: he was at once a scholar and a boxer, a poet and a good fellow.

Soon afterwards the Count de Bienne was announced, a gentleman whom I had known some years before quite intimately in Vienna. He was a man of ancient family, and the possessor of an extensive fortune. He had been left very early an orphan, and being master of his own actions, had gone to reside in America while a boy, and there he had spent his youth. He afterwards lived several years in England, and had subsequently visited almost every country in the world. He more fully realized to my conceptions the notions of a "citizen of the world," than any person I have ever met with. He spoke English, French and German equally and perfectly well; had no prejudices and no partialities; and seemed to sympathize equally and heartily with all nations and classes. He appeared to be a member of all religions at once, and an admirer of all existing forms of government at the same time: that is, he knew that abstract truth was a chimera, and that theories of liberty were a fallacy, and that there is no other real propriety or justice than that which arises upon right relation. Throwing himself into the situation and feelings of different nations, he saw that the creed and the policy of each were those that were best suited to their condition, their wants, and their circumstances. There was scarcely any subject that concerned moral or social truth, on which Count de Bienne had not thought deeply; and upon all, his views were equally original and striking. The singular independence of his opinions might be attributed to his always living alone, and to his having so fully observed the varieties and contradictions of human judgments and prepossessions, as to be alike indifferent to all of them.

After the entrance of two or three other persons, dinner was announced.

"What is the reason," said Mr. Wilkins, as the tureens were taken off, "that we always find soup served before our meats? Vermicelli is at best a tasteless affair, and only takes away that appetite which should be reserved for worthier viands."

"Sir," replied Mr. Benton, "you have hit upon the very reason. Soup is provided for the purpose of removing that keen animal appetite whose violence disturbs the mind in the nice perception of the harmony of tastes. Criticism is feeling; and it is too delicate to distinguish finely when the senses are craving the strong physical gratification which nature and habit have made necessary to them. There are two distinct pleasures in eating: the first consists in simply appeasing the appetite,—the second in calmly exercising the sense of taste. The latter is the natural delight springing from the action of one of the physical sources of enjoyment: the former is the independent pleasure caused by supplying or removing a painful want, on the general principle

> That every want which stimulates the breast
> Becomes a source of pleasure when redrest.

You are a snuff-taker, Mr. Wilkins, and you know that every pinch of snuff gives you two distinct delights,—that of pleasing the smell, and that of gratifying an animal want which custom has created. You as a sportsman also know how inconsistent is the exercise of taste with strong appetite; for at the end of a day's hunt you find cold beef as agreeable as terrapins, and perhaps more so; because the more delicate pleasure is absorbed in the stronger, and what most gratifies the latter is most acceptable. As but one of these pleasures is worthy of a sentient being, we provide soups to extinguish the other; that is, we destroy hunger to create taste."

"That is reasonable enough," said Rolle; "but surely no man of sense ever allows himself to get hungry. From the first moment that I could reflect justly on the 'end and aim' of human existence, I do not think that I have ever been hungry."

"It is curious, by the way, to observe," continued Benton, "that the wise ancients had the same custom. Their supper, which corresponds to our dinner, was preceded by an *antecœnum*, which consisted chiefly of wine thickened with honey. The commentators say that this was to quicken the appetite; but honeyed wine must certainly have had an opposite effect."

"The succession of dishes," said Rolle, "is a subject worthy of the most profound consideration. I regard the architecture of an entertainment as one of the highest of the fine arts. When, at the close of a well-cooked and well-arranged dinner,—such a dinner as Mr. Benton would choose to give, and I would choose to eat,—I review the whole, it rises upon my mind like a symphony of Beethoven's,—a succession of elements harmoniously combined and exquisitely diversified. The *beaux arts*, by-the-by, are vastly more numerous than is commonly suspected. Dancing is unquestionably one of them, and eating is another. The latter is a science, which, as Sieyes said of politics, *je crois avoir achevée:* I have brought it to perfection. But there is another of the senses to which there is no corresponding fine art; for, while the hearing has music, and the sight has architecture, the objects which address the smell have never been reduced to a system. I have been engaged in investigating the matter æsthetically, and have nearly succeeded in constructing a gamut of odors, and I hope soon to present to my friends an overture of flowers. But let us postpone this discussion till dinner is over."

"The notion of Mr. Rolle is true," said Wilkins. "The great principle of the universe, moral and physical, is relation; and the sole business of the mind,—the only thing about which it can possibly employ itself,—the primary point at which its operation begins, and the terminating bound at which it stops,—the first step it takes from the domains of the sensible, and the last progress it achieves in the regions of the intellectual,—is the perception of relation. The soul, says Plato, is a harmony; and by the soul he means that mass of organized thought and feeling which belongs to, and is our moral existence; and by harmony he means just relation; these hoarded perceptions of just relation throughout all things, make the soul. There is a mental and a physical perception of relations; that is, a perception by the mind and by the senses. The former gives rise to sciences and the latter to fine arts. The fine arts therefore may be defined the evolution of harmony in the objects of the senses. Metaphysically they are but one; physically they are indefinite in number. Wherever there is a harmony in sound, motion, size, form, smell, taste or touch, *there* there is room for a fine art. This notion, which I but obscurely hint at now, gives rise to a new metaphysical system. I am a materialist, and regard thinking as one of the fine arts. I shall some day or other publish a quarto volume on the subject, with an appendix of maps."

"I hope," said Dr. Gauden, "the chapter on the æsthetics of eating will be illustrated by plates."

"It is curious to observe," continued Wilkins, "how often poets and others, writing not from *a priori* reasoning, but from the natural instinct of impression, have alluded to harmony in matters of form. The word music which they employ denotes mere harmony; and both of these words have been restricted to or derived from matters of sound, probably because the mind, being greatly under the tyranny of vision, deemed the relation of what was perceived by another sense, more abstract and unmaterial than the perceptions of the sight, and so gave to that science or drew from it the generic name of the whole operation. Sir Thomas Browne says, 'There is a music even in beauty, and the silent note which Cupid strikes, far sweeter than the sound of an instrument.' Byron, in 'The Bride of Abydos,' speaks of 'the mind, the music, breathing from the face.' Milton says, 'The hand *sang* with the voice, and this the argument.' An old law reporter dwells with delight on 'the music of a well-written act of parliament.' From a feeling of the same sort the Greeks gave to colored stones arranged in varied order the name of 'mousaic,' which modern speech has corrupted into 'mosaic.' When the old philosopher spoke of the music of the spheres, he meant the harmony of form and motion, and had no allusion whatever to sound: neither had Wordsworth when he heard 'the still, sad music of humanity, nor harsh, nor grating,'—he was referring only to the melody of virtuous conduct in the midst of suffering. Bacon, in a similar spirit, speaks of 'the breath of flowers' coming and going in the air, 'like the warbling of music.'—There is another consideration connected with this which affords scope for talent. If these arts are the relations of homogeneous elements, mathematics, which is the science of pure and abstract relation, is certainly capable of being applied to them. There can be no question that algebra or the calculus possess within themselves the capacity of expressing composite sounds and solid forms, and all other matters, as well as numerical quantities and linear shapes. I do not yet despair of seeing the formula of a temple or an overture. Indeed I am persuaded that even thought is reducible to definite primary elements, and that an equation might be constructed which should express all the possible combinations of these elements, and so contain all that man can think on all subjects. No human head perhaps could do it, and no human sheet of paper contain the equation; but still theoretically the thing is possible."

During the delivery of this harangue, Mr. Rolle had been diligently engaged in "unlocking the hidden soul" of flavor from a *cancre commun*, and I had overheard him ejaculating audibly, "Lord! how good!"—"Oh! how delicious!"—"O—oh Lord, O—oh Lord;" and occasionally exclaiming fretfully, "I wish that Wilkins would hold his tongue; how can a man eat when there is so much talking?"

"Besides this," continued Mr. Wilkins, resuming his argument,—

Mr. Rolle rose upon his feet: "Mr. Wilkins, it is my duty to inform you, that unless you cease making a noise I shall leave the room; yes, sir, unless your discourses are deferred I shall dine in the entry, with my plate on a chair. It is impossible that, amid the distraction and mental harassment which listening and thinking occasion, any man should bring to the dishes that calmness of soul and concentration of mind which such a profession as eating demands."

"Mr. Rolle," said Wilkins, "will you allow me the honor of a glass of wine with you?"

"With great pleasure, Mr. Wilkins," said Rolle, relapsing into his chair.

"The ancients, Mr. Rolle," resumed Wilkins, "thought it well that something should amuse the mind during the moments of dining, so that the senses might be at liberty to gambol in delight 'at their own sweet will.' They therefore provided music at their entertainments, to absorb the spiritual part of man. Talking, if *you* would talk, might serve the same purpose. Is not my authority correct, Dr. Gauden?"

"But Euripides," growled the doctor, "objects to music at feasts, as being a superfœtation of enjoyment, and directs the song to be reserved for dolorous occasions. 'A concert of music in a banquet of wine,' says the author of Ecclesiasticus, 'is as a signet of carbuncle set in gold.' In general, I think, the custom has prevailed among barbarous, rather than cultivated nations. Indeed, Sam. Johnson says the Greeks were barbarians."

"The Greek mind," said Rolle, "was essentially encyclopædic; it craved totality; its perpetual strife was to embrace all; it mistook universality for perfection, and sought not the all-complete so much as the naught-defective. This glorious error led them to paint their temples, to color their statues, to dance as well as sing their odes, and to bring musicians into the dining-room. They desiderated all that the genius could do in creation, rather than all that the taste would admire in contemplation; and in pursuit of the *might be* sometimes missed the *ought to be*,—not always acting on that fine critical principle of 'Jack Birkenhead's,' which Bishop Sprat has preserved, 'that a great wit's great work is to refuse.' The modern capacity may have contracted, but certain it is that no man, as men now are, can fully taste one kind of pleasure while another is at hand to distract the perception. Architecture is the beauty of form; if coloring is superadded, it will defeat the impression of the former just in proportion to its excellence. When you are conversing and I am eating, two high delights are presented at once, and one injures the enjoyment of the other. Conscious that I must lose something, that loss fills me with regret, and that regret unfits me for eliciting gratification. Besides, you forget, most eloquent Wilkins, that, as eating is in good part a mental enjoyment, listening to you more directly conflicts with a diner's duty, by withdrawing the necessary instruments of his profession. The philosopher should imitate the bee, which sucks honey from the dust as well as from the flower; from the Pythagorean school, then, though we ought not to learn to confine our food to beans, we ought at least to learn silence. What opinion, Dr. Gauden, does your classical mind form upon the subject? Is conversation an advantage in dining, or not?"

"Why, I think of it, what Cicero has said of eloquence in a philosopher," replied the other: "'*Si afferatur, non repudianda; si absit, non magnopere desideranda.*' But the same Cicero says somewhere, that the Roman feasts were called *convivial* banquets, because the conversation and society constituted their chief pleasure, and that the Greeks gave the ceremony only such names as contemplated eating and drinking."

"Did they?" said Rolle. "Sage dogs! I'll forgive them the music. Ay! they were right; the knife talking with the meat is conversation enough, and there is no society like the society of the viands. Your Greek, after all, is your only true philosopher: honor and long life to the Greeks! They called dinner by a word which signifies 'the best!' Judicious philologists!"

"Still it must be confessed," said Dr. Gauden, "that the Romans sometimes did these things very handsomely. They rarely gave a shabby dinner. It showed that there was a very just appreciation of the case, when a single mullet sold for $250, and another for $320, and fish-ponds like those of Hirtius and Lucullus commanded $160,000."

"The ancients," said Rolle, "sought to render eating more of a mental delight than we can afford to do, and introduced refinements unknown to us. They served at their table viands whose chief delicacy lay in their intellectual elegance and poetical beauty. A dinner given by Vitellius to his brother, had, says Suetonius, portions of seven thousand most choice birds in one dish, and of two thousand equally choice fishes in another. There stood in the centre a dish, called, from its enormous size, Minerva's buckler; and of what composed, think ye? Of the livers of scari, the brains of pheasants and peacocks, the tongues of parrots, and the bellies of lamprey eels, brought from Carpathia and the remotest parts of Spain in ships of war sent out expressly for the purpose. Claudian and Statius inveigh against this extravagance; but their wisdom had shown itself more rich, if, when the feast was set before them, they had, like Jacques, given Heaven thanks and made no boast of it; but these poets are raffish fellows. I know nothing more ridiculous than the sight of little fat-paunched Flaccus condemning the pleasures of the table, and exhorting to temperance and philosophic sobriety. Another dyspeptic satirist of the times slanders the emperor, because he assembled the senate to discuss the best manner of boiling a turbot; and what more important business could they have had, I should like to know? It would be as well if the topics of senatorial debate were always as honorable, or the counsel of senators always as useful. But satire is a low-born trade, and the professors of it are base-minded growlers; they go about snuffing, smelling, and whining in every direction, and wherever they find an open door, puppy-like, in they go. Juvenal was very little of a gentleman. How different was Virgil! the most thorough-bred man of antiquity! His mind and thoughts had a pearly purity and refinement; in our days he would have been a parish priest, and have died of bronchitis."

"Aristotle," said Dr. Gauden, "wrote a code of laws for the table, and it is recorded that he was particularly fond of fish.

The most remarkable glutton of Greece appears to have been Philoxenus of Cythera, who never dined out without carrying his own castors, and being attended by several of his own pages to wait upon him. He prayed for the neck of a crane that he might prolong the sensation of taste. It is to be hoped that Pluto has changed him into a boa-constrictor."

"I will venture to say," said Rolle, "that there has never been a man of *genius* who has not been a lover of good eating; naturally, I mean; for many have been abstinent from piety or principle, as Ximenes and Warburton. Look with what gust old Homer describes the carousals of his gods. Duly as the day, they met in council; and after squabbling all the morning, they all trot off together down to Jupiter's brazen-floored palace to eat and drink, which was probably the only point on which they ever cordially agreed. Scott, too, has scarcely a novel without a good trencher-man in it; and they are dealt with so considerately; there is such a pleasant humorousness thrown over the exploits of Athelstan and Dalgetty, that you see very plainly it was a 'fellow-feeling' made him so 'wondrous kind.' Whenever his heroes stop for the night, the first thing that concerns him is to feed them."

"Another maxim may be safely laid down," said Mr. Benton, "that it requires a certain degree of virtue to dine well,—at least, that bad men are never devoted to the table. I hold La Fontaine's principle, 'that to get along well in the world, one must have a good stomach and a bad heart,' to be a contradiction in itself; the two things are inconsistent. A bad heart implies a callousness of susceptibility of all sorts, and that is destructive of pleasure from eating. Johnson, who was the relentless enemy of cant, set this matter on a just footing; 'some people,' said he, 'profess not to care for their stomachs: for my part, I attend particularly to mine; and look upon it that the man who does not care for his stomach, will not care for matters more important.' That noble thinker had a mind great enough to perceive the value of little things. Cæsar showed his sagacity when he chose to have fat and sleek men about him, and distrusted lean ones. The master-passions of ambition and hate swallow up all minor likings. Some one offered Wilks a pinch of snuff; 'Thank you!' said the radical. 'I have no small vices.' It was taken notice of at Rome, that those who neglected regularity of attendance at the dinner-party hour (six o'clock in that city) were loose in their general conduct, and profligate in all their manners. Plutarch tells a story of one Polycharmus who, when accused of various vices, solemnly appealed to the people to know whether he had ever violated the rules of the table, or been deficient in the devotion that was due to a supper. The sage Athenians perceived in this so just a sense of propriety, and such an habitual rectitude of principle, that they acquitted the fellow by acclamation."

"Yet there are some instances on record," said Wilkins, "which show that deep depravity may be united with a fine Apician taste. A gentleman who had a plum tree, on which two plums were just perfectly ripe, invited Darteneuf, the great epicure of the last century, half of whose name lives immortal in the verse of Pope, to dine with him, intending that each of them should, after the dessert, pluck one of the plums from the tree, that they might not be injured by being carried to the parlor. Darteneuf, as the dinner was waxing to a close, begged to be excused for a moment, left the room, went secretly into the garden, and plucked and ate both the plums! A baser act of villany, a darker, or more remorseless want of feeling, was never exhibited. The man who could do such an act, would fatten his mushrooms with the blood of his brother."

"Yet, my good Wilkins, the story is *bipennis*, and points both ways," said Rolle. "The man who invited any one to share such a Pomonan banquet must have had a heart to which Howard's was Pharaonic."

"The circumstance that men dine in company and not alone," said Mr. Benton, "is proof of the moral excellence of the occupation; for the virtues are all social; the vices all solitary."

"To settle the precise number," said Rolle, "at which the pleasures of eating and of enjoying society, are in aptest proportion, and neither predominates unduly, has always been a difficult problem in epicureanism. Our companies are generally too large. Among the Greeks and Romans, the usual orthodox number was between four and eleven. Ausonius says seven is the best, including the master: if there be more, he remarks, punningly, it ceases to be *convivium* and becomes *convicium*. A supper of Augustus to twelve was so unusual as to have been deemed worthy of commemoration."

"Varro," remarked Dr. Gauden, "seems to have been the first who gave the rule of not more than the muses, nor less than the graces."

"Cardinal De Retz declares," said Wilkins, "that whenever a company amounts to one hundred, it is a mob, and few men have had more acquaintance with mobs, or have written their natural history better, than Cardinal De Retz. But this limit, if the true one, applies only to politics; for the standard varies with the intention and purpose of the assembly, and a far smaller number constitutes a literary mob than is required for a political one. I take this to be the just criterion in the case; that whenever the spirit of individuality passes out of the persons assembled, and some aggregate spirit, whether patriotic, destructive or panic; whether the *genius loci*, or the *afflatus* of occasion enters into them; whenever private sympathy ceases and collective impression begins, so that men are influenced not *personatim*, but *gregatim*, not by peculiar, but by general appeals; whenever, in public companies, men harangue and not debate, and in private ones, discourse and not converse; in a word, whenever externality prevails over personality; at that point the assembly becomes a mob according to its kind and sort. As every gentleman has a hatred of mobs, this consideration, rather than any numeral principle, should regulate the amount of the persons he calls together to dine. I should consider twelve educated and spirited men at a dinner-table a decided mob; while to make a rebellious mob in a garrisoned city several hundreds might be requisite; such a number at all events as would allow collective enthusiasm to master personal fear. Under the empire three was pronounced a mob; which may be vindicated on Tertullian's authority, '*Ubi tres, Ecclesia est.*' I think it will bear an argument whether a single individual may not in some circumstances be a mob; I should be strongly inclined to maintain that George Sandt when he murdered Kotzebue, the man who mutilated André's tomb in Westminster Abbey, and most of the assailants of royal personages, are not to be considered as individuals, but as mobs sole."

"Shall I have the honor of wine with you, Sir," said the Count de Bienne to me, who, seated beside me, had been eating very quietly most of this time, and appeared disposed, for at least the first three or four courses, to be a "hearer" rather than "a doer of the word."—"With great pleasure on my part," replied I; "and if you will allow me to propose a toast, it shall be in a goblet of Johannisberg—Mr. Benton's is a gift from the Prince—to the honor of your old friend Prince Metternich." "With all my heart," said the Count; and so poured forth a goblet to the brim. "It is remarkable," said he,—apparently first inspired by his draught—"that the Teutonic nations alone, of all the people of the world, are capable of enjoying in that supreme felicity which to us it seems so naturally and so worthily to inspire—the delights of a dinner or a supper. All that Dr. Gauden has said about the Greek and Roman names and dinners is true enough; but the Gothic nations alone of all the races of mankind are capable of rising to *the just and earnest worship* of the god of wine. No doubt the Greek could sip his mild Chian pleasantly, as, with his brows rose-wreathed and languid, he reposed in the arms of his mistress; and the Roman could temper with his dark Falernian the ardors of politics, or mellow the dryness of philosophy, with his strong-bodied Massic; but the 'sublime energy of conviviality,' the deep and soul-enkindling quaffings of the cup, belong only to the blood of the Northmen. Wherever the Latin race has mingled itself with the Gothic, the same inferiority has attached itself. The Italians and Spanish are dead to the enchantment of the grape, and the French Bacchic poetry sounds like a shout whistled through a straw. In all these cases, wine is extolled as an accessory to love or conversation; the wild *abandon* of bacchanality—the adoration of the goblet for the wine—of the wine for the god of wine—is denied to all but the native of the forest. All the southern festive chants are more or less erotic; the true drinking song is essentially and exclusively northern. Is not this true, Dr. Gauden?"

"Distinctions of that kind, I imagine," replied the Doctor, "run through the whole moral and intellectual character of the two races, and may be detected in most of their monuments."

"They are, no doubt, discoverable," continued the Count, "in their architecture and religion—two things which a nation rarely borrows, and never without modification. The Greek and Latin mind was fond of the definite, the sensuous, and the precise; it held to the apparent and the known; it rested in the external. The Gothic spirit, nurtured in uncoped forests, and cradled amid shadows and concealment, longed always for the vast, the undefined and incomprehensive; it craved communion with the spiritual and unseen; it sought ever the inward and mysterious. The Greek temple, accordingly, is regular and complete; it expresses the whole idea which it contains; the Gothic cathedral is aspiring, unrestricted, and indistinct. In one, the effects of form are studied; in the other, the impression of spirit predominates; the one is the complacent shaping of a learned artist; the other, the dark utterance of a poet, restless with the movings of an immortal soul, and charged with the uneasy inspiration of undeveloped life. In the creed of the people, the same thing appears. The gods of the Greeks had finite forms; their genealogy was known, their character and functions were all settled. The god of the Goths was an infinite spirit, inconceivable in origin, unfathomable in nature. The Christian religion, a religion of mysteries, was preached to the Greeks, and was rejected by them; it was planted painfully and slowly among the Romans; it spread like the unchained wind among the Goths, and never became national but among them. Do we not see in this the ineffaceable distinctions of race? The southern nations at once materialized their religion; first by the erection of a human representative and vicegerent of God; afterwards, by image-worship, saint-worship, and the prominent adoration of the human mother of God; and among them the reformation has never prevailed. The north in the palmiest hour of Popery was always Protestant, that is, immaterial, in feeling and doctrine, however Catholic it may have been in government; the trumpet of Luther was a blast of the forest, and its echo died away there. The antagonist characteristics of society in the east and the west are also developed in the history of religion. The Goths were domestic, and Christianity, a religion of peace and union, was adapted to them. The Arabs, the Saracens, and adjoining nations, were lawless, wild, and haughty, and the proud and fierce religion of the crescent suited them. In those eastern lands in which the cross had been established, it was wholly and permanently subverted by the Mahometans; and that defeat has been the marvel of the pious, who have not considered that a social religion must necessarily yield to an anti-social one, among an anti-social people."

"Those natural differences have not been so much studied as they ought to be," said I. "They might be of infinite value to the statesman."

"The appreciation of them," replied the Count, "is the foundation of politics, and the failure of every political scheme may be attributed to the neglect of them. One nation is distinguished from another of the same origin by variations similar to those which divide one race from another. The love of popular privilege which belongs to the extreme west, takes, in France, the form of love of equality; in England, of liberty; in America, of both liberty and equality. Smaller differences, I presume, run down through every district, shire and town in each nation. But the grand distinction in European nations is that of north and south, and in every reform must be kept in sight. The south must be regenerated on the plan of France under Napoleon: one member supreme, all under it, equal. The north must be revived on the model of England, by a pyramidal system of descending classes, distinct but united, like the orders in a Palladian palace, and each having privileges in inverse proportion to the number which constitutes the class. For this distinction is to be taken, that though the south accepted the form of feudality, the north only, that is, England and Germany, was imbued with its spirit. And the principle of the feudal system was personal freedom and social connection—the independence of the individual, and the subordination of the rank. The baron was the subject of the king, but his castle was his throne; the peasant was the subject of the baron, but his cottage was his sanctuary. These dependencies were easily maintained in war, for they were its support. The danger was that they would decline in peace; they were only to be preserved in peace by the appointment of civil institutions which should be germane to the feudal spirit. This, in England, was done by the fiction of land tenures, which led to courts, baron and leet, and by the trial by jury, which is the Maxima Charta of British liberty. The English did not want equality, but independence; and the rights of the people among them, though rights of inferiority, were equally definite with those of the nobility, and for purposes of distinction equally valuable. If Germany is ever raised up, it must be by establishing a pacific system cognate with the feudal; it must be by following the English plan, moderated, of course, from its present development; the chord must be the same, but the key lower."

"Your remark is striking and, I have no doubt, just," replied Dr. Gauden.

"It is, I suspect," continued the Count, "from the want of fit civil institutions that the feudal relations of emperor, baron, and peasant, have got, among us Germans, so hopelessly entangled. The encroachments of the emperor have broken the mesne sovereignties, and the peasantry suffers in consequence. Many of the German nobility have inherited from their ancestors the obligations of princes, and from their fathers the powers of but private gentlemen. It will be a long task to restore the balance."

"Benton," said Rolle, who had not probably heard a word of this long discourse between his neighbors, "Benton, why do you suffer your cook to put mustard in the macaroni? Cooked mustard is horrible."

"Why," replied the other, "my cook has a great many sorts of ability, and among the rest a good deal of irritability; and if I were to act upon the democratic maxim and assume the 'right of instruction,' I fear he would not 'obey,' but 'resign.' But there is so little of the obnoxious article, that I am surprised that you perceive it."

"Perceive it? If it were inserted in Homœopathic doses I should perceive it. But why don't you turn such a man out of the house? I wouldn't retain such a man in my service a moment. How old is he?"

"Thirty-two."

"Too young, too young. His aspirations are yet too tumultuous, and his energies too undisciplined. He cannot have attained that splendid repose of passion amid the ardor of vigorous power, which is demanded by nature for the ruling of an empire and the cooking of a dinner."

"Ude fixes at thirty the period of life at which a man may be pronounced a perfect cook. That seems to be the climacteric of the intellect."

"Sir, you are to take a distinction. There are two climacterics of the intellect, one between twenty-six and thirty, the other at forty; the period of the first is the zenith of energy; the second, of ability. For any enterprise requiring hardy zeal and intrepidity; for the resolute execution of a daring project; for all that demands nerve and force; the powers of man are in their perfection at about twenty-seven or nine. Alexander, Charles the Twelfth, and Lord Byron, who wrote his poems in the same spirit that the others fought their battles, performed at this age their finest achievements, and all of them coincided in dying at thirty-six. Shakspeare, the all-knowing, has observed this psychological truth: Iago tells us when he commences his diabolics, 'I have looked upon the world for four times seven years.' On the other hand, no man can be prepared for the performance of a truly great and elevated work; one enacting the full development and exercised freedom of every mental faculty, and the long-trained and dependible strength of every power, before the age of forty. At that age Wieland fixed the time when a man is best fitted for a high literary work, and sat down to the composition of Oberon. At that age, which Dryden calls 'the full summer tropic of his genius,' Virgil wrote his best work. After that age Burgh, who had surveyed mankind with accuracy, forbade any one to enter on any new undertaking, perceiving that that was the era of execution, not enterprise. I should therefore conclude that while an *artiste* of thirty-two is admirably fitted for grand and gigantic experiments in his profession, he is yet unsuited for that last and noblest effort of human genius; that loftiest exhibition of serene might; that most worthy task of Olympian powers: the cooking of a dinner."

"We are told in the Acts of the Apostles, that Moses was full forty years old when he began his mission; Mahomet was thirty-nine. Forty, also, was the consular age among the Romans."

Leaving this conversation to proceed as it pleased, I turned to Dr. Gauden, who was sitting on the other side of me, and after our political disquisiton with the Count, had fallen into a kind of revery. There was a fine landscape by Gouldsborough hanging on the opposite wall, in front of him, at which he was looking intently, and muttering to himself some verses of Flaminius, with the usual intermixture of fretful nods.

"Umbræ frigidulæ! arborum susurri!
Antra roscida! discolore picta
Tellus gramine! fontium loquaces
Lymphæ! garrula aves! amica Musis
Otia!—O mihi si volare vestrum
In sinum superi annuant benigni!

That must be when I come back."

"It is to be regretted, I think, Doctor," said I, falling in with the current of his thoughts, "that the Latin writings of the Italian scholars who clustered about the morning light of modern letters, are not more known and studied than they are. There is some exquisite poetry among them."

"Beautiful, sir, beautiful. In descriptions of nature they are unrivalled. The history of the literature which Le Clerc happily calls demi-ancient, remains to be written. Roscoe's books are beneath contempt."

"I am glad to hear *you* say so, for I have always held the opinion that they were infinitely overrated. I never could get through them: they would not take hold of me."

"His popularity," replied the Doctor, "illustrates a remark of Horace Walpole: that *grace* will save any book, and without it none can live long. The gracefulness of his style and the elegance of his manner have given him an acceptance with 'the general,' who hate to think and are careless of knowing. But he is always superficial and often mistaken; he says more in a sentence than he could stand by in a volume. He sketches, but does not portray, and guesses where he ought to investigate; '*il effleure lorsqu'il devrait percer.*' His taste was delicate rather than just: and his mind, though polished, was feeble and one-sided. He could argue agreeably, but could not judge accurately. He lacked that strong grasp of mind, that stern watchfulness against prejudice, and that self-denying disinterestedness of sentiment, which are essential in exploring the mines of history."

"Among the many services," said I, "which Pope rendered to literature, his edition of some of these poets should not be forgotten; if it showed no learning, it proved at least his taste, and his interest in letters. I have sometimes regretted that Johnson did not prosecute his intention of editing Politian."

"No doubt he would have done it well; he edited Browne's 'Morals' with consummate ability. But to tell you the truth, Politian is no favorite of mine. His prose is certainly elaborately classical; but his poetry is irreclaimably dull. His personal character is anything but agreeable; he was intensely and meanly selfish; always cringing and begging. He was insatiable of favors and never seems to have had the least gratitude for them. The wife of Lorenzo, you know, turned him out of the house. It is odd that Mrs. Parr did the same thing to that splendid brute, Porson. I should have been glad if Johnson had edited Petrarch, or Vida, or had written a history of that age. That is a work which is yet to be done; the men of that time are still doubtful in reputation; posterity has formed no definite conclusion about them. Such a man would have settled opinion once and forever. Let theorists sneer as they may, there is not a critical notion of Johnson's which the nation has not accepted. Brydges and Bowles have written their volumes, and Coleridge has lectured his worst, exhausting logic and his hearers; but not a decision in 'The Lives of the Poets' has been shaken: that book stands in the history of literature like a rock in the ocean; the waves and waters of opinion may beat around it and beat against it, but it stands, 'and as it stands, forever shall stand on.'"

"I have sometimes speculated, Doctor, on the effect which he would have produced on English literature, if, with the reputation which he had at his death, he had lived on till our own times. Modern poetry and fiction would have no existence. Byron, and Wordsworth, and Bulwer, would have been crushed like peascods. I suspect that the whole radical system, with its liberty and utility, would have been scattered to the winds; for his actual power was immense and his possible power scarcely calculable. For cogency of reason; for simple ability to *convince;* no man that ever existed may be compared with him. He was a wonderfully great man."

"Sir, his greatness cannot be overstated. Form the highest notion that you can have of powerful reasoning or of brilliant wit, and then turn to some of his political pamphlets, or to certain conversations which I could name in Boswell, and you will find that the reality excels your wish. His conversations are to my judgment even more wonderful than his writings. He might have said of Boswell what Mahomet said of Ali, 'I am the city of knowledge; and he is my gate.' Boswell deserves to be remembered, for his appreciation of Johnson showed a fine spirit, and the meannesses he submitted to, were the sacrifice of dignity to wisdom. And he *will* be remembered with an immortal insignificance, for he is like the beccafica which the stork takes upon his back and carries to heights which its feeble wing could not attain. His powers were undoubtedly most respectable; for I take it to be the, not so facile, business of a biographer, simply to give you a clear and satisfactory impression of the subject of his book, and this he has done; you see Johnson as he lived; in the rude grandeur of his noble nature: '*Nihil hic elegans aut venustum, sed ingens et magnificum, et quod placet magnitudine suâ et quâdam specie immensitatis,*' as Burnet says of a view from the shores of the Mediterranean."

"Johnson's independence or defiance of the restraints of refined life," said I, "though it exposed him to cavil, was certainly of service to the freedom of his mind, for it enabled him to appreciate the world with stern and conscientious truth. Every gentleman, even the most strong-minded, is habitually under the influence of cant; and when the judgment is once resigned to prescription and usage, the limits of the thraldom cannot easily be defined. Johnson stood *alone*; early a widower,—with no children and no relations near him,—an acknowledged exception to all society,—he was free from the faintest fetter of custom,—'Custom, that result of the prejudices and passions of many, and the designs of a few, that ape of reason, who usurps her seat, exercises her power, and is obeyed by mankind in her stead.' He was thus enabled to look down upon the establishments of the world with an independence which few others could hope to attain, and where he bore testimony to their value and justice, his evidence had incalculable force."

"It is a pity," said Dr. Gauden, "that Parr and others who imitated the great moralist, should have copied the 'brute part of him' so closely. You see clearly that Johnson's rudeness was like the horns of the Fauns and Satyrs, a natural excrescence; while Parr's, like those of Bacchus, was an ornament which he could remove. In his Salmoneus' wieldings of the thunderbolt, he gave too much of the thunder and too little of the bolt. He was a man of small stature; still, when he 'summoned all the energies of his reason, and put forth the whole power of his mind,' he could 'do considerable.' His dedication of the Warburtonian's Tracts is the most splendid effort of elaborate malignity that the world has ever seen. But he had always the cramped movement of one acting a part, and was still farther dwarfed by acting a part too high for him. Johnson strode with the step of a giant; Parr stalked like one accoutred in the seven-leagued boots of a dwarf. Parr *built* up his mind on a great model; Johnson's mind grew up, and he swayed it as we sway the limbs of our body. Parr struggles to get up to his subject, as a clumsy swimmer to get upon the ice; Johnson has always conquered his topics, and holds them up with the air of a man going to grate a nutmeg. You find, too, about the latter, that natural humor and honest *bonhommie* which results from the self-composure incident to a thoroughly great mind. It may seem an odd fancy, but there is something in Falstaff which puts me in mind of Johnson."

"Warburton was more his fellow than any other eminent man of his country. But he differed in many qualities, and where he differed, there he descended."

"Warburton had logic rather than reason, and had more of mechanical intellect than moral power; he was forcible rather than strong, and energetic rather than robust. He used the sling; Johnson, the mace. Johnson was like a man who, walking through a forest, meets a lion there and slays him: Warburton was like one who, happening to pass an amphitheatre as he is going through a city on important business, throws down his bundle in the street and steps in among the beasts, from pure love of a broil: as much praise must be given to the unostentatious manliness of the one as to the gladiatorial vehemence of the other. A great mind is stable by its very weight; Warburton floated about like a gossamer,—over men's heads and in their faces. No truly great mind ever tampered with error; it has a strong love of truth,—an intellectual affection, '*qui s'attache au vrai par une espèce de sympathie,*' as Fontenelle says, '*et sente le faux sans le discuter.*' Notwithstanding the high and rich delight which the study of his works has afforded me,—for, like Lelius in 'The Arcadia,' he showed more skill in missing than others did in hitting,—yet my own opinion of him is much what Voltaire has expressed about Charles of Sweden, '*homme unique plutôt, que grand homme, admirable plutôt qu'à imiter.*' Bentley, I think, had more of the great Cham's unminted wealth and sinewy vigor than any of these men: but the most Johnsonian mortal now alive, and out of sight the first man that wears calf-skin, is Mr. Webster. What a towering monument of mind is he! He may be termed a *real* statesman according to the law's definition of the realty,—'permanent, fixed and immovable, which cannot be carried out of its place.' But there are many things in this world that are of great value and no use; and Webster is one of them. Every man has his fault, and greatness is his. But he is a glorious creature. What a pity he is honest! Sir, we'll drink his health!"

"With all my heart!"

"Mr. Webster undoubtedly has the misfortune of being too great for his condition. There is in the American system no niche for such a statue. Such a man must be often disappointed, and die at last of a broken heart."

"England has secured an eternal supremacy for her great statesmen over those of other nations by the wise device of enrolling them in the peerage. Men may talk as they will of the majesty of intellect or the kingliness of character; there is no greatness which the world will always and inevitably acknowledge save that of title. The moment a man is inscribed in the quiet rolls of the nobility, he assumes in the instinctive and ineradicable admission of all men, a superior nature. He may be a parvenu and a brute, but his name clothes him, in the imagination of all, with the splendor and homage of feudal dignity, and Tudor and Plantagenet float before our eyes."

"True: and in England that natural fealty always prevails over the opposing popularity of democratic aspirants, and enables the balance of contest to be on the side of the aristocracy; so that the English have generally the satisfaction of being, at least, enslaved by a gentleman. Britain's feudality has saved her from the political Fetichism of America, whose devotion only bows to beasts. It has also kept her from the leaden tyranny of wealth, which has here set up its altars unopposed—Temples were the banks of Greece: Banks are the temples of America."

"Of England and America we must say, '*magis pares quam similes.*' The system of civility which prevails in the two countries is different. England is a lake, calm and dignified, shaded by willows and fringed with daisies. America is a river, that dashes along, often muddy and always agitated, rarely graceful and never dignified, but in this wild and free impetuosity an emblem of all that is bold, and daring, and spirited in man, and sometimes, too, not failing in its unfettered energy to work out a high and earnest beauty. Our greatness lies in that enterprise and activity of which we can give no vouchers in the drawing-room. The Englishman walks in a narrow sphere, and in that sphere excels what his colonist can do in any one of the departments in which he figures. The American is a flambeau that stinks in a drawing-room, but burns admirably on the race-ground: the Englishman is a wax-candle, elegantly bright in its station, but which, if moved out of its place, flares desperately."

"Byron, in Manfred, has sketched the bitter degradation to which a noble mind like Webster must submit, that would mingle in the strife of public life."

"Byron doubtless described what his own brief experiences in parliament had taught him. He seems to have been ambitious to bear a part in the politics of his country, and I suspect that to his failure in that enterprise is to be attributed much of the bitter hate and defiance which has been popularly attributed to domestic misfortunes. That his nature sympathized with the daring in action rather than the tender in sentiment, is manifest from his Alp, his Corsair, and indeed the whole circle of his heroes. There was rankling in his bosom some great and independent irritation;—the stings of an ambition which the honors of poetry could not gratify. His expedition to Greece is indication of the same thing. But his character is, and will remain, a riddle. Dark and demoniac as were some of his qualities, he had many traits of a noble nature. His spirit was like the form of Eblis, in Beckford's marvellous creation; '*sa figure était celle d'un jeune homme, dont les traits nobles et réguliers, semblaient avoir été flétris par des vapeurs malignes. Le désespoir et l'orgeuil étaient peints dans ses grands yeux, et sa chevelure ondoyante tenait encore un peu de celle d'un ange de lumière; . . . une main delicate, mais noircie par la foudre, . . . une voix plux douce qu'on aurait pu la supposer, mais qui portait la noire melancholie dans l'ame.*' Virtue and vice contended for his soul, as Michael and Satan for the body of Moses."

"Byron's poetry was never to my taste. He and his set are a kind of poetical Brahmins, teaching universal hatred and contempt towards all their fellow-creatures, and nourishing in themselves, as a religious duty, pride, selfishness and all uncharitableness. The '*impar sibi*' is a charge which lies not against him, for his morals were as bad as his manners. I do not deny his talents, but I have no sympathy with his subjects. 'He that striketh an instrument with skill,' says Hooker, 'may cause, notwithstanding, a very unpleasant sound, if the string whereon he striketh chance to be incapable of harmony.' As long as Spenser and Dryden survive I shall have little inclination to read a Newgate Calendar in verse, with a running accompaniment of Satanic applause, and an occasional episode of beautiful blasphemies."

"But Byron," said I, "exhibits his heroes in colors so little agreeable, and paints the sufferings of remorse so darkly strong, that few, I imagine, would be seduced by the examples which he lays before them."

"Sir, you mistake. 'The fly,' says Herbert, 'that feeds on dung is colored thereby.' What we read becomes a part of our mind, and, even if we condemn, the thought is there, and is working its evil. But in fact no one reads this poet without admiring him, for the feelings which he excites are so strong that the book must be thrown down in disgust or devoured with transport. The natural element and protection of the virtues is calmness and sobriety; all excitement endangers innocence; all familiarity with stimulating feelings and engrossing interests, perils the heart's uprightness. Ignorance of vice is the safest virtue; to shun temptation is the best deliverance from evil. The passions are like those demons with whom Afrasiab sailed down the river Oxus; our safety consists in keeping them asleep; if they wake we are lost. Byron rouses a whirlwind of emotion in the mind; and it is much if the moral integrity is not wrecked in the tempest. Navagero, a noble Venetian, burnt a copy of Martial once every year: Childe Harold deserves the same apotheosis. If the size of Lord Byron's form be measured by the shadow which it has cast over the land, immense must be his mental proportions. He has done incalculable evil to the young, and more mischief, I suspect, to the world than any other single cause now in action. Moore may foster some of the details of vice, but Byron implants the master sin,—the demon-father of a countless brood, —Pride. At a period when the independent spirit of the times requires the bridle far more than the spur, he teaches his young disciples to follow their own headstrong will, and to defy all moral restraint,—thus feeding the most fatal serpent that lurks in the breast, and for which there is sustenance enough, in all conscience, supplied by the rebellious suggestions of the native disposition. 'Lust seizeth us in youth,' says one whose thoughts are 'quaint and solid as the best yew-hedge,' 'ambition in mid-life, avarice in old age; but vanity and pride are the besetting sins that drive the angels from our cradle, ride our first stick with us, mount our first horse with us, dream with us at night, wake with us in the morning, and never at any time abandon us. There is in the moral straits a current from right to wrong, but no reflux from wrong to right; for which destination we must hoist our sails aloft and ply our oars incessantly, or night and the tempest will overtake us, and we shall shriek out in vain from the billows, and irrecoverably sink.' Believe me, we need no incentives to the development of this inherent evil of our nature. We are well assured that dark results are reaped from such a planting. For my part, as Gray says of Rousseau and his guild, 'I can be miserable enough without their assistance,' and there I leave these *heautoustimoroumenoi* to those who can read them without being worsened."

"At all events," said I, "if Byron must suffer the '*suspexerunt viri probi*' of Pontanus's epitaph, he is fully entitled to the '*amaverunt bonæ musæ.*' No man can read Manfred or Don Juan, and withhold from the poet all that his admirers claim for him on the score of genius. Manfred's being caught by the Chamois Hunter as he attempted to throw himself over the precipice, and afterwards, when describing to the witch his unsuccessful efforts at self-destruction, mingling this reality with the fancies of a mind 'peopled with furies,' and saying that 'an all-pitiless demon held him back,—back by a single hair which would not break,' is worthy of the hand which drew King Lear."

"The worst consequence of authors who are popular from some great peculiarity," said Wilkins, striking into the conversation, "is that they raise a host of followers, who wear the badge, but lack the blood which gives that badge a meaning. Bulwer in this manner is the literary offspring of Lord Byron, as the Mahometans believe the pig to have been generated from the excrement of the elephant. Clemens Alexandrinus tells us that Alexander the Great desired his sculptor to represent him with horns, willing to bear a deformity which associated him with the gods. Bulwer mimics Byron's depravity in the hope of enjoying Byron's notoriety, forgetting that an ass wears a cloven foot as well as a devil."

"Byron, to be sure, has a wilder energy and a manlier sweep," said Dr. Gauden, "but the matter of their works is much the same."

"I have no fondness for this philosophic radicalism; this moral system which sets out with denying all that the world has accepted, and opposing all that the world has established. '*Si proficere cupis,*' says the great African bishop, '*primo firme id verum puta quod sana mens omnium hominum attestatur.*' Bacon concludes his great work by repudiating all charge of wilful eccentricity and opposition: 'if I have in any point receded from that which is commonly received,' says he, 'it hath been with the purpose of proceeding *melius* and not in *aliud;* a mind of amendment and proficience, and not of change and difference;' and Johnson makes it the worthiest praise of Newton that he stood apart from the multitude, not by deviating from the path, but by outstripping them in the march. The world may be wrong, and yet we may mistake 'reverse of wrong for right:'

> 'Tis, by comparison, an easy task
> Earth to despise: but to converse with Heaven—
> This is not easy.

It seems to me, that the principle of these men, if they had any principle, was, eternally to differ for the sake of distinction. 'A good wife,' says Damis in Lessing's Young Author, 'I do not expect. And if I cannot have a very good, I would rather have a very bad one. An every-day woman, neither cold nor warm, neither this nor that, is not fit for a man of letters. If I cannot have a wife who will assert a place in a future dissertation *De bonis eruditorum uxoribus,* let me at least have one that will not escape a writer *De malis eruditorum uxoribus.* Anything but obscurity; anything but mediocrity.' In the same spirit, these writers seem to say: 'if we cannot be mentioned as those who have written in the best taste, we will be named as those who have written in the worst; if we cannot have the purest sentiments, we will have the vilest; anything but obscurity—anything but mediocrity.'"

"Bulwer—to use a happy phrase of Walpole," said Wilkins, "always writes in *issimo.* He uses the dialect of Brobdignag. If a man's mind is uncomfortable, it is with him—a hell! If one sustains a loss which will probably never be made good, it is, in his language, a curse and an immortality! His exaggerations would make Heraclitus laugh through his tears. The passion which is stamped on his pages exists always rather in the words than in the sentiment. It is not that excited feeling finds vent in burning eloquence which swells and glows like glass under the breath of the blower, but he seems in the dearth of energy to pour forth these blustering syllables for the purpose of being himself roused by them to ecstasy; to work himself up like a bully by beating the air. This style is in description what *rant* is in acting—always growing mightier, as true passion wanes. There is a certain calmness about the acme of feeling—a security which seems to indicate that the suffering transcends the powers of language to utter it, or the strength of the sensibilities to cope with it—a composure in the midst of the *most* awful scenes —which it is the highest effort of art to portray; the rage and the violence belong to inferior grades of sensation, and are the exhibition of meaner artists. When Shylock, in fear of a loss, lances wild threats upon the city's charter, you see that he is strongly excited: when the whole prostrating truth bursts upon him, he says, 'send the deed after me: I am not well.' Compare this with Croly's Cataline, with the manner of Maturin, Godwin and Bulwer, and you will perceive the difference between the master and the man. As a general remark, by-the-by, our elder classics exhibit the best specimens of energetic feeling temperately expressed. Lord Byron may be taken as a specimen of power united with fury—the might *and* vehemence of the whirlwind. Bulwer has copied all his disorder and only forgotten his strength; he is a prose Lord Byron—without his genius."

"In looking at the productions of all first-rate artists," said Gauden, "Shakspeare, Homer, and Scott, for example—it is clear that in every case they are *above* their subject—they are never overmastered by a passion which they would develop. In the midst of the contest, in the height of the agony, the narrator is cool and judging; his own sympathies absolutely sleep, and his creations are altogether impersonal. That the excitement shall be in the action and not in the author—that the moving representative shall be the calm exhibition of a troubled scene and not the troubled exhibition of a calm one—is, I apprehend, the *experimentum crucis* of art. The strife of Byron and the confusion of Bulwer are the pictures of an ordinary interest mirrored in a disturbed fancy. Homer's song of the battles on the banks of the Simois is as passionless and calm as the reflection of them in the stream might be. His poem shows action in repose, boundless passion never tumultuous. Doubtless the interest must originate with the author, but his business is to transfer it all to his subject. If it be conceded—and I take it to be undeniable—that genius is but the highest art, and that, invention being equal, the palm must be given to him in whom judgment is most despotic, we settle the question of merit, when we say that Shakspeare and Scott write like the masters of passion, and Byron and Bulwer like its slaves."

"Bulwer chiefly aspires to the praise of portraying character," said Wilkins, "and it is there that his failure is most ridiculous. His system is Rochefoucauld caricatured. He confounds the concentrative and generalizing quality of a descriptive character with the broad and diversified substance of a dramatic one. In an epigram we may say, metaphorically and extremely, that a man never means a compliment but he makes an insult; but to introduce a Lord Aspeden actually making every speech throughout a long conversation, an elaborate rudeness, is totally to mistake the limits of art: it is to forget the person in the character; to lose the man in the manner; to evaporate the substance into the quality. It may be said that in many of the plays of the old stage-writers, Shakspeare among the number, the personages are mere embodiments of a feeling or idea—what Ben Jonson calls personified 'humors.' But this great distinction is to be taken, that Richard and Iago are characters of passion, and a passion may well leaven the whole individual into its own similitude; whereas Aspeden, Brown, and that cluster in the 'Disowned,' are but the character of manners, and manner is an affectation which can but flit over the surface, not 'enter into the soul.' The qualities of nearly all his heroes are mixed in impossible combinations: the flippancy of one, the philosophy of another, and the feeling of a third are selected; and, with the address of an Orford and the morals of a Shippen; the prudence of a sage and the gayety of a boy; a fop's extravagance and a warrior's fortitude—are all assigned to a common man of the world. This, as Piranesi told Fuselli, is not designing but building a man. It is a want of psychological truth. A Henry Pelham may have really existed, and may again exist, but the novelist has to do with generalities; he is to describe a species, not an individual. Fact is the field of the historian, and probability of the romance-writer: and when the latter errs against verisimility, although he is supported by facts, he violates truth as much as the other does when he contradicts documents for the purpose of making a credible story. Herein Bulwer wanders farther than Byron; for the poet's characters being in wild and imaginary scenes may be warped into a strangeness which we cannot venture to deny; but the novelist's personages being on the terra firma of a brick pavement, and breathing the common air of cities, are within a far narrower law. Lara, in his wild solitudes, above and beyond the sympathies of the world, is in a very different predicament from Henry Pelham, Esquire, No. — St. James's street, who reads newspapers, and keeps appointments by St. Stephen's clock. Besides, Byron's people are self-consistent; they are under the control of some one great impulse, and not swayed by a score of opposing ones. Wolfe, Glanville, Mordaunt, and all that class of choking gentlemen, are creative lies; the author does not say 'the thing which is not,' but he images the thing which cannot be. They are, like Macbeth's dagger,

> A false creation,
> Proceeding from a heat-oppressed brain.

His greatest blunder, however, is the character of Aram. His object in that story was to show that a man might be guilty of a great crime, such as murder, without having his nature depraved by it; and to demonstrate this he falsified the character of a man whose story proved precisely the reverse; for the real Aram was a dirty and vulgar scoundrel. Fortunately, Bulwer's theory is as false as it is mischievous, for wherever he has deserted fact he has erred from truth."

"Bulwer forgets," said Dr. Gauden, "that most men as well as women, 'have no characters at all.' He overlooks that class which 'Nature makes by the gross, and sets no mark upon them;' a class which largely shades the light of life, and should find a place in the tablet of the faithful portrayer of humanity. He willingly essays the complications of a Hamlet, but the exquisite nothingness of a James Gurney is beyond his skill. He discerns on the shoulders of every lackey a head that might inform the counsels of cabinets. His heroes have their dinners announced by men who might put the Duc de la Rochefoucauld to the blush. Every jockey salutes them with an epigram, and every landlord converses in syllogism. His very animals have characters: *tot canes, tot ingenia.* His philosophy, though it seems to me but a trick of words, commends him I believe to many, who, captured by anything that is brilliant and novel, do not stop to inquire if it is true. When I daily hear perspicuous writers, such as Addison, Goldsmith, and Scott, put aside as superficial thinkers, and the tripod given to those who are considered deep only because they are obscure, I am tempted to keep in mind a curious but most valuable remark of Bolingbroke upon that point. 'To speak the truth,' says that sagacious writer, 'though it may seem a paradox, our knowledge on many subjects, and particularly on philosophy and metaphysics, must be superficial to be real. This is the condition of humanity.' If Scott has no system of human action, it is because human action cannot be systematized. But one might pardon even greater charlatanry than Bulwer's, if it were set forth in tolerable English. His style, with its 'varnish of words and its garnish of flowers,' is decidedly the most vicious of the age; I can forgive almost anything but the one-legged poetry of staggering prose. He does not use comparisons for illustration; simile seems to be with him a mode of writing. It puts me fairly out of temper to see a man circling round some thin notion in endless gyrations of metaphor. Scott uses tropes very freely, but his flowers have always the significancy of an eastern garland."

"All Bulwer's conceptions," said Wilkins, "lack the freshness of true creation. There is a total want of generosity in the author's mind. It is in this wide nobility of sentiment, this sympathy with the free and the foreign, that Scott stands so pre-eminent. All his characters are sparkling with the dews of natural life. When Richard met Saladin and was challenged by the Saracen to a trial of strength, he undertook to sever with his sword, an iron bar of an inch and a half diameter. One of his attendants warned him of the magnitude of the enterprise, and his own enfeebled health from illness. 'Peace, villain!' cried Richard, settling himself firmly on the ground and looking round with fierceness, 'Thinkest thou that I *could* fail in *his* presence?' I doubt whether Mr. Bulwer would have understood the feeling."

"We may safely venture to admire personally the man who writes so," said I, "for he must have had a touch of the crusader in him, who describes crusaders so well. Bulwer never succeeds in placing his characters independent on his own mind, and looking at them quite *ab extra*. He shows them to us as they seem to him, not as they were; we see them mediately, not in their own bold individuality. He maps out their natures too analytiçally; in short, he describes, rather than exhibits them. The secret of the failure is that he is too much of a metaphysician to be a dramatist. But, after all, say what we may, he is popular beyond all rival, and I invariably bow, in all literary subjects, to the judgment of the public. Storace used to say that the merits of no musical composition could be considered as settled until it came to be ground upon the hand-organs."

"If I had not taken so much of Mr. Benton's good wine," said Wilkins, "and if I was not afraid of disturbing the audible slumbers of my excellent friend, Mr. Rolle, I should enter at large upon the subject which you moot. As it is, I will only say that it is not in the nature of a truly great work that it ever can be popular. Nothing of exalted merit is capable of being *presented* to the public; 'The Creation,' for example, could never come upon a hand-organ. That which lies in the way of the mob enough to receive a full hearing, must necessarily be very inferior. There is no music in Yankee Doodle. If I were to frame an extreme theory upon the subject, it should be upon the principle of the Greek philosopher. 'This is right,' says Epicurus, 'precisely because the people are displeased with it.' In many matters it must be so; 'the eyes of the multitude,' said Plato, 'are not strong enough to look upon truth;' and generally where they blink most there is most truth. It is constantly happening that in literature as in every thing else, those voices which make up public opinion, are baying darkly where there is no game; but the blunder is finally discovered. 'Truth,' says my Lord Coke, 'may peradventure by force for a time be trodden down, but never by any means whatsoever can she be trodden out.'"

"Your doctrine," said Gauden, "would be '*qualis sopor fessis*' to poor Chandos of Sudeley,—the *peer*-less Sir Egerton Brydges. He has reached the conclusion that all good books are unpopular, and by a very harmless *non distributio medii*, resolved therefrom that all unpopular books, like his own, are good. The theme of his musings is still the hope of Milton:

At ultimi nepotes,
Et cordatior œtas,

Judicia œquiora rebus forsitan
Adhibebit, integro sinu.

The temper of his intellect was, in fact, too feeble for the violence of his impressions. I have sometimes heard it said in derogation of Lord Byron's merits, that he was the poet of temperament, rather than of intellect. I admit the distinction between these sources of inspiration; but in this case, the delicacy of the temperament seems to me to exalt the marvel of the intellect. For immense mental power must have been required to constrain such ardor of excitement to intelligent expression. Passion furnishes materials for creation, but is, in itself, its antipodes. In the reasoning fervor and logical fury of the Giaour, I am impressed even to awe, by the fearless might of intellect which every where copes and conquers the volcanic vehemence of feeling. To break up into meaning words the inarticulate roar of suffering,—to syllable the yell of anguish, is like snaffling a tornado, or tying knots in a thunderbolt."

"But when I hear of these neglected authors praying for justice, I think of the Regent's reply to a similar request of Voltaire when he had been slapped for being insolent, '*mais elle est faite.*'"

"Poor Sir Egerton!" said Wilkins. "The history of his mind and fortunes has matter that might give us pause. Born with talents of no common order, and feelings and sensibilities of the most delicate texture,—the stuff that bards are wrought of; impelled to a career of mental exertion by a most passionate ardor for distinction, and aided in it by all the advantages which high rank and abundant wealth could furnish, he has, after a long life of toil and struggling, to look back over a dreary track of painful effort and bitter suffering, and forward to a prospect of oblivion. After seventy-five years of incessant literary labor, he is known to the world by a caricature in Frazer, a philippic in the Edinboro', and a passing encomium from Southey. Yet the old man, an exile in a distant land, with broken fortune, and unstrung and embittered mind, may teach to every author a lesson that shall make him a 'sadder and a wiser man.' With all his endowments, why is not his statue in the temple of Fame?

Merely from want of patient meditation and resolute self-study; merely because he did not master his genius and control his temperament. When he experienced an inclination to literature, he sat down to rummage among dusty antiquities; when he felt the stirrings of poetic sensibility, instead of watching them, and seizing a directing theme to the production of feeling beauties, he only speculated about their existence in all great poets, and thereupon concluded that he too was a great poet. He should have grappled with his emotions, and controlled them to creation.* I verily believe, that by intense observation of the workings of his own mind, Brydges might have risen at length to such nervous conceptions, as live and move, and have their being in Byron's pages. He studied books far too much; had he burned his folios, the flame might have lighted the fire of a great poetical genius. When he felt, he should have analysed; then he might have reproduced. The want of calm reflection, and the pain encountered in confronting one's own mind, have generated an impatient habit of thought. He is unwilling to enter upon a mine of deep inquiry; if a subject of discussion starts up before him, he defers it to a more convenient season, or lets the reader know that he is preparing a separate work upon that point. He thinks in fragments; and, uninclined or unable to continue long upon the wing, ever fails to reach any thing truly great."

"What you say is very just," said I; "he has the wildness rather than the fulness of the pulse of genius. But after every abatement, I would still give my hearty vote that he should take the very highest place among our prose authors. There is no writer whose works I have more frequently in my hands, and none to whom I feel more inclined to make those grateful acknowledgments which every man owes to him who has improved and amused him, who has informed his understanding, and gratified

* Since these paragraphs were penned, the unfortunate baronet has inherited another and a darker title, "*per legem terræ.*" His last years were passed in great poverty at Geneva; where a recent Galignani states that he lately died. The sneer of ridicule was the best return his literary efforts met in life; but, methinks, "they must have hearts very tough and dry," to use the quaint expression of Hooker, who will *now* refuse to shed a tear over the sorrows of this high-minded, but most unhappy man.

his taste. He is the English Montaigne, with vastly stronger blood. His knowledge of the world is thorough; his knowledge of the human heart singularly deep and searching. His critical perceptions are unerring; his critical principles, I think, wrong, but they never affect his conclusions, for he never follows them but in general speculations; he says, for example, that poetry should be natural and unconstrained, and adds that Gray is one of the greatest of poets. His letters on Lord Byron constitute, in my judgment, the finest piece of particular criticism that this or any language contains, though he assigns the noble poet a much higher rank than you or I would concede to him. His style is perfect; formed upon no model, but growing up from ceaseless and easy employment of the pen, it is rich, but not loaded; natural, but full of vigor; it fascinates by its refinement, and compels by its strength. The harsh points which he often presents to the reader will prevent his ever being much of a favorite with the multitude, but kinder qualities endear him to the man of letters. He seems, in truth, to possess a two-fold nature; of which one part is querulous, irritable, egotistical and assuming; the other, gentle, generous, and genial. That side of his mind which is turned towards men, is like the side of a high promontory that regards the sea, rough, abrupt, and unpleasant of access: but that which looks towards poetry and the free fields of genius, is like the other side which lies towards the land, and is fanned by the mild inland breezes, soft, smooth, and sunny, mantled with roses, and refreshing to the reposer. To despise golden opinion is too much his failing. But he is a fine thinker; and a judicious selection, in two or three volumes, from the whole mass of his works, would form a treasury of wisdom. He is, moreover, a true poet, and that he has achieved no great poem, is the fatal result of a false poetical theory. If, instead of writing fourteen thousand lines in four years, as he oddly boasts, he had written but fourteen, his fame had been secure. He has not attained the rare and fine art '*de faire difficilement des vers.*' "

"It is queer," said Wilkins, "that Brydges and his brother reprinters should imagine that the rescuing which they gave to perishing works, was of any service, or should think that they benefitted letters while they made a point of limiting their issues to 'only twenty copies,' or in some cases that I remember '*decem exemplaria sola.*' Surely, such an impression left the book, so far as the public was concerned, the same sealed treasure that it found it. Those bibliomaniacs were a worthless set."

"Harmless, rather," said Dr. Gauden. "They amused themselves highly, and they injured nobody. They erected typography into one of the fine arts, and thus extended the sources of inoffensive pleasure. The investigation of a date or an author's first name, is very capable, I assure you, of delighting and even improving the best faculties of the mind; and to bear off an '*editio princeps*,' from a circle of panting bidders, in the rich consciousness of envied ownership, is a pleasure which a sage would scarcely venture to ridicule, or a divine to condemn. To be unprofitable is not the worst quality of a mundane occupation; and I would that mankind in the pursuit of honor, wealth, and power, were always as honorably or as wisely employed as was the Roxburghe club in discussing *ekes* and *algates*."

"Sir Egerton's poetry," said Benton, "has one merit; that of being intelligible; a merit which is certainly rare and probably great; for, as a general rule, the best writing is the most intelligible. Pope and Addison every body can understand; but what can you make of the poetry of Shelley or the prose of Coleridge?"

"Shelley I abandon," said Wilkins, "for I never read him. But of Coleridge it must indeed be confessed, that if he has the truth, he has also the obscurity, of an oracle. Yet, amidst the perplexed and tangled disquisitions with which his writings abound, you meet occasionally with a splendid simile or a glorious burst of poetry, which produces upon the irritated mind the same startling delight, the same rich relief which occurs to him who, wandering through a thick and undergrown forest by moonlight, comes suddenly upon a clear, amphitheatral opening, where the moon is reposing calmly on the silent grass, and shedding its silvery lustre upon the green-topped trees; he pauses for a moment to gaze on the heaven-decked scene, and breathe in freedom the expansive air; a spring of love bursts from his heart; he blesses nature for her gladness, and plunges again into the thicket, refreshed and invigorated in soul. The obscurity of Herand and Hazlitt proceeds from a very different cause from Coleridge's; for 'true, no meaning puzzles more than wit.' Hazlitt's thoughts are like the illuminated letters in the old manuscripts; so overlaid with ornaments that you cannot get at the meaning; and when you do fathom it, it is but the fragment of the sign of an idea."

"Let not Coleridge," said Mr. Rolle, "that 'spirit, still, of height unknown,' be classed with that servile company who wore his livery and disgraced his name. In the store-house of criticism there is no line which has measured the depth of his seeing; no glass has yet described the height of his imaginings. With his works before you, it baffles you to comprehend and to measure the extent of his powers. His mind was a different faculty from that of other people; it was an extraordinary combination of perception, feeling, and imagination, and all these qualities seemed to be exerted at once; it was as if he had observed with his heart and thought with his fancy. You look upon his discoveries in the tracts of truth, with the surprise and awe with which you would watch a man performing operations by means of a new and peculiar sense. He stood at the centre whence poetry, morals, and metaphysics originate, and he commanded them all. He became a poet by piercing all the mysteries of philosophy, and a philosopher, by treasuring all the revelations of poetry. It would take a life-time to exhaust his discoveries. His sentences are heavy with rivelled thought; they are swollen with pregnant conceptions."

"Coleridge thought in metaphor," said Wilkins, "and that makes a brilliant but not an accurate thinker. His invention was endless, but he was destitute of judgment. He could analyse in detail illimitably, but he conld not compose or embrace many rival suggestions. A master intellect habitually contemplates every thought in its relations to all other kindred or opposing thoughts; the entrance of Kehama into Padalon is an emblem of the manner in which a great mind reaches truth. Coleridge could invent theories, but he could not choose between them; he could broach opinions, but he could not tell their value. He could build systems and he could defend them; but he could not demonstrate the truth. In fact, Coleridge was a poet; the greatest, perhaps, that ever lived; but he was no more than a poet. He carries into all researches the spirit of a dreamer by the lonely woods. All his thoughts have been bathed in the tide of the passions; his reasonings seem to be wet with sensibility. His breast is momently swept with the gusts of feeling; his sentences seem to tremble with feeling. There never was a mind in which the materials of poetry lay in richer or more splendid profusion."

"As a poet for this life, I prefer Wordsworth to all his contemporaries," said Rolle; "I hope to read Coleridge in another. I look upon Coleridge as one who, in the cycle of progressive being, had got ahead of the rest of mankind by two or three stages of existence. I imagine, however, that if Pericles were alive, he would prefer Campbell to all the poets of this time. But if you require feeling in poetry, there is no one richer in the wealth of the heart than Mrs. Hemans. With what luxurious Sybaritism of sensibility she atmosphered her mind! She seems to have realized to the fancy the delicious impossibilities with which Volpone tempted Celia:

> Your bath shall be the juice of July flowers,
> Spirit of roses and of violets!"

"I cannot join in the high admiration which you express of Coleridge," said Dr. Gauden. "I confess myself unable to take the distinction which is very usually admitted between the man and the author. I cannot respect even the intellectual qualities of one who lived, like Coleridge, in open defiance of the most solemn and sacred duties of life. There must have been something very unsound in the perceptions of a mind that did not see and admit that the obligations resting on a husband and father were paramount to all personal aspirations after Fame or even Wisdom. If virtue and poetry are inconsistent, no man who has just notions of the real value of reputation, would hesitate which to renounce.

Integra sit morum tibi vita; Hæc Pyramis esto:
Et poterint tumulo sex satis esse pedes."

"I fully admit the weightiness of the suggestions which you make," said Wilkins; "but before we condemn a man like Coleridge, let us consider the mighty temptations which assailed him. Let us remember how nearly we have been destroyed by the puny passions which have played through our breasts, and let us not mock the mighty ruin over which the hottest ploughshares of hell have been urged. The strong seductions and fierce trials of the heart of genius who shall estimate? Such men are in a raging tumult even from their very birth; they are living always in the midst of tempests, and never, during life, enjoy the blessing of clear vision or calm touch. They are never masters of themselves; but their will is swayed, like a wave-mounted ship, by the surgings of the sea of passion. What does an ordinary mind know of the inner storm and whirlwind, as it were, of restlessness,—the craving after excitement and high action,—the inability to calm the breast and repose in fixity,—the wild beatings and widowed longing after sympathy,—which rack those hearts which are born with the ocean's temper and the lion's mettle? The feeling which attends these high endowments is like a caged panther, that rages to leap upon some satisfying object, and if barred from that, boils and lashes tumultuously in its den. Then consider how hard a task it is for the lofty intellect to learn humility,—for the blood-royal of genius to be tutored,—for the far-glancing, eagle-eyed, eagle-spirited soul to be schooled in the dull lore of duty. About the heart of genius the passions gather as to a stately midnight banquet: hard-breathing Ambition, frowning, stone-eyed,—deep-masked Love, scattering from his censer dimming fumes and enervating odors,—coarse-vested Pride, with curling lip, ready to pluck his eye out if it be admired,—lean Sensibility, quick-glancing, pale-cheeked and vulture-beaked. Existence is to such men anguish; every pulse is pain; their breath is a sigh. The inward and incessant strife of the spirit,—the instinctive jar and discord of the feeling,—the inevitable chasing of the soul even in its calmest hours and quietest moods,—will move the heart to tears without a grief.

Shall we wonder that this constant suffering makes them reckless, and saps and shatters the moral being? It is the severe lot of genius that its blessedness should be its bane; that that wherein its heavenly franchise gives it to excel mankind, is the point wherein it should be cursed above its brethren. For its high privilege is to taste of pleasures inappreciable to mortal tongue; in the empyreal privacies of lonely thought to enjoy the manna of angelic natures; in the fragrant bowers of fancy to feast on dream-food,—

> On honey-dew to feed,
> And drink the milk of Paradise.

Thus is its taste depraved by its celestial birthright: and thus does its craving after rich and strange delights render it ever restless amid the pale joys and cold and quiet offerings of the earth. To suffering also it brings the same exquisite sensibility as to pleasure; it is Apician in its griefs; pursuing and extracting the taste of woe through all its hidden forms. The spirit that abides in the still valleys of contented mediocrity can know as little of the gigantic sorrows and sufferings and allurements and goadings of a great soul that mounts amid the shelving cloudage of the highest skies, as the shaded pool can know of the deep sweeping currents of the sea, or the swelling whirlpool of a gulf. Let the shore thick-strewn with the wrecks of gallant ships, and let the haggard and storm-stained state of the vessel which has escaped, declare the perils of the deep; and let the utter destruction of Burns and Byron and Rousseau and Mirabeau, and the rent and shattered escape of Johnson and Hall and Collins, confess that genius is an awful gift. It is, indeed, a noteworthy fact that no man possessed of that character of genius which is attended with very susceptible feelings, has ever escaped moral shipwreck, except under the pilotage of ardent religion. Long was Coleridge the sport of the wayward winds of passion; but he found at last the quiet harbor. Doctor, can you remember his opium, when you read his letter to little Kinnaird?"

"When I call to mind," said Dr. Gauden, "the history of the Popes and Spensers of another day, and the Scotts and Southeys of our own, I must hesitate before I admit that genius always requires this special dispensation. If you would compare the moral tone of true genius with spurious,—of that poetical ability which springs from the soundness of the head, with that which is generated by the corruption of the heart,—contrast Lord Byron with Mr. Southey. Byron's enervating interest is like the fatal sweetness of the panther's breath and body; Southey's untainted vigor has the fragrance of the free mountain air of virtue: the one degrades and belittles the reader; the other exalts and strengthens him: the one is 'naturally inclined to believe the worst, which is the certain mark of a mean spirit and a wicked soul;' the other is generous with 'the princely heart of innocence.' Southey is of the royal lineage of ancient genius, and has the robust and warrior-blood of the old kings of wisdom: with the lascivious pleasing of modern favorites,—the perfumed softness of these immortals of a season,—he has no kindred. Most of us 'destine only that time of age to goodness, which our want of ability will not let us employ in evil;' Southey has consecrated to virtue the best vigor of his manly days. With one or two exceptions, I confess that I rarely trouble myself to open any of these late volumes of elegant literature; and when I do, I usually find that no faculty is exercised except my memory. The remains of the old temples at Athens have served as the materials of all the structures that have been erected there during many centuries, and the quarry of Pentelicus has not been opened since Phidias and Praxiteles digged beauty from its bosom. The material condition is but an emblem of the intellectual; the moderns have never visited nature as their ancestors did, but have been contented to transpose, to vary, and reset the gems which their bold predecessors seized from the treasury of her wealth. While I allow the moderns to dictate upon all subjects relating to the economy of life,—since, that matter being founded on experiment, the latest production is likely to be the best:—for all that adorns and charms existence, for elegance in poetry, and purity and strength in prose composition, we must turn to the models of another time. The throne of science may be founded in cities—the resorts of manhood;—but the shrine of the muses is in the valley of our childhood. Thither will we retire from the mechanical and 'busy hum of men,' to listen to those masters who 'instruct without clamor, and heal without stripes.' The fresh vapors that curled about the mountain-tops, melted in the morning of our existence into streams of crystal purity, with which the narrow and muddy rivulets that gurgle at mid-day, may not be compared. Life is not long enough for all knowledge, and while we linger among the moderns, we may be neglecting the wisdom of antiquity forever. *Non refert quam multos, sed quam bonos habeas libros; multitudo librorum onerat non instruit, et satius est paucis auctoribus te tradere, quam errare per multos.* I am at least sure of meeting among the ancients, what will neither vitiate my principles, nor deprave my passions; but much that will better fit me for the duties of life, the only thing that is valuable in life. The sounding extravagances of Byron and his fellows, are to me but as music to a deaf man's ear; and I could wish," added the doctor, rising, "that on my tomb might be inscribed a sentiment like that on Evelyn's: 'In an age of extraordinary events and revolutions, he learned that all is vanity which is not honest, and that there is no solid wisdom but in real piety.'—But there is Benton, more fast asleep than ever on the sofa; '*vino ciboque gravatus.*' It is time to go. Take a seat in my carriage which is waiting."

A DIALOGUE IN A LIBRARY.

The Greek Anthology—The Superiority of the Moral Science of Heathenism to that of Infidelity—Modern Popular Education—Moral and intellectual training—A life of Meditation and Action.

"Pleasant, indeed, very pleasant it is to us—to recur for a brief hour to the themes of those sweet and silent studies in which we passed our youth; and to take a second draught at the fountains of almost all that is just and beautiful in human language."—THE QUARTERLY REVIEW.

SOME days after my friend Benton's dinner, I had rambled through the country several miles. As I was returning home, my course happened to bring me in the neighborhood of a person whom I had known some years before, and whom I had often thought of calling upon, without ever accomplishing my purpose. I determined to take advantage of the opportunity, and look in upon him. He was one of that old race of scholars, whose numbers time is daily lessening, without the prospect of a futrue crop. The tendency of mind in the present day is from thought to action. From various causes, among which the rapid extension of popular privilege, and the increasing excitement of the daily press may be prominently named, the whole system of life in all its departments is in a hurried and agitated state. In times not remotely past, a literary man in his country residence was completely separated from all disturbance, and dwelt calmly circled with the quiet of his books: now, the gazettes bring before his view scenes of perpetual movement on the political world, and a host of magazines present a prospect of still more stirring action in the literary community; and with his interests thus quickened, and his passions thus roused, he will not be able to return to the gentle studies and passive contemplation which once beguiled his peaceful hours. When, with the welfare of humanity clinging strongly about him, and the concerns of truth alive within his bosom, he sees the pennon of the cause he loves, now rising, now bending, in the turmoil of the conflict, he will pant to join the struggle, and aid the interests he so warmly cherishes.

Mr. Woodward was far from being one of the race of mere bookworms, an unprofitable company of perverse idlers. Still, mere acquisition of learning had been his profession. He was a thoughtful and acomplished man, of ingenious rather than forcible talents, of more sentiment than vigor of reason, and of a finer delicacy in perception than power of invention. He was now considerably past the noon of life, and his feelings had become regulated by the discipline of philosophy, and his opinions mellowed by meditation and experience. He had from boyhood been a student; consecrating to learning the passion of his youth, the power of his manhood, the leisure of his age. He had been, during some part of his life, a traveller; but travel to a man like him, far from a relaxation or a loss, was but a period of more diligent application. I found him "the mild, the learned, and the good;" arrived at

> That better stage of human life,
> When vain imaginations, troublous thoughts,
> And Hopes and Fears have had their course, and left
> The intellect composed, the heart at rest,
> Nor yet decay hath touched our mortal frame.

When I entered his library, he was reclining on a sofa, and musing, with half closed eyes, over a volume of the Greek Anthology. He received me with polished courtesy, for he belonged to a family of honorable rank, and had in former years mingled a good deal in society, and I began the conversation with a remark on the work which he held in his hand.

"Of all the soothing words of the wise," said he, "which have come down to us from the ancient world, there is no volume more a favorite with me than this of the Anthology. I look upon it as the minute-book of antiquity's confessional. The poems here collected were not intended for the strenuous world, nor were fitted to mingle among the household literature of Athenian gaiety; but they are the wild, and hurried, and abrupt soliloquies of deep and mighty spirits, who mutter the inward revealings of consciousness in some moment when the under eddy of feeling, setting in with the upper current of habit, throws up the sentiments that had lurked unseen beneath the surface; soliloquies, which like the story of The Ancient Mariner, seem uttered almost in despite of self. Through all of them there runs that tender sadness which always marks a deep thinker upon man's condition. In their exoteric pleas, the voice of the ancient is a voice of joy and eager invitation to the feast of life; here you have collected in golden vessels the waters of that bitterness which ever wells from the fullest fountains of earth's purest joys. The ancients compared with the moderns, seem like the actors on a lofty stage, compared with the homely spectators in the pit. In their histories, their epics, and their tragedies, you perceive a buskined dignity of sentiment, a heroic elevation in every rank of life, above the every-day familiarity of our times, the loftiness of people declaiming in blank verse. You find in their greater writings none of the humbling confessions of later days, none of the used appearance of modern literature, as of the gloss worn off, the dew dried up; the reserved muse emits never the moan of sympathy, or the winning plaint of personal emotions, but speaks always in the tone of distant command, or dignified instruction. But in this volume the secret all comes out. Here we have their real and naked sentiments of their own state, the desponding prospect, the regretful retrospect, the signs of a laden and troubled heart, the evidence 'in spite of pride' that 'life to every one that breathes is full of cares.' Here we meet the feeling confutation of the 'bold denial hourly urged amid the wrangling schools,' the vague and unsatisfied aspiration, the indefinite doubt, the startled and confused suspicion,—arising when the real and ideal clash, when conscience jarringly conflicts with belief,—that all is not right in the common creed, that there is some inexplicable blunder in the established system. Many of these epigrams I passed by in my youth, concluding them destitute of meaning; but now, in the sober twilight of declining life, I find in them a deep and supernal meaning, like the wild words of one who has spoken with a spirit. And thus have I often found it, that the discoveries of the intellect are comprehended by the reason, the creations of feeling only by the heart; and that the understanding is independent on circumstance; sensation its slave. Aristotle is penetrated by the thinker in the field and in the closet; Plato's reasoning of the heart, logic of the fancy, woven in the mystic hour of nature's ecstasy, must be viewed from the same moral point where its frame stood. Place yourself on the lonely promontory of Sunium when the last rays of the sun are gilding with a melancholy lustre the few faint clouds which survive his race, and the stillness of earth is like the silence of Heaven, and gaze upon the fathomless sky veiled in a faint mist of light. Then will thy spirit float upward to the highest heaven, and converse face to face with his; and thy soul shall breathe the thoughts which are as pure, as subtle, and as lofty 'as the ether which floats around the throne of the Almighty.'"

"The style of composition in these epigrams," said I, "seems to be altogether peculiar, and has never been imitated, perhaps could not be, successfully, in any modern tongue. They are the most finished, the most nicely wrought, the most strictly classical of all the classics."

"They have a simplicity and a sincerity," replied Mr. Woodward, "which no later writer has attempted to reproduce. They are impressive from their composure; their weight arises from their reserve. The gayer of them have something in them extremely unmodern. The sensation of *humor* appears to have been unknown to the Greeks; their perceptions and tastes were too refined for so gross a feeling, for a gross and unworthy one I think—in the sense in which I use it—it commonly is. These compositions are purely free from it, and yet there is in their cautious avoidance of force, their *naïve* shrinking from effect, something more diverting than real humor. In modern epigrams, the last line is the one on which the poet toils; all the others are prepared for it, and it is the most vigorous and highly wrought. It is otherwise here; the earlier lines are melodious and spirited, the last, generally, prosaic, pedestrian and tame. And here lies the humor, that when something sonorous and decisive is expected, the matter is thrown off with something familiar and almost undignified; the effect resembling that produced when a fool in the old English drama, having fixed attention, and raised expectation by promise of important disclosures, suddenly blurts out some droll truism in homely prose; or when a clown, having undertaken to jump over a barrier, gains the goal by quietly walking under it."

"It is a mournful consideration," said I, "for them that wish well to mankind, to reflect how much of the wisdom of the world lies unemployed, how much of the bullion of truth, which the sages have mined from knowledge, and stored in books, lies uncoined to use, how rarely from the conquered provinces of intellect, captives have been brought home to men. That ancient fund of cumulative truth, which we call 'the wisdom of ages,' whereof the materials are experience, the refiner is sagacity, and the result is gnomic wisdom, is the younger world's birth-right, and it has been voluntarily renounced. These gems have been dug from the mine to be buried in the grave; they have been drawn from ignorance to be entombed in forgetfulness. The charts are all before his eyes, but the pilot, though inexperienced, never consults them. And the philosophers in this matter are as blameworthy as the mob at large; for if the latter have disregarded many of the results of opinion, the former have neglected more of its materials. '*Multa ignoramus, quæ non laterent, si veterum lectio nobis esset familiaris.*' For in dust-covered volumes of the old speculative, and the modern skeptical writers, there lies much debased wisdom which might be profitably purified, many suggestive glimpses which might be advantageously pursued, much broken and imperfect truth which might be usefully combined and completed. These men standing by the circumference, though the position were a false one, saw and guessed at many important things which we at the centre, though it be the vantage-ground, might never think of. But the world is both an unskilful and an ungenerous combatant; for, not content with fairly vanquishing the foe in the field, it exterminates after it has overthrown. When Christianity had triumphed in argument and in fact over the ancient pagans, and the later infidels, and the enemy were become as dead men, arms were not laid down, and the war did not cease: and none, whether from fear or hatred, visited the hostile camp to see what treasures might be found there. We should at least have the Hebrew sense to despoil the vanquished, if we cannot rise to the Alexandrian wisdom of enlisting them. We hew, however, the unburied carcass into food for hounds, and break the tombs of the erring prophets."

"The course you hint at," replied Mr. Woodward, "would be wise enough for philosophers, but '*non cuivis contigit adire* Athenas.' The world is, for itself, perhaps, not foolishly prudent; for it is the nature of error never to be extinguished, but only to be smothered; and if the damper is not kept closely down the flames may again burst forth, or at least the ignorant meddler may get his fingers burnt among the '*suppositos cineres.*' Beneficial as is the study of mere morality, I think it had better not be pursued among the mere moralists of *anno Christi* times.

But no such objection lies to Greek and Roman ethicists, and amongst them the guides in this important path would be more safely sought. For morality, as distinguished from religion, may be defined a system of rules for the conduct of men, deduced by human wisdom from human experience, and having for their object and sanction the well-being of men in the present world. Of systems of morality thus founded only on human reason, it might at once be anticipated that those constructed before the revelation of Christianity would be purer, more consistent and entire than any whose growth is from modern wisdom,—distinguished from religion, as these last always must be, and opposed to it, as they too often are. You will understand me when I allude to Paley on the one hand, and Helvetius and Hume on the other. The former took his conclusions from Scripture, and tied, not grafted, them on philosophy; and in many instances,—as, for example, his chapter on The Sabbath,—his results, though perhaps just, cannot possibly be deduced from his premises. The latter fare still more unfortunately; for in their anxiety to avoid the appearance of borrowing any thing from Christianity, they have often plucked from their systems what was the legitimate growth of the 'human *mind* divine.' In resiling from the temple of revelation, they have often stumbled by the pit of error. Many a fair growth of the soil of reason is torn up because its branches, extending into the territory of divinity, it might be supposed that its roots had derived sustenance therefrom. Reason thus opposed to Christianity is maimed of its finest limbs. Such was not the position of the ancients; their morality was purer *morality* as it approached the doctrines of the Saviour. Christianity, like a vast edifice, has covered the whole ground, and the earth-born plant beneath it that would seek the light, must twist itself into unnatural deformity; the old systems grew up freely and unshadowed, and often instinctively tended toward revelation, as certain plants by nature regard the sun. The judgment, too, of the ancients in these matters was the clearer from their not being disturbed by contention, nor paralysed by doubt. Never checked by fear, and never stung by conscience,—serene and passionless, the mind of Cicero was con-

27

sistent and wise; but infidelity had wrought in the breast of Bolingbroke a storm, an anarchy of contending emotions. His understanding is always turbulent and unsteady,—sometimes paralysed by instinctive doubt, and sometimes maddened by its unavailing opposition. He has granted every thing; he has denied every thing: one while mocking in demoniac defiance, and anon trembling in an agony of fear. The burning light of his powers, unconcentrated and ineffectual, was scattered by the gusts of passion; the fire of Cicero's genius was a calm flame, that reveals little, but its aspiration is to heavenward."

"Even if the position of the two classes," said I, "in regard of opinion, is the same, their relation in respect of feeling is different: like that of the ascending and descending travellers who meet at the middle of Mount Blanc. Hume distinguished against Christianity, and Plato built towards it: their station is the same, their view opposite. When Bolingbroke and Atterbury met at Calais, the one blessed and the other cursed his country."

"On another account," continued Mr. Woodward, "the perusal of the heathen writers on ethics is more beneficial than the study of contemporary moralists. I mean the priority of the former in point of time to the promulgation of revealed truth. The imperfect revelations of St. John the Baptist were fit preparations for the teachings of Christ; had he preached the same defective doctrines after the ascension, they had been mischievous, as calculated to displace the other. When we take up a book of recent ethics, we expect something distinct from Christianity and but dubiously consistent with it, and its perusal detaches us, and perhaps aliens us, from the authority of Scripture: but we lay down our Cicero to take up our Bible, and pass from the right-minded inquirer to the divine demonstrator."

"I fully agree with you," said I, "on the value of moral science as a distinct system, and in the preference which you assign to the ancients. I neither discern the wisdom nor respect the prejudice of those who, like the monks of old, would erase the memory of the Latin bards, and write in its stead the knowledge of its own more sacred dogmas. To imagine that any sane man will rest in these and reject Christianity for them, were as vain as to suppose that any one would be willing to exclude the light that now illuminates the world, and guide his steps by the rays of the sun of some other system. We legislate not for Bedlam or for Norwich."

"One of the objections," said he, "to the value of moral rules is, that religion is a *principle* of conduct, that precepts have lost authority, and that obedience to them may even be injurious as dethroning the principle. How this argument can be admitted while the ten commandments are still read in the churches, I am at a loss to discover. I would answer it by saying that if the precepts raise the right acts, the acts will draw the right principle after them. Good actions create good principles, far more certainly than good principles occasion good actions. When the heart is won to virtue, and seeks to perform the requisitions of morality, it seeks to perform them on Christian grounds and for Christian rewards. He that is pure is ready to be pious."

"Another answer to the objection," said I, "would be that precept may be subsidiary and assistant to the principle, and even in many parts illustrative of it."

"In all parts suggestive of it. 'We frequently fall into error and folly,' says Johnson, 'not because the true principles of action are not known, but because for a time they are not remembered; and he may therefore be justly numbered among the benefactors of mankind, who contracts the great rules of life into short sentences that may be easily impressed on the memory, and taught by frequent recollection to recur habitually to the mind.' Under this view, I would be glad that, for the attainment of that sort of conduct which lies between virtuous and prudential, and is at once a duty and an advantage, the classical poets were more carefully studied in youth on account of the sententious wisdom they contain, and not merely as grammatical exercises, and for the gratification of lettered ostentation. In exquisite common sense, and elegant condensation of thought, the Roman poets have found, save in Pope, no imitator among us. The light that irradiates this path must of course be drawn from human sources, for its object is to encounter vice and folly with their own earth-weapons,—to reason down the sophistry of vice, to ridicule to silence the giddy mirth of folly. Here antiquity possessed a superiority over us. For this knowledge is to be drawn from what Sir Thomas Browne has called 'that universal and public manuscript that lies open to the eyes of all,'—the manuscript-book of nature and of man; 'and surely,' he continues, 'the heathens knew better how to join and read these letters than we Christians, who cast a more careless eye on these common hieroglyphics, and disdain to suck divinity from the flowers of nature,' or read it in the workings of the heart of man. Those instruments of worldly sagacity and natural penetration which they polished till they became at once beautiful and piercing, are laid by in our temples, to rust and grow dull by disuse. Certain minor virtues there are which Scripture has not descended to inculcate, and which human reason must be called in to teach, as Diogenes lighted a candle at mid-day to discover manliness. It is true that patriotism may be learned from Christ's weeping over Jerusalem, and friendship inferred from the Saviour's preference for St. John. But to feel these in their strength and in their loveliness,—in their beauty as affections, and their power as duties,—we must listen to the song of the ancient minstrels. A single line from Horace will urge millions to die for their country, and another of Virgil will bring a tear to the eye of the far-wandering patriot, and teach him even in death to think on his delightful native land."

"The objection," said I, "which has been made to the poets of a lighter cast—ministers of pleasure—is more futile than all. Little effect can they have upon our minds; the joyousness of their joy has long been turned to sadness, and the wild laugh of gaiety comes to our ears like an echo hurled back in mockery. Christianity, if it has not altered men's minds, has changed the whole chord of men's feelings; the commotions of nature which attended the crucifixion were but a type of the revulsions that were wrought in the breast of universal man. The motives to enjoyment adduced by all their poets frighten us from the banquet. Drink to-day—it is the burden of all their festive poetry; drink to-day, for to-morrow we are not. The Christian, like the Pagan, may despise death; but this boldness belongs to different occasions. Their genealogy will point out the distinction. The Pagan indifference is the offspring of ignorance and the sister of apathy. The Christian fearlessness is the daughter of Faith."

"Besides the loss of wisdom and knowledge," said Mr. Woodward, "which you have observed that we incur by limiting ourselves to the literature of our own religion, the injury to true feeling, to all that concerns the heart—is vastly greater. Man, historically, lives in fragments. His present being is detached from all that has gone before, and he loses the experience which centuries of curious and opposite circumstance might give him. As Wordsworth has gone back to the darkling aspiration and boundless conceptions of childhood, and found therein a proof of immortality, so would I go back to the infancy of man, and trace in the changes thence to manhood the wideness of his spirit from the many phases it has shown. I would regard the mythology of those times as past away, but not the men nor their relation to that mythology. I look on myself as a moment in the existence of MAN, and regard Paganism as one of the views which in my youth *I* took of nature. And the rather because Heathenism and Catholicism, each after its sort, are more favorable in the view they take, to the cherishment and growth of religious *feeling*, than Protestantism and our times; and I am unwilling to lose the benefit of that view, but would revive those times within me, renew the old mythology, and be for the purpose and the nonce, a Heathen and a Catholic. By every class of the writings of the Greeks and Romans we may be led to intimate knowledge and constant acknowledgment of the Creator of the earth—to bow to God manifest in the world. In the mistaken view of the Protestant Christian, God is a being to be dreaded, and to be worshipped from a distance. We do not as of old see about us a thousand tokens of his power and goodness. Herein may we be well taught by even the gayest of the bards of Latium and Cecropia, to feel what the *incarnation* of the Saviour must assuredly have been intended to bring about—a communion and a fellowship with the God of the earth which we inhabit. The period of their existence was more favorable, to be sure, to such feeling. The glimmering starlight of antique knowledge shed over the whole face of nature a charm and a significance which the penetrating ray of meridian light has dazzled away forever —a rich effulgence on the foliage, and a silver veil about the mountain's brow—a faint twinkling on every brook, and over every valley a mysterious shadow—'the glory and the freshness of a dream.' That has become science which was once devotion. They enshrined gods for every function and every attribute of deity. Their mythology was the outpouring of the piety of the national mind. Their Lares and Penates were so many mementos of a protecting providence. Their Jupiter, their Minerva, and their Venus, were but avatars of the power, the wisdom and the love of the one, felt, but unseen, God. There was in every heart an altar to the unknown God, but they externally repressed this by these various representative deities. To reproduce this healthy tone of feeling among the nation is impossible; but for the individual the effect may be accomplished by contemplating in a right spirit the effusions of the ancient muse. Often have I in the still solitude of my nightly musings gone back in imagination—and never without benefit—to these long-distant times, and felt through the feeling of another. I extend the same exercise to the Catholic religion; for it was admirably adapted to nurse and to promote the warm, the tender, the delicious feelings of the soul. It encouraged worship to beings less awful, less unapproachable than the infinite and eternal mystery of ages. The men associated kindness and commiseration with the mother of Christ. Females hoped for sympathy from one of their own sex, and felt a calm reliance upon her who had felt the storms of temptation, and knew when and how best to administer aid. The circumstances which detach *us* from our connection with the Deity, linked them the more closely. The Protestant, when he is tossed on the ocean of storms, and every rising wave presses danger on his life, trembles at the presence of the God of the whole earth: the Catholic felt the arm of his patron Saint upholding him, and dreaded no ill. When the face of nature is changed and all is hushed and quiet in the undisturbing breath of celestial harmony; when the bright moon is gilding the vault of heaven, and enlightening, calming and etherializing the earth, the pietist now is mute in wonder at the awful stillness of Almighty power; and the fair land, encircled by the arms, and reposing in the bosom, of the sea—bright but inanimate—the heavens and the waters holding communion in the mystic language of light, all seem to tell him that he is deserted, and alone. In times more distant, the mariner was charmed by such a scene; and as he reclined in his little bark—extending with one hand his spotless canvas, his other upon the rudder—he gazed upon the silent moon, in her mild majesty presiding, and breathed out in accents of fervent devotion,

> O Sanctissima! O purissima!
> Dulcis virgo Maria!

These may have been fancies, but they were not 'fancies that our reason scorns;' for whatever tends to keep alive holy and elevated love, to raise the affections and build attachments in the heavens, and to keep the heart open amidst the contracting cares of life—be it fact or fiction—should ever be welcome to the philosophic mind. All feeling is founded on fancy, and most fancy on falsehood."

"Such a practice," said I, "as you allude to would require to be undertaken with great caution, and pursued with great moderation. Sharon Turner has spoken of 'the multiplicity of error which generally follows the desertion of the simple truth;' and for the million that result is certain."

"Many evils arise," said Mr. Woodward, "from applying to general judgments derived from particulars; but the converse process occasions more. Studious and original men forfeit many advantages they might safely enjoy, by making universal fitness the test of the measures they devise for themselves, and by not limiting their theoretical schemes by 'the constant reference to convenience and practice.' What I have alluded to is certainly dangerous, and might be fatal, to the rectitude of a community; but that is no reason why you and I may not amuse our intellects and train our feelings in the fields of fancy. The world and I have long since dropped the slight acquaintance which we ever had together. The more I look within, the more I am convinced that I am unfit for it; the more I look without, the more fervently do I say within myself, '*Sit mea anima cum philosophis!*'"

"You are not one of those, then, who look with favor on the direction which mind and mental culture are taking in our days?"

"The modern system of things," he replied, "neither commands my respect nor wins my sympathy. This insane craving after 'knowledge,' this diseased exaggeration of the value of facts, and this ruinous mistake of believing information to be education, and of scrupulously separating from public instruction the only essential things, the principles of religion and the rules of duty; this disgusting flattery and stimulation of the mob; this admission of the worthless and scorn-compelling rabble to the decision of questions which they can never comprehend; this breaking of principles over the back of majorities; this utter neglect of all that improves and elevates man, of all that is honorable in conduct, ennobling in wisdom, important in politics, and indispensable in religion—offend alike my reason and my taste, and move me, I confess, to a warmer contempt than wholly consists with the coolness of contemplation. '*Quod magis ad nos pertinet, et nescire malum est agitamus,*' should be the motto of popular educationists. I concede fully the importance of scientific and mechanical knowledge in their own place and degree; but to feed with such husks a country demanding sound food, is fatal in its folly, and outrageous in its absurdity. It is not thus that nations are generated. There goes more than this to the making of a virtuous people and a wise community. A people rising to a sense of their responsibilities ask for light on the vital subjects of truth and action, and are furnished with treatises on galvanism and hydro-dynamics! They ask for counsel in the distractions and doubts of political commotion, and are furnished with 'patriotic' lives of the hireling traitor Sydney and the selfish conspirator Hampden. They are laboriously inducted into the regions of 'pure mathematics!' and gratefully entertained with 'familiar accounts of Newton's Principia!' Every man is made capable of dyeing his own coat and assaying his pocket-pieces, but not a solitary step is made towards the completion of that line whereby Plato has traced with golden pencil the image of a pefect man, 'to know what should be done and said to God and man.' For my part, I admit the test of utility in every consideration; I ask of every thing, *cui bono?* And I ask it of Lord Brougham's efforts and publications. Do they tend to make us better, wiser, happier? If they do none of these, let us at once tear from them the lying title of 'useful knowledge,' and no longer deem those benefactors of their race who amuse themselves by angling for popularity with saw-dust bread."

"'*Nec me solum ratio et disputatio impulit ut ita crederem; sed nobilitas etiam summorum philosophorum et auctoritas.*' The straightest thinker among the Latin fathers has written wisely upon this point: '*nec tam de rebus humanis,*' says Lactantius, '*bene meretur, qui scientiam bene dicendi affert, quam qui pie, atque innocenter docet vivere. Idcirco majore in gloria philosophi quam oratores fuerunt apud Græcos. Illi enim recte vivendi doctores sunt existimati, quod est longe præstabilius: quoniam bene dicere ad paucos pertinet, bene autem vivere, ad omnes;*' a sentiment of memorable truth, which Johnson has closely copied where he says, 'Prudence and Justice are virtues and excellences of all times and of all places: we are perpetually moralists, but we are geometricians only by chance;' and which he may have had in his mind when he elsewhere wrote: 'if, instead of wandering after the meteors of philosophy, which fill the world with splendor for a while, and then sink and are forgotten, the candidates of learning fixed their eyes upon the permanent lustre of moral and religious truth, they would find a more certain direction to happiness. A little plausibility of discourse, and acquaintance with unnecessary speculations, is dearly purchased, when it excludes those instructions which fortify the heart with resolution and exalt the spirit to independence.' What shall I say more, or what can I say better? But besides objecting to the sort of knowledge which they are now disseminating, I have little relish for the object itself under its best form. You and I, Sir, have, 'like all men of sense,' as Dr. Parr would say, our own notions of all this 'new conquering empire of light and reason,' and of this whole affair of popular instruction, and national regeneration, however we may deem it prudent to mask our private sentiments. I remember, however, a notion of Taylor, the Platonist, upon this point, which has often diverted me by its violence, while it has gratified me by its justness. In every class of beings in the universe, says that eccentric *frater Platonicæ familiæ*, there is a first, a middle, and a last, in order that the progression of things may form one unbroken chain, originating from deity, and terminating in matter. In consequence of this connection, one part of the human species naturally coalesces, through transcendency, with beings of an order superior to man; another part, through diminution, unites with the brutal species; and a third part, which subsists as the connecting medium between the other two, possesses those properties which characterize human nature in a manner not exceeding but exactly commensurate to the condition of humanity. The first of these parts, from its surpassing excellence, consists of a small number of mankind. That which subsists as the middle is numerous—but that which ranks as the last in gradation, is composed of a countless multitude. In consequence of this beautiful gradation, the most subordinate part of mankind are only to be benefitted by good rulers, laws, and customs, through which they become peaceable members of the communities in which they live, and make a proficiency, as Maximus Tyrius observes, not by any accession of good, but by a diminution of evil. Hence, the present efforts to enlighten by education the lowest class of mankind, is an attempt to break the golden chain of beings, to disorganize society, and to render the vulgar dissatisfied with the servile situation in which God and nature intended them to be placed. In short, it is an attempt calculated to render life intolerable, and knowledge contemptible, to subvert all order, introduce anarchy, render superstition triumphant, and restore the throne of 'night primeval and of chaos old.' Taylor was a man too thoughtful to be disturbed by passion, and too independent to be warped by interest. Such a strong expression of opinion, though the thought be woven in the loom of a false philosophy, coming deliberately from such a man, would at least make me suspect that the inevitable benefit of such institutions was, after all, not quite so clear."

"How do you account," said I, "for the fact, which seems to be undeniable, for it is the matter of statistical evidence, that an increase of crime has attended the increase of knowledge? I admit, to be sure, that Bacon's maxim is both morally and physically true, but true on the one part with entire distinction from the other; and I am at a loss to conceive how physical knowledge should be an engine of moral power. I can well understand that a knowledge of the comparative merits of the two theories of electricity is utterly valueless to the peasant at his plough-tail, but am unable to apprehend how it should do him any harm. It is at the worst merely useless."

"I can very easily comprehend," replied Mr. Woodward, "how the study of such things should work all the evil which it has done. Before the dissemination of cheap magazines and cyclopedias, the peasant, when his work was done, drew his chair into the chimney-corner at evening, and sat down to muse in quiet. In those moments of natural meditation, the drama of his days past slowly through his mind, and conscience gave her involuntary judgment. The acts of the concluded day, the enterprises of the coming morrow, were instinctively marshalled in review, and their true worth and character were tried by the wisdom of calmness. In the interval memory suggested the wholesome cautions of the parish preacher, the long-neglected counsels of the anxious mother, the good resolutions which suffering had made and safety had recanted; fancy, at her ease, revived the scenes of boyhood's reproving purity and envied peace, and the instructive incidents of another's fate and of his own escapes, or, wandering to a wider verge, painted in homely but impressive tints the sad but salutary picture of 'the hour of death, and the day of judgment.' Silence made gently audible that whispering oracle, the human heart. Ignorance left him 'leisure to be good.' The guide and witness were kept alike within his breast. But now, when the fresh number of the attractive weekly presents its fascinating pages, endorsed by high and stimulating names, every fragment of unoccupied time is given to the high-wrought description and the animated criticism; not a moment is left for self-communion and inward examination. His quiet hours are gone from him. The inobtrusive visits of reflection are shut out, and scared away: he is too busy to think, too excited to feel. In this single result of the absorption of leisure, and the consequent removal of one great barrier to sin,—himself—I find an ample resolution of the difficulty. You may add to it, however, the restless and discontented humor which imperfect knowledge occasions; the rivalry of contempt or envy which it gives rise to; the shade and inferiority which it casts on the tame and unambitious scheme of duty; and, above all, the brilliant objects with which it fills the fancy, as food for meditation, to the exclusion of the events and interests of domestic life, and the general predominance which it gives in the thoughts to the public distant over the private past."

"It would be an interesting exercise," said I, "to estimate accurately the comparative benefits and evils which learning has produced in all the stages of its history. The result to nations seems always to have been good, but the effect on individuals has sometimes been woefully different. Among the heroes of letters are to be found some of the vilest monsters of degraded vice."

"That has always struck me as a most curious circumstance. It is certainly true that both students and authors have, in numerous cases, exhibited an enormity of private flagitiousness to which the vulgar have been incapable of rising; and, as respects the former, I can but imperfectly account for the fact. I can only explain the measureless depravity of such a man as Cardan by supposing that he was naturally a man of strong passions, and that his earnest and absorbing devotion to mathematical and other studies led him to deem the external objects of acquisition and reputation the only important concerns, to the neglect of the culture of his moral nature; that while he thus looked abroad, and forgot that watchful training of the feelings which common men almost instinctively keep up, and even that knowledge of the insidiousness of the ways of temptation, which is their best opposer, his passions grew up to fiend-like magnitude and violence ere their master was aware of the danger. Ambitious men soon learn to sacrifice every thing, even soul and body, to the gain of a favorite end; but ambitious men of action have a constant check upon their savage humors in that practised coolness which their schemes demand; the poor student is left the defenceless quarry of the vulture-beaks of passion. That creative authors should be,—as they almost always have been,—men of bad dispositions, and uninfluenced by the touching sentiments of which they have been the unabsorbing reflectors, I can more readily account for. An ordinary man notes his impressions to enlighten his experience; and makes remorse and self-satisfaction the beacon and guide of his conduct. A poet observes his feelings only to portray them; treasures up every twinge of conscience, not to reform his conduct or rectify his principles, but to point a couplet for the illustration of a Giaour; he meditates on the twilight religion of nature's most religious hour, only to weave from it a white square in the chequered tissue of a Don Juan. A poet soon unappropriates and unrealizes his griefs and his joys, transporting them to that ideal region where fancy decks them with foreign beauty. He studies vice and virtue for their fine contrasts, a death-bed scene for its grouping, and a startling warning or an awful denunciation for its effect. Others contemplate the gladness of the morning sun, or the unworthiness of late repose, to emulate or avoid; Thomson studied them that he might describe them. I was not surprised, therefore, to find Wordsworth, when I met him, cold, contemptuous, and self-esteeming; nor to find Southey and Landor a couple of ferocious egotists. In the channel of the stream there blooms no verdure; it is the incumbent bank only that is vivified and refreshed. The sexton goes into the church only to arrange it for others."

"The position of susceptible authors is a most unfortunate one," said I; "for unless they are dowered by nature with unusual generosity of temper and a fund of great good sense, like Walter Scott, their feelings will make them unhappy, and the struggles of their unhappiness will make them vicious."

"You say true," replied Mr. Woodward; "authorship is the

28

most hapless trade that has yet been invented. Doubtless it is a noble thing when the poet's soul, expanding through futurity, is conscious of immortality, and can exclaim '*Nomen erit indelibile nostrum.*' But there is no sort of venture in which the unavoidable risk is so great and the possible gain is so little; even in the highest success the loss is greater than the acquisition, and in ordinary cases the contest is against fearful odds. To write for one's livelihood,—to stimulate the weary and overtasked mind at the call of necessity,—to execute from dull compulsion the treasured dreams and hoarded schemes of a literary youth,—to be obliged to think, and necessitated to imagine,—is a misery which, perhaps, more strongly than any other, deserves the name of agony. And when we look at the career of the most fortunate writer, and consider the trials and doubts and strivings which harassed his existence, and then remember how little of the final admiration reached him personally,—as in a triumph the hero who rode in the van saw but a small part of the crowd which followed,—we may well conclude with the reflection of La Beaumelle in a letter to Voltaire, '*La plus brillante reputation ne vaut jamais ce qu' elle coûte.*' In the case of a great poet, the sensibility which he pictures excites and wears his own; and while physically he is surrounded with enjoyments, his consciousness is with his imagination, and that is in the scenes of suffering. When Byron threw himself into the situation of his Giaour, he created in himself all the miserable passions which he described. As a writer his success was great; but surely that man's sacrifice to fame was the most awful that ever was made—his own heart."

"But do you not think," said I, "that many of the evils of which you have spoken are shared proportionately by all men of letters—by the student, I mean, as well as by the author—and that more happiness is to be found in energy and enterprise?"

"In spite of the *dictum* of Jean Jacques, '*L'homme n'est point fait pour méditer mais pour agir,*' I think," said Mr. Woodward, "that the miseries of a life of action are far greater than those of a life of reflection; observe, I do not say authorship, for that has the toil of action without its rewards, and the gloom of meditation without its repose. Notwithstanding the extraordinary honors which fell upon Demosthenes and Cicero—honors, prompt, palpable, and abiding—both of them in the zenith of their glories recorded their deliberate regret that they had ever entered on the field of ambition. We are told by Mr. Bushell, one of Lord Bacon's servants, that when the king had dissolved Parliament without restoring 'that machless lord' to his place, this made him then to wish that the many years which he had spent in state policy and law study, had been wholly devoted to true philosophy, 'for the one, said he, at best doth both comprehend man's frailty in its greatest splendor, but the other embraceth the mysterious knowledge of all things created in the six days' work.' Many a monarch, I suspect, has felt as Cromwell expressed himself in one of his speeches, with tears too deep for insincerity; 'I can say in the presence of God, in comparison of whom we are but like poor creeping ants upon the earth, I would have been glad to have lived under my wood-side, to have kept a flock of sheep, rather than have undertook such a government as this.' And many an ambitious statesman has exclaimed on his death-bed, like Amboise, the Cardinal-minister of Louis the Twelfth, 'Ah! Friar John, Friar John! Why was I not always Friar John!' Let the triumph be as boundless as it may, it shall never fill the meanest craving of the aspiring heart."

"But we must not," said I, "in viewing one side of the comparison, forget the darkness of the other. Solitude and meditation encourage vast longings and bring nothing to satisfy them. You remember the remark of Ximenes to Ferdinand when a riot occurred during the king's visit to his college, 'that study and studious discipline were as little exempt as ambition and worldly affairs from the influence of passion.'"

"Doubtless an unhappy temper will find 'some grudging, some complaint,' in the calmest joy and the serenest pleasure. And doubtless there is many a cloud overcasts the contentment of the scholar; yet in all the chances of fortune and the changes of mood he still has ever near him the pearl of quiet—a treasure which Newton truly estimated when he spoke of it as '*rem prorsus substantialem,'* and to which I would apply what Cicero has said of Philosophy, '*qua nihil à Dis immortalibus uberius, nihil florentius, nihil præstabilius hominum vitæ datum est.*' When the fancy, weary of building gilded domes of clay, and of picturing bright tarrying-places and inns of Mortality, floats away upon freshening pinions to the soul's future home, and calls before 'the inward eye,' that blessed spot which we term heaven, the element which casts enchantment over the longed-for resting-place is—Peace. That is a possession so estimable that I can forgive the sentiment of Erasmus, in that letter wherein he so triumphantly vindicates his own career, that quiet error is better than tempestuous truth, while I cordially adopt the exclamation of the noble-hearted Barneveldt to Gomar, 'Truth above all things! but Peace next.' The scholar, and only he, enjoys this boon on earth. To him only is given the precious offspring of silent thought—self-knowledge; for the man of action, whose spirit is absorbed by that which is without, has never an opportunity to look within, and when thrown upon himself in the latest hour of human weakness, converses darkly with a strange and frowning fellow;

Illi mors gravis incubat
Qui, notus nimis omnibus,
Ignotus moritur sibi.

Such men make acquaintance with all things save that which alone shall be their companion through eternity. But to the man of reflection it is given to ponder calmly the sky and the earth and the nature of all things, and to unsphere the soul which abides in the universe and to commune with it, and to know whence and why the world arose, and whither and how it will pass away, and to apprehend what in it is mortal and transitory, what divine and eternal, and to feel himself a member of the universe as if it were a city; '*in hac ille magnificentia rerum, atque in hoc conspectu et cognitione naturæ, Di immortales! quam ipse se noscet! quam contemnet, quam despiciet, quam pro nihilo putabit ea, quæ volgo ducuntur amplissima!*' It was in view of an elevation of heart like this, that the Italian had graved upon his tomb, as a legacy of admonition to mankind,

> Scis quis sim, aut potius quis fuerim,
> Ego vero te, hospes! noscere in tenebris nequeo;
> Sed teipsum ut noscas, rogo. Vale."

"But is it not," said I, "both incumbent as a duty, and wise as an advantage, that those who have light should show it to the world? Is it not a useful and a holy work to instruct and reform mankind by argument and exhortation?"

"Sir," replied my companion, with a melancholy smile, "to improve mankind is hopeless. I had thought once that I might be a benefactor of my race in some degree and kind, however small; but failure brought a juster knowledge. I looked for the results of my efforts, and lo! there were none, save other than I wished upon the actor; for while men grew no better for my toils, I grew worse from their unsuccess, till fretted by failure and contaminated by admixture, I retired from the contest to repair what I had lost. When with a polished blade you would shape blocks, the blade it is which suffers. No! man is incapable of improvement: or, if capable, to how small a degree compared with perfection! Refine the understanding and improve the heart to their highest elevation of strength and purity, how infinitely yet does it fall short of what man must be to make the labor useful! I therefore draw apart, and wait the issue of Almighty wisdom. When He chooses, his is the hand and his alone that can erect mortality.

> In the unreasoning progress of the world
> A wiser spirit is at work for us,
> A better eye than ours.

Labor is not always blessed, nor is idleness always unprofitable.

> God doth not need
> Either man's work, or his own gifts; who best
> Bear his mild yoke, they serve him best. His state
> Is kingly: thousands at his bidding speed,
> And post o'er land and ocean without rest:
> They also serve, who only stand and wait.

Knowing then how little I can do for others, and how much I must do for myself, I say in the beautiful words of Amalthæus,

Percurrant alii sinuosis æquora velis,
Eooque legant ardentes littore gemmas;
Ipse, nisi attonitæ mihi sit mens conscia delhæ,
Intra naturæ fines regnare beatus
Dicar, et insanis animum subducere curis;

and inscribe, with Bolingbroke, over my door, '*Hìc, alienos casus et fortunæ ludum insolentem cernere suave est. Hìc, mortem nec appetens nec timens, innocuis deliciis, doctâ quiete, et felicis animi immotâ tranquillitate fruiscar. Hìc, mihi vivam, quod superest, aut ævi aut exilii.*'"

"And you are happy in your philosophic solitude?" said I, rising to leave him.

"I may say with Burke that 'I would not exchange it for what kings in their profusion can bestow.'"

"I will leave you then in the company you love. Good morning."

"Good morning," said Mr. Woodward. "Pray, Sir, *come and see me soon again.*"

A DIALOGUE IN TRAVELLING.

Reflections as to the influence which is from above, and which is perceived by the faculties of the soul, rather than by those of the understanding—Remarks in this connection upon Coleridge, Davy, Southey, Wordsworth.

"Each with the other pleased, we now pursued
Our journey beneath favorable skies.
Up through an ample vale, with higher hills
Before us, mountains stern and desolate;
But in the majesty of distance, now
Set off, and to our ken appearing fair
Of aspect, with aerial vesture clad,
And beautified with morning's purple rays."—WORDSWORTH.

IT was early on a beautiful morning of the summer, that, along with my friends Robert Herbert and Henry Thompson, I left the village of Derwent-Water for a tour on foot among the beautiful hills and lakes of Cumberland. The gladness of the vigorous morning was yet upon us, as we set off, after breakfasting at a small inn, about four miles from the town. We had walked thus far while the earliest rays of the sun where struggling with the mists of the valleys; and when we resumed our journey, the broad march of the majestic day had begun its full and triumphant course. It was one of those delicate and delightful days when the common air seems charged with the life and inspiration of eternity.

That disposition to confound change of circumstance with succession of time which the nature of our existence gives us, has led to the error of limiting the act of creation to an epoch and an instant. To the eye of true philosophy that mighty miracle is hourly repeated. If we apprehend truly the wealth of Infinity, it will be found that every possible system and sphere that now has a being must have existed before, else that anterior condition had not been infinite. Creation, therefore, is but revelation; and daily, as the revolving sun gives glory to the shapes of earth, and form to the masses of the sky, the wonder at which the stars of the morning sang together for joy, is performed anew. Upon the rising face of the ancient sky, which is downed by the featherings of the light, the softness of infancy ever is abiding. Forth, from the bottomless abyss of darkness, day after day surges up, like the regular and resistless heaving of the sea, whose swell never hurries, and whose lapse never pauses. Thus, bathing in the oblivious tide of night, is the youth of the hours everlastingly renewed; and nothing in nature, save the heart of man, grows old. The blue of the heavens pales not with age, and on the odor-plumed wings of the wooing breeze Time can moult no quill.

Upon the first aspect of the awakened sky there is a tenderness and a charm which the advancing moments soon efface. The varied countenance of the landscape of the skies presents to us at a later period characters of majesty unsurpassed, and serenity undisturbed; there is always above us that which lights the fancy, expands the thoughts, and calms the passions,—whether floating before the western breeze, there sail beneath the sun clouds freighted with glory,—or whether along the silence of the southern horizon there glow in dreamy splendor long crimson branches sprinkled with spots of pearl, like a child's dream of Araby the Blest: yet no variety of the ever-varying scene touches the heart with half the sympathy of joy, or excites the spirit with that rush of inspiration with which the fluttering of the primal sky kindles and melts the gazer's soul. Like the first glow of passion upon the face of beauty, it has a magic of impression which can never be renewed as it can never be forgotten.

"There is a consideration," said Herbert, as we came to a point on the road, surrounded on all sides by a gay and glittering landscape, "which a divine of the George Herbert school might wisely moralize into a thousand similes; I mean *the extent to which the earth must borrow from the sky to have its own earthly beauties fully enjoyed.* When you shut out the clear smile of the blue heavens, you seem to exclude nothing upon which man is greatly dependent; his position and his powers, the scene around him and the soul within him, remain the same; yet, though the privation may not at once be felt, time will soon show that you have cast a blight upon his enjoyment which no form can resist and no philosophy compensate; an influence which deadens the affections, dims the brightness of the virtues and even taints the vigor of the intellect; converting all desires and thoughts into a single want. The iris hues of the flower-wreathed summer—the meltingness of music—the grace of marbles—the grandness of tower and temple—the age of mountains and the strength of ocean—and all the moral luxuries of kindling thought and glowing speech, and love and lofty rank—lose all their might, so long as his eye cannot hail some portion of that living color which is to him a glory and a soul. Where the glad and glancing sun-rays cannot pierce, the securest beauty droops; and that impression which possessed its cause as with a presence and a spirit, dies from its splendid magic and goes out. So are those thoughts which give respect to man and dignity to conduct, the airs and odors of an immortal world. The strong and high existence of men is not shut up within their mortal frames; the bending sky is a portion of our life and the apprehension of deity is a part of our mind; for what is the mind but a mass of thoughts? The very form and frame-work of the intellect consists of thought; principles perceived make up the intelligence, and feelings analyzed constitute genius. This truth should be the guide of our schemes of education, which would then be modes of forming the mind as well as furnishing it. It suggests a notion which may be deemed fancy or prophecy, according to the temper of our mental disposition. If every truth which the mind discovers, becomes a new centre of observation from which it goes on to make new discoveries—a new instrument of conquest—a new ward in the intellectual key, which was wanted to unlock some old difficulty—*then*, the mind extends by these adjunctions; it goes on transforming things which are without it to thoughts which are within it, and of it, and it. Thus, by degrees, all the external world shall be transformed into internal convictions, and the universe of matter be wrought into the unit of mind, and all material existence be *thought* into God. I confess when I regard the proof the physical world gives that a God once existed, and the evidence the moral world shows that none exists now, I am indeed tempted to think that deity is in abeyance in his creation; and that as the cumbrous body thus expires in detail, the divine spirit will revive in its completeness. As in the dry seed lies hid the germ which holds in narrow bands the perfect flower which shall glad the air; and in its paleness may be read by hope's prophetic eye the soft spreading of the roseate flush that shall make faint the heart with ecstasy, even so in the rude denseness of the formless globe is involved the life of the ever-living. Do I err in thinking that mind is in its essence cognate with God? Have they not the same offspring? Are not thoughts, angels? The ideas which visit and persuade the soul, are they not ministers of power and life? There are thoughts which have tyrannized over men with a sway that no god or demon can exceed. The thought of immortality, for example, has crazed and enslaved the world; and truly in its variety of influence is stamped with the seal of somewhat more than human. In times of patient anguish it is a smooth river sliding softly through a forest—bright amid the darkness—that bears the soul gently from horrid tangles into quiet meadows and smooth fields of joy; in the trying hour it is a poison-blast, that rides by in awful majesty, and while the upper sails which are yet exposed are creaking and trembling, the havened spirit clings nestling closely to the bosom of its God: sometimes it is a blind, wild terror that at noonday when no foe is near makes the wicked start to flee impending terror, or almost compels the mind to totter beneath its pressure; and sometimes it is a whirling flame-eyed fury, that cracks its whip of fire and rolls its rattling wheels of iron."

"Every language," said Thompson, "has marked a difference between the mind and the soul; and 'the universal language of mankind,' says a clear, close and strong thinker, 'is no fallacious evidence of truths that are founded in the reason and nature of things.' This difference, philosophy has not improved; for, while metaphysics has grown into a great and cumbrous science, none have explored the spiritual life of men or questioned of its origin or nature, that immortal essence which was before and will be after us. He who has possessed his soul in peace well knows that there is sphere within sphere of inward being, whose depths our mortal consciousness does never wholly apprehend or fathom; a being, to the sense of comprehension, glimmering and dim, but to the faculties of instinct, strenuous and immortal; seen as through the thin and saffron-misted dawn, but known as with the fulness of the pulse of noon. Viewed by none is the form of its nature; felt by all is the fact of its being. An apostle has suggested that by comparing the visible with the invisible or spiritual world, important truths might be discovered. And certainly if an organization so distinct as it is from both the mental and material frame of things be found to suggest a deity, the argument of his existence is indefinitely strengthened. And nothing so strongly avows divinity; it is indeed the type of the universe and the antitype of God. Of this system, he is the centre and the canopy —the spring and the spreading-forth; what it has of infinite is his, what it tells of eternal, comes from him. And it is this faculty alone in man which is capable of perceiving God; hence when the passions of lust or vanity swell and discolor the soul, it no longer feels his presence, and prayer becomes a senseless thing. God is, indeed, the life and guardian of our hearts, 'the elder brother of our spirits;' and they who banish him from their hearts, must toughen and petrify all the sensibilities of their nature. For the tender soul, exposed to struggle with the naked, atheistic world, quivers and shrinks, as would the uncovered, living flesh, blown by chilling blasts; then, aching with distress, it draws within the thought of God, and that thought is the balm of peace and gladness of repose. When intercourse with worldlings has fouled and made turbulent that atmosphere of the soul, by which its breath is healthful and its vision clear, and made its respirations convulsed and difficult, sympathy with heaven is the pure zephyr that blows away the vapors that have clogged the scene. Truly may we say with the prophet in the hour of our inward trial, 'In the secret place of thy dwelling shalt thou hide me,' and with the apostle, 'To whom should we go, Lord, but to thee?'"

"The truths which the mind produces seem to be wrought out into existence by the enginery of effort; those exhibitions of mysterious knowledge which the soul puts forth seem to be involuntary, and almost accidental. It takes no cognizance of the interests of the passing world, and the wisdom that springs from our human condition and dies with mortality, is no portion of its lore. But oracles of the knowledge of the anterior life and experience of our spirits, and of the relations which, in 'the being of the eternal silence,' it bears to the unseen powers of the universe, are wrapt within it, as phosphoric light is folded in the bosom of the wave; and casual agitation shakes them out. When a soul has for a season entertained one peculiar course of thought and feeling, and chance or change of humor sends in another, and the two currents meet—it is in that moment that great truths respecting our nature are discovered. By removing the barrier of worldly care and callousness which shuts off from our consciousness the divinest portion of our being, our life may always sit in the unclouded brightness of celestial light, and memories of past eternity will be exhaled into its contemplations, while 'winged thoughts of the "*sursum corda*" kind,' connect it with the everlasting future which awaits us."

"The man," said Thompson, "of all the English thinkers, best fitted to investigate these strange powers of our nature was Coleridge. He has, indeed, done something to estimate their character and value, and so has Davy; but a systematic display of the subject is yet wanting. Coleridge was, by his moral qualities, fearfully well fitted for the task. Owing to his long and dubious struggle with a habit which became a vice by the disingenuousness of his conduct in the matter, he lived for years in what Greville has called the 'twilight between vice and virtue;' and the dark contests and fluctuating emotions of his spirit amid these alternations gave him capacity to behold the tints of sin and purity in their broadest and deepest contrast; he bathed in degradation to renew the Houri delicacy of his appreciation of holiness, and when he relapsed to self-indulgence the stain stung deeper into his soul for the tenderness which recent absolution had produced.* His spirit writhed under the galling inconsistency of the lectures of an apostle combined with the life of an apostate, and flashed forth in its agony gleams of portentous light that are garnered into stars among his poems, and which give the reader pause, like the signs of a magician which we know to be spells though we cannot conjure with them. Davy, too, I fear, sometimes violated the majesty of his self-respect, and that may have given morbidness to a faculty which in most men is unfeeling."

"A pregnant caution, by-the-by," said Herbert, "against giving credit to facts and anecdotes gathered from report, is furnished by the host of errata which the more recent biography of that distinguished philosopher has detected in the early

* See "Recollections of Coleridge," by Cottle—the most valuable book which has hitherto appeared upon this subject. It is a skilful development of one of the most extraordinary and instructive histories ever exposed; and it is done kindly though firmly. Much of the tale is purely humiliating, yet is its conclusion proud, and touching even unto tears; when we behold this king of thought freed from the demon which had convulsed his days, and at the close of life "sitting clothed and in his right mind."

and more popular one. A few more such expositions might profitably teach the reading many what the thinking few are well convinced of, that the current class of memoirs and reminiscences, whether still ductile to the imagination of narrators, or gathered with all their improvements into books, have in no case that degree of accuracy, not to say exactness, on which one who seeks the truth may certainly depend. In a few instances in which I have been able to compare versions adopted by society of some given incident with the literal facts, I have found that the statements of the nearest and most authentic parties gambolled absurdly from the truth. The most tenacious memories have a trick of substituting one circumstance for another in the histories confided to them, in a manner which leaves the individual wholly unconscious of the change. When a narrative has passed through two or three lips, it is generally as much modified by the process as the sounds which conveyed it. It is a rare accomplishment to hear a story as it is told; still rarer, to remember it as it is heard; and rarest of all, to tell it as it is remembered."

"In the disputes which animate and exercise the world," said Thompson, "pure truth upon one side is perhaps never brought to oppose pure truth upon the other, but all the arguments are to a certain degree diluted with error. Fortunately the debasement is equal on both sides; we fight in a cloud that dims alike the adversary's eye, and the muffled weapon which we bear is compensated by the dulness of his."

"One circumstance," said Herbert, "in the characters of the men you have spoken of, gives me a higher opinion of the mind of Davy than of Coleridge's; I allude to the fondness which Coleridge had for theory, and the contempt and dislike with which, especially in his later days, Davy regarded it. Theory is essentially unphilosophical: it fetters the mind and makes the errors of the past tyrannise over the inquiries of the future. It is of no service in the investigation of subjects and the progress of knowledge; it belongs to the stationary periods or those of decline. Youth is captivated by brilliant generalisation; age values truth more highly, and cares less for the

management of them. If the principles of our classification be erroneous or narrow, we shall certainly be led into error that will be serious where the matter is still in the progress of development. A theory based on the qualities of an object will prevent its being unfolded according to its objects; and he who arranges topics in reference to their causes will cease to value them according to their results. Thus the jurisprudence of every nation will show, that when law becomes a science and a system it ceases to be justice. The errors into which a blind devotion to arbitrary and theoretical principles of classification has led the common law, will be seen by observing how often the legislature has been obliged to come forward to restore the equity which its scheme had lost."

"The English law is at present one of the most curious monuments in existence—an antique bulk, hewed and plastered and puttied into a modern shape—a fiction, retained long after the object of it has passed away. Yet it strikes me as a sublime proof of the wisdom and caution of that nation which has modified what was defective from the beginning, and has resorted even to the silliest appendages of fictions, rather than make a radical change."

"The only portion of the constitution which Southey cannot muster toryism enough to admire is the law. In that matter, he prays for reform."

"He is a wise man, is Southey," said Thompson; "and a good man; in fact, the greatest man of the times, though not enough of a quack to be popular. He and Coleridge are men of equal strength, and the only superiority of the latter lay in his charlatanry. A clamor has been raised against him for the errors of his youth; as Bembus says, '*quod puer peccavit, accusant senem.*' But Southey changed only as circumstances changed, perceiving that uniformity is not consistency. Erasmus in one of his epistles complains of a fate very similar to the Laureate's; '*rapiuntur in diversum omnia, etiam quæ optimo scribuntur animo; ne tempus quidem perpenditur, quo scripsit aliquis, sed quod suo tempore recte scribebatur, transferent in tempus incommodissimum.*' The defamers of both of those great men should have remembered, that, however they might have seemed to vary in position, they were always true to the faith of their principles and always obedient to the law of their natures. In the feelings, hopes and purposes which have presided over the life of Southey, there has been no turning; though he may have seen, as he advanced, a better mode of accomplishing what he desired, than when he set out. It is to his praise, that from his earliest youth he has been the friend and defender of virtue. The advancement which Southey has given to literature has been mediate rather than direct; it lies in what he has directed and encouraged others to do more than in what he has done himself. 'Thalaba' was a bold and defiant 'declaration of independence' on all the critical principles, models, and canons, whose authority, till then, had enslaved taste; it was an act like that flinging of the spear by the converted Saxon king into the sacred enclosures of Druidical superstition, which desecrated forever the imputed holiness which was itself the false god that had enfettered men's minds. The dull deity of classical correctness was thenceforth unsceptred, and all were at liberty to adopt what license they pleased. Accordingly, it became the shield of Ajax, under cover of which Byron and Moore came upon the field."

"The author, whose true character in these times it seems most difficult to settle," said Herbert, "is Shelley. His imagination was inexhaustible, and his creative faculties boundlessly rich; but there was in him a total want of judgment. His works are, therefore, not so much poems as splendid storehouses of poetical materials; and to estimate the exact worth of such disordered wealth, has not been an easy task. Unfortunately for the speedy determination of his merits, his works are of a kind

> Quo neque procax vulgi penetrabit, atque longa
> Turba legentium prava facesset.

What the mob canvass, they soon conclude; but that which is debated only by the learned, will long be doubtful. On the whole, I think that the reputation of Shelley has risen with time, and that Byron's has declined."

"Of the latter point, in the sense in which you mean it, I am not so sure," said I. "The intense personal interest which the peer, his position and history excited, and which at first might not be easily distinguished from the admiration of the poet, has indeed subsided: but if his name is less often in the newspapers, his merits are more freely acknowledged by the critical. He now stands where nobility is no recommendation. In the literature of the past, as in the ninth place at whist, the honors are not courted. Byron's European fame is the best earnest of his immortality, for a foreign nation is a kind of contemporaneous posterity."

"There is a cant," said Herbert, "of extolling Byron for his deep acquaintance with life and his extensive experience of society. To my thinking, his misanthropy and anger against men denoted a want of thorough knowledge of the world and a partial and defective reasoning. There is a fine anecdote related by Goldsmith of Alexander VI., who on entering a town which he had captured, beheld a portion of the townsmen engaged in pulling down from a gibbet, a figure designed to represent himself, while another part were knocking down a neighboring statue of one of the Orsini family with whom he was at war, in order to put his effigy, when taken down, in its place; Alexander, far from condemning the adulation of these barefaced flatterers, seemed pleased at their zeal, and turning to Borgia, his son, only said with a smile, 'You see, my son, how small is the difference between a gibbet and a statue.' Scorn is the most ignorant and thoughtless form of disesteem; there is a patient tolerance that lies beyond contempt, and a placid love, born of pity, is a yet profounder phase of unregard. Shelley's apathetic carelessness of men showed that he despised them from his heart; and Wordsworth's diligent cheerfulness and systematic content, indicate a more thorough appreciation of the worthlessness of life than either of the others attained."

"Byron and Shelley," said Thompson, "were friends in life, and have often been classed together in literature; but they were in truth intellectual antipodes. The feeling on Byron's pages is all personal feeling; it is actual emotion, elevated and refined into the ideal. His sufferings suggested all his sentiments; and experience was the parent of all his thoughts. Shelley's feelings were in his imagination, and he had no personality. It is the business of poetry to present to us the generalisations of ideal passions, and these are usually attained by forgetting or merging the individual and the real, and sending the mind to wander through the fabrics of fancy; in this sense it is justly affirmed, that Byron succeeded by the magnitude of his failure. He wrote true poetry without being a poet; he shaped into poetry its antagonism. The other was born a bard. Hence, if in respect of the mental qualities of the two men as geniuses, the question of greatness be made, we give the palm to Shelley; if in reference to their moral abilities as performers, we name Byron. In the first view, Shelley possessed more of the poetical faculty; in the second, it is Byron's praise, that in despite of the defect of those qualities, he wrote yet more splendid verses than the other. The first was an intellectual superiority, the last was a personal triumph; in the one you praise the mind, in the other, you applaud the man; in that you extol the gorgeous fancy, in this you reward the victorious will."

"Shelley's mind," said Herbert, "seemed to be no portion of himself; his consciousness was apart from his conceptions. It is this which makes him often difficult to be understood, for usually it is through sympathy of temper that men attain to unity of thought. A flash of mutual feeling brightens a chain of notions otherwise dark and perplexing. The poet lifted by passion to some airy seat, babbles of the golden forms which his fancy floats before him, and his words will be Pindaric to our sense, unless we are placed in the same position by similarity of mood. Notions are but the expanded flower and foliage from the germ of feeling, and we must plant the latter in our heart, ere the atmosphere of our intelligence will be gladdened by the former. In truth, we never fully comprehend a poet's lines, unless we are beforehand in possession of the poet's meaning, and his words but remember us of our own images; in that case, he is explaining our own affections to us, and giving us in ideas what we previously possessed in impressions. It is the business, therefore, of the judicious poet, by addressing the heart, to fling his feelings upon us before he expands his meaning, and thus to aqueduct the chasm between our consciousness and his thoughts. There is no trace of personal feeling from one end of Shelley's writings to the other. Compare, for illustration, his ode to the sky-lark with Wordsworth's on the same subject; the one is a record of individual emotions and a retrospect of spiritual experience, and breathes, throughout, the sadness of a pensive soul; the other displays an artificial and mechanical ingenuity, and, as exquisite as a Greek chorus, is as cold as a Greek statue. It is this same absence of conscience and want of moral impressibility which makes the atheism of Shelley so thorough and undoubting. Byron suffered so intensely from the stings of mental remorse, and labored with such agony of effort to brighten the blackness of vice into that image of light and beauty for which his spirit was self-stung to struggle, that when he most earnestly chants the glories of sin, he is unwittingly offering his tribute to virtue. The convulsion of passion under which he labored was wrought by his striving to maintain the erectness of his spirit amid the tyrannizing encroachments of the devastations of wickedness."

"On the whole," said Mr. Thompson, "Byron has done great service to virtue, and will be regarded through all time as having made in that matter a great and conclusive experiment. Before his time, men, dwelling in the region of moderate decency, have handled and smelt and tasted the forms of seductive vice, and have asserted that there was much excellence in them, and that it might be a question whether it were not a safe game wholly to relinquish truth and its restraints, and to take up with vice for vice's sake. But Byron is the first man who has devoted his life and powers to the cultivation of flagitiousness, and has been determined to find and fix in depravity all his hopes and wishes and rewards. To this new scheme of happiness he dedicated himself wholly, and with all the ardor of desperation; he sounded passion to its depths, and raked the bottom of the gulf of sin; he explored, with the indomitable spirit of Carathis, every chamber and cavern of the earthly hell of bad delights; and the result was barrenness and exhaustion; the conclusion was, that when the inspiring immortality of celestial hope was resigned, there was an end to the interest which had once been attractive; —that in atheism there was no principle of progression,—no source of vitality,—no impulse to exertion;—that virtue is, in its views, its thoughts and its hopes, prolonged, complete, and permanent,—that vice is deciduous, crumbling, fragmentary; that the one addresses itself to that within us which is deep and everlasting, while the other engages only those faculties which are mortal and transitory, and leaves the eternal soul 'to the self-torture of irremediable vacuity.'"

"When we observe the extraordinary difference in the whole system of principles, purposes and impressions between Lord Byron and all who have gone before him, and remember that every great era, whether progressive or revolutionary, has been preceded by some great author who, in the fulness of prophetic feeling has embodied all the sentiments and sources of power which lay at the bottom of that general effort, are we not entitled to conclude, that this poet is the forerunner and herald of the advent of some new, deep, fervid epoch which shall develop in action that struggling energy which his verses show, and be as violent, as free, and as selfish as he was? or, if you deny the accidental connection in time which this supposes, is it not probable that he will create such an age? 'Poets and philosophers are the unacknowledged legislators of the world.' At all events, whether or not we admit either a causative or a coincidental connection between poetry and politics, the sure and deep progress of democracy in every portion of the world seems likely to evolve in history a condition of which the bard's bold fire shall be the antitype. The radical quality which gives character to both is the same,—a passionate selfishness,—a sullen savageness, assumed by men to make their mood the master of their life. This anticipated similarity would only be giving to the age a resemblance which one of its acts already exhibits. Against the centuries-woven frame of fetters, the tide of revolution heaved up its fulness as the last race were passing from the earth, and Napoleon embodied this spirit in politics and Byron in literature. In him were gathered all the dim and vague half thoughts of liberty and strength and madness which ages of every kind of oppression had created. His genius was the feathered mounting of the waters where the recurring stream conflicted with the flow. That agitation has subsided, but I think that another, slower, calmer, more general, and stronger swell is setting in, which, as it grows mightier in its pacific fulness, will dissolve and absorb what that other more impetuous surge shocked, but could not shake. I am not one of those who can see the dawn of a new era already streaking the eastern sky; I do not believe this broad rebellion will come 'to-day nor yet to-morrow;' but sooner or later it must. The democratic sentiment is one which *will* prevail wherever it is promulgated; it has, in itself, a silent power to sap away society, as the unseen weather saps tower and castle. It addresses itself to the worst passions of our nature, and rouses all the sceptred strength that dwells in evil, while it is in these days sanctified by an imputed name of virtue, and thus unites

> In friendly league
> Etherial natures, and the worst of slaves;
> Is served by rival advocates that come
> From regions opposite as Heaven and Hell."

"I question," said Herbert, "the permanent establishment of any thing like a democratic system. Antagonism is the essential soul of democratic strength; opposition is the source of its might: when, therefore, it has conquered enmity, and that which it attacked has been dissolved to its separate elements, its virtue is departed; its triumph is its traitor. As soon as it has destroyed control, and all is free and open, enterprise, which is the daughter of liberty, creates wealth and gives employment to all, and a conservative disposition is generated among the people. Thus does the condition of a state swing round through anarchy to peace and power. I will venture to aver, that in no republic will politics ever darken to democracy where the destructive spirit is not kept up by infusions from the dregs of those countries where there is something to generate it."

"Upon that view," said Thompson, "we need not hope for either permanent establishments or prolonged, but a succession of political systems, containing in themselves the seeds of their own destruction and re-institution; and that, in truth, seems to be the destiny of the world."

"To rise, to shine, and to set, is the fate of every power and wisdom that man displays. Humanity occasionally puts forth extraordinary strength, illustrates great principles of action, or lights up great stars of knowledge, which fade and are forgotten with the age which they distinguish. Few temporary improvements enter into the general civility of the world; in still fewer cases, are faculties advanced in one epoch, kept up in the next. I mean that there is no progression in the abilities of the general race. Perhaps, some scientific facts, and, it may be, some scientific powers, may be inoculated on the universal human mind, so that one age shall be, in its fundamental character, and in the groundwork and starting-point of its capacity, placed before its predecessor; but it is otherwise with physical skill, and with moral wisdom. Men are as little able to govern themselves now as they were in those times of deep learning, ardent piety, correct principle and strong sense, commonly called the dark ages. If we admit that one century avails itself of the wisdom of past years, and is instructed by the accumulated knowledge of many eras, this age can have no pretension to that sort of superiority; for it scorns, not studies the past,—it breaks, not builds on its foundation,—it opposes, not amends its conclusions. It has assumed such a position that it renounces all the advantage of experience, and its maxims are as crude and raw as those of the first barbarians could have been. Pulling down a house is an odd way of improving it. I am the hearty advocate of reform: I repeat with the earnestness of a prayer the benediction of old Plowden, 'blessed be the amending hand:' but because I wish amendment, I do not wish destruction."

"Revolution is the greatest enemy of reform," said Herbert, "and reform is the best protection against revolution. To anticipate hostility by yielding voluntarily what will soon be exacted, is the best mode of maintaining influence. It should be the politician's wisdom to escape the tempest by outrunning the wind."

"The cabinets of Europe," said Thompson, "are now vitiated

by a circumstance which weakens the politics of all refined ages; the manners of the time and the taste of courts give pre-eminence to the subtle head rather than the strong hand, and the class who are thus called out are necessarily inferior in vigor to the more sincere and hearty races that once ruled. The artificial villains of this age, who elaborately form their character upon those of the unscrupulous diplomatists of former times, though they acquire a set of principles nearly resembling those of their prototypes, yet, owing to the process by which they reach the same point, they miss what is the very secret of the strength of the others; their principles not being the result of their passions, but the debased creation of their evil wishes, they knowingly offend the better law which is within them, and so lose their self-respect, which saps the power of gaining respect from others. The great spirits whom they attempt to copy, while they only reproduce the empty shell of the character they emulate, were so absorbed in their conflicts with the world, that they never turned their eyes in upon themselves, and were not wasted by the weakness of conscious villainy."

"Strength will go farther in ruling mankind than skill. There is a charm in the display of power, wherever it appears, that makes men thankful thralls. It is this which gives such fascination to Byron, and will always make him, in spite of criticism and morality, the idol of the many. Nothing in literature equals the power with which he tore thoughts from things, and wrung ideas from emotion, as the chorded viol wrings melody from the tortured air."

"Yet to the eye that judges of effects from causes, there is less power and far less courage in the strife of Byron than in the serenity of Wordsworth. Byron could not rise as he did to the dignity of mental calmness and the majesty of mental contentment. There is in Wordsworth none of the narrow sympathy and bigoted enthusiasm of the school of passionists. He can love his own thoughts without hating those of others. He indulges in no straining after the impossible,—no reaching after the unattainable. When he has created a sentiment with the ardor of a poet, he determines its value with the judgment of a philosopher. The temper which recognises the good that is in the world, is more maturely wise than that which searches for the evil. Compare the impressions with which Wordsworth and Southey have contemplated that class of persons who are 'content to dwell in decencies forever,' and who perform all the outward and visible duties appointed by religion, but without any of the kind gushings of a human heart. You may compare the two. Southey's dialogue is thus:

STRANGER.

Was his wealth
Stored fraudulently,—the spoil of orphans wrong'd,
And widows who had none to plead their right?

TOWNSMAN.

All honest, open, honorable gains,
Fair legal interest, bonds and mortgages,
Ships to the East and West.

STRANGER.

Why judge you then
So hardly of the dead?

TOWNSMAN.

For what he left
Undone,—for sins not one of which is written
In the Decalogue—

STRANGER.

Yet these
Are reservoirs whence public charity
Still keeps her channels full.

TOWNSMAN.

Now, Sir, you touch
Upon the point. This man of half a million
Had all these public virtues which you praise:
But the poor man rang never at his door,
And the old beggar at the public gate,
Who, all the summer long, stands hat in hand,
He knew how vain it was to lift an eye
To that hard face. Yet he was always found
Among your ten and twenty pound subscribers,

Your benefactors in the newspapers.
His alms were money put to interest
In the other world,—donations to keep open
A running charity account with heaven,—
Retaining fees against the last assizes,
When, for the trusted talents, strict account
Shall be required from all, and the old Arch-lawyer
Plead his own cause as plaintiff.

The traits of Wordsworth's description are not more similar than the tone of his feeling is different.

Many, I believe, there are
Who live a life of virtuous decency,
Men who can hear the Decalogue and feel
No self-reproach; who of the moral law
Established in the land where they abide
Are strict observers: and not negligent
In acts of love to those with whom they dwell,
Their kindred, and the children of their blood.

Have we now any indignant denunciation of these as not fulfilling the whole measure of Christian charity? No such thing! —that one blames the rich for what they do not: this considers how much they do. 'Praise be to such, and to their slumbers peace!' is the wiser ejaculation of his comprehensive mind: and he goes on to tell us that the poor man, the abject poor, does not find

In this cold abstinence from evil deeds,
And these inevitable charities,
Wherewith to satisfy the human soul!"

"No doubt," said Herbert, "the Laureate's is a younger wisdom than his friend's. He writes like one in whom nature has not done with her resentments. The other might usually take for his motto the lines of the kindly-souled *chansonnier*,

De l'univers observant la machine,
J'y vois du mal, et n'aime que le bien."

"It is in the same spirit of catholic sympathy," said Mr. Thompson, "that in a matter of taste between the two conditions, he observes a difference without disgust, and blames a fault without bitterness.

> The wealthy, the luxurious, by the stress
> Of business roused, or pleasure, ere their time,
> May roll in chariots, or provoke the hoofs
> Of the fleet coursers they bestride, to raise
> From earth the dust of morning, slow to rise;
> *And they, if blest with health and hearts at ease,*
> *Shall lack not their enjoyment*:—but how faint
> Compared with ours! who, pacing side by side,
> Could with an eye of leisure, look on all
> That we beheld; and lend the listening sense
> To every grateful sound of earth and air;
> Pausing at will—our spirits braced, our thoughts
> Pleasant as roses in the thickets blown,
> And pure as dew bathing their crimson leaves."

"The feature of mind which you have noticed," said I, "is certainly a quality of the highest character. In the proportion of the largeness of the mind is the variety of the sympathy: it was great in Scott, complete in Shakspeare. Few poets of this day may claim this praise. There is much mental intolerance and exclusiveness of feeling in Southey, and still more in Coleridge, while it overruns the writings of Shelley and Mrs. Hemans, and becomes disgusting in the pages of their followers. Wherever it exists, it indicates one who, whatever may be his faculties of intellect, is the subject of his feelings,—one who has not risen from the thraldom of his emotion, nor surveyed with discourse of reason the mood which he has left. In Wordsworth's treatment of the most disturbing passions of the soul, there is no touch of discomposure. Of the most earnest wants of sensibility, and of the most mysterious experience of the heart, he writes as one

> From such disorder free,
> Nor rapt, nor craving, but in settled peace.

'It is the privilege of the ancients,' says Lessing, 'whatever be the subject which they treat, to enter upon it with that spirit of calm inquiry which preserves them steadily in the middle line between the vice of exaggeration on the one hand, and the fault of coldness on the other.' No modern has attained so much of this moderation; none has so much mental candor, so much intellectual impartiality."

"The pervading purpose of Wordsworth," said Mr. Thompson, "is to assert the sufficientness of the world as it is, to satisfy all the honest wants of a heart which acquiesces in the wise and the good,—to declare that the scheme of Providence is equally kind when it takes away as when it gives. Therefore the sigh of regret or the groan of despair never mingles in his music. Coleridge and Hemans delight to bring us by successive descents of pictured misery down the road of discontent, till at the last they flash upon us the precipice of despair, and vanish; they fling us out of their control into the abyss of gloom. They furnish, as it were, the *reductio ad absurdum* of repining and despondency. But in the restorative suggestions of Wordsworth, you see the power which curbs and brings back to its anterior peacefulness the tempests which its might had raised. The master is never carried off his feet, but when he has displayed his magic ends in the same self-possession he began in. The one party resembles life's mock creator, the dramatist, who, when he has brought things to the last acme of despair and misery, lets the curtain fall, confessing his inability to re-arrange the fragments which he has jumbled in most admired disorder. The other resembles the true creator, who can reduce men to the last depth of ruin, and bring them back again to peace and power, without marring the interest of the scene, and displays more strength in calming the agitation of excitement than he does in raising it. He contemplates the losses of life without being deprived of the wisdom of hope. When Coleridge compares his youth with his age, the breath of unchecked melancholy simply passes over his lyre, like the melodious sigh of a Greek anthologist, which returns into itself, and is as hopeless after the utterance as before it.

When I was young!—ah! woful *when*,
Ah for the change 'twixt now and then!

This breathing house not made with hands,
  This body that does me grievous wrong
O'er airy cliffs and glittering sands
  How lightly *then* it flashed along!

Wordsworth in like manner speaks of the change that has come upon him—

From what he was when first
He came among the hills; when like a roe
He bounded o'er the mountains, by the sides
Of the deep rivers and the lonely streams,
Wherever natnre led.

He tells us of the days in which the sounding cataract,

The tall rock,
The mountain, and the deep and gloomy wood,
Their colors and their forms, were then to him
An appetite,—a feeling and a love,
That had no need of a remoter charm
By thought supplied, or any interest
Unborrowed from the eye.

As he reviews the scene, he says,

That time is past,
And all its aching joys are now no more,
And all its dizzy raptures.

Yet mark the manly judgment with which he puts by the unphilosophic weakness of regret, and the ingenuity of hopefulness with which he finds a compensation for 'what age takes away.'

Not for this
Faint I, nor mourn, nor murmur; other gifts
Have followed, for such loss, I would believe,
Abundant recompense:

and he goes on to recount the graver instruction which the landscape gives since he can hear

The still, sad music of humanity,
Nor harsh, nor grating, though of ample power
To chasten and subdue;

and can recognize

In nature and the language of the sense,
The anchor of his purest thoughts, the nurse,
The guide, the guardian of his heart, and soul
Of all his moral being.

And his resolution 'never to submit' to vain repining, is finely seen in the lines which follow these—

Nor perchance
If I were not thus taught, should I the more
Suffer my genial spirits to decay:
For thou art with me, here upon the banks
Of this fair river; thou, my dearest friend,
And in thy voice I catch
The language of my former heart, and read
My former pleasures in the shooting lights
Of thy wild eyes.

In another of his poems, the fourth book of 'The Excursion,' he declares that

If the time must come, in which his feet
No more shall stray where meditation leads,
By flowing stream, through wood, or craggy wild,
. . . . The unprison'd *mind*
May yet have scope to range among her own,
Her thoughts, her images, her high desires:

and if 'the dear faculty of sight should fail,' he consoles himself by observing that he will still be able

To *remember*
What visionary powers of eye and soul
In youth were his; when stationed on the top
Of some huge hill—expectant, he beheld
The sun rise up, from distant climes return'd
Darkness to chase, and sleep, and bring the day,
His bounteous gift! or saw him toward the deep
Sink—with a retinue of flaming clouds
Attended.

And, although the 'fervent raptures' of those young days of sensibility 'are forever flown,' 'and,' he continues,

Since their date my soul hath undergone
Change manifold, for better or for worse:
Yet cease I not to struggle and aspire
Heavenward; and chide the part of me that flags,
Through sinful choice, or dread necessity.

Since those 'soul-animating strains' were hushed, in which Milton bade us 'bate not a jot of heart or hope, but move right onward,' never has the moral or courageous cheerfulness been so nobly inculcated. Moreover, in that sublime Ode in which he teaches us that though our bodies live in time, our souls dwell ever in eternity, whose attribute for all that it contains is immortality, he indulges for a moment in a passionate regret for the departed light that lay 'about us in our infancy,' and then rises to his wonted strength of thankful satisfaction—

O joy! That in our *embers*
Is something yet doth live,
That nature still *remembers*
What was so fugitive!

And, having lodged among the eternal truths of his life the knowledge which these 'high instincts' bore about them, he exclaims,

What though the radiance which was once so bright
Be now forever taken from my sight;
Though nothing can bring back the hour
Of splendor in the grass or glory in the flower,

He can still find abundant blessing in what is left;

In the primal sympathy
Which having been must ever be;
In the soothing thoughts that spring
Out of human suffering;
In the faith that looks through death,—
In years that bring the philosophic mind.

The appreciant patience of his thoughtful heart discerning, that if the 'vision splendid' of heaven-remembered glory has faded into common light, '*Earth* fills her lap' with instructions as well as 'pleasures of her own,' and that

30*

Another race hath been and other palms are won.

If you will compare the last stanza of an ode of Wordsworth, having for its motto an extract from the ballad of Sir Patrick Spence, with the sixth paragraph of an ode of Coleridge, bearing the same motto, you will see how much more dignified and just and valuable than the unprofitable and false dejection of the more metaphysical bard is the temper in which the other, while he sees that time has 'suspended what nature gave him at his birth,' evokes as ministers of comfort those other faculties which life and the world evolve, and which are the offspring of the '*human* heart by which we live,'—

Reason . . . . . which can bring
The timely insight that can temper fears,
And from vicissitude remove its sting;
And Faith . . . aspiring to that domain
Where joys are perfect, neither wax nor wane.

The same loftiness of spirit which will not be fretted and cannot be *ennuyé*, but 'makes the happiness it does not find,' is visible in the dignity which he gives to common things. Byron delights in nothing but the exquisite and faultless; but surely it is a coarser sensibility which is only moved by some image of perfection than that which can be satisfied with the small degree of beauty which the actual and the ordinary presents. And in this we gain a view of that disposition and faculty which give to Wordsworth a loftier rank as man and moralist than any praise of poetry implies. Knowing that the world around us and all that it contains is the highest work of heaven's great King, and is declared by him to be good and perfect, he has seen that the truest excellence of grace and loveliness must be found in the daily realities that encompass us, and we may conceive that he has aimed to find in nature and in life the same satisfaction and approval which the incarnate eye of The Mightiest and Most Pure beheld in what he saw. The marks of deep and comprehensive thought that in Mr. Wordsworth's higher poems declare him to be a philosophic reasoner of the highest order, declare that in those smaller pieces, which have been called puerile or infantile, we must search for some profounder purpose than has yet appeared. Accordingly, it has appeared to me that, proceeding on the notion I have indicated, his object in that class of his poems has been to show what man might feel, or ought to feel, or what Deity intended that he should feel, rather than to declare that such feelings are the self-selected emotions of his own natural temper,—to show that in the flight of butterflies, the opening of a celandine, the trials of a shepherd and the walk of a beggar, there is enough to gratify a healthy sense of the beautiful, to fill the demands of a proper interest, and to move the sensibilities of a correct heart. And who that remembers that these are the scenes which the Infinite created for perfect and contemplates for pleasing, and of these was the discourse of Christ, will deny that his is the true system of taste?—Those poets who only 'speak of Africa and golden joys,' and those moralists who feed the expectant hopes of struggling goodness with pictures of gorgeous splendor and exciting incidents in Paradise, err alike in truth of perception and in wisdom of policy, and encourage views that are both devious and discontented. As the faculties of man grow more exalted and purified, he finds higher gladness in tamer things; and it is plain that the promised joy which the righteous will attain will be accomplished, not by elevating in degree the objects of pleasure, but by refining in kind the sensibilities of the observer. The punishment of Adam lay less in any actual change of the home of his days than in that blunting of his susceptibilities by sin, which made what once seemed paradise appear a sterile world; and conscience is the sworded cherub which keeps him from the joy he once tasted. Thus it seems that Mr. Wordsworth's theories are supported by his theology, and that we must accept his æsthetics until we can confute his creed."

A DIALOGUE IN TRAVELLING.

Reflections on travelling and its modes—Scenery of the Tyrol—Power of applying to use the common people in different nations—Remarks on the letters and character of Dr. Johnson—City and country contrasted in their effects on imagination—Acted wisdom superior to written wisdom—Napoleon a system—Prospect of liberal institutions in Europe—Vienna—Trieste—The Ocean—Voyage to Cyprus—Beauty of that Island.

"Quæ me cumque vocant terræ."—VIRGIL.

As I was turning over, some time since, one of the hundred volumes of that eccentric but very interesting man, Sir Egerton Brydges, I fell in with an observation which struck me as being odd, but not unnatural, and which, in fact, jumped with my own notions so far, that I had always acted upon it a good deal, though I had not thought of reducing it into a regular system of life. He says, that if he were not held down by the tie of a family connection, and if his means were adequate to the expense of the thing, he would give up altogether the plan of a fixed residence, and spend his days in travelling about perpetually, from place to place, throughout all the world; comforting himself amid the annoyances of to-day with the confidence that to-morrow's sun would rise over a different scene; enlarging knowledge by surveying the old qualities of humanity under new forms of manners in the marts of the world, and enriching his fancy by an endless variety of the splendors of nature. It is the same writer that, in another work, his letters on the genius of Lord Byron, says, I think, justly, that extraordinary as were the natural parts of that great poet, he yet was indebted to the wandering habits of his life for much of that flashing grandeur of imagination, that rush of soul and torrent force of an unblanching mind, and the charm of a spirit magnificently changeful, that kindle his pages as with the fires of heaven, and have made his works the worship of multitudes and a wonder of the times. And this notion of the learned Chandos has, I take it, a good footing in philosophy; for if it be well looked at, it will be found, perhaps, that those ideas which lie upon the fancy, and those thoughts, which rise upon the mind, are but the images of outward things acted on, and, as it were, sublimated, by the analysing ardors of the moral powers. He, therefore, that has seen the most, has most materials for fancies and thoughts; while by the same influence, if his faculties be not of so feeble a temper that they are oppressed and crushed down, the moral energies we spoke of, are quickened by the excitement of novelty, the stimulus of expectation and surprise, and the effect of fresh specimens of excellence on the emulations and ambitions of the soul.

"A better reason," as Sterne says, than all this,—I mean a fondness for amusement and locomotion,—has made me pass much of my time in voyaging about. And, notwithstanding the many new inventions in this way, I think that, so far at least as pleasure is concerned, we have not improved much upon the simple method that was in use among our great-grandfathers; that, I mean, of travelling on horseback. It is a characteristic of this age, that whatever it does it must do passionately. The man of the present time will not journey, unless it be furiously. If that grave ancestor of mine, who is now looking down upon me from his stately chair, with nothing ruffled about him but his wrists, could step out alive from the canvas and behold the crowded steamboat pawing madly along the water; or the long train of cars shooting like a harnessed comet over the narrow road of iron, he would surely imagine that one side of the world had caught fire, and the scorched inhabitants were rushing from the flames—or that some still more terrible catastrophe was about to happen at the other end, and mankind, with a noble philanthropy, were hastening to prevent it—or, at least, that every person in the excited multitude was pressing forward on business of a vital importance—and he would doubtless be surprised to be told that those herds of men were hurried on by interest not more weighty or more elevated than those which occupied his own bosom, to traverse in two hours the distance, which to him, followed by his careful servant, had often, for the mind and meditative heart, formed the improving employment of as many days; that one of the most tremendous powers in nature had been pressed into use only that men may save a time which they will not employ, and shorten a distance which it had been pleasant to prolong. An emblem, too, of the democratic spirit might perhaps be found in the spectacle of men pressing and pressed forward in masses, when before they moved with a more solitary and reserved independency; in the submission of individual inclination and humor to the direct will of the multitude, of which they became a part; the exchange of a path and a conveyance of limited capacity for speed, with freedom to tarry or wander at discretion, for a road and a vehicle of limitless power, but without the ability to stop or deviate at all; with many other fancies of the like nature. * * *

It was on a fine fresh day in the beginning of the summer of 1828, that, along with my friend the Count de Mardini, I crossed the Julian Alps from Lombardy to upper Austria. A soft west wind was blowing, and the deep blue sky was piled with ranges of white pillowy clouds, which rose in unsubstantial grandeur, as if to mock, by their resemblance, the imputed permanence of the lofty hills. We had passed the summit of the ridge, and were beginning to descend on the other side, when a lovely little valley upon the left rose upon my sight. I paused for a moment to look upon its pure and light green grass, and to contemplate the beautiful repose which rested upon it. Dismounting from my horse, and sending my attendant forward to wait for me at the foot of the hill, I walked on through the valley, leaving the count to come along as he pleased. The valley terminated by an abrupt and deep descent, after a short distance, and the brilliant and endless landscape of Tyrol was before me. The distant peaks rose far above the lower clouds, and their white caps were scarcely distinguishable from them; the blue of the sky shaded itself through the darker blue of the distant hills into the green of the adjacent woods, and the heavens and the earth together seemed one vast amphitheatre. I descended the mountain, and remounting my horse, continued my journey towards Vienna. Our way lay through the dominions of the duke of Swartzenburg, a prince once powerful, but whose territories were now reduced, by the policy and arms of the emperor, to less than half of their former extent. Passing through the forest of Gratz, on the borders of the duke's possessions, the sound of horns occasionally heard echoing about the hills, indicated that there were huntsmen in the woods; and I thought it possible that the duke himself was engaged in this pastime.

"The duke is fond of the chase, I believe," said I to my companion, who had long resided in these regions, and now again had joined me.

"For want of any thing better to do. But you may be sure, that if his highness* found it practicable to engage in any thing better, he would not waste his time in this barbarous and barbarizing sport."

"I should think," said I, "that as long as his dominions are covered by forests like these, and peopled with such savages as one meets with everywhere in his dominions, the duke would be at no loss for objects to employ his attention. There is nothing either in things or men which does not require improvement."

"You say true; every thing is to be done; but how to do it is the question. A man cannot work without tools. The tools of a statesman are active, intelligent men; none such are to be found, for the whole country is brutified. If the duke were to attempt to put in operation any of the many plans of improvement which I know he contemplates, his first and strongest opposition would be in his own household."

"If a man wants tools, he can make them, or he can do without them. I know no possible condition of things, in which a cool head and a strong heart cannot triumph, if it wills it."

"A prince, here," said the count, "is the slave of circumstances. Immemorial custom has petrified around him, and shut him up in a cage of stone. His privileges are compulsory, his rights are duties, his powers are fetters."

"Circumstances are rocks under which a weak man hides, and which a strong man scales and carves his statue on the top. If circumstances cannot be conquered, they may be directed. If

* The title of an Austrian Duke corresponds to "Highness," not "Grace," as in England.

the river cannot be stopped, it may be sent into a new channel. All that either the statesman or the mechanic wants, is power; the operation of that power he can prescribe himself. If custom and circumstance have a power on people, that power may be used for any end. England is a country in which the art of managing men seems to me to be better understood than in any other in the world. The method there is, not to give the people new dispositions, but to take advantage of their old ones —not to instil good principles, but to turn the bad ones to account,—in a word, not to change the wind, but to turn the rudder. The secret of success there, is to identify a cause with the natural interests or the prevailing passions of the people. Under shelter of this, adverse details may be introduced, as the fish swallows the hook for the sake of the bait."

"That," said the count, "is practicable where great and steady passions are in action, which, having been once tried, may again be calculated upon. Here there is nothing to grapple with."

"If a nation has a soul, it may be employed; if it has none, one may be put into it. There is a remedy for every national defect. If a people are dull and apathetic, war is the natural remedy. If they are servile and degraded, privileges, valuable on the one hand and safe on the other, will give them dignity and self-respect. If they are predatory in inclination, the possession of property will teach them its value. Thus for all diseases you may provide a cure. But the difficulty is, that those countries which want this wisdom, have not the experience which has taught it to others; one possesses the knowledge, and another has occasion for its exercise. It is the part of wisdom in politics to make observations rather than experiments, and if these princes could profit by the example of older kingdoms, or if one imbued with the spirit, and familiar with the tactic of an active nation, could direct the measures of these sovereigns, the union would be blessed for the latter. Light is combination, and so is truth and power."

Our conversations on a subsequent day turned upon subjects of English literature, with which the count, who had long resided in England, was profoundly acquainted; and also on the politics of France, with which, as he had been an envoy for some years to the Court of that country, it was less surprising that he was entirely versed.

"I have often amused my leisure time," said the count, "by reading some of the letters of Dr. Johnson, a man in whose ignorances there was more wisdom, and in whose prejudices there was more truth, than in the learned candor of the most liberal philosophers of the age. Nothing, by-the-by, gives me so strong an impression of the robust vigor of his mind, as his hearty love of cities and his systematic contempt and dislike of the country. His fondness for the narrow and unsuggestive walls of Bolt Court, was a preference which was characteristic of a man who loved to have no thoughts within his memory that were not of his mind; whose inly-working intellect preferred notions to ideas; to the hawk-like temper of whose reason, conceptions were more germane than sentiments. The less the mind is filled with images of external nature, the higher and fuller beats its own creative energy. I think it is Cumberland who has said that he wrote with most facility when he had no other prospect before his eyes than a dead blank wall. To one who has observed how much influence the habitual presence of a vision or pictured scene has upon the strength and activity of the mind, it might not seem fanciful to suggest that one of the reasons why America has done so little that is great in literature, may be the vast extent of its country, whereby one wide idea occupies the mental view,—one great dream absorbs the mental interest. Certainly, to that cause, and to the consequent distraction and transportation of the thoughts and fancies over a great and varied scene, assisted, doubtless, by the great facility of communicating with different parts, and the constant circulation of newspapers, may be reasonably attributed the unusual want of individuality of character which, as a nation, marks that people; for that intensity of soul which quickens the intellect into a salient fire, can only be cherished by summoning all the thoughts and interests within the spirit, and making that which is external, subject to itself; surrounding points draw silently off that electric fire which else might be nursed into a consuming spirit. And the same causes which give force to character, give vigor to intellect, for intellect is essentially distinctive and self-evolved; cleverness may be caught from the imparting of the things around us, but genius is the raying forth of inward light. The Englishman is confined to a narrow walk of material images, local impressions, and political interests; and I think that this tameness of the physical gives earnestness and power to the mind. Johnson, bred up in a prairie, had been far other than Johnson jammed up in an alley."

"For the cultivation and exercise of the logical faculties," said I, "and for all those studies that concern the '*quic quid agunt homines,*' that exclusion of the images furnished by the world of sense—'the infinite magnificence of heaven,' 'the sleepless ocean,' and 'the vernal field'—which the city ensures, is doubtless favorable. Wit, too, is a thing essentialy civic. The queer pickings of Charles Lamb from the motley ball of humor could never have been prompted but by the air of the Temple. But that elevation of the mental and moral being, around whose purity plays the light of philosophy, or the yet serener brightness of poetry, can better be attained by inhaling those fresh and high-floating thoughts, which, like air, encase the shapes and sights of nature. The majesty of nature is the curtain of deity; and the light of deity is grace and truth. As poetry, which is the highest truth, makes its haunts in the sky-coped forest and the secret mountain top, so I imagine do the lesser spirits of wisdom, in the proportion of the purity of their essence, require to be manna-fed on nature's stillness. Of the men whose footsteps daily wear the stones of London, there are few who would not gasp and stare at a stanza of Wordsworth, or even a couplet of Pope."

"And yet those persons may really be the superior men," said the count. "The truths which the poets bring into their minds are incorporated in the other's nature, and are thus too deeply inspirited in him to be objective to his mind; they lie so close within him that he does not see them. I think that the world errs in the high rank which it assigns to literary men. I look on genius as being imperfect and truncated comprehension, that penetrates like a point by reason of its narrowness, and of which the light is brilliant because the ray is broken. Poetry is but partial and narrow sympathy, which is interested in a particular because it sees not the whole. He that has never experienced a sentiment is the perfect poet; even as the only pointless thing in nature, the circle, is the only complete one. He is the universal and encyclopedic sympathist, for he holds all things before his intelligence with an equal advancement. The centre of revolution must have the rapidest motion in the system, and that is rest; the roar of the coursing spheres must be the loudest in the universe, and that is silence. To be, is higher than to describe; to do, is proof of more wisdom than to analyze the doing; to have, is rarer than to explain the having. Homer, who created by instinct, would have been puzzled to comprehend the rules which Aristotle discovered in him; yet was he the deeper critic and the profounder philosopher. In the judgment of smaller minds, an angel who saw by intuition, would be dwarfed by a logician who proved by syllogism. Newton, who, at a glance, perceived the truth of Euclid's theorems, and could not well demonstrate them, would have passed for a dunce in a class-room. The world is struck by whatever is brilliant in execution and elaborate in process; not perceiving that visible light can exist only in darkness, and that enginery is always the resort of weakness. If we consider the matter closely, we shall find that to be wise, imports a loftier order of intellect than to say wise things; that to act truly, denotes a superior order of mind to that which perceives truths. It is bookmen who settle the rank of bookmen; hence, the supremacy given them. But, in fact, not only is bookish theory a feebler thing than practical prudence, but the wisdom of the world of books is less in quantity than that of the world of action. There is more wisdom acted than comprehended; more comprehended than uttered; more uttered than written. Practice is always in advance of system; the thinking man is the unconscious plagiarist of the acting man. You will always find that the expedient of the artizan has anticipated the principle of the philosopher; and if you bring down any true poem to a peasant, you will find that the truths which it contains are familiar to his consciousness, if new to his understanding.

That philosophers and poets daily proclaim fresh truths in political and moral science, and that the world does not act more wisely for all the proclamations, proves that those truths were previously known to the action of the world. Governments are framed wise by ploughmen, and proved wise by philosophers; mobs make revolutions, and historians admire them. Might not the oft-recurring fact, that

> A few strong instincts and a few plain rules,
> Among the herdsmen of the Alps have wrought
> More for mankind, at this unhappy day,
> Than all the pride of intellect and thought—

have suggested that there is a higher way of knowing truths than by the analysis of the intellect, and a stronger way of proving them than by the machinery of the syllogism? I consider that the scales of fame and of true merit are inverse; and that the genius which we crown with applause, is but a disordered and distorted form of that silent wisdom which we despise as dullness. Poetry is the natural mind run wild; it is by a restraint of the reason that we are not all poets. But not only do I hold that the hind's mute way of taking unconscious cognizance of metaphysical verities is a higher one than the professor's, but the order of new truths, which conduct exemplifies, lies above that of the notions which speculation deals with. To act with discretion, requires the union of so many more and more difficultly acquired qualities than are required to think brilliantly, that I regard a successful clerk or beadle as more respectable in an intellectual point of view than many who probe the depths of metaphysics, or attain to the heights of poetry. Of course there are moralists who can 'act *and* comprehend.'"

"If, as your remark would teach," said I, "men are to be considered truly intellectual, in proportion as they furnish no *mental* display of intellect, we should probably be right in preferring the thought-checking labors of urban life. The principle which your observation embodies, has, I confess, sometimes occurred to me, though I have never ventured to assert it quite so distinctly as you have done."

"If we compare the two modes of life which we were speaking

of, by their effects on masses," resumed Count Mardini, "we shall find that the intellectual and moral force of cities is far greater than that of the most populous country. To the honor of the former be it said, that they have always been the asylum of liberty. In the darkest ages of feudal tyranny, cities kept alive the spirit of freedom. In every contest with despotism, they have been the first to rebel and the last to submit."

"Let us not mistake," said I, "for the spirit of liberty, the restlessness of vice or the discontent of misery. For true and valuable freedom—for freedom of spirit and of mind—for elevation of purpose and erectness of heart—for that independence which annihilates superiority by never deigning to question it—I confess that I should look to the vallies and the plains of rustic life. A king ceases to be a superior in the country, as a candle is extinguished in the sun-light; and as compared with infinitude, all finites are equal, so does the boundless regality of nature withdraw from ranks the sting of difference. The soul is born free, and if there is nothing to enslave it, will remain so; and what is there of slavish in the far-roaming wind, the piercing sun, the stream that never can be staid?—what is there to suggest a thraldom in the calm senates of the lofty oaks, or the mute hilarity of laughing roses?

Dic quibus in terris inscripti nomina REGUM
Nascuntur *flores*, et eris mihi magnus Apollo."

"That sort of moral freedom which you indicate," said the count, "is the only freedom that is worth possessing, and it is independent on the form of polity under which it is cherished, for it is the inalienable quality of the unshackled mind and the unsullied heart. But men in this world will fight for names and forms, neglecting the substance. With the efforts that are now going on to republicanise the governments of Europe, I have no sympathy; for I know that they are as foolish as I think they are vain. The honest are free everywhere; the cowardly nowhere. I have seen in democracies a vileness of subserviency that a galley slave might have pitied; and I have found in the ranks of toryism an independence and a self-respect that Brutus never knew."

"Except in the reports of journalists, and the speeches of demagogues, I do not think that the 'spirit of the age' in Europe tends at all to republicanism. The monarchies of Europe seem more likely to resolve themselves into organized military despotisms than to be dissolved into democracies," said I.

"And that mode of government, as now exemplified in Austria and Prussia," said the count, "seems to me the best that can possibly be contrived, for it is a government of law. If Napoleon had had talent enough to combine properly the elements that lay around him in abundance, he could have established a government of this nature that would have been perfect; he might have created an administration that would have combined perfect despotism with perfect freedom."

"You are the first person that I ever met with, count, who has ventured to suggest that Napoleon had not talents for every thing."

"Of all the persons of whom I have ever read or heard," said he, "there is no one for whose abilities as a ruler and a man of power, I entertain a more profound and settled contempt than for those of Napoleon Buonaparte. He was a great soldier, and nothing more. At no period of his varied life was he the master of the circumstances around him—the criterion of greatness—but always their absolute slave. He controlled not the revolution; it began without him, and its elements had been organized without him; it went forward, and he went with it. Vast energies were in dislocated combination, and were to work out their jarring course; they did it with him on their back; they did it as soon, and no sooner, as certainly, and not more regularly than if he had not been there. France, under Napoleon, was like a steam-car thrown from its track, and dashing madly through the sand to the nearest precipice: as it goes on in awful force, for a while, a man stands upon it, and vaunts his own power which directs it; it would have gone as well if a child had sat upon the box. The government of Napoleon contained within itself always the elements of inevitable ruin. Every mistake in policy which he could make, he made; while there stood beside him a pale priest, who warned him from every one of them. The true history of the empire is this, that Buonaparte's military fame had raised him to such a height that he was fourteen years in falling to the ground. A merchant may live for years in a state of bankruptcy, and still appear to be solvent. Napoleon's extravagant foreign enterprises were the desperate movements of a dancer on a slack-rope, conscious that the moment of pause is the moment of fall: he could not have kept his place, in peace. His triumph was but for the half-hour necessary for his enemies to recover from their surprise. What a contrast between him and Cromwell! who bent, conquered, and crushed circumstances, as if they had been osiers; and lived, not like Napoleon, only till the unavoidable explosion should take place, but lived secure in the confidence that his genius had broken down all danger and established his safety. Napoleon held his power at the sufferance of Talleyrand and Fouché, and a dozen more: they made use of him, not he of them; and when it suited their interest, they dismissed him. Cromwell stood on his own single, all-sufficient strength. Compare Napoleon with Mirabeau, who, instead of floating like a straw upon the whirlwind, waved the tempest into fury with one hand, and stretching forth the other, said, 'Thus far shalt thou go and no farther.' In estimating the greatness of any one, you must judge either by the effects which he wrought, or by his own inherent personal might. By both tests Napoleon is found wanting. Cromwell transformed for everlasting, the condition of the English people, and the principles of English society; kings came in after him, but the mark of his five fingers is on the government to this day, and will never vanish. Ximenes revolutionized Spain, once and forever; and the modern *guerilla* glories of the Peninsula attest his genius. These countries passed through the grip of these men like clay through the hands of the potter; the empire passed over France like a bright cloud over the earth. Where are the results of Napoleon's life? where, the political evidence of his existence? The France of Louis Philippe is the France of

Louis Quatorze. Read the histories of the times of the First and Second James in England, or of Henry and Charles in Spain; and in both instances you will say, 'There has been some mighty spirit at work in this interval.' Read the annals of the last five years in France, as a history of a century back, and you will detect no moral anachronism. Napoleon left a few roads and statues; what are these? Proofs only of wealth; any rich men might have built them. He operated on things; they on men; he wrote his name upon the ground; they stamped their likeness on the nation. If, again, you look at the individual, Napoleon had absolutely had no personality. He was a name. No man can be great, who has not great passions; *he* had *none.* Richelieu left on France the furrows of every passion that ever lightened through his breast. The country shook as he breathed. Sketch his stupendous policy in the form of a portrait, and you have a colossal image of the man. You feel inclined to call France, under his administration, Richelieu; and to call him France. What all these men did, they did alone; all their great contemporaries opposed them. But take away from the empire some five or six names, and you have nothing left but the pomp and the glitter. Some one asked Mackintosh what de Stael meant when she said that 'Napoleon was not a man, but a system;' 'Mass! I don't know,' said Sir James. But she meant wisdom: she meant that there was in France a confederate system of power, organized by powerful men, at the head of which stood Napoleon, and that, by a political synecdoche, the world has called this system 'Napoleon.' Certainly, great things were done under the empire; but Buonaparte no more did them, than Shakspeare's wig wrote Othello. The splendor of his military achievements has struck the world blind to his miserable statesmanship; the grandeur of his pacific monuments, which only showed greatness of aspiration and great command of physical means, has been deemed evidence of greatness of intellect, as the swelling robe conceals the mean form behind it. But the very qualities which his victories evinced, unfitted him for statesmanship. He fought his battles on general principles, and by the aid of grand and comprehensive combinations;

whereas politics is essentially a science of detail—a system of particulars—a rule of exceptions. When the history of France under Napoleon is truly written by an independent thinker, it will exhibit a great national triumph and a contemptible personal failure."

"The utter failure of both French revolutions," said I, "is a mournful discouragement to the hopes of the philanthropist; yet with these prospects before me, I am still not without hope that great results may yet be accomplished in the political improvement of men. The great impediment in the way of successful change from tyranny to freedom is, that the agitation which necessarily attends the process constantly rouses that ambition which might otherwise have slumbered, and sharpens those qualities of power which might else have been ineffective. But for the sounds of war, Napoleon might have lived and died at Ajaccio, and his spirit might have slept as calmly and as darkly as now reposes its possessor in his wave-swept grave. Still, as in all cases of failure, the causes of failure are evident and were evitable, there yet remains hope that, in some future voyage, the harbor rocks may be avoided, and the smooth river gained. The wreck of one vessel on a sand bar, so far from proving that another will share the same fate, affords a strong presumption that its successor will avoid it; for the danger is made known. Taught by repeated failure, man may at length devise, or guided by accident, may discover perfect institutions, and these will make perfect men, and the dream of the sanguine may yet wake to fulfilment."

"The perfectibility of things human," said Count Mardini, "is a true doctrine, but with a circumstance not always observed. The perfection of all things beneath the heaven will be their destruction; for destructiveness, or the disposition to impracticability, becomes in every thing mundane, after a certain point of improvement, an element developing itself with geometric acceleration, while the melioration goes on in arithmetical increase. The good in an institution, a machine, or a character, may now far exceed the opposing tendency to dissolution or unfeasibility, but the augmentive ratio of the latter so far exceeds that of the former, that by the time that one has reached perfection, the other will equal it and nullify the whole. Vague as this assertion may seem to you, it may be proved in physical matters by experiment, and in moral, by figures. The atheist notion of the ultimate universal perfection of humanity, and the Christian dogma of the final dissolution of terrestriality, so far from contradicting one another, are consistent and identical. At this moment, the institutions of the liberalized sections of Europe are on the point of becoming perfect and impossible. It has happened from the beginning until now—it will happen from now until the end—that men and nations advance nobly into the illuminated temple of Reform, as if led by an angel's hand, and when their hand is just upon the altar, *then*, as if a demon's eye glared on them, they are paralyzed in an instant, or start back into the darkness and barbarity of threshold times. So invariably has this happened, that it cannot be the occasional effect of falling off, but the essential consequence of going on; in fact, the pit lies at the foot of the altar.

> Jove strikes the Titans down,
> Not when they set about their mountain-piling,
> But when another rock would crown their work.

But the splendid thinker who wrote those lines—by far the most splendid of our time*—errs in imagining *that* to be the accident of defeat, which, in truth, is the essential consequence of success."

Entertaining the time with such conversations as these, among others, on different topics, we found ourselves after some days' travel in the capital of Austria, where my friend Mardini was now residing. Here I spent some weeks in the enjoyment of such pleasures as the society of that metropolis—one which I have sometimes thought was the most brilliant in Europe—could afford. Leaving the count, at the end of the time, in that city, I resumed my travels, now solitary, and directed my course towards the South. A week's ride brought me to Trieste. The faint

* Robert Browning.—ED.

summer sun was declining through the dreamy mists of the west, when the long, blue line of ocean burst upon my sight. My heart was glad within me when I beheld the glorious image of the infinite and eternal. * * * * * *

Ha! exclaimed I, as I sprang upon the broad beach of the Mediterranean, and my spirit drank the splendid spectacle of light and life that spread before me—what a relief it is to escape from the straining littleness and wearisome affectation of men, to the free, majestic and inspiring sea—to listen to his stern, exalted voice—to watch the untrammelled swell of these pure waters, till the pulse of our own heart beats in sympathetic nobleness—to behold it heave in untiring energy—changing momently in form, changing never in impression! What joy is it to be sure that *here* there is nothing counterfeit—nothing feigned—nothing artificial! Feeling, here, grapples with what will never falter; imagination here may spread its best plumed wings, but will never outstrip the real. There is here none of that fear which never leaves the handicraft of art—the fear of penetrating beneath the surface of beauty. Here, man feels his majesty by feeling his nothingness; for the majesty of man lies in his conceptions, and the conception of self-nothingness is the grandest we can have. That small and noxious passion-mist, which we *call* our soul, is driven without; and our TRUE soul—the soul of the universe, which we are—enters into us. The spirit which rests like a vapor visibly upon the bosom of the waters is a presence and a pervading power; and the breath which it exhales is life, and love, and splendid strength. Nothing in nature renders back to man the full and instant sympathy which is accorded by the mighty being who thus reposes mildly in the generous grandeur of his glorious power. We may love the forms of the trees, the colors of the sky, and the impressive vastness of the hills; but we can never animate them with a soul of life, and persuade ourselves that they experience the feeling which they cause. But the sea, as its countenance shows its myriad mutations with the variety and rapidity of the passions which sport through the breast of man, seems truly to return the emotion which is breathed towards him; and fellowship and friendship—yea, and personal affection—are the sentiments which his gambols rouse in the spectator's heart. The flashing smiles that sparkle in his eye—are they not his happy thoughts?—and the ripples that flit their scouring dance over his breast—are they not feelings of delight that agitate his frame? Whether I am amid mountains, or on plains, there is not an hour in which my existence is not haunted by the remembrance of the ocean. It abides beside me like a thought of my mind;—it occupies my total fancy;—I ever seem to stand before it. And I know that whenever it shall fare so ill with me in the world that comfort and consolation can no longer be found in it, I have a paraclete beside the shelving beach who will give the consolation man withholds. The strong, thick wind which comes from it will be full of life; the petty tumult of care will be shamed by the gigantic struggle of the elements, and subside to peace. What can be more noble or more affecting than the picture of the old priest, who, wronged by the Grecian king—his calm age fired with passion—retires along the shore of the sounding sea and soothes his breast ere he invokes the god?

Thoughts like those
Are medicin'd best by nature.

I have never stood by the banks of the ocean thus superbly fringed with curling waves, and listened to that strange, questionable, echoed roar, without an emotion altogether supernatural. That moan—that wail of the waters—which comes to the ear, borne on the wind in the stillness of evening, sounds like the far-off complaint of another world, or the groan of our own world's innermost spirit. Like some of the unearthly music of Germany, when heard for the first time, it startles a feeling in the secret mind which has never before been wakened in this world, giving us assurance of another life, and the strongest proof that our soul is essentially immortal. Little as I am inclined by nature—and I am still less by principle—to indulge in hankerings after the unattainable, still I have always sought to realize that sentiment by which the soul infers that its birth-place and home is above, by finding within itself thoughts and emotions which are germane only to that realm, and which could not take root but in a soil celestial, nor flourish unless watered in the bud by the undescended dews of heaven. Go, stand in a lonely forest at midnight, when no sound awakes the echo, and look up on the moon gliding over the pillowed clouds —go, and standing upon the topmost stone of The Coliseum, gaze upon the sun slowly sinking through the silent mists to his resting-place, the sea—or, mounting upon The Pyramids, explore the deep, blue sky, which hangs above you—and this feeling will come to you in all its fulness, and you will know its truth and will confess its power. Upon such scenes I have looked, and, looking, wept at my own incompetency to grasp in its completeness this mysterious instinct, and to fathom it to its foundation. But I have calmed my agitation and descended to the business of life with the hoarded assurance of deep bliss in store for me hereafter, when, through a long futurity in another world, with an eye brightened, a heart quickened, and an understanding infinitely more comprehensive, I may attain unto that which in this sphere has baffled me, and repose throughout eternity in the fruition of glorious thoughts, which here I can but dimly apprehend, and splendid truths which here I only doubtfully discern. * * * * * *

I found in the port of Trieste, a vessel about to sail for the island of Cyprus. I took passage on board of it, and on the following morning, the silvery waves of the Adriatic were whitening in front of us, as sailing round cape Parna, we emerged from the narrow bay into the broader gulf. The crew of the vessel consisted of that motley sort of company which is usually found in the ships of the Mediterranean,—Jews of Lombardy and Istria on their way to the Morea and the islands of the Archipelago—Candiotes returning home from the sale of olives at the Austrian markets; here was a young Turk who had been pursuing his medical studies in Italy, and there was a Dervish on his way to Khorassan. Each individual or party, according to their national distinctions, though strangers to one another, gradually withdrew from the rest, and retiring to some particular part of the vessel, maintained a haughty reserve as to the remainder of the passengers. The Jews were crouching in the dirt of the forward deck, or thrusting themselves stealthily into little knots of talkers with the offer of opium and tobacco, and other wares, for sale: the solemn Turk was pacing the stern, with his long pipe in his mouth, and a shining dagger in his belt; and a small party of shivering Frenchmen, with their hands in their pockets, and their bodies shrunk with the cold, were laughing at a sickly dancing dog, as the miserable animal was jumping to the sound of a cracked violin.

On the fifth day of the voyage, we touched at the island of Meleda, off the coast of Dalmatia; and I trod with some interest, the ground which later and more learned investigations have proved to be the scene of the shipwreck of St. Paul. Thence we sailed along by the wild and picturesque Ionian Islands—Corfu and Theaki, the famed Corcyra and Ithaca of the Homeric poems. We anchored for a day in the bay of Candia, and I landed to trace the memorials still remaining of that protracted defence, which, whether we regard its moral importance or its physical efforts, is one of the most striking and honorable events in modern history.

The sun had declined into the western sea, and the mild moonlight was streaming far and wide through the clear, still air, when about midnight, the isle of Cyprus was descried from the rigging. I was standing alone upon the forward deck, leaning over the bowsprit, and watching the finely-feathered waves that rose like an imperial banded plume around the majestic on-step of the ship. Thence, raising my eyes to where the moon, in her mild purity presiding, smiled light and love throughout the adoring air, I let float through my pensive mind, those feeling thoughts of which the holy scene seemed redolent. Not a cloud interrupted the flood of light which rained through the air; not a breath of wind disturbed the lone, white slumbers of the deep.

Fair is the morn upon the monarch sea! when the day's broad and burning eye flings one swift flash over the waters, and ere the glancing light has rested from its bounding, springs above the horizon and goes thundering on its course: and the waves wake and tell one another the story of his coming. Fair is the noon upon the lusty sea! The heart of the born king of day thrills with intense dominion, and the general pulse of nature feels its fullest, deepest beat: in that fervid struggle in which the unconquered sea flashes back defiance, flash for flash, there lies the mightiest interest of power, energy and action, that the universe can show—the manliest scene beyond the breast of man. Fair falls the evening o'er the sombre sea! when nature pauses to consider that another breath of her life has been drawn; for the day and the night are the respirations of the universe: the face of the waters darkens with regret that their so glorious rival hath succumbed, and a melancholy smile plays upon the brow of the lagging surge. Fair rests the night upon the placid sea! O fairer than all is the smile of the midnight! It is a Christian calmness—a domestic quiet! Every phase of nature is a manifestation of love, but through modes and sorts of infinite variety. The morning bounds with the wild ardor of the young man when he first meets his destined bride; the noon is rich with the undeficient gladness of the newly-married husband; the evening dreams, an emblem of parted lovers; but the lonely midnight watches with the affection of a pale mother over her sleeping child—still, though earnest—serene, but anxious—O! how anxious!—If the Christian scheme be a mortal fancy, it must have sprung to being amid a scene like this. * * *

When I awoke on the following morning, the gay, glad hills of Cyprus were around me: I was in the chosen home of beauty—the native land of love. Nature, here, is as luxuriant as the teeming wish—as fair as the fancy's holiest forms—as various as the robe of the many-vestured day. Every thing here is animated with swelling life. Morning rests upon the hills like the breath of Love upon the breast of Beauty. Not softer are the virgin odors that nestle in the folds of the opening rose; not clearer is the water of the crystaling diamond, than the aspect and impression of that atmosphere, and the spirit melts into union with it. The air seems to be a feeling and the breezes to be vocal thoughts. The seasons, in which the sterner and fiercer passions of the soul find an answering voice in

Nature, are many; when there is a concord between the selfish or savage tempers of the mind, and the spirit of the earth and skies. The bitterness of cold Misanthropy; the jealous fires of Ambition; the Gorgon severity of Hate; Lust, and Fear, and Frenzy; all these will seldom fail to find a kindred mood in "the great brotherhood of Ocean, Earth, and Air," whose responsive throb shall deepen the beating of their own wild pulse. It is more rarely that the softer emotions of the heart are either suggested or sympathized in by nature. The reason of it may be that the spirit of nature is always so majestical and strong that to cope with it we must summon within ourselves the sterner and grander passions; which are usually the worser ones.

But now the scene was as gentle as the first dream of Love: it was calm almost to religion. It was an holy day. To such a time belonged only

> Thoughts as pure as the chaste Morning's breath,
> When from the Night's cold arms it creeps away.

The yellow sunbeams, shed through the foliage that surrounded the casements, were casting a latticed light upon the floor of my chamber, and the vigorous but delicate young air of June was floating over my breast with a gentle rapture of joy, and gladdening my senses with the inodorous perfume of its virgin freshness. Except the occasional chafing of the branches of the shrubbery in the garden, when the soft wooings of the wanton breeze waxed stronger than might beseem their gentleness, no sound whatever disturbed the stillness of the day. I lay for a while in a waking reverie of pleasant feelings, tasting the sweetness of the morning health and breathing placid joy. As the cool wind played about my limbs, and its mild inspiration thrilled more and more through my frame, the tide of life swelled with the flowings of the fountains of the air. I arose, and, dressing myself, walked towards the casement to look out at the beauty of the bright-robed summer. I was inhabiting an ancient palace on the brow of an eminence, which commanded the distant vallies and the neighboring sea. The grounds stretched far along the shore, and were marked by varied and enchanting beauty. The unfathomed morning, spreading through the air, had dappled the shadeless blue with its faint featherings of hazy light; and the long and definite shadows lay upon the ground as if they had been carved for ages in unchanging ebony. There was a Sabbath feeling in the time, and almost I could persuade myself that I was standing in some quiet rectory in religious England. Fancy acting upon this suggestion, carried me back to my native country, and to scenes which had passed away with long-past times. I seemed to stand, as in a dream, on the porch of my father's house, with my parents and my sisters beside me. I drew a sofa towards the window, and reclining upon it, indulged the memorizing dreams that pressed upon my heart. Upon the view before me was stamped the intensity of peace; and as, with a spirit yet too tender to cope the interests and hopes of the active world, I sympathized keenly with the holiness of the scene, my soul yearned for that *domestic* affection to whose white hand the golden key of life's fullest and most satisfactory joy is given. It seemed to me as if I had left my father's house but yesterday, as if I was again a child, privileged to ask for boundless love, and beneath all the wearisome restraints of appearance and opinion. I seemed to have returned to that state of infantile inexperience in which the *world* appeared to be a visible sphere external to my knowledge. With what earnestness I longed to renew that happy state around me, as I had restored its feelings within me! What would I not have given to exchange the flickering and unsteady brilliance of those attachments which accident might hereafter promise for the tried certainties of *natural* affection, for that solicitude which we know must wait upon consanguinity for its own satisfaction,—for love without passion, interest without excitement,—devotion that does not look for gratitude! Not with thought, nor with study, nor with hope, but with suffering does wisdom dwell. Long years of sad experience must pass over us, ere we learn that nature is wiser than our heart, and that duty is a kinder monitor than hope. We must be mocked by the deluding revelry of pleasure, and cheated by the false fires of unstable fondness, before we can perceive that the only perfect love on earth is that which glows in those eyes that have kept watch above our cradle. Alas! that the knowledge should come when the blessing has departed!

I found in Cyprus a friend of my college life, Charles Maynard, with whom in that pleasant season I had passed nearly three years as a class companion. Like myself, he was a lover of letters, a man of leisure, and a lover of travel: and, guided by similar influences no doubt, we found ourselves, by a coincidence at once very singular and very natural, sojourners alike beneath the skies of the Mediterranean, and worshiping in Cyprus at the altar of its beauty. We resolved to visit in company portions of this delightful island. That we might escape the greater heats which in those latitudes are sometimes oppressive, we rose at an early hour for our visit to the Villa Angelani, distant about a half day's ride. [The rest of this MS. is wanting.]

MISCELLANEOUS PIECES.

LIFE.

"MAN," says Sir Thomas Browne, "is a noble animal! splendid in ashes, glorious in the grave; solemnizing nativities and funerals with equal lustre, and not forgetting ceremonies of bravery in the infamy of his nature!" Thus spake one who mocked, while he wept, at man's estate, and gracefully tempered the high scoffings of philosophy with the profound compassion of religion. As the sun's proudest moment is his latest, and as the forest puts on its brightest robe to die in, so does man summon ostentation to invest the hour of his weakness, and pride survives when power has departed; and what, we may ask, does this instinctive contempt for the honors of the dead proclaim, except the utter vanity of the glories of the living? for mean indeed must be the real state of man, and false the vast assumptions of his life, when the poorest pageantry of a decent burial strikes upon the heart as a mockery of helplessness. Certain it is that pomp chiefly waits upon the beginning and the end of life; what lies between, may either raise a sigh or wake a laugh, for it mostly partakes of the littleness of one and the sadness of the other.

Human life is like a dream in the after-dinner sleep of a demon, in which an image of heaven is interrupted by a vision of hell; a thought of bliss breaks off to give place to a fancy of horror, and the fragments of happiness and discomfort lie mingled together in a confusion which would be ridiculous if it were not awful. The monuments of man's blessedness and of man's wretchedness lie side by side; we cannot look for the one without discovering the other. The echo of joy is the moan of despair, and the cry of anguish is stifled in rejoicing. To make a monarch, there must be slaves, and that one may triumph, many must be weak.

"Who is married?" said the gay and thoughtless Emma, as she took up that important chronicle of passing events, The Daily Times. "Married, on Wednesday morning, at the residence of her father, in Wiltshire, the Honorable Lady Charlotte Howard, to Captain Beauclerk, of the Royal Navy;" and the reader passed on.

Six months afterwards the servant put into the same hands the same gazette. "Who is dead?" said the fair querist, as she opened the expansive pages. "Died, on Wednesday morning, at the residence of her husband, in Wiltshire, the Honorable Lady Charlotte Beauclerk, in the 21st year of her age;" and the reader passed on.

Thus did the world notice and forget the two events: yet in the simple record of that marriage and that burial, there resided what might startle the voluptuary in the midst of his delights, and what the hermit might ponder in the loneliness of his cell. I was at the house of feasting and at the house of mourning. I saw the bride in the spring-blossom of her loveliness, and beheld the narrow coffin that housed her till eternity.

The painter who searches earth and heaven for shapes of beauty to invest the loved Madonna of his toil, is not visited in his twilight musings by face more exquisite than was hers. An Arab, had he found her by a fountain in the desert, would have bowed in speechless wonder; he would have enshrined her delicately in a crystal niche, and offered his daily worship to the image, and never *thought* of love—she was so fair.

With the fortunes of one who was rich in all that makes life enviable, she was about to mingle the gentle current of her fate, blessing and to be blessed. Around the scene of her bridal, as it now rises before me, there seemed to float, as it were, an atmosphere of delight—a perfume of happiness shed from the bright object who was the marvel of the time. As she stood before the priest, in her father's ancestral hall, in the elegant timidity of patrician refinement, surrounded by the high-born and the illustrious, fancy could not picture a being more favored, or a destiny more brilliant. Her glance was a memory of joys; her smiles a prophecy of bliss. Long and cloudless must be the summer-day that waits on a morning so splendid as this!

A few months afterwards I had returned from a short tour to the continent, and, without stopping in the metropolis, I went down to fulfil an engagement which I had made to visit the young couple in the country. I left the road a few miles from the house, and walked over the fields, for the day was delightful, and the rural scene showed full of charms. When I reached the park, I met an old servant of the family, whom I had long remembered. "Well, John," said I, "and how is your young mistress?" "I am grieved to say, sir," said the old man, in a husky voice, and a tear gathering in his eye, "I am grieved to say, sir, that she died last night." "Died!" cried I, in utter amazement, almost staggering with the shock, and overcome with a sickness of heart which I cannot describe—"Good God! can life never *blunder* into satisfaction? This incessant tale of disappointment is a story too commonplaced to be listened to —too regular to be believed!"

It was a brief and ordinary tale of life and death; but brief and common as it was, it started feelings which philosophy could not compose, and waked thoughts which religion herself but dubiously resolved.

There *is* a moral to this history of life, which no language has yet been able to bring out, and which, perhaps, no mind will ever be capable of embracing in its fulness. All our remarks, though struck out of the heart by impetuous anguish, sink in expression to the merest commonplace. The sage explores the realms of thought, and the poet dives in the remotest depths of language, for adequate reflections, and they both come back to the simplest dialect of the street, as being all they can say. A grief falls upon us, whose magnitude, we think, might shake the world, and our fullest comment is a shake of the head or a motion of the hand.

I stood in Windsor Castle when the coffin of the third George was borne to its vault. The longest and the brightest reign recorded in any annals was concluded; all that could elevate and bless humanity, in the tributes of power, the offerings of wealth, the esteem of the wise, and the affection of the good, had waited on his life; and to dignify the closing scene, prince and peer, the lords of genius and the ministers of virtue were assembled in the imposing pomp of power and the majestic splendor of distinction. Yet, with all, how ordinary was that life and how ordinary was that character! Focus of all the brightest rays that permeate the universe, he trod the common earth, a common man. To my thought, this history of a great good man, this record of power used and not abused, of merit always rewarded, excellence always protected, talent always fostered, and religion always respected, spoke a profounder commentary upon the utter vanity of life than the glaring failures of a Charles or a Boabdil. I had pondered these things, and was now gazing on the mockery of the funeral pageant, and knew that a knell was then sounding throughout England which would arrest the steps of the thoughtful, and melt the hearts of the feeling; yet what could I say, what could I even feel, commensurate with the demand of the scene?

I stood by chance at a window in London, and saw the remains of Lord Byron pass by on their way to the parish churchyard. He who had spurned all accepted usage, and sedulously scorned established habit, was borne along like the humblest citizen to rest in an obscure grave, like the lowest peasant of the fields. He whose temper had defied a nation, and whose genius had held high war with truth and virtue, and come from the contest not ingloriously, was jolting along the street like the carcass of a dog, and what could man do?

It is recorded of both Merlin and Zoroaster, that as soon as they were born they burst into a fit of laughter—the quack and the philosopher. And in sooth the world seems to be but a material sneer. Of God considered purely as Creator, every act and motion must be creative; I imagine that a smile awoke the angels from nothingness, and that man was laughed into being. Life seems perpetually burlesquing itself, and one-half of existence is a running parody on the other. On the stage the farce succeeds the tragedy; off, they are mingled in alternate scenes.

To one limiting his belief within the bounds of his observation, and "reasoning" but from what he "knows," the condition of man presents mysteries which thought cannot explain. The dignity and the destiny of man seem utterly at variance. He turns from contemplating a monument of genius to inquire for the genius which produced it, and finds that while the work has survived, the workman has perished for ages. The meanest work of man outlives the noblest work of God. The sculptures of Phidias endure, where the dust of the artist has vanished from the earth. Man can immortalize all things but himself.

But, for my own part, I cannot help thinking that our high estimation of ourselves is the grand error in our account. Surely, it is argued, a creature so ingeniously fashioned and so bountifully furnished, has not been created but for lofty ends. But cast your eye on the humblest rose of the garden, and it may teach a wiser lesson. There you behold contrivance and ornament—in every leaf the finest veins, the most delicate odor, and a perfume exquisite beyond imitation; yet all this is but a toy—a plaything of nature; and surely she whose resources are so boundless that upon the gaud of a summer day she can throw away such lavish wealth, steps not beyond her commonest toil when she forms of the dust a living man. When will man learn the lesson of his own insignificance?

Immortal man! thy blood flows freely and fully, and thou standest a Napoleon; thou reclinest a Shakspeare! it quickens its movement, and thou liest a parched and fretful thing, with thy mind furied by the phantoms of fever! it retards its action but a little, and thou crawlest a crouching, soulless mass, the bright world a blank, dead vision to thine eye. Verily, O man, thou art a glorious and godlike being!

Tell life's proudest tale; what is it? A few attempts successless; a few crushed or mouldered hopes; much paltry fretting; a little sleep, and the story is concluded; the curtain falls—the farce is over.

The world is not a place to live in, but to die in. It is a

house that has but two chambers; a lazar and a charnel—room only for the dying and the dead. There is not a spot on the broad earth on which man can plant his foot and affirm with confidence, "no mortal sleeps beneath!"

Seeing then that these things are, what shall we say? Shall we exclaim with the gay-hearted Grecian, "Drink to-day, for to-morrow we are not?" Shall we calmly float down the current, smiling if we can, silent when we must, lulling cares to sleep by the music of gentle enjoyment, and passing dream-like through a land of dreams? No! dream-like as is our life, there is in it one reality—our DUTY. Let us cling to that, and distress may overwhelm but cannot disturb us—may destroy but cannot hurt us; the bitterness of earthly things, and the shortness of earthly life will cease to be evils, and begin to be blessings. "*Eheu! fugaces, Posthume, Posthume labuntur anni!*" says the Roman. But there is no "*Eheu!*" to the Christian.

A SERMON IN A GARDEN.

"Lessons sweet of spring returning,
Welcome to the thoughtful heart,
May I call ye sense or warning,
Instinct pure or heaven-taught art?"—KEBLE.

"AND what are you going to do with yourself this Sunday afternoon?" said a fair "church-going *belle*," who happened to be passing a week in summer, at the same pleasant villa with myself.

"Pardon me," said I, "I am going to church, as well as yourself, though not, I confess, to hear the same minister that you are;" and I took my hat and walked into the garden.

"I know not why it is," said I to myself, as I drew on my thread gloves, and took my way along the gravelled walk, "that persons should think that 'God' is only 'in his Holy Temple.' Doubtless his presence is vouchsafed within the walls of temples made with hands; and whenever men are 'gathered together in his name.' And such assembling of ourselves ought not to be forsaken. But he may be seen in the earth, and seen in the sky, and all creation's forms are frost-worked with his love. The Providence of God, as it seemeth to me, hath in nothing been more bounteous than in the rich provision which hath been made for nurturing our moral being by the food of moral wisdom. Upon all the shapes of earth, and all the shows of life, there is charactered a moral; instruction is wrapped like a garment around all the state of man, and blooms like a rose upon the front of Nature. Each of the thousand little dramas that are daily rounded in the great scene of human life, folds up its grave conclusion; and Time is daily chiselling the couplets of wisdom on the adamant of the past, in ineffaceable events, so that experience hath become a great pyramid, carved all over with the hieroglyphics of knowledge. Wisdom, too, is the spirit of the inanimate world; instruction is lapped in the perfumes of the flowers, and mingles its voice with the chantings of the brooks; it finds a pulpit on every hill, and makes a tent of every leaf.

"But there is this difference between the benefits of Nature and those of experience," continued I, taking a distinction where I had at first perceived but a resemblance. "Counsel must be wrung from the folds of observation, and struck from the close fist of History; we must wrestle with the angel of the past, ere he will impart his blessing: whereas it is freely exhaled by Nature, and floats like a summer odor around the gardens of all creation. Mingle but among the forms of Nature, trees and flowers, and flowing streams, and your soul will partake of the purity and freshness wherewith she has invested all the subjects of her kingdom. For, as on the faces of the flowers, there glow no colors but those which they have seen in the heavens—the sapphire of the sky, the opal of the stars, the ruby of the orient clouds—so are all the thoughts which they suggest, and the feelings which they inspire, tinged with the sanctity of heavenly light. The breath of the violet's eye is peace; the smile of the rose's cheek is innocence. There is great benefit in being conversant with pure and genial thoughts, as there is great bane in breathing the atmosphere of foul ones; by communion with generous and clean imaginations, the tone of the desires is insensibly purified, and the vigor of the virtuous affections imperceptibly strengthened.

"Wisdom is daily crying aloud in the business of the streets, and voicing the stillness of the forest with her teachings; yet where is this knowledge garnered, and where are these lessons recorded? They perish not, for the spirit of wisdom, as the spirit of life, is immortal. Where, too, are the forgotten thoughts of man—his evanished fancies? Have they become spirits? And are they now winged with a life of their own? Will they greet us as we enter eternity? And will our future be colored by their complexion?

"Doubtless," thought I, seating myself upon the grass, "doubtless much of

> 'The gentle moral of the gale,
> And wisdom written in the tulip's dye,'

lies in that splendid world of unthought ideas and unseen perceptions. But while upon the ear of our inner spirit there swells a symphony of thoughtful feelings, it may be permitted to our mind to spell out in stuttered syllables some fragments of that song.

"When man for a moment stills the tossings of his heart, and curbs the sallyings of his restless temper to listen to the gentle music of fair flowers, their chorussed whisper is, 'Be calm—be quiet!' What a lesson of counsel, and what a suggestion of grace is that! Quiet is the element of wisdom. The calmest man is the wisest. For the mind is a coral-stone, around which thoughts cluster silently in stillness, but are scared away by tumult. Men in this time are spurring invention, and agitating all the waters of knowledge; whereas the effort of the truly philosophic mind still is to look at its subject in the calmest manner. Peace is the parent of patient thought—of passionless judgment; and if the calm suggestion of the flower could be uttered in the ear of the heated politician, the restless religionist, the enthusiast scholar, they would receive the holiest counsel that yet had visited their thinkings. It is not asked that in the drear air of stillness, keener thought should be exerted, or wider scope be given to the purpose; peace is itself a voice of wisdom, and quiet is a robed prophet from on high. Old fables tell that when descended deities, disguised in flesh, mingled in assemblies of men, they were still recognised by the unmoving eye-ball; and the legend shadows the essential calmness of divinity. In literature, and in philosophy, whether human or heavenly, mark where the star of peace is shining, and beneath its crest you will find cradled the kingliest knowledge, the whitest sanctity, the mightiest power. In things mortal, and in things divine, the spirit of wisdom descendeth like a dove. Mistrust as well the strength as the honesty of the ever acting; respect the counsel and revere the goodness of the quiet and the still. In the throng of them that have pretensions to be the spirit of God, in the form of man, we see many a piercing eye, and many a jewelled hand, and many a sceptred arm; we see but one whose brow is crowned with the light of peace.

"When I say that peace is a conservative of piety, and an inspiration of the moral perception, I say but what holy writings every where declare. It is a revelation to the heart—an illumination of the mind in things divine: '*Be still*, and know that I am God,' said the spirit on high; '*The peace* of God preserve thee in the knowledge and love of God,' says that ancient prayer, the prayer of Christian benediction: indicating that that quiet is a sympathetic mirror of the truths of heaven, furnishing, what Archbishop Leighton has finely called, 'an inexpressible kind of evidence' of the reality of faith, an evidence that all may feel but none communicate. Against evil passions, habitual calmness is the best preservative, for, if the storm of excitement be once roused, even in the cause of virtue, none can tell whither it will blow. 'Commune with your own heart, *in your chamber*,' says the royal harper of Israel, 'and be still.'

"In action, as well as in thought, the man who has learned to pause, has learned the last and highest lesson which wisdom has to teach. In worldly things, I need not dwell upon the value of this counsel: but in that warfare which on earth never ceases, it is equally precious. Christian man! thou hast often felt that in thy safest moods some strong temptation has come upon thee, and wrestled with thy spirit, and disquieted thee, and the vexation of spirit which it wrought has made thee reckless, and thou hast fallen. The struggle was momentary, although bitter; thou wast struck down by a blow. When thou art again assailed, remember my words. Pause, and the temptation will pass from thee; be still for a moment, and that stillness will be thy salvation!

"The sin which assaults thee, seems to thee sweet, and thou thinkest that it will be always so, that to vanish it were hard, to live without it were a dreary prospect. But pause, and thy mood will change; thy appetites are corrupted by the proximity of evil thought; let it slip from thy mind, and the craving for it will fall with it. It is only in their first rankness, in their panting novelty, that sins have a force to paralyze the will and melt down the moral purpose; if thou canst make them wait two breathings at the door, they will fade and fall to earth. The first moment of attack is not the moment to put forth thy strength; thy vigor is then racked by the keenness of temptation: but pause, and by that recuperation of vigor in repose, which is a law of both the physical and the moral life, thy energy will be augmented and concentered, and with one sally thou wilt disperse the foe.

"The contemplation of flowers opens to us other ends and objects of existence, than those that lie in the open view and worldly recognition of mankind, and teach the great lesson of contentment. In many a lonely vale and many a hidden nook, there flowers and fades a gem, whose beauty has drawn forth the choicest wealth of heaven, and which, to mortal seeming, was only framed to lie along the breast of love, or nod above the regal brow of beauty; yet where it waved, it wanes; no mortal eye hath ever sparkled o'er its splendor, and on earth no record lives of its exceeding fairness. Yet not in vain did it pass through the silent mystery of birth, nor can its placid smile be saddened by reproach of uselessness: such marvellous skill the All-wise would never waste, and if he formed, he first had fixed a purpose; yet in the world's valuables that flower had passed uninventoried. Hence, stranger, if the world shower her pearl and gold wide of thy dreary path, and if the voice of praise or sympathy come never nigh thee, nor conscious proof of usefulness console thy life, and thou thinkest that thy being is divorced from purpose, yet be not disquieted: fret not thy gentle fancy with such thought: thy breathing has its benefit. The lonely flower is telling thee that God is pleased with that which, in its appointed place, but buds, and blooms and dies; it lives to show thee, that while the whirlwind executeth wrath, and the breeze conveyeth mercy, those 'also serve, who only stand and wait.' Possess thy soul in peace; ripple not the current of thy years by pining or regret, for he that fashioned thee in secret, 'curiously wrought thee in continuance,' sees a use in thy existence.

'Tis Nature's law that nothing shall exist
Divorced from good—a spirit and a pulse of good.
A life and soul to every mode of being
Inseparably linked!

"The white feet of the moonlight gliding on the lonely Ararat —the music of the wind that sighs among the ice-cliffs of Arctic desolations—the desert spring that hath never moistened a mortal lip—all, all are useful in their great Creator's eye. In the orchestral harmony of being, they make up the full-channelled stream of praise;—they swell the columned incense that daily voyages from earth to heaven; they are a feature in the world-mirrored face of God. So, the contentment that sits and sings by its own grey hearth, and the armless, voiceless resignation, that rolls its coat of frieze about its limbs and smiles—they 'bear His mild yoke,' and bearing it, are blessed. Thou who sighest in obscurity, repress these rising murmurs; sweeten the air with calm submission; and let the watery beams of Hope silver the stainless element of Peace.

"From the enfeebling and pernicious distractions of externality we may in some measure be delivered by the soothing gentleness of thoughts a-field, and taught a quiet inwardness of feeling. An anxious and busy conscience, finding that it has a work to do, looks out for earnest action, forgetting that the best 'good work' it can perform is to preserve its own garment white, and to keep its vestments unspotted from the world—to calm down its own passions—to keep its own will resigned. I abhor and deprecate that restless rage of action, that incessant enterprise, that is abroad in the Christian world—that outwardness of interest, which never inquires if all is well about the heart; it is the opposite of 'pure and undefiled religion;' it begins in folly and a feeble judgment, and it ends in vanity, presumption, and self-righteousness. It forgets those high and solemn duties which every man owes to that immortal being—his own soul. Doth not the prophet rebuke this pious frenzy when he saith,—'Thy strength is to sit still?' And doth not the apostle disclaim these works when he saith—'The fruit of the spirit is peace?' O, that the Christian

Would pause awhile from *action*, to be wise!

"Nothing can better display to us the true value of our own state and nature than the thought of that world which is walled within a garden. When from the heated interests of life, its breathless anxieties, its leaden cares, we turn to this white-robed commonwealth of flowers, and behold how large a sphere there is, on the threshold of which all the concerns which we have weighed, sink into naught, the burthen of those cares is lightened, the sting of those anxieties is drawn. When we see how large a share of the love and the power of God, is hourly shed upon objects from which man is shut out, we see how small a space life fills in the broad eye that scans the universe.

"The hourly fading of the brightest flowers shows us how valueless is their existence, and may teach us how small is the claim our merit gives us. Viewing all things from ourselves as a centre, we seem to occupy the foremost ground and highest platform of creation, and think that the arm of vengeance will be arrested from regard to our eminence, or, in truth, to our native excellence. Turn, thou that measurest with the high and lofty one that inhabiteth eternity, and that thinkest thyself of consequence to him, turn to the lessons of the withered lily—the wisdom of the drooping rose. Sparkling beneath the morning sun, behold a city of delights where an angel might refresh his spirits, and a seraph make glad his inmost heart; where skill is lavished in unceasing fulness, and the music-breath of beauty floats like a vapor round the forms of grace. If earthly thing, unaided, could win his love or gain a title to his sparing mercy, it were surely this—the only mundane thing that never sinned. But in the noontide gladness of their rarest grace—in the summer sweetness of their most enchanting loveliness—in a moment he blots out their being, and turns their beauty to darkness and decay. Let us learn then that if God hath no need of 'his own gifts,' neither hath he of 'man's work.' Between them and us it is but a difference of days and years.

"While thus their present splendor bids us uncrest our pride, and plant the knee where stood the foot, so will their sometime meanness counsel us to caution how we use contempt. We daily meet with those in whom the inner and diviner life of man is no more developed than is the eyelet in the stone-dry bulb, or the yet ungreened bud upon the bush. Yet, reverence mortality wherever it moves, and let the foot of scorn come never near to hurt the meanest of the manly race. For as that bulb and bush, stone-dry, ungreened, e'en now fold up unseen within their rudeness the perfect flower which shall deck the air, so in the darkest, rudest breast, there lurks a soul—a thing, even now, God-like and awful, but which, anon, will gem the long line of Christ's attendant train. The cold and clod-like savages that chill the earth—they are but angels in the wintry state. He that regrets a leafless plant may be scorning that which shall win him love from them he loves; he that had struck the goatherd of Admetus, had smitten the sun-god. As, then, the time-forgetting seedsman smells the orient blossom in the death-browned wood, and as in cottaged humbleness the prophetic eye of maternal love vails to the sceptre in her infant's grasp, so let the heart of faith respect a seraph in each mortal form. Contempt is a feeling that is rarely just, and never wise: however degraded an object may be, until thou hast thoroughly known all its history, and hast clearly seen its destiny, thou hast no right, as an honest man, to despise, and none then, as a philosopher. What thou wouldst scorn, has its place in some system: and he that understands the elevation of the statue, will never sneer at the lowliness of the pedestal.

"Such," I continued to myself, drawing up my feet as I felt the ground growing damp under my limbs, "into such, and a thousand other hints of virtue, might this scene be moralized. But there is in the mere atmosphere, that floats around these gentle urns of loveliness, a draught of virtuous power, for that atmosphere is a mild sadness.

"'There is often found,' says the sweet prophet of the moral muse, my master Wordsworth—

> 'There is often found
> In mournful thoughts, and always might be found,
> A power, to virtue friendly.'

"All joy and complacency tends to unnerve and enfeeble the spirit, and all saddening thoughts are wholesome, and have airs of virtue breathing about them. And when gay scenes pass before the eyes, and the heart is not interested, there is always raised a feeling of regret. In the gladness of beauty, the aged heart's second sight discerns a something mournful, and the brightest pageant, when the hopes are elsewhere, is a melancholy thing. The mere ambition of the scene excites these pensive thoughts, and when we add to the feeling with which we look on flowers, the remembrance of their evanescence, the consideration is full-fraught with that sorrow which leadeth to wisdom. As they fade momently, beneath our eyes, let the young and the lovely remember, that if one beauty decks their front, one destiny binds their lives."

RELIGION AND POETRY.

THE one essential characteristic of the material man is life, and the one essential characteristic of the moral man is religion. As in the physical system there are two sources of vitality—the heart and the brain,—so in the spiritual system there are two sources of piety—the intellect and the feelings. As in the former both must exist, so in the latter. As in the one both must be distinct, so also in the other.

During one of the most oppressive summers which I ever remember to have felt in Persia, I left Bacdat, which was then my residence, to æstuate in the delicious village of Soora, a place which may or may not be on the maps, about five hours north of the city. Whatever part the love-crowning roses and the "rosy-crowned loves" of the place might have had in carrying me there, the pleasure of enjoying the society of decidedly the most intelligent man I ever met with, constituted a large share of the inducement. Our cottages were in two vallies, on the opposite sides of a respectable hill, and as to accomplish the passage in the middle of the day was a thing impossible, we paid each other alternate visits every morning, measuring them as the pendulum of the world oscillates,—by the day. One morning, as I walked down his side of the hill, I saw him sitting by a fountain before his door: "Mirkaun!" cried I, "what is your opinion of the origin of evil?"

"Separation," answered he, and he monologized till sunset in proof of his position that all moral errors arose from the separation of things which ought to be united.

The next day when he called on me, he said, as soon as he came within speaking distance, "H., what is your opinion of the origin of evil?"

"Union," answered I; and I employed the day in demonstrating that all error was occasioned by the union of principles which ought to be kept separate.

I am surprised, by the by, that those who have sought for the first germ and cause of evil in the universe, have not rather looked for it in the confusion, division, or misapplication of good, than attempted to refer it to a distinct and independent principle. I may add, that when I met my companion on the following morning, he asked me what opinion I held of the merits of the two days' discussion. I replied that either was a good theory as theories went, but that the truth would probably be found in both joined together.

"True," replied he, "and that proves my position."

I have wandered from my purpose, which was to remark that the true cause of the final corruption of every pure religion, and the original fault of every impure creed, has been joining with the divine and systematic portions of the belief matters which, though a part of the whole scheme of *religion*, were yet no part of the assured creed, being, in fact, implied results from it, or collateral connections with it, rather than definite elements of the original principle. I have no intention to develop this idea in all its applications; that belongs to a work which yet remains to be written by some independent thinker, and which, when written, will be the most valuable addition to human knowledge which it has received since the time of Bacon—"The History of Religion." I am only wishing to indicate the effect on the pagan and Roman Catholic religions, of incorporating feeling with conviction, and the propriety of keeping them asunder in the modern Protestant systems. In Greece, religion was the natural offspring of feeling; in the elder Christian world, feeling was the adopted issue of religion; the two matters are now separate systems, for the most part, and should be so entirely.

The delicate Grecian, placed by nature in the land of beauty's chosen seat, amid all tender and impressive influences, felt as the child of nature needs must feel when every breeze that blew was instinct with delight. There is in all sentiment something sacred; and the Greek, following the mild impulse of natural inclination, deified the whole system of his feelings, and the wondrous mythology of his country was created. Of a religion thus fashioned, many were the advantages. The earth was a consecrated pantheon; and every moving, every resting thing, a caryatic or columnar support of the divine entablature. Wherever he looked were altars—wherever he listened was the chant of praise—wherever he tended, spread a chancellated ground. In every spot was seen a God, or the garments of a God; mementoes of adoration were every where abounding. From off the morning hills the sheeted mists arose with silent pomp of homage; and with a gentle burst of holy joy the bubbling fountain bounded to the earth. The commonest act of life was worship; for over all a deity held sway, and aureoled all with piety. It was the peculiar blessing of this creed that there was nothing, and there were none, *beneath* religion; the lowliest feeling had its warder in the skies; and the chosen representative of every sentiment being but an exalted *man*, always retained a sympathy with humanity. When the timorous mariner called upon the name of Neptune, or, gazing on the lowering sky, sighed for the aid of the storm-assuaging brothers, he felt that his hopes were suspended from them by the chain of a common nature. When the warrior, about to loose the dart, or lanch the spear, cried to "the God of the Silver Bow," he knew that while his patron had the power of an Olympian, he had the feelings of an honest brother of the chase; the Christian would have trembled at the profanity of such a prayer. But while this religion secured more general and constant acknowledgment of God, it brought many great and fatal evils, for as Moses in the presence of his God shone celestial, so did the brightness of those deities always among men, fade into human pallor, and they descended in sanctity as they did in station. The mythology even became an instrument of evil: for as religion was the offspring, it soon became the slave, of passion; and the feeling which had wrought, could warp, divinity. Whatever inclination prompted or indolence invited, imagination was at hand to stamp with the approbation of some divine example; "and conscience, drunk as with wine, could sanctify to them all bloody, all abominable things." Thus was piety, like the Britons, destroyed by its allies, and the dome of religion, like the fane of Errool, fell by the weight of its own pillars.

As when the thousand stars of night rush out, the single power of the sun comes on, so did the Christian Lord reveal his awful splendor as the heathen gods passed away. Under the new faith, and naturally distinct from it, feelings of course arose, and were all baptized into the church. But it was soon perceived that these feelings had no sympathy with heaven, when heaven was filled by the exclusive terrors of Jehovah, and that they could no more cling to the naked doctrine of "GOD over all, always, and in all places," than the myrtle could entwine itself about the red-hot thunderbolt. They therefore invented the demi-divinity of the virgin, as a rock on which to hang, screened from the brilliance of almighty power, and proceeded, like sagacious jewellers, to set their God in saints. It has been the fashion of late years to class the saint-system of the papal church among the most conspicuous monuments of human folly; but folly was not the fault of the Romish hierarchy; the "wisdom of the serpent" did nothing unwisely. They who made the calendar were wise for their own generation: the evils of it fell, like England's national debt, on posterity. The progress of the matter was in this wise: Religion, as it came from God, was not an affair that could whistle through the key hole of a nursery, or be made the umpire of a market-house dispute; many acts must therefore be done apart from all religious consideration, else religion becomes degraded: that which is done beyond the eye of piety soon becomes a sin, and the practice of sinning soon makes men sinful. To obviate this result, the saints were created to be representatives* *sub modo* of the Lord, to keep alive a sense of the divine existence and obligation, and bear the truth to many places where the master in person would not venture without compromising his dignity; for the rosary might be carried into a corner when the cross would stick fast in the door. Again, there are constantly occurring in life a large number of little miracles, and a still larger number of false stories of them; if these be referred to chance, the notion of a constant providence is lost; if they be assigned to the intervention of the Almighty, omnipotence is degraded. By the happy insertion of saints into the chain of agents, the good is secured and the evil prevented,—religion is made "familiar,"

* I remember a fable, I think in Athenæus, of Jupiter stopping one night at the house of a peasant, with a couple of thunderbolts on his back. The cottager, fearing that the bolts might set his house on fire, refused to admit the thunderer unless he left his load in the yard; this was impossible, for the deity and his power were "one and inseparable," and the poor god was obliged to sleep under a shed. The saints of Christianity were so made as to be gods in all respects, only that they did not carry thunderbolts, and were therefore admitted as a much safer sort of people.

but deity by "no means vulgar." All hands shared the advantage. Such were some of the motives that led the framers of the wisest system that the earth has ever witnessed to this wonderful device, and contributed to make the papal church, what it has always appeared to those who observed without prejudice, and thought without passion—the very sublimest monument of human ingenuity that ever existed. The evils of this invention were doubtless foreseen and despised. Those evils I need not dwell upon—every thing was brought into the bosom of religion,—politics, domestic arrangements, science, war,—and "*quicquid agunt homines*," was the concern of the priesthood; till the ark of the Christian covenant became like Noah's, a mere menagerie, in which when human concerns, like the beasts, came in at the doors, purity, like the dove, went out at the window. The master's prediction became history; his mustard-seed had grown into a tree, and birds, of which most were "*obscœni aves*," found shelter in its branches. The spiritual church had for its type the monasteries of the time, in which men ate, drank, and slept, and performed all the business of life within the consecrated walls. The temple became utterly defiled, and the church fell into a state which called forth the sorrow and scorn of all good men. I think that I am right in finding the germ of all these abominations in the original error of introducing into Christianity affairs which did not belong to it, of extending religion much too far in its influence, and of thinking that feeling must be consecrated to the Lord. When you cut blocks with a razor, the razor it is which suffers.

The sum and substance of Protestant Christianity is, "Repent and Believe;" that much, and no more, of precept came from God, and that much, and no more, of performance should go back to him. We have seen the evils of joining feeling and religion; let us keep them distinct; let revealed faith be preserved the same narrow and distinct path which it was made by the Almighty finger, and let the natural piety of feeling flow like a brook by the side of it, to refresh, but not seduce the traveller—to relieve, but not convey him. While sentiment is trellised on the outer wall of the temple, it adorns and protects it; if it finds its way within, it rends the walls and disorders the building.

Here then lies the true use of poetry in these modern times; I mean human and unreligious poetry,—poetry as a system independent on religion in its origin and end,—the poetry of Wordsworth, Coleridge, Wilson, Brydges, and Shelley. Let us never look on their conclusions as sacred, nor imagine that they form any part of Christianity; let us not believe that we fulfil any direct portion of our vocation and duty as Christian men, when we renew within us the mood they exhibit; but let us read them to keep our sympathies tender, our moral perceptions delicate, our hearts free and open, our hopes fresh and springing, and our whole nature elevated, pure, and unselfish. When this is done, then let us go to prayer.

Another advantage springs from the fictions of poetry as long as it is kept apart from religion. In these latter days, when philosophy has explained all the material phenomena of the universe, we are in danger of resting on second causes, and losing the many excitements to pious feeling which the ancients had; and the golden lies of the poet are of infinite benefit in keeping open in our breasts the springs of wonder, and preserving in the world some traces of mystery. The heathen poet tells us that he was converted by hearing a clap of thunder in a clear day; *now*, it is only by a bold poetic fiction, that in the thunder "God in judgment passes by;" and these fictions, though not accepted by the intellect, have their effect upon the heart. When poetry leads us among the false mysteries of the outer world, it keeps alive a sense of the real mysteries of the hidden world. I need not say that under this view the line between fictitious poetry and true religion must be strictly kept up; for divine revelations must never be married to human inventions.

I therefore regard "Religious Poetry" as full of evil.

MONOLOGUES AMONG THE MOUNTAINS.*

BY A COSMOPOLITE.

[*Extract from the Author's Correspondence, March 3rd*, 1843. "I have been overrun, my dear Henry, by ten thousand armies of occupation ever since I received your request; engaged daily at my office fron nine in the morning till ten at night; investigating some important trust titles, and with other engrossing concerns. They have left me little time, and no eye-sight. However, I have *whirled* you off some rhapsodies which you can kick into sense or lick into shape. I am only afraid that they are too late for your purpose. No thanks for them; for such things I can write by the foot, yard, perch, mile, or if necessary even by the league. Don't let me be known in any way as author. The preface 'To the Reader,' put in editorially, of course. Some persons will probably take it as literally true: others will not 'undergo the fatigue' of thinking any thing about that matter; and it may entertain the rest who know or who don't know that the arts of the drama belong to modern literature as much as to the stage at any time. Adieu! Send me some good *French and German* autographs, if you can. I have most English and American worth having, and at all easy to be had; though I should like one, if you can get it, of George Ross, the signer of the Declaration, which is rare. I have scores of many of the others, which I will exchange three to one for a *good* George Ross."]

TO THE READER.

The following piece belongs to a series of papers which have been given to us to be made use of in this paper. The author has too little vanity to be diffident; and therefore when we state to our readers that he is one of the most extraordinary persons of this age, a man of splendid passions, and bearing on every feature of his character and mind the unquestionable stamp of genius, we are sure that his modesty will not be offended any more than it would be were we to say that he is above six feet in height, with a countenance of antique and almost royal dignity, glowing and generous, yet furrowed with thought and suffering; showing the fatigues rather than the fires of passion. His history has been wild and romantic to the last degree. His birth placed him in the first position of distinction and enjoyment in his own country, at a time when the pacific revolutions of commerce and the more violent inroads of democracy had not confused or shaken the distinct supremacy of the old-landed families: but the restlessness of his temper and the impatience of a mental energy to which repose was almost madness, made him a wanderer from his youth. From the elegant and exclusive luxury of the English no-

* These pieces, originally designed, as is conjectured from the author's correspondence, for another publication, appeared, in part, at a later date in a Magazine of Philadelphia. —ED.

bility as it was before the younger Pitt, had "*soused* it with a flood of spurious creations," and from the still more selected society of the French peers before the revolution, among whom he spent some years; this singular man set forth to travel through some of the most unexplored and inhospitable parts of Europe and Asia. He travelled on horseback over Russia and Siberia; penetrated into China; lodged for several months in a monastery of Buddhist priests in Thibet; traversed Central Asia; and passed two or three years among Bedouin Arabs. This last-named people he has visited several times, as he claims relationship with some of their chiefs; his great-grandmother, as we understood him to say, having been the daughter of one of the Sheiks, who had come to Constantinople to arrange with the Sultan some dispute about tribute money. The singular and original style of beauty of this child of the desert so much impressed one of the ancestors of the person we speak of, being then Minister at the Porte, that he married her and brought her the next year to England. This anecdote we remember to have seen related in the first edition of Dr. Kippis' "Biographical Dictionary;" it was omitted in the subsequent impressions, from what cause we do not know. This remarkable man has been mixed up with most of the tumults of Europe and the intrigues of the eastern world; besides carrying on a crowded scheme of private enterprise and adventure. His age would weigh about seventy years; but if his vigor and activity were thrown into the scale of the numbers, fifty would give his effective age. As we were conversing the other evening, over a few bottles of Metternich hock of the matchless vintage of '34, he fell into a discourse about the advantages of old age, which led him to give a few particulars of his history and adventures.

"The Cardinal Alberoni," said he, "is reported to have expressed the odd wish that he had been born old; I suppose because he would have escaped the errors and mistakes of youth. Could a man be born old, yet with the recollection of a past to look back upon, and with all those different strata which successive floods of passion deposit upon the character, and with all the quaint, gnomic scrawls which Time writes upon the spirit—just as the world, (we must suppose, to reconcile Scripture with geology,) was created with all the formations that belong to an advanced stage of its existence—I know not but that I would join in the Italian's wish: it would be simply so much time saved. But as things are settled here below, it is to youth and its fatal blunders, to manhood and its fruitless acts, that age is indebted for its powers and its privileges. I deem it a cheap tutelage that through such painful rudiments my soul has learned that dauntless secret of wisdom—*nil admirari;* an element and a conclusion of philosophy that is not to be found in the study, nor a-field; but is taught only in the merciless college of experience. I rejoice that through many toils and after laborious wanderings I have *grown* old: for I am '*donatus rude.*' Time, at the end of my pilgrimage, presents me with a full charter of emancipation from all prejudices and all delusions. Opinion, custom, cant, the authority of schools, the practice of multitudes, the narrow maxims with which men love to delude themselves—these give not the smallest bias to my judgment; but free, unfettered, and with the force of genuineness and sincerity, I see into the heart of truth. I have learned never to consult the dead reckoning, but always to take an observation for myself. I who have seen the Queen of France attended with all the magnificence of Versailles, with that unrivalled radiance of countenance which made her, indeed, 'a star to all the glittering throng,' and have seen the same woman with thin, wan features and dishevelled hair, riding in a cart to the guillotine: who saw the Emperor Napoleon seated

High on a throne with trophies charged,

His feet on sceptres and tiaras trod;

and a few years later saw a fat, bilious man, in a green coat, on the bleak rock of St. Helena, who, they told me, was the same person; I who have seen a mighty empire created in India within the space of half my life, and in the same period a battalia of European kings crowned and cashiered; you may imagine that I am tolerably disenchanted from all the prestige of royalty and greatness. As to wealth and luxury, I saw something of that before the Jacobins rendered it necessary to keep a sword in one hand to protect the fork in the other. And such as it has been since, I have seen something of it too. I have passed months with Beckford at Fonthill, when we kept some days the simplicity of an anchorite's meal, and some days sat down to three hundred dishes between us, with music and women, and such elaborate elegancies as you may conceive when, with an unlimited exchequer, we joined the best inventions of our genius to contrive what should be most delicious. I have revelled, too, with the Prince at Carlton House, where, through many a midnight hour, we drolled it gaily. Often, too, have I passed the night in a tent with an old sheik, counselling whence we should steal a kid for our morning's broth. The adventitious differences of states and conditions do not, therefore, greatly dazzle my imagination. I have spent years in the different universities of Europe, '*approfondissant les choses*,' of speculation and morals; and I have battled among the sands of the east till my face was bronze and my hand as hard as the iron it wielded. For I abhorred, above all things, narrowness of thought and feeling; and I loved to bring my soul into sympathy with all the possible emotions which the heart of man can experience, and to multiply my consciousness through all the forms and modes of life. Most of all, I have taken care to know and be familiar with all the great intellects that the time has produced in either continent; that, communing with their minds and studying their farthest speculations, I might know all the varieties of the possible as well as the actual, and see all the wonders of the world that is not. I have seen systems of philosophy, each more infallible than its predecessor, rise in succession only to be displaced. In one word, I knew Europe and literature before the names of Byron and Buonaparte had been heard by the world; I know them now when they fill it. Others will obliterate their impression, and the curtain which has now fallen, will rise again over mightier intellects and more astounding changes. Do you wonder, then, that I reverence nothing; that I approach every thing with an impression of contempt; and, following nothing but the force of my own soul, I think what I like and speak what I list?"

Pausing a few minutes, and somewhat musing, while he was quaffing down another goblet of this delicious wine, which, he said "mnst have grown close under the Castle, and indeed partly over the cellars," and which he assured us was much better than any of the 1350 bottles, which coming from the same spot had been divided as a rare possession between George IV. and the King of Prussia—this extraordinary man began again: and rising to a strain which was of a higher mood, thus broke forth: "I cannot live with men. The horizon of my being hath not been wont to be bounded by their narrow circle. In that tangle of small interests and mist of little passions, which is called society, my soul cannot get its breath. I go forth to breathe and find in the vast theatre of nature a chamber large enough for it to dwell in. I despise not men; I have learned to despise nothing that my Creator hath made; but I forget, I ignore them. I cannot live so lonely as they do—divorced from nature. I must be among my brethren, the forests, the mountains, and the sea, whom I may love; else my heart pines within me. I have seen those to whom the silence of nature was dreadful; but I have kept my purity, and can dwell among the pure. The dark-browed fiend remorse intrudes not within my cottage; my memory is not a whirling cess-pool which heaves up the carcasses of old sins to poison the atmosphere of the spirit. I have followed virtue; I have never degraded my character by vice. By my station I was born to great thoughts. Pride and dignity of mind and nature have kept me from ever doing a selfish or a wicked action. I have been useful to my race. I have labored to be good; and I have my reward. The good Being whom I have served and loved, sendeth his angels, Peace, and Strength, and Freedom, to stand around me in mine age.

"To that cause, too, I owe it that, though grey-haired, my vigor is as fresh and my sensibilities as delicate as in the first fervor of my youth. The ardors of virtue, like the fires of heaven, kindle without consuming; the heats of evil exhaust to ashes. I am old; but much, both for evil and for good, may be done in extreme old age. At a period of life later than that which I have reached, Dandolo acquired his greatness, and Bacon lost his honor. The minds that break in the decline of life, are usually such as have been stretched on the racks of paradox and subtlety; but minds originally strong, that have been occupied, though never so laboriously, with truth and sound sense, rarely give way even in the decrepitude of the body. The wanderer in many lands, and the worker of stern deeds, in whose veins the blood of Plantagenet flows, mingled with the wilder tide of the Arab, never knew fatigue but when compelled to rest, and never tasted repose save in the whirl of action. *Otia nescit.* To me there is a sting in idleness. Here I shall labor greatly, as I have always labored. And the intervals of stronger toil I shall relieve by lighter compositions upon letters and taste, which the world may care for or condemn, as it sees fit. My ancestors ever did battle against usurpation and tyranny, and they have left me as the motto of my mind and my life: 'Above all things—FREEDOM.'"

"From what we had the advantage of seeing of this eccentric person, it struck us that he had attained a more thorough independence in every part of his character than any one whom we had met before. In his habits he seemed never to consult what was usual; but considered only what was convenient. In expressing his opinions he appeared not even to be aware that the world had some settled way of thinking upon any of the subjects he spoke of. What seemed to him reasonable, that he uttered. Upon all subjects he seemed perfectly delivered from prejudice; and to possess, not the bigotted skepticism of Voltaire, but that more complete Pyrrhonism which is skeptical even of its own doubts. His descent is probably as illustrious as that of any man in Europe, and he was well conscious of it: but he never, in judging of the merits of others, paid any attention to their origin. He was easy and familiar with the lowest as with the well-born. He did not seem to know what *hauteur* was. Though boundless in the pride of his soul, he had not the smallest pride of manner. The papers which we shall, from time to time, present to our readers, contain reflections upon literature, philosophy and life. The author resides at present a recluse among the mountains where he has built himself a beautiful home from which he never now goes, except to refresh himself at a picturesque spot of lofty ground which he owns near the sea. He writes a vast deal, and with great rapidity. The papers which we give below are perhaps the most careless compositions of the whole; but as they are not without something characteristic of the writer, we have thought them worth printing.—EDS.

No. I.

ONCE more, back to the life of the Mind!—to the spring and the flash of Thought, and the boundless sweep of the Feelings! In the atmosphere of the world I can no longer get my breath; in its keenest enterprises I live but half my being: but, here, amid the solitudes of the mountains and the sky, I once more feel my soul within me. The glow and might of Nature inspire again that luxury of conscious power, which, in my hours of young enthusiasm, once made existence ecstasy, when the brave children of the Soul flew forth, with rush of strength, over Life and Earth, to revel in the wealth of conquest. By sympathy with her sublimeness, my spirit is refreshed and comforted.

For my own part, I have always been of opinion that the only sort of life worth leading, is that intense and fiery life, in which the poorness of our mortality is merged and drowned in the flood of the soul's eternal forces,—that fierce existence, in which the buried lustre of our creation-flame is flashed out from the depths of our nature, to gild and glorify our career—that thronged, still-crescive vehemence of feeling which presses the heart into calmness through rapture. Of every pursuit I have made a passion, and never deemed the car of life worth mounting, save when its axle was a-blaze with swiftness. With the blank half-vitality of those who dream out the dulness of their years, lacking "sense to be right, and passion to be wrong," I had no sympathy; but wherever there was turmoil and effort, the dash of action, or the daring of the mind, there was something kindred to my thoughts. Born with these impetuous tempers—with a spirit that loved to breathe itself in the chase of the splendid and the great, and in the full stretch and strain of the faculties to taste the relish of the Infinite,—I plunged into society and the world, equally ready to dally with their softnesses or grapple with their strength. *Vixi.* I have lived indeed. I have wrung from life some of its deepest, dearest treasures,—the pearls of its sweetest pleasantness,—its blazing diamonds of delight. The joy that is in the fresh, bold dreams of Power—the purple luxuries of Passion—the glory of the far-gleaming visions of Love—the wild, trancing promises of its pursuit—and the rapturous madness of possession—these I drank largely from Youth's foaming cup. *Sed, hæc prius fuere.* That cup is now empty. Those interests are exhausted. I have lived *through* them; I have consumed them by partaking. That quick galvanic action which took place when boyhood first plunged into the stream of affairs has ceased. Merely to enjoy what exists around me is no longer sufficiently exciting: I must *make* the life I would partake; and in that stress of soul, which is creation, I must find a refuge from the terrible fatigue of listlessness. So then, the resources of the earth being spent, I come back to dwell amongst the energies of Thought.

This life of ours seems to me to be a kind of desperate encounter between the world, which is Time's eldest champion, and the soul of man, which is the youngest offspring of Eternity; in which, while the latter seeks to snatch pleasure and knowledge from its mortal enemy, the former strives to paralyze the vigor, to kill the hopes, and to convulse the serenity of its angelic antagonist. To withdraw from the struggle, like Solomon, overwhelmed with exhaustion and despair, or, like Byron, maddened with resentment and flaming with the hate and indignation of a deceived and duped existence, is surely proof of weakness and defeat. I own no such faint and yielding soul. The world and I have met in conflict: I have gained from it a thousand trophies; from me it boasts not one. I now fling from me the powerless foe, and, calm, confident, and strong, I go forth to glad myself in fields of nobler force. Were I one as impotent to endure as I am sensitive to feel, memory were to me a staple from which I might spin out the thread of an everlasting sadness. For me, that sun of expectation which lighted life's vapors into magnificence and splendor has sunk below the horizon—and the chilly scene has grown cheerless, gray and desolate. The friends who cheered me once, the companions to whom I was of importance, have disappeared. She—the endlessly beautiful—profuse of charms as prodigal in vows—the girl, *amata nobis, quantum amabitur nulla*—has deserted me; and that other being—that great and graceful spirit—august with loveliness—the glory and the anguish of my life—whose flame of soul was wont to mix and blaze with mine—has fled from the earth, and left me the legacy of eternal solitude. The gilded train of passions, fancies and desires, that once girt my proud and conquering soul, has vanished, and I am indeed alone. But what is this to me? The stern, wild force of a spirit like mine laughs at calamity like this; and roused into its savageness of strength, hurls away from it the tyranny of the Past, and draws back into the eternity of its own self-born and self-sufficing power. What are the rattling arrows of the storm to one who sits above the clouds? The mortal of my being I give to agony and dissolution; but the death of the mortal is the delivery of the immortal. That ethereal energy within me which hath the temper and the touch of everlasting, rises with swan-like beat of wing, and, spreading its unmoulted plumage to the morning, soars upward, breasting the golden light.

Time has somewhat blanched my cheeks, but not paled the

fires of my bosom. My heart hath done battle with the wastingness of troops of griefs; but neither the strong assault of the days, nor the crushing uses of our daily existence, nor wrong, nor solitude, nor remorse, have had power to tame the soul which they tortured, or beat back one of the deathless aspirations of my nature. As gaily and as glowingly as ever does my spirit launch forth its eager forces; my breast still thrills with the exulting sense of conflict and victory. Confidence goeth out with the morning; and blue-eyed Joy with fair-fronted Peace come smiling to me in the evening. From the failure of the outward, I have learned the vigor of my own being; and my maturer life realizes what mine youth would not be taught, that Action is the child of Time, but Thought is an inhabitant of Eternity.

It has been said by an eminent French pilosopher that there is no glory on earth but the military. Doubtless great memories are connected with the sword, and deep feelings answer to its flash. When we behold the famous conqueror of our own days, going out in the splendor of his power, and all the pageantry of force—moving like the thunder-cloud, to strike like its fire—and listen to the tramp of the host, a sound so ominous and terrible, and to the pealing music which seems to shatter the heavens, and whirls our feelings for a moment into forces beyond mortality, and gaze on that marvel of discipline wherein manhood itself seems to render homage to intellect, as the suggestions of one understanding operate to mass multitudes together and infuse into them an instinct to serve, to suffer and be slain—the group of horsemen from out whose midst issue the rapid syllables that are spells to oversweep the force of fate—the flying messengers that convey to the kindling mass the electric fires of one glowing will—the keen survey of the field, the quick combination, the advance, the victory, and in the midst of all this breathless turmoil—the spirit of the hero then reposing in the prophetic calmness of the triumph—the despatch written on the saddle-bow, to fix the destiny of distant nations—the couriers coming and going with intelligence of battles in the north, and with words that shall be the history of the west—when we look with terrified amazement on this scene, truly we feel as if the crowning greatness of our condition were before us.

But, mightier and more majestic yet is the spectacle, when, sublime and still, in mystery of strength, the mind of man proceedeth forth through the void unknown of meditation. Its march is creation, and glory is in its repose. Star-like, advancing to the sound of its own inherent music, the lustre of beauty which swells from its presence, thickens into crystal forms of truth which beam with the brightness of the life forever. With pomp of cloud-like grandeur, the dreams of the passions move on before and waste themselves through the infinite, while the armed hosts of the thoughts, with a spontaneous glitter beyond the sun, plant, on all the pinnacles of time, trophies that tower through the blue vault of eternity. In the purple of the rays that stream from that far-effulgent essence, the trivial things of earth are seen to be symbols of a profound significance, and signatures of a wondrous import; and even the torn vapors that fleet in the train of the fair procession of the morning, when lit by the flame of its coming, gleam like banners of celestial texture, stamped with the watchwords of Purity and Hope. When thus the faculties of man move upon the deep of existence, to gather into stars of Truth the pale, primal light of Nature, or to fashion new worlds of Art and give to their orbits a being among the eternal things of the universe, we behold a witness that our souls are portion of the Divine Spirit, and that our destiny is co-eternal with His element; for to create is the incommunicable attribute of Godhood, and an everlasting progeny cannot be born of the mortal.

To me, here dwelling alone amidst the old serenities of nature, thoughts are ever coming and going, and feelings touch me and pass on. In the silence of the early morning, I am visited by the wandering scouts of the Intellect, who report to me of the distant, the wonderful, the divine; and, in the musings of the darkness, gazing into the depths of the soul, the myriad forms of sentiment reveal to me their beauty by their own phosphoric lustre. To unsphere these angels of the mind from the universe of the spirit, and send them forth, in language to bear to men the greetings of a brother, and woo for me the love of noble hearts, is necessary to the quiet of a nature that never knew repose but in the tension of the faculties. Not to remit or rest have I come hither, but for loftier toils in larger tracts of effort. A breast that hath been wrung as mine has been—that, fated quickly to feel, and never to forget, went out into life, and in its youthful fervor filled its depths with pleasures in whose recesses anguish had its birth-place—whose sad destiny it has been to regret its best feelings, and curse its very virtues as the cause of its ruin—to which misfortune has been for guilt, and the sins of others for a remorse—such a bosom may be silent in its strength, and calm in pride of power; but that austere tranquillity is not rest, and the stillness of that self-mastery is born of the storm. From the mountain-heights of meditation, I look down upon low, earth-born mists that no longer come near me, and I taste a clear, and pure, and wholesome atmosphere; yet, ever and anon, forming itself out of sun-light and summer airs, the dark cloud, which is the shade of Nature's offended countenance, gathers around, and the secrets of the Great Fear that awaiteth in the invisible are syllabled in the tones of thunder, or shot forth in the rubric signals of the lightning. Such is the moral mystery of our being! Our very existence seems to be a sin, and life is a perpetual repentance for itself. The blood of youth is joy, and the old age of joy is contrition; pleasure is the sweet spring-blossom of feeling, and pain is its bitter autumnal berry. It is well! it is well! For as it is the unquiet of the sea which forms the crest that sparkles on its shores, so from the tumult and agony of the spirit is splendor of thought flung forth. Grief of heart is the quickening spell of the mind's inspiration; and the ruin of the individual is the glory of the race.

It is the waning-time of night. Let us leave these morbid musings with which we have beguiled the midnight hour, and go forth to look upon the dawn.

No sound, no motion! yet it is the mighty coming of the day. All night, no cloud hath been seen abroad; no mist hath dimmed the effulgent ether between the glittering stars. All is solitary, still, and cold. The first wave of the light rolls forward, and scatters its snowy foam throughout the air. For the tide of the great ocean of Infinity, whose flood is darkness and whose ebb is day, has begun its resistless flow; and the bark of the sun-god, who stands prepared to spring upon the heavens, nears upon the swelling waters. The pure bosom of the sky is flushed at the rude invasion of its beauty, and as the glowing presence of the day-prince grows more intense and instant, its blushes deepen from roseate into purple, till it seems as it would faint with excess of feeling. It throbs with the quick-darting pulses of emotion, and its white breast, made delicately carmine by its virgin wishes, lies, like the bride of the morning, passioning with expectancy.

What wild and solemn rapture the silent heavens flash down upon the soul! The Spirit of Power, that inhabits in the bosom of man, struggles forth to press to itself the Spirit of Beauty, which smiles down upon it from the depths of the blue air; and, as they wrestle in that strong embrace, Joy shouts aloud the honors of the contest. Limitless splendor! Ineffable delight! I ask no immortality but this! In the bliss of moments such as now, I feel that I partake Eternity. In truth, these deeps of spiritual consciousness contain, and are, forever, that unlocal, dateless Heaven, which men, duped by the dazzling images of the tribe and the market into mistaking succession of visible existence for degrees of moral life, have vainly pictured as future and far-distant. The infant day lies in pearly loveliness, cradled between the earth and heaven, while its smiles of light float wreath-like through the air. As I gaze into the unbounded scene, the remote and viewless gates of the Infinite seem to be opened, and the lustrous atmosphere, forth-streaming, rolls over the world a surge of glory which wafts with it the breezy freshness of a celestial bliss; the soul bathing in the stainless waters is made pure with holy strength. The Present and the Distant, the Actual and the Impossible seem to be tumbled together in this tumultuous prodigality of splendor; the softest forms of Memory are revived, and Hope's most golden aspirations are made real; and the faculties, expanded by the swell of passion, seem to pervade and to possess the universe.

I never understood so feelingly as to-day what the Prince of Denmark meant when he said that he was only mad nor' nor'-west. If the bold breezes that hail from that quarter rushed on Elsineur as they rush upon this headland where we stand, I do not wonder if they dashed into his soul an inspiration whose wildness might seem like an insanity in one whose spirit, when the wind was southerly, was sicklied over with the paler cast of thought, or flushed by sweet affections to a hue no deeper than the rath primrose. As the stimulating influence sweeps stronger and fuller from the windows of the sky, the mind becomes charged with a sensitiveness of fervor, which would be calm and rational if it might cope with those divine interests which in the earnestness of this moment it blindly apprehends, but which is a drunkenness of the faculties when turned among earthly objects. For my own part, I can withstand the *graciousness* of nature, and can harden my spirit into a wanton kind of ingratitude when she woos my love with spring airs from the west, or summer breezes of the south, for well she knows that the turbulent and torn heart of her son is mocked more than soothed by such gentleness; but when she condescends to loftier pains of pleasing, and, waking the harmonies of strength, and sounding the lower notes of her organ of the winds, pours over the earth the free, wild music of the north, I am stung into a delight that overflows to tears; for with those deep, melancholy tones of might my nature is accordant. To be great, I ask little but north winds and leisure.

No. II.

WHEREFORE should the soul of man droop or be disquieted within him, while God has vouchsafed to us such sublime sources of consolation as the mountains, the sea, and the splendors of the sun-rise ?—The watches of the night are over : Silence guarded the stern vigils of suffering and gloom, till, like a gush of love, the melody of morning burst from the skies, and scattered the coward troop of solitude. Calm with the confidence of joy—happy as he to whom his friends have returned—I have stood upon this mountain-rock, from the budding dawn of light, till now, when the full-expanded flower of day is blooming on the stalk of Time, shedding the odor of brightness through the universe. Exalted scene of might made beautiful by boundless Love! There are, to whom Night with her stars and stillness is a fascination: the deepest, wildest throb of delight that quivers through *my* being, is when the first red gleam of the sun is flashed across the abyss of air, like the signal-gun of a monarch's coming. Beyond every living thing in Nature, my feelings are with *him:* when I behold his shining, all the faculties of my existence swell forth to meet his forces. The slackened nerve of energy once more is bent up, and "a short youth runs warm through every vein."

August and sovereign Sun! Presence of grandeur! Image of high command! Thy rising is a sacrament of strength; and in our souls' communion with thy rays, the eternal covenants of Hope are renewed, and our being's high sympathy with Truth and Virtue is again established. Power is born within thy palaces of Light, and influences of Pleasure ride on thy rushing beams. Stern orb of Destiny! what issues attend upon thy coming! Thy motions are our Fate, and thy progress up yonder blue arch of Heaven shall be the Anguish or the Joy of Nations. Fierce firstling of omnipotence! in whose form Infinity grew palpable in splendors, when earliest its excess of energy overflowed into creation. Almost titles of divinity are thine. Thy changes are earth's epochs: our passions and our actions wait on thee: thou goest up in glory, leading the hosts of Being. Author of order! Token of Him that made the universe! To thee it is given daily to renew the wonders of the primal miracle, and call the earth into beauty, from the deep of Night and Nothingness! Nay, even beyond the marvel of that type, thou makest each morning as many worlds as there are minds within it, for that dawning which seemed as general as the heavens is as particular as each human heart. The mingled music of thy seven-toned lyre rolls over the earth; childhood's gentle spirit, light-slumbering on its violet-bed of visions, catches the *finest* sound of the rich symphony—the joy-note of the strain—and, trembling into fine accord with it, wakes to its fairer, falser dream of real life: the strong, full tone of Duty sounds, swells, and echoes through the soul of manhood; the laxer ear of age faintly hears the deep, harsh note of Custom, heavily vibrating with weight of memories. From thy golden fountains wells forth that perennial stream whence all drink Life and Consciousness; to different lips, how various is the taste; to some, as sweet as praise; to some, more bitter than the draughts of Death! Proud, melancholy orb! lone in thy lordliness! thou dwellest in thy solitudes of splendor, and pourest thy bounty ceaselessly on all things, and meetest with no return. Sublime in thine unsocial greatness! beyond the sympathies of those on whom thy blessedness is lavished! sustained by the great happiness of doing good without reward! satisfied, through a thousand ages, with the pure consciousness of duty! Thou art the type and teacher of the life of man. Shine on, most glorious orb; we hail in thee the elder brother of our souls, in whose grandeur our nature is ennobled.

Wearied by the fret and wretchedness of society—vexed and saddened in spirit by its miserable monotony of littleness—I have come to dwell amidst the expanses of Nature, that I may find that companionship which the world does not afford me, and inhale that bracing air of loftiness and force by which my youthful soul was nurtured. From the exhausting fervors of action—the rage of ignoble passions—the excitements which convulse—the experiences which deprave the heart—I turn, with what large relief of feeling! to these wide, kingly scenes, which, while they stimulate and stir, still raise, invigorate, and calm. I have ever loved to have my being the subject of *great* impressions; and I find nothing that is great in the politics, the business, or the literature of this time. But when I seek the forests or the hills, I am sure of being in a majestic presence. Severe or soft, serene or in storms, Nature at least is always grand. In all her moods, she wears an aspect of sublimity. Qualities of might dwell among her retreats. The springs of energy are amidst her depths. Peace spreads her courts of mystic power within her valleys: sentiments of Purity float, like their snowy mists, around her monumental hills. As we breathe her atmosphere of greatness, that generosity of feeling, which the world had well nigh strangled, lives again within us. From her fellowship, we knit to our souls that magnanimity which is the noblest treasure of our nature, the ornament and crest of character, a god-like quality above the name of virtue. Her solitudes are inspiration; in them we meet with sensations which are not of Time—impressions, weird, startling, not exempt from terror—suggestions of the Eternal. Her breezes, to me, are spirits of power from the far home of the soul, issuing forth with ghostly visitation, to whet the almost blunted purposes of Ambition, and sting the mind into Resolution through Remorse; they search the chambers of the spirit, and champion all its strength. Flushed into tameless force, by those influences which light the gyr-eagle's blazing eyes, and charge his feathers with swiftness, Thought springs into the boundless vast, and, with sounding pinion, wings the wide, silent sleep. From her choirs, the poet's strain snatches sounds that out-voice the tempests of a thousand years. Those endless, ever-swelling harmonies that roll in upon the soul from the broad sea of Homer's verse, were fashioned of her echoes. Hers are the eternal fires that kindle up the soft transparencies of Spenser. Mighty as were Lord Byron's native faculties, it was to his communion with nature, chiefly, that he was indebted for that flashing grandeur of imagination, that rush of soul and torrent-strength of an unblenching mind, and the charm of a spirit magnificently changeful.

In my earlier days, while the cloud of the Infinite yet hung around the soul, informing it with the electric might that dwells in mystery, I needed not the sight of outward objects to delight, nor the force of outward agencies to strengthen me. My youth is to me a recollection of delight. Existence then was energy; Thought was beauty; Consciousness was joy. The musing spirit teemed with creations of loveliness and light; I thought that its spontaneous wealth could never be exhausted. *Fulsere quondam candidi tibi soles.* That time is gone—that pleasant time, when, every morning, soft, budding thoughts were clustering round my mind—when, within the inward empyrean of meditation, shapes of enchantment, sparkling as morning on the blue Egean, spotted with splendor, rose and floated through the sapphire atmosphere, as the wreathed clouds beneath a stainless sky slowly unveil themselves out of the invisible air. But though the day of that ethereal susceptibility is gone, in which the pulsations of the blood were impressions of the Intellect, when I *felt* Fancies, and Thought was almost a physical sensation, yet my sensibility to the effects of excellence in outward things is as quick and tumultuous as ever. The faintest appearances of that nameless divine essence wake my feelings into kindling life. There still remains within me, undiminished by calamities and cares, that calm, intense, and exquisite perception which can distill from beauty the drops of ecstasy. Time, who as often plays the sudden robber as the subtle thief, has snatched from me many a gift of strength and many a grace of pleasure; but he has left me still the power daily to hang against the eastern sky a picture whose glow of gorgeousness fires my nature into rapture; the power to be delighted almost to delirium with the rising of the sun; to apprehend in the beautiful a majesty which almost bows down and prostrates my being before it. And though that mantling luxury of strength which for its own relief threw forth the forms of grace, and that warm flush of sentiment which colored them into celestial loveliness, have vanished—not fading by their own weakness, but burned out by the blaze of the passions—their removal has discovered stronger and more enduring faculties in the resources of the resolute Will. And I have learned to see in the fictions of the mind a far deeper value and significance, and a far loftier office, than I had conceived of in the wantonness of boyish fancy. Let no man regret the decline of youthful fervor; for the world brings to us a knowledge and a power beyond all that our birth bestowed. The revelations of Time are full of wisdom. I have learned to see in that dreaming which was the idleness of childhood, the true dignity and highest destiny of man.

There is in Life an idea above Life. The being of man is infected with the apprehension of a state and character of existence beyond the experience of his daily consciousness. Toward this condition, his nature is stung by a perpetual and inherent uneasiness; and in it alone it rests. This Life above Life is Beauty; and the mean of its realization is Art.

When we attain to the Beautiful, we pass to a different region—we rise into another world. For though the Ideal is, in its direct analysis, but the development, completion, and perfectness of the Actual, yet in impression and effects the change is of essence. In those subjects of more complex and intricate relation which lie above the range of mechanical considerations, form constitutes character. The chymist can reproduce the substance of every element and every organ in animal life; the form, he cannot produce. In the capacity to impart Form, consists the mystery of creation.

Sensible images being the most dominant in our constitution, the Beauty of material shape is that with which we are most conversant; and to the laws of its existence and evolution, we give, by emphasis, the name of Art. But to every faculty of our nature, and every subject of our cognizance, belong its peculiar beauty, and its appropriate Fine Art. Truth is the beauty of Intellectual form, and Science is the art which deals with it. Goodness is the beauty of the affections, and Religion is the fine art which undertakes to produce it. Virtue is the beauty of morals, and Philosophy is the æsthetics of that perfectness. Society is the beauty of the grand *ensemble* of human action, and Politics is the sublime and profoundly difficult art by which it is attained. There are minds to which the abstract beauty of mathematical forms presents itself so objectively that they perceive in it a richness beyond even the luxury of pictures; but they are rare souls, fashioned in Nature's pride.

To evolve the Beautiful, in all its various departments, is the end and object of man's existence; it is the great duty of our species. We were formed, not to enjoy, but to produce. The life of the race is a grand and continuing process of creation in which Deity acts, not directly, but through the medium of man's nature. And this glorious purpose of our being is accomplished mainly by those things which we blindly call the defects and evils of our nature and condition. For suffering is the source of action, the moving power of the moral being. Man never moves, and cannot move, but upon the impulses of suffering; even when led on by foregoing pleasures, he advances because the thought of a pleasure unpossessed is pain. Were we happy, we should be cyphers. Moral evil is therefore the servant of God's design, and a minister of man's greatness; for goodness renders men happy, and wickedness is necessary to fill their souls with the forces of wretchedness. It is thus, by throwing imperfection and the consequent power of pain into the world, and evil with its attendant energy into the human heart, that the sublime career of life has been set going. Beauty is in its own nature immortal, serene and satisfying; and its immortality is the appointed refuge of our souls from the stings and punishments of Time. Our disappointments and our sorrows are our truest friends; for they compel us to create. Our sufferings are our glory. Pain is the kindly discipline of him that would have us to be great. We are hunted into greatness: we are whipped and scourged into Fame. Cast thine eyes upon the splendid productions of the past, thou that murmurest at the dispensations of Providence, and see the sublime monument of man's woes and wants, his privations, his inward agonies; and behold the justification of creative love. Persons may be destroyed; hearts may be crushed; but the beaming car of Intellectual Life moves on in glittering majesty and sounding pomp. God is glorified; and man, made honorable in despite of his wishes, leaves the tracks of Time strewed with the spoils of Eternity.

The treasures of Art are the trophies of our race. Of an essence beyond mortality—gleaming with an inherent, star-soft lustre—they hang on high along the firmament of Fame, the appropriate and imperishable evidences of the lofty destiny of him from whom they emanated. They are the sublime and silent signals by which the Past converses with the Future. Time, whose touch is the tarnish of the earthly, is to them a handmaid and a beautifier. They gather those rays of another sphere which are wandering through our atmosphere, and reflect them down upon our spirits. They are a presence of Eternity amid the changeful strifes of the world.

And why has not this age and country given forth its contingent of immortal works? Why should we remain forever appalled and paralyzed by the perfections of Grecian excellence? Who shall set up the pillars of literature, and say, "Beyond the daring of the Past, Futurity shall never go?" Men still are men; the inspiring forces of sky and earth, of rock and water, are not diminished. On each new morning of creation the majestic life of Nature rouses itself in all its beauty, and, shaking magnificence from all its motions, goes forth in power, and joy, and thrilling youth; shall not our spirit attend its march, and be incorporate with it in ever-living force? There is no lack of energy in the character of our country; but it is wasted upon interests, transitory and deciduous. The power of the modern soul, swept by passions which the elder world knew not of, often foams into splendor; but it is a flash as wild and evanescent as the yellow gleam of the morning ray upon the dashing waves of the Adriatic. Instead of that intense concentration of power and purpose which brought all the light of Being to one star-like focus, we behold, in the instincts of the modern character, a tendency to disperse and scatter the rays of mind. Single, almost to narrowness, calm, self-controlled, and patient, the Greek sought ever to turn every shape to beauty, to garner up every feeling into the perpetuity of art; hence, while our results are fragmentary and fugitive, his productions have a character of Everlasting.

The causes of the inferiority, or rather the utter and absolute failure, of modern effort, I think that I can in some slight degree unfold. They consist mainly in our not understanding the true nature of Art, in what it consists, and of what dignity it is. I love my fellows, and I love my country; though I associate not with the one, and extol not the other. I cherish, above every other wish, the desire to see my countrymen come forward into the line of the true greatness of the race; and at some future time I hope to find, among the youthful men of genius in our land, a few hearers of the views which I have to offer

Taking up their writings, and those which have been their models, I shall suggest to them that they have not yet attained one correct conception of what Art is—that they have still to acquire the first elements of æsthetical education.

No. III.

How glorious, above all earthly glory, are the faculty and mission of the Poet! His are the flaming thoughts that pierce the veil of heaven—his are the feelings, which on the wings of rapture sweep over the abyss of ages. The star of his being is a splendor of the world.

The Poet's state and attributes are half divine. The breezes of gladness are the heralds of his approach; the glimpse of his coming is as the flash of the dawn. The hues of Conquest flush his brow: the anger of triumph is in his eyes. The secret of Creation is with him; the mystery of the Immortal is amongst his treasures. The doom of unending sovereignty is upon his nature. The meditations of his mind are Angels, and their issuing forth is with the strength of Eternity. The talisman of his speech is the sceptre of the free. The decrees of a dominion whose sway is over spirits, and whose continuance is to everlasting, go out from before him; and that ethereal essence, which is the untamable in man—which is the liberty of the Infinite within the bondage of life—is obedient to them. His phrases are the forms of Power: his syllables are agencies of Joy.

With men in his sympathies, that he may be above them in his influence, his nature is the jewel-clasp that binds Humanity to Heaven. It mediates between the earthly and celestial: in the vigor of his production, divinity becomes substantial; in the sublimity of his apprehensions, the material loses itself into spirit. It is his to drag forth the eternal from our mortal form of being—to tear the Infinite into our bounden state of action. What conqueror has troops like his?—the spirit-forces of Language—those subtle slaves of Mind, those impetuous masters of the Passions—whose mysterious substance who can comprehend—whose mighty operation what can combat? Evolved, none knoweth how, within the curtained chambers of existence —half-physical, half-ideal, and finer than all the agencies of Time—linked together by spells, which are the spontaneous magic of genius, which he that can use, never understands—the weird hosts of words fly forth, silently, with silver wings, to win resistlessly against the obstacles of Days, and Distance, and Destruction, to fetter nations in the viewless chains of admiration, and be, in the ever-presence of their all-vitality, the immortal portion of their author's being. Say what we will of the *real* character of the strifes of war, and policy, and wealth, the accents of the singer are the true acts of the race. What prince, in the secret places of his dalliance, uses such delights as his? Passing through the life of the actual, with its transitory blisses, its deciduous hopes, its quickly waning fires, his interests dwell only in the deep consciousness of the soul and mind, to which belong undecaying raptures, and the tone of a godlike force. Within that glowing universe of Sentiment and Fancy, which he generates from his own strenuous and teeming spirit, he is visited by immortal forms, whose motions torment the heart with ecstasy—whose vesture is of light—whose society is a fragrance of all the blossoms of Hope. To him the True approaches in the radiant garments of the Beautiful; the Good unveils to him the princely splendors of her native lineaments, and is seen to be Pleasure. His soul lies strewn upon its flowery desires, while, from the fountains of ideal loveliness, flows softly over him the rich, warm luxury of the Fancy's passion. His Joys are Powers; and it is the blessedness of his condition that Triumph to him is prepared not by toil, but by indulgence. Begotten by the creative might of rapture, and beaming with the strength of the delight of their conception, the shapes of his imagination come forth in splendor, and he fascinates the world with his felicities.

Art is greater than Science; for to create is more than to know. In science, we explore the harmony and order of things in their relations to a centre infinitely from them and us: by Art, we compel, through the transmuting ardors of our moral being, things to assume a new order and harmony in relation to ourselves as a centre. The natural sciences are God's fine arts; the fine arts, as we know them, are the manifestations and monuments of man's divinity.

The scientific faculty is the pure Intellect: artistic energy lies in the conjunction of the Passions and Intellect. Intellect, warmed, animated and urged by the interfused fire of the Passions—Passion, illuminated, informed, and guided by the pervasive light of Intellect—is the creative faculty or force in man. Material instinct, raised and rarified by thought, is the ideal. In the race and in the individual, the era of art is at the commencement of the middle period of existence; for then the passions and the intellect are in the due degree of equipoise.

True Science, then, consists in a subjection of the mind to the forms actually existing in the outer world: Art is the subjecting of the substance of outward things to the forms preexisting in the mind. Art, therefore, through all its multiform illustrations, is of two parts; the natural substance and the imparted form: the vital union of the two is Beauty in some department of æsthetics. In sculpture, painting, music and poetry, the material is the stone, the color, the sound, and the language; the form is the soul's conception of the fair or great: their combination constitutes all the immortalities of Phidias and Raphael, of Mozart and of Milton.

Wherever you have a substance capable of being made subject to the forms which feeling paints upon the understanding, you have scope for a fine art. The life of man, then, is the greatest of the Fine Arts. The stuff that it is wrought of, is the condition, acts, and circumstances of humanity. The instinctive efforts of each person to cut or mould these into shapes conceived by his own Ambition, Vanity, or Love of Pleasure, give us a work of art; sometimes magnificent, and sometimes ridiculous; brilliant or burlesque; fine or fantastic; wonderful or worthless; in most cases a simple failure; in the greatest instances, a melancholy torso.

The current of Things flows ever on toward the throne of God: man's being is an element cast in to take or make its fate: the man of perceptions, who is the philosopher, arranges his feelings according to the laws which he sees established, and floats with the stream: the man of passions, who is the actor-artist, sets his nature traverse to the course of events, endeavoring to soothe or storm them to his will. This poetry of action, this architecture in history, demand a front and force almost divine; for the particles of social life are kept in form by a magnetism whose axis is the sceptre of the heavens; to overcome and change that order, the soul of man must be intensely charged with power. Nature, more than our will, sets us on this desperate enterprise; for at a certain period of existence, Imagination, winged by emotion, assumes a kind of personality distinct from ourselves, and whirls us headlong into the lists. For my own part, I have not become content to trifle with the airy essences of thoughts and words, without having first fought with the rougher substances of Life, and exhausted in that contest the last contingents of Hope. But I have no instructions to impart respecting this life-craft. I understand it not: it is to me a mystery and a puzzle. My observation has shown me many courses that are fatal; none that are wise. It is to me an inextricable tangle of contradictory principles and conflicting purposes; a system, of which different parts seem to be under the jurisdiction of distinct and jealous deities—the constitution of man being planned upon one design, its development being directed by another, and the end and result of the whole being regulated by a third law thwarting both—as also the wise fabling of the ancients showed in the fiction of the three Fates; a scheme, in which success and failure are but different modes of punishment, and good and evil but varied methods of arriving at it—in which nothing is certain but the suffering of man. For myself, the glory of my life has proved its bitter perplexity: when I touched the glittering prize it exploded with ruin and amazement. How gorgeous was that conflagration of the Feelings, which in youth wrapped the battlements of life in splendor, to leave them in ashes! How wild, that swelling strength that then sprang forth in insolence of power, to win the terrible defeats of victory, and reap that cureless disappointment which lies in the success of the passions! Never to have tasted Joy, is a privation; to have commanded all its resources, is the saddest of human calamities. The failures of Love are bitter; but triumph is the most hopeless of them. A stout mind endures repulse, and even is strengthened by it; but from the moral overthrow of boundless gratification, there is no re-action. *Talis frangit fortia corda dolor.* The pleasure-tides of Hope have ebbed away, and return to me no more: thrown high upon the beach, I lie amid the wrecks and rubbish of old and ruined schemes. From the profession of life-artist, therefore, I have retired, having totally failed in it. But, alas! it will not give up its liens upon me. By the keen enjoyments of earlier being, I have provoked the animosities of Pain, which seems, with mad resentment, to take its revenge on a nature which had defied it, by stinging it through madness into insensibility—and have accumulated upon the hours of thought, an agony beneath whose weight the darkened mind reels. The passions need no scourgings but their own. Intense delights, even of the purest kind, seem to be a kind of sin against the moderation of nature; and the recollection of them is a species of Remorse, which, like a deadly arrow from the quiver of the great hunter, Nemesis, drinks from the side of its victim, drop by drop, the streams of life. From the delirium of that passionate influence which maddens to emasculate, we wake in weakness and anguish; and can only utter the wild, hopeless cry of Atys—"*Jam, jam dolet quod egi, jam, jamque pœnitet!*" My day, then, being ended, let me creep into the cave of Death, and lie snugly housed there, while the flying troops of Existence sweep to and fro over my head.

But thought survives when the Passions have been slain; and from its depths, creations divinely delicate, yet dauntless in endurance, may still be made to give themselves forth. Those exquisite porcelain moulds of poetic fancy, which, when pressed upon the rude matter of actual life, were shattered into fragments, may here impart their loveliness of form to essences as fine as light. The pride that was lost by Action, may be recovered in Art.

Literary art is the chief subject of our present concern; let us understand its nature and development. Æsthetic power, I have said, consists in a certain harmony and conjoint action of the affective faculties with the intellectual: but this union constitutes the Sentiments, which, therefore, are the creative elements in our nature. Phrenology recognizes this triple division of our mental organization; assigning the passions to the rear and base of the brain, the intellect to the forehead, and the sentiments to the central parts between them: and beyond this grouping, the classifications of that science are hardly to be relied on. Sympathy with the merely physical emotions may so predominate in a literary work, that it shall not rise to the character of art at all.* On the other hand, the reaction of the intellectual element may be so strong, that the production passes quite out of the region of genuine art, into the thinner air of metaphysics: it is in the due proportion of the two that the perfectness of art consists. The mistake of approving the former of these conditions, is not common or lasting; the imposture, indeed, could never take effect, but in an age when the mob are the arbiters of reputation; who, imagining that they are raised to the level of literature, when in truth literature is let down to their level, are of course delighted with productions which they know how to appreciate. But the latter evil, as an error in opinion, and a fault in practice, is in modern times nearly universal; and in view of this, it can hardly be too often or too strongly insisted that the sensuous quality is the true and peculiar characteristic of art. According to my view of it, art is nothing else than an intellectual image of passion: it is passion, so far abstracted as, without parting from its own essence, to assume a mental form; or, it is a rational conception made concrete and palpable in something which addresses itself to that part of our nature which is not purely intellectual. It is a creation; and the affective energies, whether for re-production

* To this class, I refer the writings of Dickens, Sue, &c. Their power over every one that reads them, is intense and irresistible; but it is impossible to treat them as works of art. Whoever *admired* an execution? Who but is fearfully *interested* by one?

or for new production, are the creative in man, the others having capacity of perception, selection, and repression, not of generation :—it is a thing of power; and the more physical qualities being the more sympathetic, must enter into every thing which is to have power over men :—it is not notional, like science, but is substantial, and must be wrought of those constituents which are the most material in our intelligent nature.

We see from this how large a part the consideration of Language must have in our conceptions of Art. It is no part of science; it is of the essence of art—it is its hypostasis. Science is the separate action of the intellect, which is merely analytic. Art is the heroic offspring which is engendered when the divinity of mind embraces with the human voluptuousness of passion: it is the magnetic energy that is evolved when intellect and feeling re-act on one another in all the power of their mystic co-relation. The first and most natural shape in which artistic action within man's nature gives itself forth, is gesture and motion, which, therefore, might be called the earliest and simplest of the fine arts. Sound, likewise, is a natural menstrum of artistic spirit. When the constructive instinct predominates among the feelings, Architecture is the form in which Beauty is born of the marriage of the mental with the material. Language is the highest and most general of all the modes of utterance. In its first and true nature, it is less an expression than an emanation —a natural effect of this dynamic condition of the faculties—a gesture, as it were, produced by the struggle of instinct and intelligence, and propagated through the organs of speech. As passion predominates in that state of relation between the different parts of our being from which language proceeds, it is obvious that the language will be picturesque and musical in its character, concrete and definite, material, a-glow with sensuous life: as intellect gains head in the combination, and language grows to be less the spontaneous overflow of emotion than the ductile expression of the thoughts, it becomes abstract, speculative, thin and dry. In the *language* of the poet, then, you read the degrees in which the affective and the intellectual, respectively, have contributed to his work; in other words, the degree in which his work is truly Art. The censure of language is, therefore, a criticism upon the genius : when you judge the style, you are analyzing the mind. Language is the clothing of science, it is the organization of art; it serves the former for intercourse with the world, it is the life and being of the other.

The sentiments, blended of passion and intelligence, the true seat of creative vigor, have, in like manner, a triple division; they are the moral, the spiritual, and the merely natural; so distinct from one another as almost to be opposed; in the development of all which consists the civility of the race. In the great work of effecting this civility, the task of educating the moral sentiments was assigned to the Romans; of the spiritual to the Hebrews; of those which I have called natural, to the Greeks: and in the literature of these three nations, you have the same phenomena of life and man exhibited under the natural point of view, under the spiritual, and under the moral. These natural sentiments acting æsthetically, result in the conception of the Beautiful; and their display in the Greek organization took place under the conditions of an immense intellectual development, a very limited moral one, and little or nothing of spiritual perception : Greek art, then, embodies natural emotions with a most exquisite fineness of illustration, and presents a most subtle analysis of the natural sensibilities, but is unplagued by moral questionings, or the morbid apprehensions of spiritual consciousness. That predominance of the moral faculties, which evolved, in the Roman state, the greatest system of law, society, and politics that the ancient world had seen, while it condemned the Latins to rather a debased species of art, led them to the invention of one form of poetry unknown to the Greeks, that of moral satire. In the Hebrew organization we behold an enormous excess of the spiritual functions with a very defective moral faculty, and even a mean intellectual ability: passion, therefore, overmastering reason in the composition of their poetry, it became the most vehement, substantial, and intense, that man has ever produced. These three distinct elements of civility flowed into one at the commencement of the Christian era; and modern life and modern art are the mingled action of all of them.

Effluent from the feelings, tempers and fancies of an humanity that claimed no higher origin than the flower-bearing Earth, yet inerrant and exact as geometry itself—combining the freedom of nature in the conception of thoughts with the precision of science in the expression of them—infinitely refined in its sympathies, yet simple, strong and never offering at any thing false or unsound—sensitive, with an equal fidelity, to the most material instincts that inhabit the depths of our nature, and the airyest gleams of emotion that flit over its surface, and sovereign, with equal ease, to summon them to become the eternal, life-giving spirits of some fair form of words—searching every thing with the lights of philosophy, that it may decorate every thing with the lustre of beauty—subduing passion to the yoke of logic, and giving to pure reason almost the warmth and loveliness of feeling—able, by the telescopic powers of its language, to advance the indefinite into distinctness, and to make reality recede away into a vagueness as dim as air—intense, yet expansive, comprehensive and yet particular, fervid without faultiness, glowing and still controlled, natural but refined—daring any thing except deformity, fearing nothing but to violate grace, regardless of all laws but those of Beauty—delight of the sense and wonder of the mind—Hellenic Art stands on high, like the grouped stars of Heaven, at once a superstition, a rapture, and a science. The forms of Grecian brightness do not flare and blaze like the fires of modern ardor, nor are they, as the priestly poetry of Israel, distorted by the inspiration with which they swell; but, serene and genial, they glow with a native brilliance that softens the surrounding atmosphere with the light of joy and the warmth of repose. From the quiet of their lofty seats they seem to look down upon the rivalries of ostentatious Rome, the fanatic furiousness of Judea, the madness of Gothic fervor, and to say, "*Quare fremuerunt gentes, et populi meditati sunt inania?*" That literature is not plagued with those desperate "questionings of outward things," that abnormal apprehension of things not palpable and nigh, which has infected our poetry from Judea, nor tormented with that analytic temper that will not enjoy but moralize, that too profoundly meditative, Roman mood, which draws out a bitterness from every pleasure, which regrets the Past, or desponds over the Future, instead of exulting in the Present. It was this want in the Grecian nature, of the spiritual and moral sense, that made Grecian art peculiar and unimitable: for Art, in the purity of its philosophical conception, is essentially a heathen thing; that is to say, is constituted of those carnal apprehensions of the grand, the graceful and the fair, whose integrity is impaired by the influence of any thoughts not of earth and the present. Glad and innocent as childhood, yet, like childhood or summer, overcome sometimes in the very acmé of brightness by a dark cloud whose origin and nature and purpose were utterly inexplicable, the Greeks seem to be moving about in that paradise of careless, joyous ease, which the world was, before the wretched knowledge of good and evil had invaded it. When I seek for Purity, let me be aided by the suffering song of David; but I desire to be all Pagan in my appreciation of the Beautiful. What relief it is, to turn away from the frantic fooleries of theological contests (the vice and shame of this age), and from the metaphysical perplexities of recent poetry—to the rich and soft repose of Grecian art—to that calmness which is strength and wisdom, that silent grandeur which is freedom and peace! Greek literature!—delight of my boyhood—only friend of my inmost being—how should I live without it? Fair Spirit of true art! pure, beautiful, divine—comforter, companion, and enchantress—that in the white dawn of Ionian glory, unveiling thy kindling fascinations to mortals, didst infuse a love that grew to inspiration! Thou art delicious, to wake affection; and august, that thou mayst deserve our worship. The admiration of thy charms is cleansing; the influence of thy nearness purges our privacies of thought. Over the glossy streams that gush from thy sacred mountain is written—

. . . . Purâ cum vesta venite,
Et manibus puris sumite fontis aquam.

Reigning over our Fancy, thou servest in the cause of virtue: for, showing us what marvels may be accomplished by those who are possessed with the Idea of the Perfect, thou dost incite us to mightier and unceasing efforts in the higher æsthesis of virtue and goodness.

Latin art in letters has been underrated by critics from not being well understood. It is not that, being of one nature with Greek art, it is inferior to it in quality; in its elements and purposes it is essentially different. It is not composed of those merely physical sentiments which Attic genius sought indeed to elevate, but not to modify; it does not seek for a pure and purged apprehension of natural beauty: it has a conscience—which Greece never knew. It is fashioned of the moral instincts and sympathies; and if any one would behold these, under their various development of personal dignity, domestic affection social regard, and political relation, embodied in strong and graceful forms of feeling, fancy, or thought, and arrayed in the dazzle of a language full of sensibility, surprisingly suggestive, and capable of accomplishing, by a kind of elegant indirectness, effects almost as exquisite as the arrowy certainty of Grecian phrases—he will find them in their best loveliness in Latin poetry. In dealing with this moral species of art, the test of artistic merit is the degree in which the work proceeds from the moral sentiments and instincts, and not from the dry analysis of a moral ratiocination: and under this view, the Latin bards are genuine poets. Their craft is as truly art as Grecian is, and their mastery of it not inferior: but the more vital clay with which they wrought was incapable of those firm, cold, glittering forms which shine forever in the Parian stone.

Idolatry of the classics is part of the religion of a gentleman: and, bred as I have been from my father's arms, into the most intimate familiarity with Grecian letters, and beholden to them inexpressibly for comfort and joy among a thousand troubles, and almost for sanity amidst the torrent of false reason and base superstition that now sweeps over the world, they are to me at once a passion and a pride: they are a refuge from care, from fear, from solitude, from remorse; I turn to them with the same confidence and affection with which one seeks his home and fireside; and I feel an assault upon their supremacy as a wrong done to myself. And yet—reluctantly—against my will—in spite of earnest endeavor—I am overborne by the despotizing might of Jewish inspirations, and am compelled to admit that Israel is greater than Greece. Bowed down and driven away from the darlings of heathen witchery, by an irresistible sympathy, I recognize at last that there is in art something yet higher than Beauty, and that there may be a power in Spirit above the fascinations of Form. And whence is this superior vigor—this amazing vehemence and vitality of Jewish art—this fervor of enthusiasm, whose words are weapons, whose cadences are like the thick drivings of the tempest? It is because the spiritual instincts and sensibilities, of which Hebrew poetry is the bold, imperious utterance, are yet deeper, more impetuous and absolute than either of the other kinds; as the experience of the world attests. The spiritual, the natural, the moral—such is the successive development in the history of the individual, and such is the order in which the several civilities of Judea, Greece and Rome have evolved themselves: that is the sequence as you pass forward from the merely affective to the intellectual organs, and that is the gradation in the degrees of force and substantiality exhibited by these respective schools of art. Fit to be the winged messenger of that tremendous law which was born amidst thunderings and lightnings—whose fearful courts are held in the shadowy sanctuaries of the soul, and the ministers of whose judgment are Frenzy, and Horror, and Self-damnation—it flies forth in the solemnity of a delegated Omnipotence: by the force of its sincerity, extravagance becomes venerable and absurdity august. Hebrew literature is the fresh, morning effort of that deity in man whose calmer work is Grecian art, and whose later toil is Roman. It is the native residence of the sublime. Grecian sentiment, never soaring without the jealous accompaniment of Grecian intellect, could never reach Sublimity, but, like Aurora in pursuit of Night, still drove the dusky fugitive before it. Of range unlimited—defiant of the graceful shackles of Greek decorum—flashing like the lightning from pole to pole in wantonness of might and freedom, it sounds with equal energy the highest and the lowest notes of mortal consciousness; from the physical sympathies of the mere animal who warmeth himself and crieth "Ha, ha! I am warm!" to the infinite delicacy of spiritual being which to an *Idea* says, "Thou art a place to hide me in." It gives vitality to matter, and form and action to the subtlest phenomena of mind and soul. In its harmonies Ocean claps its hands, and corn-fields laugh and sing. Among all the deep minds of Greece there is none that may be measured with the unfathomed soul of David. The storms of the Andes have no tones more terrible—the melodies of the summer winds among groves of myrtle and orange are not more ravishing—than those that mingle in the bursts of his lyre. From the recesses of his spirit, there seems to surge forth a stream which is but the tiding overflow of the sea of Heaven. With the roar of a coming deluge, headlong it rushed over the world—a resistless stream of Light, and Power, and Glory—absorbing the confluent courses of Greek intelligence and Roman morals. It rolled on in unresisted conquest, till it met the great refluent wave of Milton's soul, which, with audacity and strength divine, forced back the gathered torrent even till the returning tide echoed against the throne of God.

No. IV.

THE splendor and blaze of summer are in the sky! Afar, and faint, her yellow banners float, flame-like, through the blue ether: nearer, the air, thrilled into voice by the warm touches of the light, gives forth her iris-like melodies in breezy sighs of pleasure: while around and beneath, upon an hundred hills, the thick forests stand, like emerald cressets streaming towards the Heavens. It is the passioning of Nature. Wild, fervid, fiercely-voluptuous, as youth's first, full embrace with guilt,—the spirits of Earth and Sky glow together into an union, intense as fire and glorious as Sin. We dwell to-day beneath the tyranny of Light, and in the very porches of the Sun. The lustre is vehement, almost to gloom. Swelling in crested strength,—travailing with conscious boundlessness of Vigor,—

Existence seems about to be self-born into some higher and more emphatic type of being. In earlier days, this was the season of my deepest joys. There was something in its godless glow that fascinated me. The Arab-soul of youth,—half-savage in its love of freedom,—craving sensation,—struck and enchanted by Power,—revelled in the raging of the Summer's ray. Lover and worshipper of the Sun, the sting of his heat smote strength into my frame; I exulted in the dazzling deluge of his beams. Through the madness of the mortal energies, the sympathies of the deep soul were reached and roused. But that delight is over; the might of spirit whence it was engendered has been struck forever. And I regret not their [MS. wanting.] Rather, I say in daily thanksgiving, Blessed be God for the *infirmity* of our Nature. Betrayed by Strength, and ruined by Joy, redemption cometh to us at last through our weakness and sufferings. It is that lingering residue of distress and cowardice, which still will haunt our hours of Pride, and soil our brightest raptures, that becomes our strength and salvation. That is the consciousness of our Immortality, which, reproducing itself within our finite life, compels our inverted being to right itself, through madness and misery. In worldly schemes and action, we mistake our nature, and perplex our fate: for we have inherited a portion of that high angel essence, whose greatness is in humility, whose only comfort is in the consciousness of Duty; whose energy is convulsed by selfishness and its sight extinguished by [MS. wanting.] Our shame is our Dignity; our force is in our fears. It is our failures that save us. For myself, desolate, but not in despair; I send on high the earnest breath of gratitude, for this chiefly: that amidst the ecstasies of Sin, I never could escape the exquisite sense of its degradation; that, sated with raptures, I could not harden myself into contentment: but that the living consciousness of a better destiny, growing more intolerably keen within my bosom at each lower step in the descent, whirled me at last with the volcanic strength of frenzy into the regions of an exulting penitence. Wild with love and anguish, mad with enjoyment and remorse, my soul tore itself away from the warm oppressions of its pleasures, to tell its misery to the mountains and the silent skies, to the lonely forests and the stars of Night. Nature is still, as she ever was, my refuge, my restorer and support: but it is her sterner, chaster aspects that I now take [MS. wanting] in,—her ruder lineaments, her suffering moods,—those rigorous scenes and times, that, repelling sense, urge forth the Spirit. Alone and thoughtful,—with regrets to urge and hopes to guide me upwards,—I dwell amongst the grandeur of the hills,—the varying clouds for Memory and the changeless sky for Faith,—sending on high the eternal aspiration after good;—my feelings my only friends, the higher sorts of poetry, my companion and teacher.—But we forget our purpose, amid these reveries. Our business is with criticism. Having distinguished the kinds of ancient Art, let us sketch the outline of its character as displayed in modern Europe.

Civility, as I have said, consists in the development of the sentiments: if you compare a savage with a civilized person, you will see that the difference between them lies not in the passions, which are quite the same in both, nor in the mere intellect, which may be more piercing in the savage,—but in the sentiments, which are the offspring of their combination. Jewish, Greek, and Roman society exhibit three several kinds of civility, each of them partial; one, spiritual, another æsthetic, and the third, moral. To bring them into union,—to lead forth a family of nations in which all these elements should be combined in one grand and harmonious civility, was the problem which Nature proposed to herself in modern history. During the fourteen first centuries of our era, the object of her efforts was the moral and spiritual education of a race of glorious barbarians; and the machines by which it was accomplished, were the feudal Law-system, and the Church. Those who correctly appreciate the effective purpose of those two great institutions, can never cease to admire the wisdom which their organization exhibits, and the priceless excellence of their beneficent results. Being designed to operate upon a human nature grossly full of vices and defects, they were of course adapted to it; and some have erringly supposed them to have been the causes of faults which they harmonized with, only that they might remove them.

Others have misapprehended the value of these systems, because they have looked for intellectual results from schemes designed to produce only spiritual and moral ones. That deep and, as it now seems, ineradicable moral intelligence and spiritual consciousness, which give character to modern Europe, are nothing else than the effect of ages of discipline by the feudal and Catholic systems: they are now the birth-right, and spontaneous faculties, of every individual; but he who imagines that these perceptions and feelings are strictly *natural* in man, forgets that Greece had no spirituality, and that Judea possessed scarcely more of that social and moral instinct or sagacity, which all Europeans now are born with. When these two great systems had done their work of educating the race into an enlightenment beyond their own measure, and had thus become useless and contemptible to man, they gave way, and perished with different degrees of suddenness in different nations; and the intellectual or scientific faculties, covering the æsthetic energies in their sortie, rose forth upon the world, like a new dawn upon the full day. Bacon and Shakspeare were contemporaries,—the Sun of science which lightens all the world,—the Sirius of poetry, around whom all the stars of Art revolve. Galileo and Dante, Vico and Milton, flourished at the same time. Since that epoch, the task which society had been engaged in, is the intellectual civility of men.

The characteristics of Jewish, Greek, and Latin art, are each single and uniform: the peculiarity of modern Art is, that all these are blended together and interfused, like the gorgeous colorings of a forest in autumn. In English poetry, what rich varieties of form, what infinite diversities of effect! There is Chaucer, who is a Greek poet: and Milton, who is a Hebrew poet: and Pope, who is a Latin poet: and Shakspeare, who is a World poet.

It is impossible to make any progress in the philosophy of æsthetical criticism, without recognizing that there are these three distinct kinds of Art, founded in distinctions inherent in the nature of man, and illustrated historically by the three great nations of antiquity to which we have referred. They may differ in the degrees of their power and beauty; but one is as genuine as another. It may well happen that a man, by reason of the predominance of one set of sentiments on his nature, is fitted to sympathize with one of these kinds of poetry, to the exclusion of the others; but if he cannot enjoy the rest, he should at least endeavor to appreciate them, for the limits of one's taste ought not to be made the measure of one's judgments. If we group the English poets according to an historical law, we shall find, perhaps,—though, of course, in a very general way, and liable to disturbance by very slight causes,—that the earliest English poets are of a Heathen or Greek family of art; the middle ones of a moral cast; that the spiritual predominates in those most eminent in our own day. Now, critics, who are familiar chiefly with these more recent models, and have schooled their taste and informed their understanding by their examples, fall into the error of imagining that the spiritual consciousness is the very faculty of poetry, and that the mystery and power of art can consist in nothing else; forgetting that there are three Graces, and that though we may love one, we should be wise enough not to deny the others. It is thus that there has been constructed a school of criticism, very limitary and insular in its sympathies, and, on that account, morbid in its tastes; a school whose canons would, on the one hand, consign Homer himself to neglect, and set Euripides above Æschylus; and on the other, push Horace and Virgil quite out of the line of poets. All these narrownesses are very unphilosophical: Wordsworth is undoubtedly a poet; but it does not follow that Campbell is not as great a one; and Pope greater than either. The summit of Ida is triple.

In passing the great poets of England in hasty review, we shall distribute them according to the three several styles which we have recognized, though of course that classification is extremely far from rigorous; indicating only that the Greek, the Roman or the Jewish spirit predominates, not that it is exclusive. But first we should speak of two who certainly cannot be referred to one class more than to another; one of them belonging equally to all, the other being different from any; I mean

Shakspeare and Spenser. Shakspeare is, I grant, "the divine, the matchless, what you will :" yet Spenser is that poet, of all modern times, in whom the spiritual, the moral, and the natural, combine in the most exquisite justness of proportion, and result in an absolute unity of effect; composing one divine faculty, constituted of three, yet distinct and entire. In Shakspeare, these three join, but do not unite. He is not a triple one, he is three. In his plays, three separate intelligences seem to execute different parts of the work; sometimes, it must be admitted, in a diversity of manner not very promotive of the harmony of art. In one scene, I behold before me the re-arisen spirit of the most wonderful, the most delightful of the Grecian dramatists,—Aristophanes; in other parts, I listen to a mind instructed in all the lore of Cicero and breathing all the dignity of Cato: while beneath and beyond both of these, there are sometimes gleams and sometimes lightnings of that lurid fire of the infinite, under-lying life, and disturbing it now with uneasy tremblings, and now with volcanic overthrow: but so separated, and even discordant, in their characteristics, are these three creative emanations, that I lose the sense of the identity of their origin. His genius was boundless in comprehension, but it was not homogeneous, and it was not proportioned. Spenser,—expansive yet harmonious as the spheres,—gracefully uniform amidst limitless extension,—rich as autumn and freshly various as the spring,—is the faultless exemplar of Gothic art.

First and greatest of the bright-eyed band that wear the golden grasshopper in the bonnet, is cheerful old Chaucer. To no poet in the world, may he be named as second. Genial, exuberant and changeful,—like the abounding Dawn, his spirit diffused itself over existence, coloring nature into fresh, peculiar splendor, and waking life to animation and delight. Possest of a quick, true eye for the picturesque, both in scenery and in society, which he reproduces in his verse, not by sketching impressions, or indicating general effects, but by means of particular traits, caught through minute observation, and conveyed in language, precise, simple and lustrous: instinct with that true poet-spirit, which, instant to seize and faithful to record every suggestion of the infinite which the mortal teems with, sees in the actual the best materials of the ideal: full of that efflorescent energy of Fancy which causes every seed of thought and observation which falls within it to bloom into vital beauty, —that artless propriety of sentiment "*qui ne sait ce qu'elle fait, et fait tout avec grâce, qui ne sait ce qu'elle dit, et dit tout avec esprit*"—of that classic restrained vigor, that is at once voluptuous and pure: brilliant yet delicate in his tints, exact but free in his touches, natural but exquisitely finished in manner, concise but easy in expression: flowing forth in strains of melody, free, rich, and ceaseless as a summer brook, which no familiarity can render tiresome, and no perversity make discordant. Fashioning his work with a severe correctness, and then shedding over it those alchymic hues of pleasure which turn all things to golden grace, this enchanting minstrel presents us with images at once accurate and glorious, and processes at the same time logical and delightful,—the elements of Truth under the outlines of Beauty. Never was Art made more delicious. Able to embody the most profound moral conceptions in imaginative forms of surpassing grandeur, force and terror, yet liking to enjoy more than to create; teeming with invention, and yet preferring to observe rather than contrive; his greatest enterprises of strength are accomplished without effort, and his longest excursions wear no appearances of fatigue. His sympathy with humanity is as widely-ranging and as fine as his love of nature is eager and joyous: easily capable of constructing brilliant air-palaces of the purest Fancy, as in that immortal fragment of Kambus-Khan, which of all Chaucer's productions seems to have left the strongest impression upon Milton's feelings, he seems always to feel that the rightful dwelling-place and employment of his thoughts, was amid objects and social interests: specially master of the pathetic, and knowing his mastery, yet never displaying his power at the expense of his art, not pressing sympathy into pain, but thoughtful and dignified even amidst the impetuosities of feeling, operating not by a blind aggregation of emotions, but by distinct and well-analyzed strokes, to which a craving sensibility could add little and an exacting taste object nothing, exhibiting the reserved, suppressed intensity of Euripides, and not that wild and morbid abandonment to distress into which Virgil and Catullus fell when they sought to emulate the energy and earnestness of Ionian passion: a perfect artist, not Gothic, to sublimate reality away into the indistinctness of the heavens, but Greek, to bring down the golden atmosphere of the skies to shed magic radiance around the familiar and the near: seemingly discursive but really direct: the last inheritor of that Homeric secret of elevating without distorting, and transfiguring without change.

[The rest of these MSS., which were several in number, are lost: what follows is a mere lead-pencil fragment, but belonging apparently to the same subject, is here added.]

Pope for the moral poets: eulogize him as working with moral sentiments, and even in Abelard to Eloise moral passions: not trains of ratiocination; not metaphysical: Jeffrey and Allison. We might name Wordsworth as the person in whom the spiritual develops itself more exclusively than in any other poet: he has little of moral sentiment as distinguished from spiritual, and mere natural sympathy—the [MS. wanting]... in him, though delicate and true, is feeble. Of the capacity of the spiritual to constitute a great and powerful poetry, no man that has read the Psalms of David can entertain any doubt; yet Wordsworth, I think, falls far short of being a great poet. The intellectual predominates far too excessively, and physical emotion is far too weak in his mental constitution to give him that mastery of human sympathies which is the wand of the poet. Exquisite in apprehension, subtle in discrimination, the pure stream of refined emotion winds around the forms of nature and the exterior of life: its passages are not forced through by its own resistless violence, but are opened before it by the antecedent analysis of the intellect. If any man would know the difference between a speculation and a creation—between a thought and a thing—let him pass from the rarified and fatiguing tenuity of the Excursion to the [MS. wanting.] The metal which he works upon is the genuine stone of Ophir,—nay, if you please, it is the refined, essential gold of the heavenly throne;

it is the quantity that is defective. The economy of the poet is truly amazing to behold. It is beaten out past any analogy with the leaf of the gold-beater, into an infinitesimal degree of fineness : when, occasionally, it is massed into a point of visible magnitude, that point is as bright in purity of essential lustre as the very lamps of the sky. His organization is defective in tone,—in capacity to re-act with vigor and effect on the objects of its apprehension—in that muscular energy and force which moulds and masters and gives form. When he approaches a great subject, instead of being fired and raised and maddened by it, he is paralyzed, and his faculties are thrown into a state of mere collapse. He possesses a fancy susceptible of the forms of grand and lovely images; it is the force of creative energy that is so marvellously lacking. His Greek odes—as Dion, Laodamia—are cast in the genuine mould of Euripides: but they are the hollow shells of exquisite sculpture not solid masses of [MS. wanting.]

DRAMATIC CRITICISMS.

MR. MACREADY.

THAT portion of the community to whose cares, or whose more fatiguing want of them, the drama is wont to prove a nightly solace, will be gratified by the intelligence, now rendered certain, of Mr. Macready's appearance in this country early in the coming autumn. His reception, we well know, will be cordial and cheering. By the delicacy of his social deportment—by the dignity of his public aims, and the studious ability with which he has devoted himself to the life-long labor of realizing the loftiest conception of a dramatic career, he has secured a more honorable place in the confidence of the best classes of our community—the educated, the reflective, the refined—than any foreign performer who has ever come among us. These persons are happy to hail his arrival, as a gentleman who brings to private intercourse the most select contributions of taste and scholarship, and as an artist who displays on the scene of his peculiar distinction, an intellectual capacity which elevates him to the level of the great philosophical critics and analysts of Shakspearian life. While he has raised himself to an enviable respectability by the decorum of his personal demeanor, he has raised his profession in the scale of mental consideration by the superiority of thoughtful power which he brings to bear upon its most exalted difficulties. The present impression produced by other actors—we allude only to the very first order of them—may perhaps have been more intense; the sympathy of the passions under Kean or Cooke may have been more vivid and absorbing; but we have met with no player upon whose exhibitions we reflect with deeper rational interest and satisfaction than Mr. Macready. We viewed *them* with a confused and indistinct tumult of emotions which subsided when the occasion had past, and left nothing behind it but the memory of a physical excitement. We recall *his* great illustrations as having been the means of giving us a grander impression even of the genius of Shakspeare himself—as having been memorable revelations of the *mind* of the immortal contriver of characters which Nature might mistake for her own noblest creations—as being gilded with some rays of that admiration which glitters forever around the bard whom he interprets. It is in his relation to these vast and weighty monuments of histrionic fame—the tragedies of Shakspeare—that we consider Mr. Macready's name as specially distinguished; and we hope that it is this matchless scene that will be illuminated by the last splendors of his art that go forth upon American soil. We would suggest to him, as a thing woithy of his own position and eminently grateful to his friends, that he should give in each great city of the Union a complete series of his Shaksperian personations, in regular sequence. Let him close his engagement in America by that full *diapason* of professional display.

From the time that we first grew acquainted with the merits of this profound illustrator of the drama, we have cherished his reputation with something of enthusiasm. We have read, since then, many depreciating criticisms—many effusions of faint and partial praise; but our conviction of the justice of our own earliest impressions, and of the genuine worth of the subject of them, has remained unshaken. The vivid effects of the scenes, under his control, we are told, are but an elaborate and complicated mechanism; all is fore-planned and settled with minute and measured particularity; what seems the rapid improvisation of passion, is the deliberate result of calculation and arrangement. So be it: but what, then, shall we think of the capacities which contrive, combine and manage this intricate system of display? How can we sufficiently admire the invention which conceives, the vigor which executes, and the taste which controls these alleged dynamics of the drama? Admit that the result attained by Mr. Macready is as effective as that reached by artists of less laborious skill—a position which we cannot allow to be at all questionable—is it not obvious that the methods ascribed to the former as the means of his success imply far more than all the abilities which are possessed by the others?—as much genius and a greater measure of discipline and accomplishments? The imaginative sensibility which, in the quietness of the rehearsal, apprehends the impressions which are to be worked out with careful exactness in the exhibition, is surely the same with that which moves the performer whose action is spontaneous in the presence of the audience. In addition to all this, the sustained strength which carries out, through a series of arrangements, all the spirit of the first conception; the tact, the judgment, the delicacy of execution which must preside over the whole; the energy which, in the final moment of delivery, must vivify the performance with the freshness of an impulsive movement; all these call for new admiration and distinct honors. Is there not as much inspired invention in the complex construction of a piece of clockwork as is displayed by him who, by a glance at the sun, or a felicitous guess from the shadows, tells you the hour of the day? If the elaboration imputed to Mr. Macready be really undergone by him, it only proves that he is a man of consummate genius, who preëstablishes such a system of operations that the conceptions of his genius cannot fail to take effect with exact and absolute precision. In truth, the habits alleged as a derogation from the fame of this great tragedian, would be quite indispensable to make out the highest titles to it. Wherever we can penetrate into the interior system of men of the first greatness in any department, we find that the anxious employment of instruments and aids of success is not less striking than the richness of those native resources that might well seem able to do without them. It is a secondary ambition which is content to rely upon the unassisted suggestions of the mind or feelings. Napoleon was accustomed to make the most copious and thorough preparations for his enterprises; he provided for every possible want; he anticipated every rational contingency;

and when success had thus been reduced to demonstration and victory rendered a logical necessity, he talked about his destiny, and bade men marvel at the might of his genius.

After all, the merit of an artist of any kind, is to be judged by the excellence of the final result which he accomplishes; and certainly no personation, that we have witnessed, informs the great drama of Shakspeare with a nobler life, or makes its colossal characters flash forth a higher and truer splendor of moral revelation, than the histrionic efforts of Mr. Macready. He does not possess the fascinations of countenance—the witcheries of tone—the graceful charm of captivating manner; he may not enchant the senses by qualities half physical in their nature. He is the actor of intellect. He plays to the mind of the spectator. He begins by fixing the curiosity of the understanding keenly upon the inward condition of the character he is dealing with, and then leads the passions on in unbreathing suspense through a progression of scenic power in which the acuteness of the metaphysician subserves the brilliance of the artist, until the blaze of the denouement flashes back over the whole the conviction of reason and the satisfaction of the conscience. We have seen no artist of the drama who infuses into his exhibitions such poignancy of mental interest. It is that intimate union of the rational with the sensuous in his performance that gives such intensity of gratification to the most reflective among his auditors. He holds the sympathy of the lowest, while he commands and sways the admiring respect of the best cultivated. We may witness in other performers occasional displays of greater power—outbursts of startling but irregular force—it will be long ere we shall behold, in any one, a higher tone of classic dignity, a more continuous grandeur of moral impression, than is shown in the best personations of Mr. Macready.

—

MR. MACREADY'S MACBETH.

IT is evident that a deep impression has been produced by the Macbeth of Mr. Macready, and that the interest of the audience has been powerfully engaged; but probably most people would feel themselves somewhat at a loss, if called upon, to say seriously what has been the cause of this undefinable delight, and wherein lay the secret of this fascination.

When we first saw this great actor, during the two first acts, we did not know exactly what to think of him; we could not make up our mind. It was obvious, that here was a scheme and style of acting essentially different from any thing we had seen before. The actor was very clearly contemplating a different purpose from other actors, and employing different means thereto; but what his system was, and how his excellence should be characterized, was something of a puzzle. As the piece went on, the prospect cleared, and we left the house at the end of the play, with the consciousness of having been as strangely affected, and as intensely delighted as we had ever been in our lives.

That which we had in our mind, throughout, as the key to Mr. Macready's design, was Charles Lamb's essay "On the Tragedies of Shakspeare, considered with reference to their fitness for stage representation." In that paper, the acutest critic of our times ventures upon saying, that Shakspeare's plays are those which, of all others, are the least fitted for performance, because the chief interest of Shakspeare's persons lies in the mind, and the workings of the mind of those persons; whereas, what we see upon the stage, is body and bodily action. That which Lamb thus considered to be the grand peculiarity of Shakspeare, and which he supposed it was the nature of acting to leave out, it has been Mr. Macready's purpose to seize upon and to portray;—to display before you the *soul* and mind of the person, as it was conceived by Shakspeare,—not simply to pronounce each speech with that effectiveness of voice and attitude that might best attend those words considered by themselves, but to reveal the moral clockwork of the feelings which resulted in striking out that speech from the depths of the speaker's heart. From the beginning, it was the individual, moral nature of the royal homicide which was bared to view, and upon which our attention was riveted, and to trace that moral nature through all its changes and declension—to follow it through all the complexity of the passions—to see that those lusts of the mind which are at the beginning spirits to animate, are afterward furies to punish—to mark how a noble nature is first convulsed and then hardened by the consciousness of guilt, —this lofty and profound exhibition it was which fascinated our attention through five acts, and left us, at last, breathless with interest. Who does not feel, in reading Shakspeare, that the unwritten part of the character is a vastly larger part than the written? That there exist between the speeches vast intervals of passions, which nothing but Shakspeare's own genius could entirely fill up, and *that* only in folios of moral metaphysics? It is this unwritten portion of the character which Mr. Macready give us. His acting fills up these chasms, and is the *complement* of the worded part; he not merely tells us what Macbeth thought when he spoke, but shows us all he felt before he spoke. Other actors enact the character by reciting the words. Mr. Macready illustrates the words by displaying the character. They start from the language that is set down, and work inwards to the character as far as they can; he starts from the soul of the person he is representing, and works outward to the language, modifying its impression by a knowledge of its cause. If you would know what such or such words mean, when their meaning is brought out in the most effective way possible, these actors are your men. If you would learn what Macbeth meant by speaking those words, and why he spoke them, Mr. Macready must be your oracle. They detach the speech from the character and deliver it with all the grace and power of elocution; they are orators; attitudinizers. Mr. Macready is nothing of these—he is nothing but Macbeth. Doubtless, elocution and attitude are very valuable qualities, and to make Macbeth a series of reading lessons, and the stage a succession of *tableaux vivans*, is a very fine exhibition. But it is not enacting the character, or, if it be, it is not Mr. Macready's method of acting it; and without suggesting any thing unfavorable to others, we take leave to say that Mr. Macready's method is, to us, a very agreeable method. We take leave also to think, that Shakspeare's dramas are those which, beyond all others, require that illustrative and supplementary style of acting which Mr. Macready employs: not that Shakspeare's personages talk less than those of other dramatists, but that they obviously *think* and feel a great deal more. We are willing to admit, that if Mr. Macready had the countenance of Conway, or the limbs of Hamblin, he would have—something which he has not now. He does not command the senses; he does not strike and overawe the fancy by the flashes of imposing form. He addresses the imagination and intellect. Let the reader be pleased to turn to that essay of Lamb's which we have referred to above, and he will understand what we mean by saying, that to witness the performance of this great actor is, to us, like *reading* Shakspeare, gifted, for the nonce, with powers of perception to see all that Shakspeare meant but has not expressed. This profound style of explication is very exacting, and perhaps at last fatigues. Perhaps, too, this actor's moral analysis, always subtle, is sometimes morbid. But take the whole together, and we venture to utter our opinion: that the tragedy of Macbeth, performed by Mr. Macready, is the highest of dramatic enjoyments.

The character of Macbeth is a great psychological study. It appears to have been a favorite opinion with Shakspeare, that evil is not spontaneous in the heart of man, but that it results from good qualities acted on by perverting circumstances; and that that sort of vice which is active and ferocious, is commonly generated of feelings too intensely sensitive to abide the whips and stings of life, which at length torture them into the moral madness of wickedness. It may be said that the heartless Richard, "born with teeth," does not bear out this assertion; but turn to that astonishing soliloquy of the guilty king, when he starts from his dreadful dream, and hear the sharpest cry of anguish that bursts from that self-confessional—

"There is no creature loves me;
And, if I die, no soul will pity me!—"

This volcano of the soul gives us to see, by one glimpse, how

38

the ardors of love once burned in the bosom of that unhappy deformed; and that the thick incrustation of hate, which had so long hardened over the surface, was only affection chilled into its opposite by the cold scoffings of the world. But in Richard, this hardening process was complete before he appears upon the stage—in Macbeth it all goes forward upon the scene. Mr. Macready enables us to see, in this character, a consistence and unity which we had not perceived before, and we shall very briefly give the view of this character which we understand that gentleman to have embodied.

Macbeth is obviously a person of very sensitive feelings, and, at the same time, of highly excitable fancy. We may remark, in passing, that such a combination must often produce the results of cowardice, and such Macbeth does certainly often exhibit. When he first appears before us, his breast is free from sin. His imagination is soon intensely excited by the vision opened before him by that "supernatural soliciting" which "cannot be ill;" and the first scene shows us how unhappy he was made by the struggle between ambition and virtue. Afterwards, reviewing the excellence of Duncan, and anxious to cling to that place in the affections of his fellows which he had so honorably won in war, he resolves to abandon all thoughts of the murder. But it is his fate to be linked to a woman whose despotic nature and commanding intellect give her a natural ascendant over him. She reproaches him with wavering, with want of love, with abject cowardice, with breach of his oath. Too feeble in mind to control her, and too susceptible in feeling to be insensible to these sarcasms, he is stung and maddened by these taunts, and his nature recovers, by an enforced cruelty of heart, that place in its own self-esteem which the vigor of the principles could not vindicate. But it is all effort:

> "I am settled, and bend up
> Each corporeal agent to this terrible feat."

The act being done, he is a prey to all the anguish of remorse; his whole being is convulsed and agonized. But mark what justice it is "the self-condemned deals on his own soul."

Remorse is the natural pain resulting from inconsistency between one's principles and one's acts. If the acts be past and irreparable, this inconsistency can only be removed by assuming principles which agree with those acts, and make the man no longer at conflict with himself. When the agony of that self-contradiction becomes unbearable, to this the victim is forced, and with Satan he exclaims—"Evil, be thou my good!" He hardens himself in wickedness, and that penetrable stuff, conscience, whose piercing had given such pain, is expelled from his bosom. In Macbeth, this transition takes place near the close of the third act. After the terror and disgrace of the exposure of the feast, he sits down to contemplate his position, and the lost condition of his soul is forced upon him:

> "I am in blood
> Stept in so far, that, should I wade no more,
> Returning were as tedious as go o'er."

And then he excuses himself to his wife for the exposure at the banquet, by promises of braver behavior for the future:

> "My strange and self-abuse
> Is the initiate fear, that wants hard use:—
> We are but young indeed."

This is the cardinal scene of the play—the hinge on which the soul of the sufferer swings round "from soft to stern." Thereafter, Macbeth is a different being; hard, composed, and terribly consistent. This process of moral transmutation it is, which, as we suppose, constitutes the main interest of the play; and this it is which Mr. Macready sets himself to illustrate. In the earlier acts, his manner is that of a man whose soul totters beneath the weight that is laid upon it; we have the irresolution, the lapses or trances of the thoughts, the regret, the whine, of one whose spirit, still meanly clinging to that humanness of feeling from which its acts have forever cut it off, is trampled upon and goaded by its own fiercer thoughts and passions, and is the living victim of its own self-gendered serpents. In the ghost-scene at the supper-table, which is perhaps the finest part of his performance, Mr. Macready exhibits Macbeth as suffering intensely, agonized in mind and heart under the maddening consciousness that this fixed, unmoving image of horror, is the creation of his own brain, and that he is smitten down and abased before his own being, and that one-half his nature has become a devil to persecute the other half. Then follows the hardening of the heart, the stopping up of all "access and passage of remorse," the petrifying of the spirit, as it turns to gaze boldly on the Gorgon countenance of guilt. Here, the voice of the actor changes—his manner for the future is decided and firm; from the slave, he has become the hero of wickedness. In the three first acts, almost as sensitive as Hamlet, in the two last, he is almost as ruthless as Richard. Yet still, his ferocity is very distinguishable from "the hardness by long habitude produced" of the misshapen son of York. His vigor is passion; his severity is impulse; his courage is the frenzy of shame. To the last, through the rings of the steel-armor of sternness with which he has encased his breast, you catch a glimpse of the same susceptible, excitable, quick spirit, which, in the morning of his days, had made his appreciation of virtue so intensely keen, and his sense of the departure from it so fierce an anguish.

On the whole, we look upon Macbeth as a character scarcely less complicated and subtle than Hamlet, and the study of it as one of the finest employments and pleasures of the thoughtful mind; and we confidently accord to Mr. Macready the praise of having apprehended, distinguished and illustrated this fine combination and progress of passions in an able and brilliant manner.

MRS. ELLEN KEAN.

THERE is an order of women who, from their first approach, fix the admiration of our minds, and, after the longest familiarity, have failed to wake one response from the sentiments: there is another class, whose presence is a witchery of people's hearts, inductive of an enchantment which the understanding vainly endeavors to explain to itself: but it is only the Mrs. Keans of life and art to whom it is given at once to charm and be approved, —first to fascinate and then to be admired;—who, at the same time, kindle the fine resentments of the enthusiasm, and satisfy the searching skepticisms of the judgment; whose effect is both a mystery and a reason. If we were to give utterance only to the undefined feelings of delight which rise spontaneous to her coming, and attend the progress of the scene, we should convey a wrong impression as to the particular and high character which we suppose to belong to her as a professional artist: and if we dwell upon the peculiar and rare attainments in technical or mechanical skill, which, obviously enough to us, contribute largely to the effect, we offer violence to the nice instincts of the heart which assert a higher influence than examination can account for, and are more disposed to worship than to analyze. Her voice, her countenance, her motions, upon her earliest appearance, are in tone with our conceptions of the ideal in elegance and beauty, and pleasure antedates consideration: but her more intellectual and acquired powers hasten to vindicate and justify the foregone homage which she has snatched from our bosoms, eager to testify to us, that the light of fascination which played so tremblingly before her was not, like the nightly flickerings of the north, causeless and fading, but, like the messenger ray of the morning, the growing promise of a more palpable and continuing brightness: and we thus have the double interest of being enraptured, and of knowing that it is right that we should be enraptured. We can easily reconcile the two points of view, of nature and science, in our own mind, but cannot so readily explain their consistency to others. For ourselves, we have no conception of inspiration except as a more extended and more exquisite rationality. We look on genius as only a more subtle, intense, and rapid kind of sense. But, after we have explained all the mechanical and chymical and vital elements that constitute humanity, we have yet imparted no just notion of a man: and when we have explained the talent and acquirements of the performer, we have given no sufficient view of the excellent merits of the performance. In both cases the power which is the result of many components is as entire, instinctive, and natural, as the components are varied and curious; and the effect must still be described by epithets not referring to its causes.

Mrs. Kean is obviously in possession of some of the most unusual and difficult accomplishments of the stage. When the curtain rises upon a play, the object proposed is, not the pronouncing of some speeches, or the display of certain gestures, but the *acting of a scene*. The elements of the scene in words and motions, are of course given by the author: but much of the crystalizing power which shall group these into the intended form—the vital energy which is to associate them into an organization—must come from the actors; and chiefly from the leading actor. To combine the several sayings and doings which are set down by the poet, into the unity of a single joint action, is, we take it, the true problem of the boards. In real life, if two people, or half a dozen of them, come together in some animated encounter of passion, pleasure, business, mirth or anger, their separate acts and words interlink with, and re-act upon, one another, so as to develop one entire impression and effect. The capacity of realizing this result, in himself, and in others, by the effect which he has upon them, is the master faculty of the tragedian; the one central, essential characteristic of the profession, to which all other talents, graces, and attainments, of any sort or degree whatsoever, are secondary and collateral. Mr. Macready, we must admit, had this great quality beyond any one whom we have ever seen upon the stage; and certain parts of "Hamlet" and "The Bridal" seemed to us to bring out in him the perfection of acting. Second to Mr. Macready only, among men,—and before any woman of this time—Mrs. Kean stands eminent in the possession of this queen virtue of her art. There is another talent kindred to this, but exhibiting itself rather where a single performer predominates in the scene, than when several parts are equally considerable; it is that of properly emphasizing the different actions and speeches which are to be delivered,—fore-shortening the different portions of the scene, in accordance with the perspective in which they are to be seen with other parts—throwing the proper light and shade upon the picture by the degrees of prominence given to different positions. The black and white of the printed play give no hint of these delicacies of real existence: there all is monotone: the lightest passages are not distinguished from those which are to be dwelt upon and made to ring again. All this must come from the intelligence and taste of the actor; what speeches are to be flung impatiently from the lips, and spoken quite by the by, and what are to be deliberately and fully uttered —what movements ought to escape the notice of the audience, and what should strike and detain it;—this unwritten part of the play, larger and more important than that which is "set down," must be the performer's contribution. In this respect Mrs. Kean's felicity is beyond any one we have seen. Mr. Macready is, in this particular, her inferior. He occasionally lacked delicacy; the iron of his weighty manner sometimes entered into the soul of the passage, and killed it. The brilliant and refined effects accomplished by this means, in the performances of Mrs. Kean, it is scarcely possible to overstate. It imparts the charm of a glowing and fine original, to the most hackneyed plays. In her it seems less to be the result of study and taste, than the effect of a highly vivid imaginative faculty, idealizing the scene before her, as she advances. But the suggestions of the strongest imagination could be availed of, for attaining such rich and just impressions, only by a judgment of the truest delicacy, and a felicity of manner singularly various.

Beyond question, Mrs. Ellen Kean is the first actress of the present day. Since Mrs. Butler, she has had no rival. These two great performers we need not contrast. They were equal, but extremely dissimilar. We entertain the hope of seeing Mrs. Butler again upon the stage. The two, alike in grandeur, as unlike in nature, may move in freedom in their several spheres— the eagle and the swan; and neither moult one feather.

MRS. KEAN IN "AS YOU LIKE IT."

THE most graceful, the most imaginative, the most delicate actress of moderate times, appeared in the character of ROSA-

LIND, for the first time, at the Chestnut Street Theatre, in Philadelphia, on Friday last, September 19th, 1845. The house was full, and the performance was attended to throughout with the most animated interest and delight. At the close of the piece, in acknowledgment of the protracted and enthusiastic applauses of the audience, Mrs. Kean, conducted by her husband, came out in front of the curtain, where bouquets and wreaths of flowers were showered upon her. In our opinion, the present generation is hardly likely to see a more just illustration of the refined and frolic spirit of one of the most exquisite and characteristic of the female creations of Shakspeare; and surely will not witness, in finer completeness, that combination of selected excellencies, in aspect and demeanor, of

Cleopatra's majesty,
Atalanta's better part,
Sad Lucretia's modesty,

which in Rosalind ought to be exhibited to the eye of the spectator, that the mental qualities of the original may be perfectly apprehended. For ourselves, we were, simply, enchanted. The recollection of "the arms sublime that floated on the air,"—the gliding, liquid movements—the light and springing tread—the quick yet soft transition, wave-like, from thoughtfulness to sport, from mirth to majesty of temper—the grandeur, just melting into voluptuousness, of the arched and swan-like neck, the yielding attitude, the speaking eye—comes to us now like a strain of rich, soft music. Dignity joined with grace, is the true characteristic of this fascinating performer; in whose displays, grace often becomes gayety, and dignity never verges upon stiffness. Her action seems to be taking place within a visible atmosphere of grace; to exhale and throw off, as it were, a halo of sparkling elegance. An ethereal delicacy gives a charm to every motion, and an influence to every word and look. A captivating simplicity seems to prompt each thought, and a spontaneous loveliness to crown every effort. Her sportiveness is the wayward, yet vain, endeavor of a gleesome spirit to escape from its own inherent and inevitable gracefulness. Grace is the condition of her being; like lustre to a star. In laughter, and in tears, and in the more delicious union of the two,—in movement and in rest—in pensive sentiment and swift-glancing repartee—in all that she does, and all that she is—the attribute is, grace—still grace.

In the *romantic* class of Shakspeare's female characters,—Portia, Beatrice, Rosalind, we would add Miranda,—Mrs. Kean's supremacy is as absolute and exclusive as Mrs. Butler's special adaptation is unquestionable to the *passionate* order of the same author's conceptions,—Juliet, Constance, Lady Macbeth. The two sorts of creations are distinguished by the same qualities which peculiarize the two performers; the characteristic of one being *imagination*, of the other, *emotion*. With regard to that kind of comedy, so essentially Shakspearian, which is at once familiar and highly ideal, natural and poetical, in which social interests and ordinary scenes are exhibited to us through a heightening and refining veil of fancy,—Mrs. Kean seems to be native to the element. On the other hand, of the visionary realm of pathos and of passion, Mrs. Butler is the undoubted queen. The styles of the two are widely apart. Mrs. Butler's exhibition of a character was a brilliant succession of occasional effects; a series of intense and splendid impressions. It was a manner highly emphasized; in which ordinary scenes were past lightly over, in order to concentrate an irresistible power upon passages and situations capable of extraordinary expressiveness. In Mrs. Kean's personations, that genius which was accumulated upon separate points, is diffused over the whole exhibition. Her style is elevated, sustained and equable. If you are not agitated and astonished by the wonderful exhibition of parts, you are interested and gratified by the general excellence of all. If Mrs. Kean has less force, she has more delicacy; if the feelings are less morbidly engaged, the taste is more uniformly pleased and improved. In any of her performances, she may be said to have but one brilliant scene; but that is the whole.

MR. KEAN'S OTHELLO.

At the Chestnut Street Theatre, last night, October 30th, 1845, we saw the master-piece of the English stage—the greatest dramatic production of the world. Under the guidance of Mr. Kean, and his more delightful wife, we watched the development of that immortal scene, which, familiar in its rise, natural in its progress, and piteous in its close, engages the sympathies, one after another, until the total being of the spectator is absorbed in the event; were enchained by the weird influences of that *Fate*, shadowy and sublime, which, springing from an ill-assorted union, impels the hapless pair, consciously, yet uncontrollably, to destruction, making the kindliest feelings of one her betrayers, and the noblest passions of the other, the authors of their common ruin; and were profoundly interested by those contending storms of emotion, which rage together for a while in the bosom of the Moor, like opposing tempests on the Caspian Sea, till they burst in the ruin of his happiness, his fortune, his honor, his life, and his soul. It is no mean praise to sustain such a character in any way; to satisfy the observer, in its performance, is, undoubtedly, to win the highest honors of the stage.

Mr. Kean did an injury to his just pretensions by making his first appearances in Philadelphia, in comic parts. His Don Felix, and Benedick, had, of course, very many meritorious qualities; yet, substantially, and in respect of the essential requisites of the performance, they were, comparatively, *failures:* they displayed taste and talent and study, yet, on the whole, they were *from* the purpose of the plays. In fact, all that there is about him is of tragic build: he carries such weight of metal, as sinks the light crafts of comedy. We missed his Hamlet: in Othello, we saw him, for the first time, in his native proportions and true character. In the lowlands of gayety and mirth, he had appeared to feel the constraint and awkwardness of a false position and a borrowed title; but his first movement in the Moor seemed to declare "My name is MacGregor." We have been wont to think Mr. Macready's Othello the greatest histrionic exhibition that we had witnessed; we are now satisfied, after a close consideration of Mr. Kean's, that Macready had given us some erroneous views of some of the characters of the play, and of the agency by which the catastrophe is worked out; or rather, to be candid, had confirmed certain wrong impressions which our own thoughts had long before suggested to us; impressions, we mean, unfavorable to the delicacy and perfect integrity of Desdemona's character. The resistless grace of Mrs. Kean's simplicity and frankness, soon set us right upon this point: the majesty of her "I am your wife, my lord:—your true and loyal wife," scattered and swept away the last remnants of doubt; and at the feet of her "His unkindness may defeat my life, but never taint my love," we beg permission to recant and unsay all heresies in any wise impairing the spotless and angelic nature of the "gentle lady." Mr. Kean made the action of the piece turn chiefly upon the peculiar organization and temperament of the Moor, as the child of a different and lower race; honorable from conscious rank, controlled and mild through the necessities of official position, yet essentially dull of intellect, . . . astute enough, but lacking strong courageous sense . . . and capable, by the operation of the passions, of being transformed back to his original turbulence and wildness. The *moral* influence of this conscious inferiority, as leading easily to suspicion, jealousy, distrust and subjection to the guidance of others, is easily comprehended: but Mr. Kean brought out, in a distinctness we had never before seen, the physical or physiological operation of these natural peculiarities of race and nation.—When Iago brings his infernal machinery to bear upon him, you are less impressed, in following Mr. Kean's conceptions with the varying progress of opinion, in Othello, than in the utter change of nature that takes place: the slumbering sympathies of a savage origin are reawakened within him. We feel how significantly his sagacious lieutenant had characterized him, at the opening of the play, as a "barbarian." He is passion-struck: the intellect has sunk; the blind, mad instincts of animal fury are roused in this drunkenness of the feelings. You are no longer in company with a civilized and educated man: the savage is before you, in all the wild and crested turbulence of native ferocity. His nature falls at once below that of his intellectual companion: he reverences and follows the mental lead of Iago, as a savage worships his *Fetiche*. In carrying out this striking and fine conception, the surprise and awe with which Mr. Kean makes Othello turn to look at Iago when he begins to pray beside him, were electrifying. The readiness with which he gives up his own intention and adopts Iago's advice, as to the *method* of putting his wife to death, was exhibited as belonging to the childishness and weakness of a fallen and degraded understanding. When, in the later acts the storm has subsided, and honor, justice, self-control, and, with them, reason, have returned, the foregone conclusion of the passions is too deeply seated to be shaken: the *fact* of guilt has been settled in a mind, too resolute, now, to re-examine the grounds of belief, and the conduct that follows is such as any man, absolutely persuaded of his opinion, might adopt.

Such is the impression which Mr. Kean gives us of Othello; to us it is, in part, new, and it is certainly ingenious, reasonable, and in the highest degree effective. Were we required to say what passages appeared to us to be particularly striking, we should indicate the whole of the scene in which intelligence is brought to Othello of his recall to Venice, and Cassio's appointment in his stead—the exclamation to Emelia,

> "She's like a liar gone to burning hell;
> 'Twas I that killed her;"

and the "Farewell" speech, which we heard pronounced, as we are very sure it has not been since the death of the elder Kean; the last line, "Othello's occupation's gone," in which each successive word seemed to echo from a profounder abyss of gloom and despair, was admirable. But brilliant parts cannot make a great whole, and little special decorations of manner do not constitute a grand personation: the one, conclusive question still remains—did the performance give truer and clearer views of the character, and render the entire play more probable, more consistent, and of a higher intellectual interest? In view of this test, we give to Mr. Kean's Othello our full approbation.

We may express, in conclusion, the satisfaction we have in seeing that Mr. and Mrs. Kean have rendered the theatre, once more, the resort of the class called "fashionable," and that, in the revival of the Shaksperian drama, the circus and the pantomine and the ballet are falling into discredit. Without affirming that the moral influence of the drama is ever of the highest kind, we yet think that as counteracting the natural tendency of *fashion*, which with us, especially, is to the lower grade of exhibitions, the regular drama, in promoting refined taste in a community, and in elevating the subjects of social concern, and the topic of conversation in the drawing-room, exercises an influence friendly rather than otherwise, to purity and virtue.

APPENDIX.

APPENDIX A.—See *Ante*, p. 66.

PROTOCOL of a Constitution of a Society for the publication of Letters and other Documents of the War of the Revolution—to be incorporated under the title of "Contributors to the JOHN MARSHALL Fund, for the printing of Letters and other Writings of the War of the Revolution."

OBJECTS AND PLAN.

The purpose of this Society is, the publication of Original correspondence, and other writings, relating to the Revolution of 1776, and bearing date between the first meeting of the Continental Congress, in Philadelphia, in 1775, and the adoption of the Federal Constitution in 1789. It is not intended to form a *collection* of MSS., but to effect the printing and publishing of MSS. remaining in the possession of private persons, and of societies. MSS. presented to this association, shall be handed over to such of the Historical Societies of the States, as shall agree to place MSS. in their possession, at the disposal of this Fund for publication. Persons having papers of importance which have not been printed, shall be invited to allow such papers to be published. If entrusted to this Society, they shall in all cases be immediately copied, and be printed from the copies, and the Society engages to return promptly to the owners, without injury, the originals of all papers thus entrusted to them: or if the proprietors choose to part with the originals, they shall be deposited in such one of the State Historical Societies, acceding to the agreement above stated, as shall be deemed most appropriate. Persons not willing to entrust papers to the Society for the purpose of being copied for publication, shall be requested to furnish copies, or allow copies to be made in their own possession by agents of the Society. But no papers shall be printed but with a certificate by some person of character, that such copies are entire and accurate, and with a reference to the person or society in whose possession the original is.

The labors of the Society shall also be directed to the ascertaining of what letters and documents of the Revolution have heretofore been printed, and to the facilitating of reference to them, by the compilation of *Classified Indexes* of Letters, &c., in which such Letters, &c., shall be arranged according to their subjects and dates, and their contents briefly described, so as to bring them readily under the view of the students of history.

ORGANIZATION.

The officers of the Society shall consist of a President, four Vice-Presidents, thirty Managers, a Standing Committee of Publication consisting of nine persons, a Secretary and Treasurer. The officers at the time of the organization of the Society shall be the following persons:

PRESIDENT—Daniel Webster.

VICE-PRESIDENTS—John Quincy Adams, James Kent, Albert Gallatin, —— ?

MANAGERS.

New England.	*N. York and Philadelphia.*	*The South.*
Dr. Warren,	Hon. John Duer,	Dr. Moultrie.
Josiah Quincy,	John C. Hamilton,	—— Middleton,
The representative of Artemas Ward.	Charles King,	Mitchell King, Charleston,
[Seven more.]	Joseph R. Ingersoll,	Dr. Stevens, Augusta.
	John Penington,	[Seven more.]
	J. F. Fisher.	
	[Four more.]	

STANDING COMMITTEE OF PUBLICATION.

Philadelphia.	*New York.*	*Boston.*
William B. Reed,	John McVickar,	Jared Sparks,
Edward D. Ingraham,	George Gibbs,	—— —— ?
H. B. Wallace.	George Bartlett.	R. H. Dana, Jr.

Secretary.

—, *Treasurer.*

BY-LAWS.

All persons, not corporations, shall become members by subscribing annually five dollars; but no one who has once subscribed shall cease to be a member, or to be liable to the payment of five dollars annually, unless before the end of the year he gives notice in writing of his withdrawal. Subscribers shall be entitled to receive a copy of every book and engraving published by the Fund during the year. Subscribers paying eight dollars a year shall receive copies of books on large paper, and India proofs of engravings. Corporations and governments may become subscribers, but shall not be members.

The President shall summon a general meeting of the members to be held at New York, whenever he is requested to do so by a majority of the managers.

The Managers and other officers shall meet at New York, on the 1st Monday in September of every year. Vacancies which have occurred in the Board of Officers during the previous year, shall be supplied by an election by ballot, from the members of the Society. Any members of the Board of Officers may be removed by a general meeting of the members, called as above provided, and others elected in their room.

The Standing Committee of Publication shall consist of nine persons, of whom three shall be residents of Philadelphia, three of New York, and three of Boston. Vacancies occurring shall be filled by the committee from the members of the Society: but the Board of officers at their annual meeting, may remove any members of the committee and elect others in their room. This committee shall be the Supreme Council and Executive Board of the Society, in the intervals between the annual meetings of the Board of Managers; and shall have authority to dispose of funds, enter into contracts, and transact all business on the part of the Society.

A statement of the proceedings of the Standing Committee of Publication shall be read at the annual meeting of the Board of Officers, and printed.

At the annual meeting an address shall be delivered publicly by the President, or some one appointed by the Board of Officers at their previous annual meeting.

The Society shall print annually three volumes, and one engraving from some portrait, not before engraved, of a person eminent in the War of the Revolution.

Every volume printed by the Society shall be carefully *edited* by one or more persons, selected by the Committee of Publication.

Persons conferring important benefits upon the Society by the communication of original papers for publication, may be elected honorary members of the Society, by the Standing Committee of Publication, and their names shall be printed in the annual statements.

www.ingramcontent.com/pod-product-compliance
Lightning Source LLC
LaVergne TN
LVHW020936110826
845150LV00004B/882

* 9 7 8 1 4 2 5 5 5 1 8 6 5 *